THE POLITICS OF
IMPERIALISM
AND
COUNTERSTRATEGIES

THE POLITICS OF IMPERIALISM AND COUNTERSTRATEGIES

Editors
Pratyush Chandra
Anuradha Ghosh
Ravi Kumar

AAKAR BOOKS

THE POLITICS OF IMPERIALISM
AND COUNTERSTRATEGIES

© Aakar Books, 2004
© Contributors for their Respective Essays, 2004

First Published, 2004

All rights reserved. No part of this book may
be reproduced in any form without prior written
permission from the publisher.

ISBN 81-87879-35-1 (Hb)
      81-87879-36-X (Pb)

Published by
AAKAR BOOKS
28-E, Pocket-IV, Mayur Vihar Phase-I, Delhi-110 091, India
Phone : 011-22795505 Telefax : 011-22795641
E-mail : aakarb@del2.vsnl.net.in

Typeset at
Nidhi Laser Point, Shahdara, Delhi-110 032

Printed in India on behalf of M/s Aakar Books by
Arpit Printographers, B-7, Saraswati Complex,
Subhash Chowk, Laxmi Nagar, Delhi-110 092
Phone : 011-22825424, 30971860, 33339192

Acknowledgements

We are grateful to all our contributors who have been so kind and patient. Special thanks to Prof. Peter McLaren, the "poet laureate" of revolutionary praxis, for his pedagogical ability to enthuse and make us work. We are grateful to comrades in the Indian Institute of Marxist Studies (Delhi Chapter), especially to Pothik Ghosh. Thanks to Mr. K.K. Saxena of Aakar Books, without his committed endeavour this project could not have been successfully completed, in such a short time and with such perfection. Ms. Ritu Singh has done a wonderful job of copyediting.

Finally, we would like to acknowledge Comrade Ganeshan's encouragement and guidance. He and his struggles will always remain close to our heart, a constant source of inspiration wherever our political compulsion leads us to. We dedicate this book to him.

Contents

	Acknowledgements	5
	List of Contributors	9
	Introduction —*Pratyush Chandra, Anuradha Ghosh & Ravi Kumar*	13
1.	Imperial America & War —*John Bellamy Foster*	25
2.	Globalisation and the Emerging Global Politics —*Prabhat Patnaik*	37
3.	Imperialism at the beginning of the 21st Century —*Doug Lorimer*	59
4.	Dynamics of American Foreign Policy: Economic Aspects —*William K. Tabb*	88
5.	God's Cowboy Warrior: Christianity, Globalisation, and the False Prophets of Imperialism —*Peter McLaren & Nathalia E. Jaramillo*	110
6.	The US Imperialism and the Middle East —*Samir Amin*	154
7.	Empire Building and Rule: U.S. and Latin America —*James Petras*	197

8 : *The Politics of Imperialism and Counterstrategies*

8.	The Left in Latin America: Questions of Theory and Practice —Ronald H. Chilcote	249
9.	Beyond Crisis: On the Nature of Political Change in Argentina —Ana C. Dinerstein	263
10.	Anti-Globalisation versus Anti-Capitalism: The Dangers of Nationalism, Racism and Anti-Semitism —Werner Bonefeld	302
11.	Building a New World, Bottom Up —Massimo De Angelis	330
12.	Where is Power? —John Holloway	361
13.	Analysing Imperialism in the Age of Globalisation: Some Problems —Pratyush Chandra	367
	Index	399

List of Contributors

Samir Amin is Director of Forum du Tiers Monde in Dakar, Senegal. His numerous books include *Eurocentrism* (1988), *L'empire du chaos* (*Empire of Chaos*, 1991) and *Au-delà du capitalisme* (*Spectres of Capitalism*, 1998) and *The Liberal Virus* (New York University Press, 2004).

Massimo De Angelis teaches at the Department of Economics, University of East London, Essex, UK. His recent works include *Keynesianism, Social Conflict and Political Economy* (Macmillan, 2000). He is the editor of a web journal, *The Commoner* (http://www.commoner.org.uk/).

Werner Bonefeld teaches at the Department of Politics, University of York, UK. He recently co-edited *The Politics of Europe: Monetary Union and Class* (Palgrave, 2001) and *What is to be Done? Leninism, Anti-Leninist Marxism and the Question of the Revolution Today* (Ashgate, 2002).

Pratyush Chandra is a political activist and freelance writer in Delhi, India.

Ronald H. Chilcote is Managing Editor of *Latin American Perspectives* and a Professor of economics and political science at the University of California, Riverside. He recently edited *The Political Economy of Imperialism* (Kluwer Academic Press, 1999) and *Imperialism. Theoretical Directions* (Humanity Press, 2000).

Ana Cecilia Dinerstein is teaching at the Department of Social Sciences, Bath University, England. She is on the editorial boards of Argentine Marxist journal, *Herramienta* and British *Capital & Class*. Besides co-editing *The Labour Debate* (Ashgate, 2002), she has authored a forthcoming book *Against the Violence of Stability. On Labour, Crises and the Politics of Resistance in Argentina* (Verso, 2004).

John Bellamy Foster is one of the editors of *Monthly Review*. He has authored a number of books and articles on ecology and imperialism with a Marxist perspective. His recent contributions include *Marx's Ecology* (Monthly Review Press, 1999), *The Vulnerable Planet: A Short Economic History of Environment* (Monthly Review Press, 1999) and *Ecology against Capitalism* (Monthly Review Press, 2002).

John Holloway teaches Sociology in the Instituto de Ciencias Sociales y Humanidades of the Autonomous University of Puebla, Mexico. He has written widely on Marxist theory. His most recent book is *Change the World without Taking Power: The Meaning of Revolution Today* (Pluto Press, 2002). He was the co-editor of *Zapatista! Rethinking Revolution in Mexico* (Pluto Press, 1998).

Nathalia E. Jaramillo is a doctoral student in the Division of Urban Schooling, Graduate School of Education and Information Studies, University of California, Los Angeles.

Doug Lorimer is a member of the Political Committee of the Democratic Socialist Party of Australia and the author of *Trotsky's Theory of Permanent Revolution: A Leninist Critique* (Resistance Books, 1998).

Peter McLaren is a Professor in the Graduate School of Education and Information Studies, University of California, Los Angeles. Much acclaimed as one of the most important proponents of Revolutionary Critical Pedagogy, he has written widely on educational theory and revolutionary politics. His recent works include *Che Guevara, Paulo Freire, and the Pedagogy of Revolution* (Rowman & Littlefield, 2000) and *Schooling as a Ritual Performance* (Rowman & Littlefield). He co-authored *Red Chalk: On Schooling, Capitalism and Politics* (Institute for Education Policy Studies, 2001) and co-edited *Marxism against Postmodernism in Educational Theory* (Lexington Books, 2002).

Prabhat Patnaik teaches at the Centre for Economic Studies and Planning, Jawaharlal Nehru University, New Delhi, India. He is one of the most important political economists from India. His recent works include *Accumulation and Stability under Capitalism* (Clarendon Press, 1997) and *The Retreat to Unfreedom: Essays on the Emerging World Order* (Tulika, 2003).

James Petras is Professor Emeritus of Sociology, State University of New York, Binghamton. His most recent works include *Globalization Unmasked: Imperialism in the 21st Century* (Zed Books, 2001) and *System in Crisis: The Dynamics of Free Market Capitalism* (Zed Books, 2004), both co-authored by Henry Veltmeyer.

William K. Tabb is a Professor at the Economics Department, Queen's College, City University of New York, New York. His recent books include *Economic Governance in the Age of Globalization* (Columibia University Press, 2004), *Unequal Partners: A Primer on Globalization* (New York: The New Press, 2002), *The Amoral Elephant: Globalization and the Struggle for Social Justice in the Twenty- First Century* (New York: Monthly Review Press, 2001).

Introduction

—*Pratyush Chandra, Anuradha Ghosh, Ravi Kumar*

Imperialism, or for that matter every stage in the capitalist development, has its genesis in the relationship between capital in general and particular capitals, the administration of competition (involving collaboration and conflict) among the latter. And, it all depends on how and how much living labour is valorised and transformed into capital – a social power. This entails the whole process of dependence and subordination. Hence, imperialism is not simply 'export of capital', 'domination of one nation over another', 'expansionary policy of a country', etc. It involves every aspect of social existence. This multifaceted nature is reflected in the human 'scream' against inhuman being, which is a product of the contradictory process of fetishisation, "existence against-and-in-capitalism" (Dinerstein & Neary, 2002; Holloway, 2002). Recent global and local struggles all reflect this multi-nodal upsurge from diverse pores of capitalist contradiction—be it international mobilisations against global institutions, or Zapatistas in Mexico, recent upheavals in Argentina, Bolivia and Venezuela.

    The present collection is a product of our effort to understand the present state of capitalism and political conflicts marking it. We started off by identifying the concept of Imperialism to put in perspective evermore intensification of global process of capitalist accumulation through 'financialisation' and 'lean production'. We sought to understand how do these processes have generated a crisis of much-acclaimed celebration of postmodernity, problematising the autonomy of local struggles. We saw the older debates between Marxists, like Hilferding, Kautsky, Luxemburg, Lenin and Bukharin continuing to illuminate various strategic-tactical questions concerning the anti-capitalist struggle in general, but they have to cope up with more complexities now as 'imperialist' processes are evolving new dimensions. Indian capitalists and various 'national' capitalist interests which were till now seen as having an anti-imperialist tenor, although an inconsistent one, are seen merging with the 'core' capitalist 'transnational' pursuit for profits. Innumerable questions were posed to us: is this phase really that of "imperialism without colonies", as one of the most respected Marxists, Harry Magdoff (2003) has been defining it since the late-1960s? Does it show an evolution of 'multilateral' imperialism? Or, has the political superstructure associated with all these processes really ceased to be centred, and has an "empire" really evolved, as another revolutionary intellectual, Antonio Negri, with Hardt (2000) has posed it? But then how do we explain the political economic function of 'unending' wars and militarisation? There are so many pros and cons to all these formulations and conceptualisations of doomed but 'ever-evolving' capitalism. How do we visualise class struggle and proletarian internationalism at the present juncture? We have a firm conviction that only by grounding our praxis in re-reading of the whole Marxist critique of political economy that we can define and undertake our tasks for the complete emancipation of humanity which is possible only by establishing the society based on "each according to one's ability, to each according to one's needs."

The papers in this collection grounding themselves in diverse Marxist traditions are united in their pursuit for understanding the ongoing political conflicts around the globe. If alternative has to be anti-capitalist, its evolving forms/contents have to be identified. One cannot simply go on rhetoricising ad infinitum— "another world is possible". Even if we refrain from identifying that 'world', the system will give its own content. "Anti-capitalist indifference" (as Bonefeld defines it) leads to barbaric conclusions, reflected in nationalist vandalism of Shiv Sena and RSS in India, Al Qaeda in the Middle East, anti-immigrant racist resurgence in the "advanced" societies—"anti-capitalist capitalism". We will have, as we have, a circular clash of barbarisms – terrorism and war against terrorism. And there is always a danger of being trapped in this systemic dungeon of mystifications if the processes leading towards it are not comprehended—once again quoting Bonefeld, "in the false totality of bourgeois society it takes courage to demystify abstractions". The present collection is a small endeavour to demystify the political economic processes and their ideological ramifications represented in the political conflicts that mark these initial years of the 21st century.

Introduction to the Chapters

This collection was never intended to present any 'the' theory of imperialism, or capitalism, hence the way diverse themes related to the capitalist reality have been posed and dealt within the essays definitely at times diverge and even contradict each other. Hence, the chapterisation too does not follow any specific principle, except some loose notion of thematic architecture in the minds of the editors. The following summaries too do not pretend to bias the readers with the manner in which the editors have read the essays. The only purpose that this collection fulfils, as we perceive, is to present the readers some representative Marxist modes of understanding the politics in present-day Capitalism, i.e., the politics of Imperialism and forces against it.

John Bellamy Foster attempts to focus on the theories of imperialism from a Marxist perspective in order to understand the relationship between imperialism and war. The shift in characterizing America from "a traditional nation-state to an imperial power" is an attempt in finding legitimacy as well as acknowledgement for the hegemonic aspirations of the United States, invested with an unparalleled role on the world stage. For Forster, the differences between formal and informal nature of imperialist control was never a matter of enigma. Imperialism essentially is a historical process associated with capitalist development in all of its complexity (economic/political/military - core and periphery) that has within its very structure the deeper globalising tendencies because of the accumulation dynamic of the system itself. The Marxist perspective tries to analyse imperialism not simply through the policies of states but also through the actions of corporations and the mechanisms of trade, finance and investment within which is embedded a whole constellation of class relations, including the nurturing of local collaborators or comprador elements in the dependent societies. It is imperative to point out that the inner logic of imperialism alone explains the wars on Afghanistan and Iraq in the post Cold War phase and that the heightened militarism and aggression are a necessary fall-out effect of the imperial aspirations of America, the most evident impact of which is seen in the rising gap in income and wealth between rich and poor countries and in the net transfer of economic surplus from the periphery to the centre that makes this possible. It is important to understand that those seeking to challenge imperialism must oppose the essential oneness of economic, political and military domination under capitalism and call into question the entire system as a whole.

Prabhat Patnaik finds an increasing mobility of capital-as-finance, which is more speculative, as opposed to capital-in-production as the characteristic of 'new' imperialism. Commensurate to the needs of finance capital, the character of the nation-states too have undergone change and to overcome the challenges of post-war setbacks and socialist assertion, the "bankerization of capital" or "debt imperialism" under the auspices of IMF and World Bank were imposed under "conditionalities" that protect the global interests of multinational banks and other creditors. Consequently there emerges a world super-state that does not eliminate the existing nation-states but rather gathers its legitimacy from the hegemonic control exerted to defend and consolidate the interests of global capital leading to a progressive abrogation of the sovereignty of a host of them and its subsequent appropriation by a small number of them acting in unison. Wars are nonetheless inevitable in order to maintain the strategic interests of imperial, global capital and the authority of the super-state so that the ascendancy of the dollar over other currencies are maintained by the centralization of explicit political control over the world's oil reserves and the economies of these countries (and hence the wars in Iraq and Afghanistan); isolation of 'recalcitrant' states like China with a view to bending them eventually to the will of US super-imperialism; and the fracturing of internal unity in countries like India and China or Yugoslavia by opening up latent social divisions (but never class divisions) on the lines of identity or community based secessionist politics. The present phase of globalisation like the old "white man's burden" theory imposes a predatory despotism over much of the world but within its very womb lies embedded the seeds of its destruction.

William K. Tabb explores the two faces of American imperialism: economic coercion through the global state economic governance institutions to foster regime changes in the areas of trade, investment and finance and the actual use of military force. The emphasis is on the need to understand the relation between the State and the structural logic of capitalism that ushers in the dynamic of policy formulations that serve only certain interests in the society. The legitimisation of the policy of aggressive military interventions within the American people emanate from the populist notions created about the ideas of the era of freedom and democracy that the US proclaims to augur in countries where the governments are not conducive to the will of the empire. Again it is important to understand that oil interests are not the only stakes for US policy-making; more essential is the need to understand how behind the oil interests hide the real agenda of the economic coalition supporting current policy making relating to the arms industry. Military expenditure and emphasis on research related to the needs of the US army with the view to commanding the synergy of space superiority with land, sea and air superiority makes US hegemony quite unchallenged in the international arena. The dire implications of such policy making threatens the human interests of the global community and the only way out of this to build an international people's movement to confront the empire by challenging the very capitalist economic system that perpetrates inequality and injustice through the policies of globalisation and imperialism in the 21st century.

Doug Lorimer focuses on the analysis of the present phase of transnational, corporate, finance capitalism invested with an imperialist character under the aegis of the economic and military' strength of the United States of America. A historical approach to the development of capitalism the world over is adopted to understand the dynamics of the 'globalised', 'post-industrial', 'financialised' capitalism that has emerged at the end of the 20th century. The post-World War II extension of the internationalisation of the forces and processes of production that formed the substratum for the rise to dominance of transnational corporations of course entailed a substantial deepening of the fundamental contradiction inherent in the capitalist system, i.e. the contradiction between the increasing social and economic interaction and interdependence among people throughout the world vis-à-vis the political division of the world into a series of nation-states dominated by the ruling elite. Since September 11, 2001, under the cover of a global war against terrorism, the trajectory that the US and other imperialist ruling classes have embarked upon will result in progressive curtailment of democratic rights and public expressions of dissent along with deteriorating standards of living both at home and abroad unlike the period of the Cold Wars. The increasing lack of social and political stability favours the perspective of revolutionary mass political action as the only way out of the endless horrors that imperialist capitalism present to humanity.

Major proponents of revolutionary critical pedagogy, *Peter McLaren* and *Nathalia Jaramillo* try to provide a holistic perspective tracing linkages between the crisis of democracy, which allows the US to raid Iraqi raw materials and exploit their labour-power for the US corporations, imperialist thrust of capital and the strategies employed by the forces in power (capital). The whole purpose of US, representing the interests of capital is to weaken and cheapen labour in order to compensate for a major loss of profits and dramatic increase in debts over the last several years. However what comes to us is the United States defining its empire building exercise as an extension of its democratic project, which is linked to the desires of free market. American 'national interests' wants the free market democracy in the rest of the world. The Iraqi experience is a continuation of the same project, wherein after the transition to the neo-liberal marketplace, "the Iraqi business elite will be able to purchase for themselves the best democracy money can buy, and the bogus freedom that goes with it." In this global strategy of the imperialist capital even bodies made to enforce peace—UN—have become "more like vaudeville stage for the political charades of Powell and Blair than a viable organ for peace." Bush *hijo* (a Spanish word for "son", "junior") uses the fascistic rhetoric of 'family-values' and religion. The whole exercise being undertaken in this paper also unravels the way imperialism has evolved over years to the current phase where the logic of capitalist global integration is intrinsically linked to this new phase of US military aggression. Rejecting the bourgeois anti-capitalism, which critiques civil society but sees market capitalism as the best solution, the localist anti-capitalism stressing on self-sufficiency achieved means of micro relationships among producers and consumers as well as reformists who want a more regulated capitalism at the level of the nation state, the paper treats working class as the most important agent of anti-capitalist social transformation, adopting a multi-racial, gender balanced, anti-imperialist approach that struggles to bring about a world in which everyone has equal access to the resources that they need in order to live a valuable and worthwhile life. There is a need to wage an anti-imperialist struggle on the triple continents of reason, faith, and passion, on the picket-line or protest march, schools, places of worship, libraries, shop floors, and corporate offices – "in every venue where people come together to learn, to labour, and to love."

Samir Amin studies the location of the Middle East in the global imperialist strategy of the US. Starting with a historical analysis of the emergence of US supremacy and the collective triadic imperialism under its leadership and the Trojan horse of Atlanticism, Britain. The dual danger of the existence of a Soviet bloc and its spreading support base in the Third World forced the bourgeoisie of Europe and Japan to accept the US leadership. After the 1991 collapse of Eastern regimes, there has been anxiety among the US leadership to reassert itself. The Middle East owes its startegic importance to three factors: "its oil wealth, its geographical position in the heart of the Old World, and the fact that it constitutes henceforth the 'soft underbelly' of the world system." Amin sees a liberatory potentiality in the resistance from the nations of the old world not ready to be subjected to the "empire of chaos". The United States will behave roguish flouting international law slipping on the fascist slope with its "patriotic laws".

James Petras finds that the expansion of empire is accompanied by the decline of the republic wherein the military aggression is undertaken at the cost of masses, which face a cut in facilities as well as massive unemployment while the MNCs get huge subsidies. US in its drive to expand has also violated and opposed human right provisions. Today the US imperial expansion takes place with the active approval of the vast majority of US citizens despite the worst social and economic suffering imposed on them. This support is based on the consumption of state propaganda via the mass media, symbolic gratification in being part of a victorious 'world power' and a servile attitude to established state authority. The lack of a credible left wing political party or movement further undermines popular opposition. There have been also significant changes in class formation after a quarter of neo-liberal rulership. Given the nature and frequency of changes, any theory of anti-imperialism must be by its nature tentative and contingent as it attempts to deal with the fluid nature of class and national subjectivity – consciousness. This imperialism is characterized by inter-ruling class conflicts, especially among the militarists and the corporate empire builders, the economic empire builders and the Zionist strategists, Rumsfeld and the military-intelligence professionals and the military and economic empire builders. Despite the differences within and the differences between MNCs and Bush

Introduction : 21

Administration the former back him because of the favourable policies that he has pursued like waving environmental regulations, providing subsidies, protection against competition, decreased taxes, covering up of corporate corruption, tolerating loose banking regulations, and control over minimum wages. The major challenges to the empire do not exist in the US but it comes from outside, from the ongoing mass struggles in the Third World. Change will only come when the reality of Third World resistance and revolts undermine the US military will to conquer.

Ronald Chilcote while assessing the state of the Latin American Left starts contextualises it with a brief examination of the analytical value of the globalisation perspective, how it realises itself in the "historical experience" of US domination and future potentialities in the capitalist system. He finds globalisation to be a "way of describing a world" akin to theorisations of Kautsky, Schumpeter and diffusion who stressed more on "peaceful alliance", "interdependence" etc. He assesses the political changes heralded by 'the age of Gorbachev' with continued US interventions in Latin America that impacted upon the left strategies - a move towards participation in elections, but this has heralded new difficulties, with constant threat of abdication or accommodation. But he too like some other authors in the collection finds potentialities in new forms of organisation and struggle with experiences in participatory democracy in Argentina, Brazil, Ecuador, Peru and Mexico. He envisages a left research agenda based on these developments to "mitigate the crisis of Marxism" reasserting the centrality of class analysis and class struggle, yet explaining new social movements.

Ana Dinerstein's paper explores the nature of political change in post crisis Argentina. Undertaking an analysis of relationship between the crisis and the popular mobilization, new territories of participation vis-à-vis the reorganization of State power during the period 2002 and partly 2003, this paper suggests that the importance of political change in Argentina can be traced in (i) the recovery of collective action and the political instrument of social change after a period of intense dominance of capital and the economy over the political capacity of transforming the society and (ii) the reinvention of political subjectivity, i.e., the identities, organizations and forms of democratic and participative actions. Though these changes did not reflect totally in the reorganization of the State, both constitute the fundamental basis for a process of change, whose form cannot be foreseen as yet, but which would, indubitably, form part of a regional process of political change of greater expanse in a long term.

Werner Bonefeld counter-poses the bourgeois critique of capitalism which is so prominent within anti-globalisation movements against anti-capitalism that aims towards the revolutionary destruction of capitalism with human emancipation in "the democratic organisation of socially necessary labour-time by the associated producers themselves." Anti-capitalist indifference to such project is contradiction in terms. Bonefeld provides a comprehensive critique of nationalist anti-globalisations and their eventual degeneration into a barbaric re-enforcement of capitalism, since their "nerve-centre... is a fetishistic critique of global relations that projects a class-ridden society as a national community, subsuming, through an murder, class relations into the abstract identity of national sameness—the national 'we'." Racism and anti-Semitism all have done this (we can include by logical extension, the anti-Islamism, so popular globally and of Hindu nationalism). Bonefeld hints at the blurring of the distinction between the rightful critique of Israeli nationalism and concrete persons. He shows how like the management of the Israeli class conflict through the militarisation of its policy towards Palestine, Islamist struggle for self-determination is reduced to similar mystification. Characteristically, Bonefeld marks with Horkheimer that "whoever wants to talk about Fascism but not about capitalism should up".

Massimo de Angelis weaves in his contribution the relationship between capital and different dimensions of social life. His point of departure is the current debates on alternatives that are not rooted in a strategic understanding of the social force we face (capital). He warns against relying on emerging 'co-opted' critical voices from within the camp of international financial institutions such as that of economists like Joseph Stiglitz. A critical attitude must guide our engagement with them. The dangers of cooptation can be avoided through thinking of alternatives in terms of commons, which suggest alternative, non-commodified means to fulfil social needs, e.g. to obtain social wealth and to organise social production. There is an increasing need to consolidate a social force that begins to constitute spaces of life beyond capital. Basing his arguments on Marx's theory of capital accumulation and analysing *enclosures* as creating and reproducing the commodity-form, he argues that the state deploys institutional force to maintain, protect or extend commodity relations. The capital through the different forms of state can overcome its crisis either by extending its domination through repression and war and corresponding wave of enclosures and the extension of disciplinary integration or by co-opting and dividing the forces that oppose it. The new discourse, articulating the diverse alternatives emerging out of the crisis of the neo-liberal capital, must echo the needs and aspirations coming from below giving coherence to their plurality.

John Holloway in his short piece deals with the location of power, which he finds central to the discussion on empire and imperialism. He talks about capitalist spatiality that exists through a fracturing of space. Holloway poses the central contradiction determining the political conflicts in capitalism – between "the free, frontierless flow of social doing" and "the fragmented, frontier-dominated and linear space of capitalist command." "Our power is everywhere, without frontiers or straight lines. Capitalist power, prior to being in any particular place, lies already in the concept of a spatiality marked out by separations and highways." He finds the de-territorialisation of capitalist command in the form of recent financialisation and the increasingly belligerent politics of the US and other governments to be complementary as "both are aspects of the flight of capital from insubordination, aspects of the protracted crisis of capital." Holloway argues for moving against-and-beyond the reassertion of capitalist spatiality.

Pratyush Chandra in his chapter endeavours to read the

phenomenon of imperialism and globalisation on the basis of the fundamentals of Marxism. He presents a survey of literature on the topic, and locates recent politico-economic changes in the operation of the circuit of capital. He presents a rereading of Lenin's text on imperialism, followed by an explanation of recent imperialist belligerence, and movements against globalisation and war.

REFERENCES

Dinerstein, Ana & Michael Neary (2002), *The Labour Debate: An Investigation into the Theory and Reality of Capital Work*. Aldershot: Ashgate.

Hardt, Michael & Antonio Negri (2000), *Empire*. Massachusetts: Harvard University Press.

Holloway, John (2002), *Change the World Without Taking Power: The Meaning of Revolution Today*. London: Pluto Press.

Magdoff, Harry (2003), *Imperialism without Colonies*. New York: Monthly Review Press.

Imperial America and War

*John Bellamy Foster**

On November 11, 2000, Richard Haass—a member of the National Security Council and special assistant to the president under the elder Bush, soon to be appointed director of policy planning in the state department of newly elected President George W. Bush—delivered a paper in Atlanta entitled "Imperial America". For the United States to succeed at its objective of global pre-eminence, he declared, it would be necessary for Americans to "re-conceive their role from a traditional nation-state to an imperial power". Haass eschewed the term "imperialist" in describing America's role, preferring "imperial," since the former connoted "exploitation, normally for commercial ends," and "territorial control". Nevertheless, the intent was perfectly clear:

> To advocate an imperial foreign policy is to call for a foreign policy that attempts to organize the world along certain principles affecting relations between states and conditions

---

* This is a slightly revised version of the introduction to a collection of essays by Harry Magdoff, *Imperialism without Colonies* (Monthly Review Press, 2003). Footnotes providing full documentation are included in the book.

within them. The U.S. role would resemble 19th century Great Britain.... Coercion and the use of force would normally be a last resort; what was written by John Gallagher and Ronald Robinson about Britain a century and a half ago, that "The British policy followed the principle of extending control informally if possible and formally if necessary", could be applied to the American role at the start of the new century (Richard N. Haass, *www.brook.edu*).

The existence of an American empire is no secret. It is widely, even universally, recognized in most parts of the world, though traditionally denied by the powers that be in the United States. What Haass was calling for, however, was a much more open acknowledgement of this imperial role by Washington, in full view of the American population and the world, in order to further Washington's imperial ambitions. "The fundamental question that continues to confront American foreign policy," he explained, "is what to do with a surplus of power and the many and considerable advantages this surplus confers on the United States." This surplus of power could only be put to use by recognizing that the United States had imperial interests on the scale of Britain in the nineteenth century. The world should therefore be given notice that Washington is prepared to "extend its control", informally if possible and formally if not, to secure what it considers to be its legitimate interests across the face of the globe. The final section of Haass' paper carried the heading "Imperialism Begins at Home". It concluded: "the greater risk facing the United States at this juncture...is that it will squander the opportunity to bring about a world supportive of its core interests by doing too little. Imperial understretch, not overstretch, appears the greater danger of the two."

There is every reason to believe that the "Imperial America" argument espoused by Haass represents in broad outline the now dominant view of the U.S. ruling class, together with the U.S. state that primarily serves that class. After many years of denying the existence of U.S. empire, received opinion in the United States has now adopted a position that glories in the "American imperium", with its "imperial military", and "imperial protectorates". This shift in external posture first occurred at the end of the 1990s, when it became apparent that not only was the United States the sole remaining superpower following the demise of the Soviet Union, but also that Europe and Japan, due to slowdowns in their rates of economic growth relative to that of the United States, were now less able to rival it economically. Nor did Europe seem to be able to act militarily without the United States even within its own region, in relation to the debacle of the Yugoslavian civil wars.

After Washington launched its global War on Terrorism, following September 11, 2001, the imperial dimensions of US foreign policy were increasingly obvious. The US empire is therefore now portrayed by political pundits and the mainstream media as a necessary "burden" falling on the United States as a result of its unparalleled role on the world stage. The United States is said to be at the head of a new kind of empire, divorced from national interest, economic exploitation, racism, or colonialism, and that exists only to promote freedom and human rights. As Michael Ignatieff, Professor of Human Rights Policy at the Kennedy School of Government, Harvard University, proclaimed in the *New York Times Magazine* (January 5, 2003), "America's empire is not like empires of times past, built on colonies, conquest and the white man's burden.... The 21st century imperium is a new invention in the annals of political science, an empire lite, a global hegemony whose grace notes are free markets, human rights and democracy, enforced by the most awesome military power the world has ever known".

Such high-sounding words aside, what makes this "21st century imperium" an overriding concern for humanity today is Washington's increased readiness to use its unrivaled military power to invade and occupy other countries whenever it deems this absolutely necessary to achieve its ends. Yet, as Indian economist Prabhat Patnaik observed more than a decade ago, "No Marxist ever derived the existence of imperialism from the fact of wars; on the contrary the existence of wars was explained in terms of imperialism". Once the reality of imperialism has been brought back to the forefront of world attention as a result of such wars it is important to search out its underlying causes.

Classic Imperialism

One of the most influential mainstream historical accounts of British imperialism in the nineteenth century was presented in an article entitled "The Imperialism of Free Trade", written a half-century ago by economic historians John Gallagher and Ronald Robinson. A part of this analysis was utilized by Haass to advance his "Imperial America" argument. The central thesis of Gallagher and Robinson's article was simple: *imperialism is a continuous reality of economic expansion in modern times.* Those who associated imperialism primarily with colonies and colonialism, and who therefore took the scramble for Africa and late nineteenth century *colonial* expansion as the basis for a general model of imperialism, were wrong. British imperialism throughout the nineteenth century remained essentially the same in its inner logic despite the concentration on expanding free trade in one period and on annexing colonies in another. As Gallagher and Robinson elaborated (in the same passage from which Haass quoted):

> British policy followed the principle of extending control informally if possible and formally if necessary. To label the one method 'anti-imperialist' and the other 'imperialist,' is to ignore the fact that whatever the method British interests were steadily safeguarded and extended. The usual summing up of the policy of the free trade empire as 'trade not rule' should read 'trade with informal control if possible; trade with rule when necessary.'...Despite...attempts at 'imperialism on the cheap,' the foreign challenge to British paramountcy in tropical Africa [in the late nineteenth century] and the comparative absence there of large-scale, strong, indigenous political organizations which had served informal expansion so well elsewhere, eventually dictated the switch to formal rule.

For those seeking to comprehend British imperialism in the nineteenth century, this argument suggested, it is the "imperialism of free trade" and not colonialism that should be the primary focus. Only when the economic ends of Britain could not be secured by informal control did it resort to formal imperialism or colonization—that is, direct and continuing use of military and political control—to achieve its ends. If it has often been said that "trade followed the flag", it would be far more correct to say that there was "a general tendency for British trade to follow the invisible flag of informal empire". The "distinctive feature" of the "British imperialism of free trade in the nineteenth century", these authors argued, was that its use of its military force and hegemonic power in general were primarily limited to establishing secure conditions for economic dominance and expansion.

The clearest example of such informal imperialism was the British role in South America in the nineteenth century. Britain maintained its control in the region through various commercial treaties and financial relationships backed by British sea power. As British Foreign Minister George Canning put it in 1824: "Spanish America is free; and if we do not mismanage our affairs sadly she is *English*." At all times, Gallagher and Robinson state, British influence was exercised so as to convert such "areas into complementary satellite economies, which would provide raw materials and food for Great Britain, and provide widening markets for its manufactures." When left with no other way of enforcing its dominance, Britain was always ready to resort to active interventions—as it did repeatedly in Latin America in the nineteenth century.

As the distinguished German historian Wolfgang J. Mommsen noted in his *Theories of Imperialism*, the significance of this concept of informal imperialism was that it tended to bridge the gap between non-Marxist and Marxist approaches, since it stressed the historical continuity of imperialism as a manifestation of economic expansion (not confusing it simply with its more formal political-military occurrences):

> By recognizing that there are numerous informal types of imperialist domination which precede or accompany the establishment of formal rule, or even make it unnecessary, Western [non-Marxist] thinking on the subject of imperialism has drawn closer to Marxist theory.... Generally speaking, most non-Marxist theoreticians admit nowadays that dependency of an imperialist sort may well result from the

most varied kinds of informal influence, especially of an economic nature. Imperialist forces at the colonial periphery were by no means obliged constantly to resort to the actual use of political power: it was generally quite enough to know that the imperialist groups could count on support from the metropolitan power in the event of a crisis. Formal political rule thus appears only as the most specific, but not the normal type of imperialist dependence.

Ironically, Gallagher and Robinson distinguished their approach from the classic accounts of John Hobson (in his 1902 *Imperialism: A Study*) and Lenin (in his 1916 *Imperialism, the Highest Stage of Capitalism*) by associating both Hobson's and Lenin's views with a narrower spectrum of cases involving formal control or colonialism. By identifying the last quarter of the nineteenth century, when colonial annexations were at their height, as a qualitatively new stage of capitalism—the monopoly or imperialist stage—Lenin in particular, these authors argued, had come to associate imperialism with formal rather than informal control.

However, this criticism fell wide of the mark, since Lenin himself had emphasized that imperialism did not necessarily involve formal control, as witnessed especially by British imperialism in Latin America in the nineteenth century. "The division of the world into...colony-owning countries on the one hand and colonies on the other," he observed, did not exhaust the core-periphery relations between nation states. Indeed Lenin pointed to "a variety of forms of dependent countries; countries, which, officially, are politically independent, but which are, in fact, enmeshed in the net of financial and diplomatic dependence...the semi-colony", including cases like Argentina, which was so dependent financially on London that it was a virtual colony.

The reality of an informal imperialism of free trade (or imperialism without colonies) was never an enigma to Marxist theory, which viewed imperialism as a historical process associated with capitalist expansion—only secondarily affected by the particular political forms in which it manifested itself. The reason for characterizing the last quarter of the nineteenth century as the imperialist *stage* in the work of Lenin and most subsequent Marxist theorists, did not have to do mainly with a shift from informal to formal imperialism, or the mere fact of widespread annexations within the periphery, but rather with the evolution of capitalism itself, which had developed into its *monopoly* stage, creating a qualitatively new type of imperialism. It was this historically specific analysis of imperialism as a manifestation of capitalist development in all of its complexity (economic/political/military—core and periphery) that was to give the Marxist theory of imperialism its importance as a coherent way of understanding the deeper globalising tendencies of the system.

In this interpretation, there was a sense in which imperialism was inherent in capitalism from the beginning. Many of the features of contemporary imperialism, such as the development of the world market, the division between core and periphery, the competitive hunt for colonies or semi-colonies, the extraction of surplus, the securing of raw materials to bring back to the mother country, etc. are part of capitalism as a global system from the late fifteenth century on. Imperialism, in the widest sense, had its sources in the accumulation dynamic of the system (as basic as the pursuit of profits itself), which encouraged the countries at the centre of the capitalist world economy, and particularly the wealthy interests within these countries, to feather their own nests by appropriating surplus and vital resources from the periphery—what Pierre Jalée calls *The Pillage of the Third World*. By a variety of coercive means, the poorer satellite economies were so structured—beginning in the age of conquest in the late fifteenth and sixteenth centuries—that their systems of production and distribution served not so much their own needs as those of the dominant metropoles. Nevertheless, the recognition of such commonalities in imperialism in the various phases of capitalist development was entirely consistent with the observation that there had been a qualitative change in the nature and significance of imperialism that commenced in the last quarter of the nineteenth century, sufficient to cause Lenin to associate this with a new stage of capitalism.

Marxists have therefore often distinguished between an older imperialism and what was called the "new imperialism" that began in the final decades of the nineteenth century. What distinguished this new imperialism were primarily two things: (1) the breakdown of British hegemony and increased competition for control over global territories between the various advanced capitalist states; and (2) the rise of monopolistic corporations—large, integrated industrial and financial firms—as the dominant economic actors in all of the advanced capitalist states. The new mammoth corporations by their very nature sought to expand beyond national bounds and dominate global production and consumption. As Harry Magdoff observed, "The urge to dominate is integral to business". Monopolistic firms engaged in this imperial struggle were frequently favoured by their own nation states. The Marxist theory of the new imperialism, with its focus on the rise of the giant firms, thus pointed to the changed global economic circumstances that were to emerge along with what later came to be known as multinational or global corporations. All of this became the context in which older phenomena, such as the extraction of surplus, the race for control of raw materials and resources, the creation of economic dependencies in the global periphery and the unending contest among rival capitalist powers, manifested themselves in new and transformed ways.

It was this understanding of imperialism as a historical reality of capitalist development, one that took on new characteristics as the system itself evolved, that most sharply separated the Marxist approach from mainstream interpretations. The latter frequently saw imperialism as a mere policy and associated it primarily with political and military actions on the part of states. In the more widely disseminated mainstream view (from which realist economic historians like Gallagher and Robinson dissented), imperialism was present only in overt instances of political and territorial control ushered in by actual military conquest. In the contrasting Marxist view, imperialism occurred not simply through the policies of states but also through the actions of corporations and the mechanisms of trade, finance and investment. It involved a whole constellation of class relations, including the nurturing of local collaborators or comprador elements in the dependent societies. Any explanation of how modern imperialism worked thus necessitated a description of the entire system of monopoly capitalism. Informal control of countries on the periphery of the capitalist world system by countries at the centre of the system was as important, in this view, as formal control. Struggles over hegemony and more generally rivalries among the leading capitalist states were continuous, but took on changing forms depending on the economic, political and military resources at their disposal.

Imperial America in the Post-Cold War World

If the main distinguishing feature of modern imperialism, in the Marxist view, was associated with the rise to dominance of the giant corporations, the ordering of power within the system, as reflected in the relative position of various nation states, nonetheless shifted considerably over time. In the late nineteenth and early twentieth century the principal global reality was the decline in British hegemony and the increased rivalry among the advanced capitalist states that followed, leading to the First and Second World Wars. The rise of the Soviet Union in the context of the First World War posed an external challenge to the system eventually leading to a Cold War struggle between the United States, the new hegemonic power of the capitalist world economy following the Second World War, and the Soviet Union. The fall of the latter in 1991 left the United States as the sole superpower. By the end of the 1990s the United States had gained on its main economic rivals as well. The result of all of this by the beginning of the new century, as Henry Kissinger declared in 2001 in *Does America Need a Foreign Policy?*, was that the United States had achieved "a pre-eminence not enjoyed by even the greatest empires of the past".

This naturally led to the question: what was the United States to do with its enormous "surplus of power"? Washington's answer, particularly after 9/11, has been to pursue its imperial ambitions through renewed interventions in the global periphery—on a scale not seen since the Vietnam War. In the waging of its imperial War on Terrorism the U.S. state is at one with the expansionary goals of U.S. business. As *Business Week Online*, in late January 2003, expressed the economic benefits to be derived from a U.S. invasion of Iraq: "Since the U.S. military would control Iraq's oil and gas deposits [the second largest known reserves in the world after Saudi Arabia] for some time, U.S. companies could be in line for a lucrative slice of the business. They may snag drilling rights too". Companies in the oil service industry, which is dominated by the United States, might "feel just as victorious as the U.S. Special Forces". Indeed, the main object of such military invasions is regime change and the subsequent restructuring of the economy of the "rogue state"—so-called because it stands outside the imperial order defined primarily by the United States—to make it conform to the dominant requirements of the capitalist world economy, which include opening up its resources to more extensive exploitation.

Richard Haass (whose responsibilities in the present administration were extended to include those of U.S. coordinator of policy for the future of Afghanistan) pointed out in his book *Intervention*, that regime change often can only be accomplished through a full-scale military invasion leaving the conquered nation in ruins and necessitating subsequent "nation-building":

> It is difficult to target specific individuals with military force.... US efforts to use force to bring about changes in political leadership failed in the cases of Qaddafi in Libya, Saddam in Iraq, and Aideed in Somalia. Force can create a context in which political change is more likely, but without extraordinary intelligence and more than a little good fortune, force by itself is unlikely to bring about specific political changes. The only way to increase the likelihood of such change is through highly intrusive forms of intervention, such as nation-building, which involves first eliminating all opposition and then engaging in an occupation that allows for substantial engineering of another society.

Such a "nation-building" occupation, Haass stressed, involves "defeating and disarming any local opposition and establishing a political authority that enjoys a monopoly or near-monopoly of control over the legitimate use of force". (This is Max Weber's well-known definition of a state—though imposed in this case by an invading force.) It therefore requires, as Haass observed quoting one foreign policy analyst, an occupation of "imperial proportions and possibly of endless duration".

It is precisely this kind of invasion of "imperial proportions" and uncertain duration that now seems to be the main agenda of Washington's War on Terrorism. In the occupation and "nation-building" processes following invasions (as in the case of Afghanistan), explicit colonialism, in the most brazen nineteenth century sense, will be avoided. No formal annexation will take place, and at least a pretense of local rule will be established from the beginning, even during direct military occupation. Nevertheless, a central goal will be to achieve some of what colonialism in its classic form previously accomplished. As Magdoff pointed out,

> Colonialism, considered as the direct application of military and political force, was essential to reshape the social and economic institutions of many of the dependent countries to the needs of the metropolitan centers. Once this reshaping had been accomplished economic forces—the international price, marketing and financial systems—were by themselves sufficient to perpetuate and indeed intensify the relationship of dominance and exploitation between mother country and colony. In these circumstances, the colony could be granted formal political independence without changing anything essential, and without interfering too seriously with the interests which had originally led to the conquest of the colony.

Something of this sort is occurring in Afghanistan and is now being envisioned for Iraq. Once a country has been completely disarmed and *reshaped* to fit the needs of the countries at the center of the capitalist world, "nation-building" will be complete and the occupation will presumably come to an end. But in areas that contain vital resources like oil (or that are deemed to be of strategic significance in gaining access to such resources), a shift back from formal to informal imperialism after an invasion may be slow to take place—or will occur only in very limited ways. "Informal control" or the mechanism of global accumulation that systematically favours the core nations, constitutes the normal means through which imperialist exploitation of the periphery operates. But this requires, on occasion, extraordinary means in order to bring recalcitrant state back into conformity with the market and with the international hierarchy of power with the United States at its apex.

At present, U.S. imperialism appears particularly blatant because it is linked directly with war in this way, and points to an endless series of wars in the future to achieve essentially the same ends. However, if we wish to understand the underlying forces at work, we should not let this heightened militarism and aggression distract us from the inner logic of imperialism, most evident in the rising gap in income and wealth between rich and poor countries, and in the net transfers of economic surplus from periphery to centre that make this possible. The growing polarization of wealth and poverty between nations (a polarization that exists within nations as well) is the system's crowning achievement on the world stage. It is also what is ultimately at issue in the struggle against modern imperialism. As Magdoff argues in *Imperialism without Colonies*, there is an essential oneness to economic, political, and military domination under capitalism. Those seeking to oppose the manifestations of imperialism must recognize that it is impossible to challenge any one of these effectively without calling into question all the others—and hence the entire system.

Globalisation and the Emerging Global Politics

Prabhat Patnaik

I

Capital can function only with the backing of the state. As the nature of capital changes over time, e.g. from the era of free competition to that of monopoly capitalism, the nature of the state whose backing is needed for its functioning undergoes a corresponding change. Capital however is not organised in only one single national bloc with only one single nation-state backing it. There has historically been a multiplicity of national capitals, each operating with the backing of its own nation-state. The relationship between these nation-states, or what one may call the nature of the international state-system, is determined by the relationship between the different national capitals. Over time therefore as the nature of capital changes, not only does the nature of the state whose backing it enjoys and the nature of its relationship with that state change correspondingly, but so also does the nature of the relationship of that state with other states. This is why different phases of capitalism throw up different patterns of "international politics".

This was one of the essential points made by Lenin's theory of imperialism. As capitalism moved from the free competition to the monopoly phase, a small financial oligarchy presiding over an enormous amount of finance capital, representing a coalescence of concentrated banking and industrial capitals, came to hold sway in each advanced capitalist nation. Each of these financial oligarchies, tied together through "personal union", also came to have close "personal union" with the personnel of the state and thereby developed a close and direct relationship with the state, unlike in the era of free competition when the links between capital and the state were neither close nor direct. In the process of course the nature of the state itself underwent a change: the state became more rigid, heavy, opaque and bureaucratised, more of an ossified behemoth.[1] But since each of these nation-based finance capitals was in intense rivalry with other finance capitals based in other advanced nations for enlarging/defending its sphere of influence in a world that was already partitioned among them, this "inter-imperialist rivalry" meant that the imperialist states were engaged in a relationship of conflict which would periodically develop into wars. Global politics in the era of imperialism that Lenin wrote about was therefore the politics of inter-imperialist rivalry. This defined the relationship *among* the "handful" of advanced capitalist (or imperialist) nations, and *between* these nations and the oppressed countries (often nations-in-the-making) over whom they held sway and over whom they struggled.

All this is well known. But Lenin also drew attention to another important point. The oppressed countries were not all colonies. Likewise the world was not divided only into two mutually exclusive and all exhaustive categories, namely the oppressor and the oppressed nations. There were many countries between them and some of these even had their own colonies; to gain access to these colonies to enlarge their respective spheres of influence, the "handful" of "imperialist" nations sought to acquire hegemony over these middle-level colonial powers themselves. In short, while inter-imperialist rivalry was the defining feature of global politics in the Lenin era, this rivalry itself was expressed through highly complex relationships within the international state system. Lenin gave three examples to underscore this complexity which was superimposed on the more "straightforward" colonial relationship such as existed between Britain and India. The first was the case of Argentina, a nominally independent country but tied to Britain as a satellite economy. The second was the case of China which was not the colony of any particular country and which actually had an Emperor enjoying titular suzerainty but which was carved out among the different imperialist powers (what Mao Zedong called a "semi-colony"). The third was the case of Portugal which actually was a colonial power itself but which was under the British sphere of influence, with Britain thereby gaining access to Portuguese colonies. The *form* of the international state-system, it follows then from Lenin's analysis, must be distinguished from its *essence*, the latter referring to the basic driving force behind global politics in a particular era. This driving force however expresses itself through the prevailing (and historically inherited) form of the international state-system, with the latter neither arresting the former nor being reducible to it.

While this insight of Lenin is of great value, the world of today is not the same as what Lenin had written about. The question therefore arises: how do we analyse global politics today? What is the driving force behind it and how does it express itself through the form of the prevailing international state-system? The purpose of this paper is to examine these questions.

II

Most people would agree that the contemporary era is characterised by an unprecedented process of "globalisation". Saying this however is not only not enough but can be positively misleading. The specificities of the current process of "globalisation" must be analysed. There is for instance a suggestion that "globalisation" refers to the process of the world coming closer together and that in this respect something special is currently happening. But it is not clear that on this definition there is anything *sui generis* about the present. The world has been coming closer for a long time, and even though the internet and the telecommunication revolution represent major landmarks in human history, it is a moot point whether the telegraph and the telephone, when *they* came on the scene, were not as profound in terms of their effect in shrinking the world.

Likewise if the specificity of the present globalisation is seen to lie in the much greater global mobility of *capital*, then it is doubtful if anything special is really happening at present. In the heyday of capital exports prior to World War I, Britain, the leading capital exporter of the time, ran a current account surplus on the balance of payments of between 5 and 10 per cent of her GNP for over four decades, averaging 8 per cent during the two decades prior to the war. By contrast the largest capital exporter of modern times, Japan, has run current account surpluses averaging only 2.8 per cent of her GDP during the decade 1984-93. (Ghosh & Sen, 1998) "Globalisation" is clearly not accompanied by any significant relative increase in long-term capital flows (for which current account surpluses could be a proxy), and certainly not from the North to the South. What is true however is that there has been an enormous increase in the global mobility of *capital as finance*. As is well known, only about 2 per cent of the cross border capital flows are trade-related, which only underscores the importance of the globalisation of finance. It is not capital-in-production but capital-as-finance which has become immensely mobile in the current epoch, and this certainly constitutes one exceedingly important specificity of the current process of globalisation.

Through this process of "globalisation" of capital-as-finance a new kind of international finance capital is coming into being. This finance capital differs from what Lenin had written about in at least three ways:[2] first, Lenin's conceptualisation referred to finance capital that represented a coalescence of banking and industrial capital, while contemporary finance capital is an autonomous entity with little interest in production as such and concerned primarily with quick speculative gains through rapid global movements. Secondly, Lenin's finance capital and financial oligarchy were essentially nation-based (closely tied up with the nation-state), while contemporary finance capital, while having clear national origins does not let that origin influence its behaviour in any essential way; it is in that sense detached from its national moorings and has an international character going beyond what Lenin had written about. Thirdly, Lenin's "finance capital" was engaged in acute rivalry with "finance capital" based in other imperialist nations, while inter-imperialist rivalries today are far more muted, reflecting perhaps the "international" character of the contemporary finance capital just noted. Given these differences, it follows that the configuration of consolidated, ossified, hardened, imperialist nation-States engaged in intense rivalry with one another that characterised the Leninist conjuncture would be wholly out of place when it comes to serving the interests of contemporary finance capital. An entirely new configuration is needed by it and such a new configuration is in fact coming into being.

III

Before examining the contours of this new configuration however a point should be made clear. From what has been said above it should not be inferred that in our perception the world has remained stuck at the Leninist conjuncture all this while until all of a sudden things started changing only recently. On the contrary, the configuration of state systems in the advanced capitalist countries has undergone remarkable changes not just since Lenin's days, but, more particularly since the days marking the end of the Leninist conjuncture (which roughly means the end of the Second World War). At least two phases of such change can be distinguished: the first is the immediate post-war phase when metropolitan capital was attempting to recover from the blows it had received and to consolidate itself. These blows were the result of the war itself, and the legacy of the war, entailing an expansion in the strength of the socialist world, decolonisation of the third world, and the growing assertiveness of the metropolitan working class which enforced near-full employment through Keynesian demand management (the socialist threat, together with the fact that military expenditure in the U.S. was used as the chief demand stimulus, made metropolitan capital go along with it). This however, as we now know, was a temporary phase. Many observers at that time had thought that "Capitalism had changed" in a permanent sense, but that turned out to be false. The consolidation of capitalism, its recovery from the post-war setbacks, the progressive retreat of the socialist challenge, the gradual emergence of international finance capital in its new form, through stages marked by the accumulation of Euro-dollars and petro-dollars, created a new conjuncture.

Globalisation of finance capital initially took the form of metropolitan banks giving loans to countries not only in the first world but even in the third world, the period of the so-called "bankerisation of capital" or "debt imperialism". A monitor, in the form of the Bretton Woods twins (the IMF and the World Bank), supervising over the third world countries, holding them under the thraldom of "conditionalities" and thereby protecting the global interests of multinational banks and other creditors, was quite enough. It could be superimposed on the already existing structure of post-war nation-States.

But this very phase, opening up the till-then protected economies of the world to "free movements" of goods and finance, and hence giving rise to the ascendancy of the current form of international finance capital with its enormous mobility, appetite for speculative gains, and deflationary consequences, has created the need for an alternative configuration of state system. In other words, the need for an alternative configuration of state-system in the new context is not just for an alternative to the state system that characterised the Leninist conjuncture, but also to what have been its successors till now.

Given the international nature of finance capital it is obvious that the state-system needed to defend its interests must itself have a global character, i.e. it would be more in the nature of a world superstate. But this super-state would not eliminate the existing nation-states; rather it would emerge from them and would be superimposed upon them. We would in other words have a world where the nation-states continue to exist but there is an abrogation of the sovereignty of a host of them and its appropriation by a small number of them acting in unison, and thereby constituting, for all practical purposes, a world superstate. This need not entail a whole separate set of identifiable state institutions which belong exclusively to this super state but exist side by side with the national state institutions, as super-powerful, parallel institutions (in the way for instance that parallel central and provincial institutions co-exist in any federal polity). There would of course be such specific super-institutions, of which we already have examples like the WTO and the international war crimes tribunal that is currently trying Slobodan Milosevich (though this particular institution is at present finding it difficult to sustain itself). But the world superstate would not necessarily be a replication at a higher level of the national state institutions. It would mean essentially a changed relationship within the existing configuration of nation-states. We come back to the question: what would be its precise form?

IV

The emergence of this new form of international finance capital has been accompanied by another phenomenon, namely the emergence of the U.S. in a hegemonic role that is without any precedence, a role for which the term "super-imperialism" is not inapposite.

Arguing against Karl Kautsky, the principal theoretician of the Second International, who had visualised the possibility of a stage of "ultra-imperialism", or "joint exploitation of the world by internationally-united finance capital", Lenin had said that any such "agreement" among imperialist powers, which must be based on their existing relative strengths, would necessarily be short-lived, since the relative strengths change over time owing to "uneven development" under capitalism. "Ultra-imperialism" therefore can at best be a transition between two phases of inter-imperialist rivalry, a brief period of "truce" interposed between phases of conflict. There can however be an alternative trajectory away from "ultra-imperialism", not towards *inter-imperialist rivalry* but towards *super-imperialism*. Once a critical minimum gap in terms of strength comes to exist between the leading power and the others, it is quite possible that it is the *former* that would grow relative to the others, making the gap even wider and thereby setting off a process towards *super-imperialism*. The other powers then would have to remain content with whatever "agreement" is drawn up by the leader (so that super-imperialism *in a formal sense* can be seen as a new phase of ultra-imperialism, though substantively it means domination by the leader). But unlike the trajectory visualised by Lenin, this trajectory may even represent a more stable equilibrium, not in the sense that it would actually last longer but in the sense that the immanent contradictions in the *economics* of super-imperialism may be more capable of being manipulated by the leader (as the U.S has demonstrated by capturing Iraqi oil and thereby strengthening the dollar).

A number of writers have seen a phase of "ultra-imperialism" in the post-war years, different ones among them designating different segment of this period as constituting the "ultra-imperialist" phase. To what extent this is a rigorous characterisation is a matter we need not go into; but even if a phase of "ultra-imperialism" in some sense is accepted, the trajectory from there has clearly been towards "super-imperialism", which is hardly surprising since the collapse of the Soviet Union has emboldened the leading imperialist country to assert its own will more aggressively.

V

The term "super-imperialism" is apposite, not only because the collapse of the Soviet Union, one of the two "superpowers" of the post-war world, has left only one country enjoying overwhelming military dominance, but also because no matter how sharp the inter-imperialist contradictions, and they are not too sharp as yet (even on Iraq the gap between the position of the U.S. on the one hand and that of France and Germany on the other was not so large as to be unbridgeable), these cannot be elevated to the status of "inter-imperialist rivalry", at least in the sense that Lenin used the term.

The question may be asked: even though the U.S. may not be militarily challenged, can it not be economically challenged by other advanced capitalist countries (or their groupings) in a manner where its military superiority ceases to matter? For instance if it cannot undertake military expenditures owing to its economic travails without support from other advanced capitalist countries, then its mammoth war machine cannot be put to use without their consent, negating its "super-imperialist" status. Even on this score however the U.S. has, for the present, developed considerable invulnerability. As long as wealth-holders all over the world are willing to hold US dollars or dollar-denominated assets, the U.S. would never have any difficulty financing its military aggression, *no matter how much the governments of rival capitalist countries differ from it with regard to such aggression*. Wealth-holders would have this confidence as long as the value of the U.S. dollar vis-à-vis certain crucial commodities is not expected to fall significantly. Gold used to be until recently one such commodity. There can be little doubt that oil occupies such a role today (so much so that it would not be an exaggeration to call the current international monetary system an implicit "oil standard"). As long therefore as the value of the U.S. dollar vis-à-vis oil is not expected to fall significantly, the U.S. can afford to run balance of payments current account deficits with full confidence that wealth-holders across the globe would be perfectly willing to hold its currency or currency-denominated assets. Even if, for some reason, the dollar falls vis-à-vis, say, the Euro, there would still be no tendency for a "flight from the dollar", since the dollar would still be considered a "perfectly safe bet"; wealth-holders in general would expect the fall vis-à-vis the Euro to either come to a halt at some new "equilibrium", or even to reverse itself. By acquiring control over the Iraqi oil reserves, the U.S. has ensured that whatever threats existed to the supremacy of the dollar and hence to the economic ability of the U.S. to launch military aggression have now been removed. The aggression on Iraq thus constitutes as much an expression of the status of the U.S. as a "super-imperialist" power as a means for further strengthening this status.[3]

VI

Now, to come back to the original question, the world superstate, corresponding to the needs of the new form of international finance capital, would, in the prevailing concrete conditions, take the form of a U.S. super-imperialist dictatorship. This would be the means of establishing the hegemony of imperialist powers acting under the undisputed leadership of the U.S. The circumstances of, and the sequel to, the invasion of Iraq make this particularly clear. That act, totally reprehensible in itself, was part of an even more ambitious project, namely, the imposition of a global dictatorship by U.S. super-imperialism, which seeks to destroy all *independent* nation-states and substitute them by states which would fall into only one of three categories: "allies" (such as Blair's Britain), "clients" (such as Turkey), and "puppets" (such as Hamid Karzai's Afghanistan).

To say this does not mean that the Bush-version of the U.S. super-imperialist dictatorship is the one that would necessarily institutionalise itself. But even if, as seems likely, there is a move away from the Bush-version, and the establishment of an apparently more "reasonable" world superstate, that too, in its essence, would still be a U.S. super-imperialist dictatorship. *Imperialist globalisation, entailing the ascendancy of international finance capital, and the phenomenon of super-imperialism, are deeply enmeshed in the contemporary world.*

It may be asked: "Why should U.S. super-imperialism display any explicit tendency towards a global dictatorship"? Why cannot super-imperialism function solely, as it was doing, through the more conventional, and more "peaceful", means of drawing different countries into the web of "globalisation", thereby destroying the autonomy of their nation-States, and making them subservient to US-dominated agencies like the IMF and the World Bank?

There can be little doubt that war (and by implication explicit political control) represents, to paraphrase Clauswitz, a continuation of imperialist globalisation by other means. The conduct of war itself is eased by the prior "softening" of countries through imperialist globalisation: in the war against Iraq for instance a whole range of countries from Turkey to Poland to

Pakistan became directly involved, or at least complicit, just for the money they got from the US, which they desperately needed because their economies had already been brought to their knees through the process of "globalisation". "Globalisation" thus facilitates war; but why does war become necessary when "globalisation" is already unleashed?

The reason lies in the fact that "globalisation" is not sufficient for the purposes of super-imperialism, that *war is indeed immanent in super-imperialism*. There are three reasons for this: first, if the ascendancy of the dollar is to be maintained, if the pre-eminent position of the US within the imperialist world is to be maintained, in short if super-imperialism is to flourish, then control over the world's oil reserves becomes necessary, which in turn requires explicit political control over those particular economies. And since any such explicit control calls forth opposition from other states including some which had already been indirectly controlled by making them adopt neo-liberal policies, a further tightening of political control over even larger areas becomes necessary. In short, the necessity for military intervention arises from the very dialectics of political control itself. Secondly, there are some nation-states which do not give up their autonomy so easily, China being a classic example here (no matter what one thinks of China's current economic policies *as a means of bringing about socialism*). Mere "globalisation" therefore is not enough. For isolating such recalcitrant states with a view to bending them eventually to the will of US super-imperialism, a whole series of military interventions becomes necessary. Thirdly, large nation-states like India or China represent, by their very size, a potential threat to US super-imperialism, no matter how malleable they are made through their pursuit of neo-liberal economic policies. These policies themselves of course have the effect of fracturing the unity of such countries, as the example of the former Yugoslavia has shown, but this effect is slow and uncertain; what is more, such large countries are often slow to adopt the set of neo-liberal policies, and are even capable of reversing their drift into neo-liberalism. A degree of political intervention to ensure and hasten their fracturing, e.g. by sniffing out their open or latent social divisions (such as between Hindus and Muslims, between Shias and Sunnis etc. *but not between classes*) and exacerbating those divisions to the point of open conflict, and armed intervention, becomes necessary for the project of super-imperialism. For all these reasons therefore, super-imperialism is impelled towards imposing over the world its global dictatorship.

VII

The question would naturally be asked: what is wrong with this? Does this not represent the beginning of a new world where national barriers, the cause of so many conflicts in the past, are finally getting to be transcended? Are we not going to have an abrogation, through the exercise of enlightened world public opinion, of the licence to practice tyranny with impunity by authoritarian and fascist governments within their national borders, invoking national sovereignty to prevent any "outside interference" (such as for instance what the Indian government did when it endorsed the government-sponsored carnage in Gujarat even while debunking of all "outside" expressions of concern over the Gujarat events as infringement of Indian sovereignty)?

There are two different levels at which this question can be answered. The first relates to the present American dispensation whose callousness and unilateralism have caused so much discomfort even in bourgeois circles that a negative answer to it may be readily given. Few would disagree that the last thing that *Pax Americana* in its latest edition has brought to the world is *pax* itself. Not only is there an absence of peace as one act of aggression follows another (as the first Gulf War, the war against Yugoslavia, the attack on Afghanistan, and the invasion of Iraq have followed one another), but even when a country has been apparently "pacified" there is no internal peace within it. Afghanistan is an obvious example of the latter situation. The US attack on Afghanistan, while it removed the *Taliban* from power, has not succeeded in bringing any peace or order to that country: different warlords control different segments of it, with the authority of the US-sponsored Hamid Karzai not extending beyond Kabul and its outskirts, and with that gentleman himself being protected by American bodyguards; and some countries which participated in the "war against terrorism" in the hope of getting some money from the Americans have not even been paid what was promised. A similar situation is unfolding in Iraq. The Shia clerics are virtually administering Najaf and Karbala, and it does not seem likely that the Americans would be dislodging them from that position. The Kurds in the north are most unlikely to go back meekly to the old positions they occupied. Ahmed Chalabi, or whoever else the Americans anoint as the ruler in Baghdad is likely to be the titular figurehead of only a truncated Iraq. As in Afghanistan, the war would have been followed by anarchy, disorder and a virtual dismemberment of the country.

In short, US super-imperialism in its present form does not appear to be too concerned about the state of the country after its invasion, as long as what it perceives to be its strategic interests, e.g. dislodging the *Taliban* in Afghanistan, or securing control over the oilfields in Iraq, are served.

But, as we have already noted, there can be a more "enlightened version" of super-imperialism that transcends the crudities of the Bush-version. Can such an "enlightened superimperialism" not usher in a better world? After all, since super-imperialism is not the whim of a George Bush but must respond to the present needs of international finance capital, it would have to rest upon the support not only of the other imperialist nation-states, but also of significant segments of the capitalist strata everywhere, *including in the third world countries*. This fact surely would result in a tempering of the present aggressiveness of super-imperialism, and a removal of several of its ugly features. When this happens, would it not lead to the establishment of a more enlightened world order where there is a diffusion of development all over the globe, and a protection of human rights everywhere?

One would indeed rejoice over the coming into being of a world imperialist superstate if it meant a diffusion of human rights and of development all over the world. Such however is not the case. Those who argue that there would be such a diffusion are mistaken about the basic nature of contemporary globalisation, and, in particular, oblivious of the essential distinction between capital-in-production and capital-as-finance.

VIII

The standard argument advanced in favour of the proposition that globalisation would lead to a diffusion of development, runs roughly as follows: if a country opens itself up to capital movements (and has a complementary neo-liberal regime that encourages and facilitates such movements) then it would experience larger capital inflows and thereby raise the pace of its development beyond what its own internal savings would permit. The presumption in other words is that it is capital-in-production that has become highly mobile, in contrast to what had been the case historically. Capital-in-production had *not* been historically very mobile, especially from the North to the South, for, had it been so, the dichotomy between the developed and the underdeveloped regions of the world would have disappeared long ago. The present conjuncture, so the argument goes, represents something *sui generis*: capital-in-production has at last become mobile, so that if only the underdeveloped countries opened their doors to capital inflows, they would overcome their state of underdevelopment quite effortlessly.

Once we recognise however that it is capital-as-finance that has become mobile and not so much capital-in-production, we get an entirely different conclusion. Opening the economy to the free flow of global capital yields very little by way of additions to productive capacity; on the other hand it makes the economy acutely vulnerable to the caprices of globally-mobile speculative finance, retaining whose "confidence" becomes the inevitable obsession of economic policy. To this end, the long-term real interest rates have to be jacked up, and the fiscal deficit has to be cut (even in the midst of a recession as is the case in India today), which, together with the reduction in tax-GDP ratio that necessarily accompanies a "liberalised" economy, entails cuts in public expenditure and investment. In short, the economy has to be kept deflated, with *adverse consequences* for poverty, employment, growth rate, social expenditure, the state of infrastructure and the level of capacity utilisation in industry. The economy necessarily gets bogged down in a state of pervasive and worsening demand constraint. Together with these come a loss of economic sovereignty, efforts to attenuate democracy (so that the alienation of the people does not spill over into an abrogation of the "liberalised" economic regime), and growing threats to the unity of the country as the project of nation-building launched through the anti-colonial struggle becomes increasingly undermined by ethnic, communal and secessionist conflicts bred by unemployment and deprivation.

But this is not all. There is an even more basic point to be considered.[4] A capitalist economy cannot function without a stable medium of holding wealth. Gold has traditionally played the role of such a stable medium. To be sure, in the contemporary world wealth-holders do not actually hold gold. They hold some currency (or financial assets denominated in terms of that currency) which is considered by them to be "as good as gold" (i.e. whose price relative to gold is not expected to go down at a rate large enough to offset its "carrying cost" advantage). The US dollar typically is such a currency. When they hold other currencies (or financial assets denominated in terms of these other currencies), as indeed they do, the reason for their doing so is their conviction that the values of these other currencies in terms of the US dollars would not decline (often the economies of these other currencies have to be deflated to ensure this); and this is generally true of the non-dollar currencies of the first world. By the same token, however, if wealth-holders do not have confidence in some currency, then they would shift their wealth out of it, which itself would give rise to a secular decline in the value of that currency, justifying retrospectively the wealth-holders' lack of confidence. If the absence of confidence in the long-run relative value of these currencies vis-à-vis the dollar (thought to be "as good as gold") is pronounced enough, then even deflation of the economies of these currencies would not be enough to prevent a secular decline in their relative real values. And this is true of most third world currencies. It follows then that once a third world economy is drawn into the vortex of globalised finance, it can experience a combination of *both* deflation *and* a secular decline in its real exchange rate vis-à-vis the currencies of the advanced capitalist countries. And indeed in practice it does.

As a result, *in addition to* the poverty-increasing and recession-engendering effects of deflation referred to above, third world economies pursuing neo-liberal economic policies also experience a secular decline in their real exchange rates vis-à-vis the US dollar owing to *autonomous capital account transactions* (i.e. wealth being slowly shifted from their countries, by both foreigners and domestic nationals, to the metropolitan centres). This has an adverse terms-of-trade effect for their economies which accentuates the adverse effects on poverty and unemployment mentioned above. In short, far from there being a diffusion of development through globalisation, what actually comes in its wake in third world economies is economic retrogression,[5] which necessarily brings forth opposition, resistance and protests from the people.

The world imperialist superstate would *necessarily* constitute the new political arrangement through which this resistance would be countered. And the method of countering would necessarily entail a violation of human rights of vast masses of the people. Thus, far from representing an instrument for the diffusion of human rights and development, the imperialist superstate would become a weapon for the suppression of the people so that they remain reconciled to the state of accentuated misery and deprivation to which the process of globalisation of finance condemns them. This is not to say that occasional individual instances of violation of human rights by third world governments would not call forth intervention in defence of human rights from the imperialist powers. But these individual instances typically happen to be cases where the imperialist powers are themselves not directly involved in the role of oppressors. And, in any case, these individual instances should not make us miss the wood for the trees. The basic orientation of the world imperialist super-state is authoritarian and oppressive. It is sheer apologetics to pretend that under its aegis there would be a diffusion of development and human rights.

IX

We can in fact get a preview of how this authoritarian world imperialist state would manage domestic opposition in third world countries. Three mechanisms for the exercise of this authoritarianism/dictatorship are immediately obvious. The first, which has been discussed above, is through direct military intervention. Even before Iraq, the U.S., acting in concert with other advanced capitalist countries, had arrogated to itself in the post-September 11 period, the right of intervention, including armed intervention if necessary, in the affairs of any country in the name not just of fighting "terrorists", but of getting rid of "rogue states". If any organisation in any third world country advocates and campaigns for national autonomy, sovereignty, and the reversal of neo-"liberal" policies, then that organisation can be branded as "anti-US" and a potential terrorist outfit, and "joint action" can be initiated, by imperialist troops and local armed forces together, against such an outfit.

There is a further point here. In the name of fighting terrorism, the nation states in several third world countries have arrogated to themselves the right to deny civil liberties to "suspected terrorists" (The Prevention Of Terrorism Act 2002 in India is an obvious example of this). With the imperialist super-state exercising hegemony over the third world nation-states, and the latter in turn intensifying their authoritarian grip over the people through "anti-terrorist legislation", there is in effect a significant strengthening of the control of the imperialist superstate on the people of the third world. Opposition to "globalisation" can be dubbed "anti-West", hence *ipso facto* potentially terrorist, and invite repression on the basis of the law books of the domestic nation-state itself.

The second mechanism is to bind countries with international agreements, like the WTO, such that even if there is a change of regimes within any country, the fact of this change would make no difference to its policies. Interestingly the US itself repeatedly flouts the WTO with complete impunity, even though the WTO has been drafted keeping its interests and those of other imperialist countries uppermost in the mind. While the latest example of such flouting is the steel tariff it has imposed, instances such as the continuation of Special 301, Super 301, the formation of NAFTA, etc. constitute earlier violations of WTO. The third world countries on the other hand not only have their arms regularly twisted to force them into signing on the dotted line, but also face strict punishment in the event of their violating any part of the agreement. Such agreements constitute an imposition of an alien will on the juridically sovereign institutions of a third world country, and hence instruments in the armoury of the world imperialist dictatorship.

The third mechanism is the following. Unemployment, growing poverty, and material insecurity provide a breeding ground for secessionist, fundamentalist and fascist movements that divide the people along ethnic, religious, and communal lines, and hence run counter to any effort to unite them against imperialism. Such movements play into the hands of imperialism both by disrupting popular unity, and by enabling it to intervene on the side of whichever force happens to be pro-imperialist (some Islamic fundamentalist movements, for example, as opposed to the communal-fascist *Hindutva* movement in India, have an anti-imperialist thrust, and in their case imperialism intervenes in the name of "preserving civilization"). In short, dictatorship by the emerging imperialist super-state becomes that much more easily manageable when the third world is riven by divisive movements.

X

These divisive movements have the effect of weakening the third world nation-state, which is the chief weapon of resistance against super-imperialism. The undermining of the third world nation-state that came into being after decolonisation has been a constant endeavour of imperialism. In retrospect, globalisation was essentially a means of undermining the third world nation-state. It did so indirectly of course, by opening up economies to the movements of international finance and by forcing them, under pain of ruin through capital flight, to become obsessed with "maintaining the confidence of investors" which precludes any independent role of the state. But what is less commonly recognised is that it does so directly, through its continuous refrain about "bad governance", through its continuous harping on the theme of "public sector inefficiency", and through its obsessive emphasis on "corruption", even though many of these claims do not necessarily have empirical support, even though in all these respects the situation in the third world is in no way demonstrably any worse than in the metropolis, and even though a good many of such assertions amount to no more than racial slurs that the third world is incapable of governing itself, and needs to be taught "good governance" by its former colonial masters. This barrage of propaganda has the desired effect of truncating the support base of the nation-State, and together with more direct forms of coercion through Fund-Bank "conditionalities" and WTO-type "agreements", of "rolling back" its independence of operation.

To be sure, the post-decolonisation nation-state over much of the third world contributes heavily to its own historical demise through its own acts of omission and commission which result on the one hand in continuing poverty, poor health and nutrition, low levels of literacy, civil strife, and internecine conflicts along regional, communal and ethnic lines, and on the other hand in growing disparities, and aggrandisement by a small section of the population. But the "rolling back" of the state, as is demanded by imperialist agencies, far from removing these dichotomies, would accentuate them immensely, and has done so wherever such "rolling back" has occurred. In short the ills of capitalist development in the third world are laid at the door of the nation-State, and the panacea is seen not in a transcendence of capitalist development but in unleashing an even more blatantly aggrandising form of capitalism and undermining the nation-state.

XI

Let us recapitulate the argument advanced so far and draw

certain conclusions. Different phases of capitalism are associated not only with different forms of the state domestically but also with different relations between states internationally, or, in other words, different global state-systems. The current phase of capitalism is associated with a process of globalisation of finance and the formation on this basis of an international finance capital quite different from the finance capital of Lenin's time. Corresponding to this we are also seeing the emergence of a world imperialist superstate that defends the interests of this international finance capital and protects its freedom of operation worldwide. This superstate is formed out of, and on the basis of, the already existing system of nation-states, with some nation-states, i.e. those belonging to the advanced capitalist countries, acting in unison, under the undisputed leadership of the US, abrogating the sovereignty of the other, third world nation-states, and taking upon themselves the responsibility of "looking after the world economy and polity".

Since the process of globalisation is associated with economic retrogression and accentuation of poverty over much of the third world (and even large parts of the first world), it necessarily engenders resistance; resistance is also engendered by the abrogation of national sovereignty which means a rolling back of the independence won by many colonies and semi-colonies after years of bitter struggle against their "master nations". Faced with this resistance, which in certain circumstances may take the refracted and entirely counter-productive form of "terrorism", the world imperialist super-state increasingly, and necessarily, takes on authoritarian forms. It increasingly becomes a dictatorship, not just in the sense in which a state based on class rule can be described as a dictatorship, but in a more direct sense. Indeed a dialectic develops in certain periods whereby dictatorship and terrorism feed on each other, call forth each other, and justify each other to their respective protagonists, though of course the two sides in *this particular struggle* are vastly unequal. It is only the decisive action of the masses, as opposed to terrorism, that can help in transcending the situation.

The fact that such decisive mass action has not yet broken out does not mean that we are coming to "the end of history" where imperialist oppression perpetuates itself forever. There are to be sure contradictions in this emerging order. The very fact of oppression represents a major antagonistic contradiction, which, though it can be managed for a while, is bound to become more intractable over time. Dictatorship cannot be a permanent phenomenon in this day and age. Secondly, globalisation of finance has brought higher unemployment and greater inequalities in the advanced capitalist world itself, so that opposition to the new order, which is already quite considerable, is bound to grow over time. (The isolationist fascist movements growing in the advanced countries represent a grotesquely distorted initial expression of this fact). In short, developments within the advanced capitalist world may well provide increasing space for oppositional movements in the third world itself. Thirdly, even among the hegemonised nation-States in the third world, some may become more ambitious and try to carve out an autonomous space for themselves, in which case "managing them" would become more difficult than appeared at first sight. There is in other words plenty of room for the play of contradictions in this new situation. Nonetheless, the tendency towards a super-imperialist dictatorship, or, putting it differently, an imperialist super-state in the form of a dictatorship that is overarching and functions through establishing its hegemony over existing nation-states, is quite unmistakeable.

Understanding this phenomenon is an important prerequisite for fighting it. But this understanding is thwarted by the fact that many have detected in it a tendency towards an universalisation of humanist values, of freedom, democracy, and civil liberties. They could not be further from the truth; indeed they have imbibed imperialist propaganda about itself, which like the old "white man's burden" theory, pretends that it is spreading human values against barbarism when it is actually imposing a predatory despotism over much of the world.

NOTES

1. For a discussion of the change in the nature of the state between the free competition and monopoly phases of capitalism, see Oskar Lange (1970).
2. What follows has been discussed in Patnaik (2000).
3. The term "super-imperialism" was used by some writers earlier to describe the US position during the 1950s and the 1960s, when, among other things, the Bretton Woods system prevailed and conferred on the US dollar the official status of being "as good as gold". But while it is true that the US had a pre-eminent role *among imperialist powers* during that period, it was nonetheless constrained by the presence of the Soviet Union, which is why its capacity to enforce a super-imperialist status was limited then. This is no longer the case. The term "super-imperialism" therefore constitutes a more apt description of the US position today than during the 1950s and 60s.
4. This point is discussed in Patnaik (2002).
5. For an examination of the consequences of liberalisation and globalisation for the Indian economy, see Chandrasekhar & Ghosh (2002).

REFERENCES

Chandrasekhar, C.P. and Jayati Ghosh (2002), *The Market That Failed*, New Delhi: LeftWord Books.

Ghosh, Jayati and Abhijit Sen (1998), "Capital Flows and Macro-economies: A Historical View" in Deepak Nayyar ed. *Economics as Ideology and Experience: Essays in Honour of Ashok Mitra*, London: Frank Cass.

Lange, Oskar (1970), "The Role of the State Under Monopoly Capitalism", in *Papers on Economics and Sociology*, Pergamon Press.

Patnaik, Prabhat (2000), "Introduction" to V.I. Lenin, *Imperialism the Highest Stage of Capitalism*, New Delhi: LeftWord Books.

Patnaik, Prabhat (2002), "Globalisation of Capital and Terms of Trade Movements" in *Agrarian Studies* edited by V.K.Ramachandran and Madhura Swaminathan, New Delhi: Tulika Books.

Imperialism at the Beginning of the 21st Century

Doug Lorimer

A lot has been written, and will doubtless continue to be written, about how Marx's theory of capitalist development is a relic of a bygone era, irrelevant for understanding the complex dynamics of the "globalised", "post-industrial", "financialised" capitalism that is supposed to have emerged only at the end of the 20th century.

Contemporary capitalism, however, can only be scientifically understood using Marx's theory of capitalist development. The proof of such an assertion is demonstrated by the fact that Marx himself, in analysing the dynamics of capitalist economy in the 1860s, predicted that its further development would give rise to the fundamental features that characterise contemporary capitalism.

Marx's Analysis of Capitalism

Marx began his analysis of capitalism by discerning that it was an economic system in which the direct producers of goods and services are dispossessed of the means of production and forced to sell their ability to produce goods and services to those who possess the means of production as capital, as means to accumulate surplus labour in the form of monetary values. In the capitalist system, capital is accumulated through buying the commodity labour-power.

The two basic social classes that are engendered by the capitalist system are the "personification" of this process. The working class are those people, Marx says, "who produce and valorise `capital' and are thrown onto the street as soon as they become superfluous to the need for valorisation possessed by `Monsieur Capital'". They are people, for instance, who comprise many different kinds of workers, engaged in many different kinds of social activity, and who dress in many different kinds of clothes. But whether they wear a suit or overalls or are highly or poorly educated, or live in a comfortable suburban house or a squalid inner-city slum, if their income is solely derived from having to sell their labour-power to owners of capital, they are members of the class of wage-workers. Everyone, Marx quips in the first volume of *Capital*, "who lives only so long as they find work, and who finds work only so long as their labour increases capital" is a member of this class. In the *Communist Manifesto* Marx and Engels observed that those "who must sell themselves piecemeal, are a commodity, like every other article of commerce, and are consequently exposed to all the vicissitudes of competition, to all the fluctuations of the market".

Here, of course, one's class definition hinges on one's relationship to the process of accumulation of capital. Marx put a lot of emphasis in his theory of capitalism on this process. He describes in almost glowing terms its prodigious power to burst through every historical and geographical restriction it encounters, its power to conquer the world of social wealth, creating a whole array of new values along the way. Yet, at the same time, Marx was appalled by the brutality the process of accumulation of capital unleashes, by the horrors it inflicts upon the human race.

The drive to accumulate capital, Marx explains, pits capitalist against worker and worker against worker. But it also pits capitalist against capitalist. It subordinates, Marx says, "every capitalist to the immanent laws of capitalist production, as external and coercive laws". So, as capitalists strive to accumulate capital, as their actions become mere functions of the process of capital accumulation, they inevitably clash with other capitalists.

But over time the process of capital accumulation and the competition between capitalists lead to the concentration and centralisation of capital in the hands of fewer and fewer capitalists as big capitalist fish gobble up the little capitalist fish. According to Marx, this enhances the scale of operations for both capital and wage-labour, leading both of them to become increasingly socialised in their actual operations.

The labour of each individual worker becomes interdependent upon the labour of other workers, not just within their direct place of employment, but across whole branches of production within a nation and between nations.

The effects of concentration and centralisation of capital upon the capitalists also accelerates the *socialisation of capital*. This is because competition and the obligatory development of the credit system become powerful levers for the merging of private capitals into associations of capital, into joint-stock companies, in which capital in the form of the means of production is no longer the possession of any individual capitalist but of an *association of capitalists*.

The formation of joint-stock companies leads, Marx says in the third volume of *Capital*, firstly, to a "tremendous expansion of the scale of production" which would be impossible for individual capitalists operating on their own. Secondly, it leads to a situation in which one or a few firms are able to dominate whole spheres of social production. The production enterprises controlled by these firms no longer produce goods and services for a handful of wealthy people, but for the entire society, and they have thus become in fact social enterprises. Thirdly, it leads to the owners of capital ceasing to be the managers of the labour process, of the direct process of production of goods and services. This function is turned over to salaried employees, while the capitalist becomes, as Marx puts it, "a mere owner, a mere money capitalist".

From this analysis of the nature and dynamic of joint-stock companies, Marx drew the conclusion that joint-stock companies, which were only just beginning to be formed in the second half of the 19th century, represented "capitalist production in its highest development" because they are the "abolition of the capitalist mode of production within the capitalist mode of production itself" and are therefore the "necessary point of transition towards the transformation of capital" as means of production "back into the property of the producers, though no longer as the private property of individual producers, but rather as their property as associated producers", that is, as social property. Joint-stock companies are "abolition of the capitalist mode of production within the capitalist mode of production itself" because they contradict the *essence* of capitalist relations of production. That is, rather than private ownership of means of production for private production of wealth, joint-stock companies give rise to social ownership of means of production for social production of wealth. But they do so within the framework of the private appropriation of the surplus labour embodied in the wealth of goods and services that are produced.

As this contradiction develops, Marx says, it "presents itself as such a contradiction even in appearance" by, firstly, giving "rise to monopolies", which in turn demand increasing state intervention in economic activity and by, secondly, producing a "new financial aristocracy, a new kind of parasite in the guise of company promoters, speculators and merely nominal directors, an entire system of swindling and cheating with respect to the promotion of companies, issues of shares and share dealings".

In a supplementary note to the first edition of Volume 3 of *Capital*, Engels wrote in 1894 that when Marx wrote these words in 1865, "the stock exchange was still a *secondary* element in the capitalist system", but that since then "a change has occurred that gives the stock exchange of today a significantly increased role, and a constantly growing one at that, which, as it develops further, has the tendency to concentrate the whole of production, industrial as well as agricultural, together with the whole of commerce — means of communication as well as the exchange of function — in the hands of stock-exchange speculators, so that the stock exchange becomes the most pre-eminent representative of capitalist production as such."

The Imperialist Epoch of Capitalism

Utilising Marx's theory of capitalist development, Lenin concluded 85 years ago that all the features which Marx had forecast in 1865 as characteristic of "capitalist production in its highest development" had become dominant in Western Europe, North America, Japan and in his native Russia.

On the basis of economic data compiled by bourgeois economists in the early years of the 20th century, Lenin argued in December 1915 that "at the end of the 19th and the beginning of the 20th centuries, commodity exchange had created such an internationalisation of economic relations, and such an internationalisation of capital, accompanied by such a vast increase in large-scale production, that free competition began to be replaced by monopoly".

The dominant type of capitalist businesses was, Lenin wrote, "no longer enterprises freely competing inside the country and through intercourse between countries, but monopoly alliances of entrepreneurs, trusts" which were carving up the world market between themselves.

"The typical ruler of the world", Lenin wrote, "became finance capital, a power that is peculiarly mobile and flexible, peculiarly intertwined at home and internationally, peculiarly devoid of individuality and divorced from the immediate processes of production, peculiarly easy to concentrate, a power that has already made peculiarly large strides on the road to concentration, so that literally several hundred billionaires and millionaires hold in their hands the fate of the whole world". (Lenin, 1977: 104-05)

Lenin further concluded that the domination of the economic and political life of the advanced capitalist countries by these financial oligarchies had given rise to a new epoch in the history of the world which had superseded the epoch of the comparatively peaceful extension of the domination of capitalist production across the entire globe, "marked approximately by the years 1871 and 1914". Of course, he noted that even this epoch of "peaceful" expansion of capitalism had "created conditions of life that were very far from being really peaceful both in the military and in a general class sense". He pointed out that: "For nine-tenths of the population of the advanced countries, for hundreds of millions of peoples in the colonies and in the backward countries this epoch was not one of `peace' but of oppression, tortures, horrors that seemed the more terrifying since they appeared to be without end."

"This epoch has gone forever", Lenin said. "It has been followed by a new epoch, comparatively more impetuous, full of abrupt changes, catastrophes, conflicts, an epoch that no longer appears to the toiling masses as horror without end but is an end full of horrors." This new epoch, Lenin explained in his 1916 book *Imperialism, the Highest Stage of Capitalism*, would be marked above all by the drive by each of the financial oligarchies of the advanced capitalist countries to use the coercive power and organised violence of the state machines they commanded to maintain their imperial domination over the economic and political life of the backward countries and to increase their wealth at the expense not only of working people at home and abroad but also in competition with the financial oligarchies that dominated the other advanced countries. Consequently, the new imperialist epoch of capitalism would be marked by repeated colonial wars, uprisings by imperialist-dominated peoples and inter-imperialist military conflicts that would create the political conditions for abolishing capitalism through successful working-class revolutions.

The Global Economy Today

It is often claimed that the extent of internationalisation of production today has far outstripped the levels that existed when Lenin made his analysis of imperialist capitalism and that his analysis, which was based on a world market still fragmented into many national economies, is therefore "outdated".

It is certainly true that there was a phenomenal increase in international movements of money-capital over the last two decades of the 20th century. Trillions of dollars flow in and out of bond, share and currency markets on a 24-hour basis. The massive inflation of these markets has been dramatic. In 1973, a typical day's trading on the world's currency markets amounted to US$15 billion. By 1983 it had risen to US$60 billion; by 1992 to

US$900 billion. By the end of the 1990s it has risen to US$1,300 billion. In comparison, the total foreign currency reserves of the Western governments amount to only US$64 billion.

The total stock of financial assets — company stocks and derivatives, government bonds, etc — increased from US$5 trillion in 1980 to US$35 trillion in 1992 and is expected to be more than US$80 trillion this year — three times the total value of goods and services produced in the advanced capitalist economies.

However, claims that there has been a dramatic increase in cross-border trade in goods and services, or in transfers of productive capital, are vastly overstated. In 1913, for example, world trade in goods and services amounted to 16% of world output. After a sharp fall in the interwar years, it gradually climbed back up to 15% only in 1990. Similarly, the world's accumulated stock of foreign direct investment was equivalent to 12% of world output in 1913. By 1990 it stood no higher than 10% of world output.

Today, it should be obvious to everyone that the features that Marx forecast back in 1865 as characteristic of "capitalist production in its highest development" — joint-stock companies, separation of capital ownership from managerial functions in the direct process of production, monopolies, extensive state intervention in economic activity, the existence of a "financial aristocracy" consisting of "parasites in the guise of company promoters, speculators and merely nominal directors" — are the dominant form through which the process of accumulation of capital occurs on a world scale.

Just about everyone can see that stock exchanges today do not operate to raise new money for investment in the production of goods and services by issuing titles to a share in a company's profits in exchange for handing over one's spare cash to its directors, which was their original role in the capitalist system. Today it is obvious to everyone that the stock exchanges are really billion dollar markets for speculation on already existing stocks, and that the responsibility of any CEO has little, if anything, to do with managing the production of goods and services but, rather, to make the shareholders, particularly the biggest shareholders, as much money as possible, as fast as possible, through ensuring a rapid and continuous rise in the price, the market value, of the company's stock of money-market instruments (stocks, bonds, etc.). This is the logical outcome, and highest development, of a mode of production based upon the drive to accumulate capital, to accumulate paper values.

Of course, the big investors today are not mere money-capitalists. Finance capital is a new form of capital, in which the owners of capital in the form of stocks own not only banks and other financial institutions but industrial corporations as well.

In the 19th century industrial capital and banking capital had distinctly different owners, reflecting the smaller scale of capitalist operations. The rise of joint-stock companies as the dominant form of capitalist businesses at the end of the 19th century brought about a merger of industrial and banking capital into finance capital. The 60 or so families that Ferdinand Lundeberg identified in the 1930s, and again in 1968, as constituting the US financial oligarchy — the Rockefellers, Morgans, Mellons, DuPonts, Whitneys, Warburgs, Vanderbilts, etc. — did not just control all the major banks and insurance companies in the US, but also all the major industrial corporations. The Rockefeller family, for example, had effective ownership not only of the Chase banking corporation and the Met-Life insurance corporation, but also industrial corporations such as Exxon, Mobil and — in combination with the Mellon family — Westinghouse. The Morgan and Whitney families were not only the effective owners of the banks J.P. Morgan and Bankers' Trust, but also of US Steel, General Electric and — in combination with the Du Pont family — of General Motors.

It is thus utterly misleading to talk about the explosion of speculation on the money markets over the last two decades as the rise to "dominance" of finance capital — as though there are the "good", productive, "industrial" capitalists and the "bad", speculative, finance capitalists, and the latter today dominate over the former.

Since the beginning of the 20th century, capitalist production and capital accumulation has been dominated by finance capital.

The financial oligarchs invest their money-capital in both the production of commodities and in speculation in the money markets. Speculation on the money markets has absorbed more and more of their investments because, since the end of long post-war wave of expansion of capitalist production of goods and services, continued reinvestment of the profits they derive from investment in the production of real values has become less lucrative than the diversion of a growing share of these profits into gambling on the stock, bond and other markets for paper values.

Rise of US Imperialism

As a consequence of World War I, US imperialism gained pre-eminence over its European imperialist rivals. US capitalism, which Lenin called "the only full beneficiary from the war", emerged in the 1920s not only as the capitalist world's chief creditor, but also its leading industrial power. Nevertheless, its standing as the world's chief imperialist power remained subject to challenge from its rivals, whose colonial empires in Asia and Africa remained largely intact, in some instances even expanding.

In the mid-1920s, the Bolshevik economic theorist Yevgeny Preobrazhensky noted that the United States had already acquired a pre-eminent position in the world economy and drew a momentous conclusion. "American expansion", he wrote, "cannot encounter an unbreakable resistance in any country of the capitalist world so long as the country undergoing attack and pressure remains capitalist". The reason for this, in his view, was that US dominance was a function of the commanding technological and financial superiority of its monopolistic corporations in an increasingly integrated world market, and that this very superiority ensured its eventual triumph in any competition in that market. Elaborating on this idea, Preobrazhensky wrote:

> The very economic structure of the present-day capitalist countries excludes the possibility of serious resistance to American conquest, because the already attained level of the world division of labour, of world exchange, with the

existence of the huge and ever-growing economic, technical and financial superiority of America over all the rest of the world inevitably subjects this world to the value-relations of America. Not a single capitalist country can, without ceasing to be capitalist, break away from the operation of the law of value in its changed form. And it is just here that the avalanche of American monopolism falls on it. Resistance is possible only perhaps, on a political basis, specifically on a military basis, but just because of America's economic superiority this would hardly prove successful.

Preobrazhensky concluded:

A struggle against American monopolism is possible only through changes in the whole structure of the given country, that is, through going over to a socialist economy, and would not allow American capitalism to get hold of one branch of industry after another, subjecting them to American trusts or banks, as is happening with the "natural" contact between present-day American capitalism and the capitalism of other capitalist countries. (Preobrazhensky, 1965: 157-9)

A decade and a half after this was written, the US rulers' German and Japanese imperialist competitors made a bid to resist and overcome by military means the challenge of US monopolism, and, as Preobrazhensky forecast, this bid proved disastrously unsuccessful.

At the end of World War II, the US monopolists looked set to realise their goal of world domination. At the end of 1945, the US accounted for 50% of world industrial production, and its rulers had overwhelming military supremacy among the imperialist powers. On this basis, the propagandists of US imperialism trumpeted the beginning of the "American century".

This "American century", however, ran into a major obstacle the US rulers did not count on—an enormous wave of political rebellion and social insurgency by the world's working people. In Europe, German imperial expansionism had been smashed by a combination of the mass resistance of the Soviet workers and peasants and local worker-peasant movements under

Stalinist leadership. A revolutionary wave of revulsion against capitalist rule in Italy and France threatened the survival of capitalism. On the mainland of Asia, Japanese imperial expansion had also been smashed by a similar combination of action by the Soviet workers and peasants in uniform and local Communist-led national liberation movements.

Under the impact of the "Get us home" movement among US soldiers at the end of 1945, the massive US conscript army was temporarily disabled as an effective instrument for large-scale counter-insurgency operations. The US rulers were therefore unable to block the destruction of capitalist regimes and the capitalist economic structure in a series of eastern European countries in the late 1940s and in China in the early 1950s.

To restore capitalist stability in western Europe and Japan, Washington had to provide huge public loans to its imperialist rivals in Europe and Japan, which enabled them not only to revive production but, over the course of the 1950s and 1960s, to modernise their technology, bringing them into a position to offer increasing competition with US corporations at home and abroad, thus undermining the virtually unchallenged dominance the latter held within the world capitalist market at the end of World War II.

To rebuild their military forces as effective instruments for policing the world, the US rulers launched a campaign to instil fear and stifle political dissent among the US masses. This campaign became known as McCarthyism after a Republican senator, Joseph McCarthy, who conducted televised hearings in the early 1950s into an alleged Communist conspiracy within the US government. However, the anti-leftist witch-hunt was initiated by Democratic President Harry Truman, who signed an executive order in 1947 requiring 2.5 million government employees to be investigated by the FBI for potential "disloyalty", defined as "membership in, affiliation with, or sympathetic association with … any … organization, association, movement, group or combination of persons, designated by the Attorney General as totalitarian". Soon afterwards, this "loyalty check" was extended to include the three million members of the armed forces and three million employees of defence contractors—a total of 8 million people.

At the same time, on the basis of the rise in the rate of exploitation of labour resulting from the mass unemployment of the pre-war depression and wartime inflation, US capitalists were able to invest profitably in the technological innovations stimulated by war production. These in turn, particularly the use of electronically controlled semi-automated production systems, enabled the monopolists greatly to cheapen the cost of the production of whole branches of industry, and thus to expand the markets for these products.

This provided the economic basis for a twenty-year period of accelerated accumulation of capital, during which they were able to create a substantial enough aristocratic layer within the US working class to extinguish the embers of mass labour radicalism that had exploded in the 1930s.

Combined with the anti-leftist witch-hunt, this process eliminated the need for the US rulers to move outside the framework of capitalist democracy to maintain political stability at home as they pursued their global counterinsurgency strategy, which centred on blocking the anti-colonial struggles of the workers and peasants in the Third World from being transformed into successful anti-capitalist revolutions.

Decolonisation and US Imperialism

The disintegration of the colonial empires in Asia under the combined impact of the military and economic exhaustion of the European colonial powers, the military defeat of Japan and the rise of national independence movements, enabled US imperialism to expand its economic interests and military influence throughout the former colonies. Before the Second World War, for example, US corporations owned only 13% of the oil production of the Middle East; by 1960 they owned 65%.

With some exceptions, US imperialism did not seek to replace the European colonial empires with its own overt political control. For many liberal thinkers, the end of colonialism signalled the end of imperialism. However, colonialism was only a politically contingent phase of imperialist development.

Lenin recognised this and as early as 1916 suggested that "some slight change in the political and strategic relations of, say Germany and Britain, might today or tomorrow make the formation of a new Polish, Indian and other similar state fully 'practicable'" since, as he put it, "the domination of finance capital and capital in general is not abolished by any reforms in the sphere of political democracy; and [national] self-determination belongs wholly and exclusively to this sphere..." (Lenin, 1977: 144-45)

What fundamentally distinguished the imperialist stage of capitalism, in Lenin's view, was the replacement of the free competition of many small and medium-sized capitalist firms by the domination of the world capitalist market by a new form of capitalist ownership—finance capital—in which a small number of super-rich capitalist families and associations of these families held controlling ownership of monopolistic industrial corporations and monopolistic banks and other financial enterprises.

While in his 1916 book *Imperialism, the Highest Stage of Capitalism*, Lenin noted, "Finance capital is such a great, such a decisive, you might say, force in all economic and all international relations, that it is capable of subjecting, and actually does subject to itself even states enjoying the fullest political independence", he tended to regard the conquest of colonies as the culmination of finance capital's striving for domination. Thus, he argued, "finance capital finds most 'convenient', and derives the greatest profits from, a form of subjection which involves the loss of political independence of the subjected countries and peoples". (Lenin, 1977: 259) He therefore regarded the semi-colonial countries, countries which were, as he put it, "formally independent, but in fact, are enmeshed in the net of financial and diplomatic dependence" on the imperialist powers, as being in a "transitional form of state dependence" on their way to becoming direct colonial possessions of one of the imperialist powers. (Lenin, 1977: 263)

The scramble among the European capitalist powers to acquire colonial possessions, however, occurred in the period 1875-1900, that is, in the quarter-century before the imperialist stage of capitalism. While there cannot be any doubt that it was strongly influenced by the growth of national monopolies in the major capitalist countries and their drive to secure cheap sources of raw materials, the two countries in which monopolisation proceeded earliest and fastest—the United States and Germany—were either absent or latecomers in the "great game". The leading players were the oldest of the industrial capitalist powers—Britain, France and Belgium. For the British capitalist rulers, the drive to acquire colonies represented a reversal of the previous trend of policy. Thus in 1852, British treasurer Benjamin Disraeli declared, "These wretched colonies will be independent in a few years and are millstones around our necks" (quoted in Horowitz, 1971: 47), while 20 years later he announced his conversion to a policy of colonial expansionism.

What had changed in the intervening period was that Britain had lost its world monopoly of industrial production. During the period when Britain held this technological monopoly, its rulers advocated open competition in international markets. From the late 1860s, however, two new industrial powers—the United States and Germany—began to challenge Britain's economic supremacy. In a world of increasingly competitive and internationally oriented rivals, a movement by any of them to secure monopoly control of markets or supplies of raw materials by political means would inevitably tend to provoke a general pre-emptive scramble for colonial possessions to prevent the loss of presently held or potentially valuable markets. In retrospect, this appears to have been the major—even determinant—factor in producing the rush to acquire colonies.

This pre-emptive and preventive nature of imperialist colonialism is most clearly seen in the foreign policy of US imperialism, which eschewed formal for informal empire. This policy was first articulated by secretary of state John Hay in his "Open Door Notes", circulated in 1898, which sought to prevent European colonial expansion in China and preserve open access for all the imperialist powers to the Chinese market. This open door, as Woodrow Wilson aptly described it, was "not the open door to the rights of China, but the open door to the goods of America". (Quoted in Gittings, 1967: 186) As a political strategy, the open door policy represented the natural policy of a new great economic power, which recognised that open competition, in foreign as well as domestic markets, was the most efficient way of ensuring domination for the strongest. As the financier Andrew Carnegie argued shortly before the policy was announced:

> The United States does not know the destiny that is lying immediately at her feet, provided she turns from ... phantom schemes of annexation of barbarous peoples in distant lands and just looks down ... and sees what the gods have placed within her grasp—the industrial dominion of the world. (Quoted in Horowitz, 1971: 70)

The US annexation of the Philippines following the US-Spanish war of 1898, while seemingly contradicting the open door policy, in fact was in part motivated by it. The Philippines was seen by the US rulers as the gateway to the markets of China, and in the context of the global colonial scramble the only guarantee of US access to China, at the time, seemed to be annexation.

The US war with Spain over Cuba and the Philippines also brought to the fore a central element of subsequent US foreign policy—military intervention to protect imperialist interests from national liberation movements. Spain's inability to suppress rebellion in its empire was a major motivating factor for US military intervention. Thus Spain's inability to control revolutionary unrest in Cuba, where US corporations already had substantial interests, was regarded by President William McKinley as a condition which "causes disturbance in the social and political condition of our own people ... and tends to delay the condition of prosperity to which this country is entitled". (Quoted in Williams, 1962: 34)

Unlike the Philippines, which was annexed as a US colony, Cuba was placed under US military rule until 1902, when it was granted formal independence under a government subservient to US corporate interests. The Cuba intervention set the subsequent pattern for US imperialist policy toward the underdeveloped countries. Between 1900 and 1917, for example, Washington intervened militarily on more than 20 occasions, in countries from Colombia to China, to suppress threats to US property during revolutionary outbreaks, and to impose nominally independent governments prepared to protect these interests.

In the face of anti-imperialist rebellions in the Third World after World War II, the US imperialists pursued the same strategy. During the 1950s and 1960s, they managed to register some significant successes in suppressing the tide of anti-imperialist revolution in the Third World. These included blocking the extension of anti-capitalist revolution to the southern half of the Korean peninsula in the early 1950s, the smashing of incipient revolutions in the Congo and Brazil in the early 1960s, and, most important of all, the almost complete extermination of the anti-imperialist movement in Indonesia in 1965-66.

Washington's global counter-revolutionary counter-offensive also suffered two significant defeats in each of these decades. It was unable to prevent its French imperialist allies from suffering defeat at the hands of the Marxist-led national liberation movement in Vietnam in 1954 and the creation of a workers' state in the north of that country. And it was unable to stop the overthrow of its puppet regime in Cuba in 1959 and the subsequent consolidation under Marxist leadership of the first workers state in the western hemisphere.

However, on the back of their counter-revolutionary success in Indonesia, the US imperialists began a huge escalation of their counter-revolutionary military assault on the revolutionary movement in southern Vietnam, dispatching half a million combat troops to save Washington's puppet regime in Saigon and launching a massive bombing campaign against the workers state in the north.

Vietnam War

In Vietnam, Washington's huge military machine proved unable to crush a mass insurgent movement headed by a revolutionary leadership. This undermined the credibility of its global counter-revolutionary strategy among the US masses and destroyed the reactionary McCarthyist atmosphere of hostility to anti-capitalist ideas.

Already in the mid-1950s, the reactionary political climate began to be undermined by the mass actions undertaken by African-Americans against the legally sanctioned apartheid regime they had to endure in the southern US states. These mass actions increasingly drew a new generation of white working-class and middle-class Americans into progressive political activity.

As it became clear that the US rulers' war against the Vietnamese revolution could not achieve a quick and easy victory, rifts emerged within the ruling elite about how to conduct the war. While these were merely tactical differences, they helped legitimise public expressions of outright opposition to the war and placed an obstacle in the way of a repressive crackdown against such public expressions.

Increasing numbers of young people in the US advanced from criticism of the hypocrisy of the ruling elite's denial of democratic rights for black Americans and the non-white peoples of the Third World to a consciously anti-imperialist and anti-capitalist outlook.

The attitude toward the war in Vietnam of the mass of US working people turned from apathy to deepening opposition as it became clear to them that the ruling elite was willing to sacrifice the lives of tens of thousands of young conscripts in an unwinnable war. This shift in the attitude of the masses provided the social base for the building of the largest anti-war movement in us history, a movement that increasingly found sympathy and expression among the ranks of the US conscripts in Vietnam, which in turn rendered the US conscript army utterly unreliable as a world police force. It was this factor that in the end led to the defeat of the US rulers' counter-revolutionary enterprise in Vietnam.

The US defeat in Vietnam was the culmination of the shift in the international relationship of class forces to the detriment of imperialism resulting from the wave of mass insurgency in the Third World that flowed out of World War II. In a few semi-colonial countries, such as China, Korea, Cuba and Vietnam, this mass insurgency led to the creation of workers' and peasants' governments and the destruction of the capitalist economic structure. The overwhelming majority of Third World countries, however, remained dominated by the world capitalist market and oppressed by the imperialist system. Most are saddled with governments that represent domestic capitalist exploiters subservient to imperialist finance capital.

'Marshall Plan' for the Third World

Between 1948 and 1952 the US rulers provided billions of dollars in long-term loans that were used to rebuild the foundations for renewed industrial production and political stabilisation in war-ravaged capitalist Europe and Japan. The expansion of the developed capitalist economies over the subsequent two decades rapidly narrowed the large initial post-war gap between the level of productivity in the US and the other developed capitalist countries.

Many liberal commentators have called for a similar "Marshall Plan" to be applied to the Third World in the naive view that this would have similar results there. However, imperialist domination of the semi-colonial countries prevents the development of a class structure and value of labour power capable of supporting an internal market that can either meet the profit needs of a broad developing local bourgeoisie or absorb massive imports of capital and commodities from the imperialist countries. These semi-colonial class relations permit the emergence of isolated pockets of "prosperity": layers of wealthy export and service-oriented capitalists and a narrow, relatively prosperous, middle class. But there neither is nor can be a relatively well-off population of employed wage workers or prosperous farmers able to purchase a wide range of consumer durables on a level comparable to the imperialist countries.

Since the late 1960s imperialist governments, banks and international finance agencies have foisted hundreds of billions of dollars in loans on the semi-colonial countries. The Marshall Plan has been repeated. Its main result has been a disaster for the workers, peasants and even the bulk of the urban middle class in the semi-colonial countries. Nor has it proved possible for local capitalists to reproduce the successes registered in postwar Europe and Japan. Just the opposite has occurred: the gap between the economic strength of the imperialist and semi-colonial countries has widened. The Third World debt has not been a blessing preliminary to a historic developmental take-off, but a trap preliminary to a devastating crisis. The contrasting experiences of the results of the Marshall Plan in Western Europe and Japan, on the one hand, and its repetition in the semi-colonial capitalist countries on the other, demonstrate that debt is a social relation, one that has diametrically different effects depending on the relative power of the lender and borrower.

In a handful of semi-colonial countries—South Korea, Taiwan, Mexico, Brazil and Argentina—imperialist loans facilitated a process of broader industrialisation in the 1980s. In the 1990s these countries became the targets for a substantial shift of international capital flows, as the bulk of imperialist capital flowing into the Third World switched from loans into portfolio investments—that is, into buying up stocks and bonds in the big private companies and newly privatised state enterprises of what are known as the "emerging markets". As the experience of each of these countries has demonstrated, this buying up of shares is simply a stepping-stone to imperialist capital directly taking over and running the largest and most profitable enterprises in these countries, which were formerly in the hands of local capitalists—that is, to reversing the limited gains in independent industrialisation that were made by these capitalists during the 1980s.

The US defeat in Vietnam in the early 1970s coincided with the exhaustion of the factors that had sustained a twenty-year wave of rapid expansion of the imperialist economies, a sharp fall in the rate of profit and the resurgence of the "normal" tendency of monopoly capitalism toward increasing economic stagnation and financial instability.

During this "long boom", the imperialist economic system underwent a new stage of development in which the international concentration and centralisation of finance capital, particularly US finance capital, proceeded at faster pace than at any time in history.

Transnational Corporations

This new stage of imperialism was marked above all by the emergence of transnational corporations, corporations based upon an international division of labour, as the dominant form of capitalist business organisation. Such corporations had existed before the Second World War, but they were largely confined to the sphere of extraction, processing and distribution of raw materials such as petroleum.

In his 1969 book *Imperialism and Revolution*, David Horowitz noted that between 1946 and 1966 US direct foreign investment had grown by almost 800%. He went on to give the following description of the forces that propelled this post-war overseas expansion:

> "To develop commercially the new technologies (many of which received immense stimulus from the war) required heavy research and manufacturing investments and hence mass markets over which to spread unit costs. At the same time modern communications and mass media standardized tastes in different countries, while resurgent economic nationalism, often coupled with foreign currency shortages, induced governments to ensure that international goods they bought were manufactured on their own soil.

> In the course of these developments a new corporate form emerged—the "multi-national" or international corporation. Carrying out both manufacturing and marketing operations in literally dozens of countries, such corporations, as distinct from even their giant predecessors, no longer merely look to foreign sources for an independent share of sales, profits and growth, but rather seek "to apply company resources on a global scale to realize business opportunities anywhere in the world". Once placed in "external" markets, international corporations seek to expand their control of these markets as such; for they are locked in mortal combat

with similar giants for control of markets at an international level." (Horowitz, 1971: 242-3)

Referring specifically to US transnational corporations, Horowitz observed that in 1964 "only 45 U.S. firms account for almost 60 per cent of direct U.S. foreign investment, while 80 per cent is held by 163 firms". (Horowitz, 1971: 244)

At home and abroad, US corporations invested in the mechanisation, semi-automation and massive expansion of factories producing automobiles, refrigerators, washing machines, vacuum cleaners, television sets and other consumer durables. Consequently, the great bulk of US foreign investments went to mass consumer markets for these products provided by other imperialist countries. By the late 1960s, 80% of the foreign assets of US corporations were in Western Europe, Canada, Japan, Australia and New Zealand. Similarly, as the big capitalists of the other imperialist countries, particularly those of Western Europe and Japan, recovered from the ravages of World War II, and began to transform their companies into transnational corporations, the bulk of their foreign investments also flowed into other imperialist countries, including the United States.

The post-war extension of the internationalisation of the forces and processes of production that formed the substratum for the rise to dominance of transnational corporations entailed a substantial deepening of the fundamental contradiction inherent in the capitalist system. This is the contradiction between, on the one hand, the increasing social and economic interaction and interdependence among people throughout the world and, on the other, the political division of the world into a series of nation-states in which a small number of wealthy families own the commanding heights of the economy, which enables them to control all major decision making in the interests of furthering their own private enrichment rather than meeting the needs of the vast majority of humanity.

Imperialist capitalism had already brought this contradiction to maturity, as the editors of the *London Economist* openly acknowledged when they wrote in October 1930: "The supreme difficulty of our generation ... is that our achievements in the economic plane of life have outstripped our program on the political plane to such an extent that our economics and politics are perpetually falling out of gear with one another. On the economic plane, the world has been organized into a single all-embracing unit of activity. On the political plane, it has remained ... partitioned. The tension between these two antithetical tendencies has been producing a series of jolts and smashes in the social life of humanity."

Imperialist capitalism deepens this contradiction not only from its economic side by extending the internationalisation of production and centralising capital in the hands of "a few hundred billionaires"; it also deepens it on the political side, by strengthening the coercive power of the capitalist state in the imperialist countries through a massive growth of its armed forces and by extending the capitalist state's role in guaranteeing the surplus profits of the capitalist monopolies, mainly by providing them with subsidies and state orders—above all, but not exclusively, for armaments.

Imperialism and State Economic Intervention

In the 19th century, during the era of freely competitive capitalism, the attitude of the capitalists toward the state was summed up in the classical liberal aphorism, "The best government is the least government". State revenues and expenditures in the capitalist countries were kept to a minimum, accounting for around 5% of gross domestic product (GDP).

By contrast, in the imperialist epoch, the epoch of the domination of world economy and world politics by finance capital, the share of state revenues and expenditure steadily rose, accounting for around 40% of the GDP of imperialist countries since the Second World War. A substantial part of the growth of these state revenues and expenditures, particularly in Western Europe and Australia, reflected the expansion of the socialised portion of wages in the forms of welfare payments, publicly funded housing, health care and education. This expansion of the socialised portion of wages was undertaken during the post-war "long boom" as a political response to counter the attraction that the social security measures inherent in the Soviet bloc's post-capitalist planned economies exercised over large sections of the working class in these countries.

However, the greater part of growth of the imperialist state's expenditures was the result the increasing need of the monopoly corporations for state subsidies. This can be most clearly seen in the growth of state expenditures in the United States, where the post-war McCarthyist witch-hunt completely marginalized those sections of the working class that were attracted to the Soviet alternative to capitalism and the US rulers therefore had no political need to create a large "welfare state". Instead, the large post-war expansion of state expenditures in the US was connected with the creation and supply of a huge military machine. In fact, as a share of GDP, non-military expenditure by the US government remained roughly what it was in 1929.

The qualitatively greater role that the capitalist state plays in the economic life of the imperialist countries is a reflection of the inability of imperialist capitalism to spontaneously reproduce itself by simply relying on the laws of the capitalist market—a reflection of the fact that, as Lenin pointed out, imperialist capitalism is the epoch of decaying capitalism, capitalism which has reached the stage where it has to be propped up by the use of mechanisms that run counter to its own spontaneous laws of motion.

The neo-liberal offensive launched against "big government" by the imperialist rulers at the end of the 1970s might seem to contradict this, but this offensive has not been aimed at reducing the overall levels of state expenditures in the imperialist countries. Rather, it has been aimed at cutting back the share of these expenditures allocated to working people's welfare and increasing the share that goes directly to provide subsidies to the corporations and their rentier owners: it is part of the drive to increase finance capital's exploitation of wage earners in the face of the return of monopoly capitalism's long-term tendency toward economic stagnation.

The Last Empire

While she was President Clinton's secretary of state, Madeleine Albright stated, "The United States is the world's indispensable nation". While this comment might seem to be nothing but an expression of US imperial arrogance and national chauvinism, from a Marxist viewpoint it has a rational content: the United States is the world imperialist system's indispensable nation. The economic and military strength of the United States is indispensable to the survival of the imperialist system.

While the other imperialist ruling classes inevitably seek to advance their own interests against each other and against the US rulers and US-owned corporations in the world capitalist market, they know that there is no imperialist power that can displace the dominance of the US, either economically or militarily.

This situation is new in the history of world capitalism. In the 16th and 17th centuries, the Spanish and Dutch empires, through bloody colonial expansion in the Americas and Asia, accumulated much of the wealth on which capitalism based its initial spurt of growth. By the 18th century, they had been displaced by Britain and France, and by the end of that century, British agricultural, banking and manufacturing capital had laid the foundation for what was to be a century of world dominance before being displaced by US capital.

While US imperialism has suffered a relative decline in its position since the end of World War II, this has not brought any of its imperialist competitors closer to establishing its own predominance in the capitalist world.

The US has 63% of the imperialist world's naval tonnage, 46% of its land-based and 91% of its sea-based military aircraft, and 39% of its ground troops. Its armed forces are the backbone of NATO and of the military alliance with imperialist Japan and Australia. The US rulers' international military supremacy, however, is not simply based on being the most massively armed power within a system of military alliances with other imperialist powers. Nor, like Britain in its heyday, does Washington rely primarily on its unchallenged position as the world's leading naval power. Unlike any of its predecessors, Washington's imperial might reaches directly into every part of the world.

All of the imperialist powers are dependent on the massive presence of US ground, air and naval forces on every continent and every ocean to maintain the "security" of the world capitalist order.

In addition to Washington's military power, the enormous size and weight of the US market and productive capacity also preclude any replacement of US imperial dominance in the capitalist world. The US market absorbs some 25% of the goods imported by all the imperialist countries combined. Between the beginning of the 1960s and the mid-1980s, the US share of world exports declined from 15% to 11%. While this reflected a relative decline in US economic power, it was compensated for by the growth in exports from factories owned by US corporations in other countries. In total, commodities produced and exported by US-owned corporations accounted for 17% of world exports in the mid-1980s, roughly the same share as at the beginning of the 1960s. And between 1985 and the mid-1990s, US corporations' share of world exports rose to 20%, while the world market shares of Japanese and European corporations all declined.

When we look at the commanding heights of corporate power, US economic dominance stands out sharply. In 1999, for example, sales of the 200 largest corporations accounted for 27.5% of world GDP. Eighty-two of these 200 corporations were US-owned, and they accounted for 11% of world GDP. In 1999 the world's twenty largest corporations had sales of $2.3 trillion and profits of $90 billion. While only seven of the 20 top corporations were US-owned, they accounted for 42% of their sales and 61% of their profits.

The agreements among the 12 West European governments that make up the European Union to remove all intra-union barriers to trade, labour and capital flows and to create a common currency zone cannot fundamentally challenge the dominant position of US finance capital in the world economy. Even for this project to be stabilised would require the transformation of the European Union into a federal multinational state on an equal military footing with the US, and a rapid process of international mergers among the largest European transnational corporations to attain a level of capital ownership and productive capacity equal to their US rivals.

And without such a process of international fusion of the European big capitals, there is little prospect that the German or French or British financial oligarchies will surrender their existing national sovereignty to a pan-European imperialist federal state.

Among the world's 200 largest corporations, 71 are owned by European capitalists, and of these, only three exhibit multinational ownership and two of these—the Anglo-Dutch-owned Royal Dutch-Shell oil company and the Anglo-Dutch-owned Unilever food and beverages firm—have been in existence for nearly 100 years. The process of international fusion of big capital within the EU has thus been extremely slow.

The present relationship of forces among the imperialist powers could only be fundamentally changed by a war between them in which the United States' economic and military supremacy was shattered. But US military supremacy rules out a repetition of direct inter-imperialist military conflicts such as the first and second world wars.

Growing Social and Political Instability

At the beginning of the 1990s, the imperialists won the Cold War when the bureaucratic ruling elites in Eastern Europe, the Soviet Union and China finally decided to secure their material privileges by attempting to transform themselves into capitalist ruling classes. The imperialist rulers triumphantly hailed this long-sought victory for capitalism as marking the emergence of a "new world order" of peace, prosperity and democracy. But in the context of the continued trend of the world capitalist economy toward stagnation and the growing social and political instability it is provoking in the Third World, the real perspectives that imperialism in the 21st century presents to the working people of the world are continuing cuts to their living standards, new wars and a curtailment of democratic rights.

The imperialist rulers will continue the drive they began in the late 1970s to take back all the economic concessions they were politically forced to cede during the Cold War to the working people of their own countries and to local capitalists in the semicolonial countries, and to squeeze even greater amounts of wealth out of the workers and peasants of these countries. This means eroding the real purchasing power of the wages of the big majority of workers, extending their working hours and drastically paring back social welfare programs. It means whipping up nationalist xenophobia and racism in order to increase the divisions among working people and to prevent the development of international working-class solidarity.

It also means cutting down on the social legacy bequeathed to future generations—a habitable natural environment, schools, hospitals, public housing, etc. It means increasing social dislocation: petty crime, drug addiction and mounting social alienation.

There will be repeated imperialist military interventions in the Third World tributaries to counter the inevitable popular resistance to the imperialists' demands for greater and greater tribute and the collapse of stable bourgeois rule in these countries that such resistance will lead to.

At every opportunity, the US imperialist rulers will push as far as they can to reverse the Vietnam syndrome, by instilling a siege mentality and whipping up patriotic fervour among the US masses to stifle any opposition by these masses to again becoming willing cannon fodder in Washington's new counterinsurgency wars and its military assaults on unpliable tributaries.

To carry through their domestic war on workers' living standards and to stifle opposition at home to a new series of wars abroad, the US rulers will seek to curtail the democratic rights of dissidents through a new McCarthyism and through the legitimisation of the increased use of naked police force against public expressions of dissent.

This is, of course, the trajectory that the US and other imperialist ruling classes have embarked on since September 11, 2001 under the cover of a global war against terrorism.

The last time the US rulers attempted such a global counterinsurgency strategy, it was able to be sustained without serious domestic opposition for more than two decades by their ability to grant economic concessions and social improvements on a scale sufficient to imbue large sections of the US masses with faith in the social justice of the capitalist system. But the central dilemma facing the US rulers as they again launch a bid to create an "American century" is that they and their allies must wage war not only on recalcitrant forces in the Third World, but also against the living standards of their own working people.

In these circumstances, their prospects for stifling a domestic radicalisation and political polarisation are vastly more limited than they were in the late 1950s.

The situation today has little in common with the early Cold War period of counterinsurgency wars abroad and rising prosperity at home. Rather, it more closely parallels the situation of war abroad and deepening impoverishment at home that prevailed in the imperialist countries in the period between the first and second world wars. At the beginning of that period, the revolutionary opponents of imperialist war were far more isolated and marginalized than they are today. But as the initial wave of pro-war patriotic fervour was drowned in the brutal realities of a prolonged foreign war and sharply deteriorating living standards at home, the radical opponents of imperialism found a growing base among broad masses of working people for their perspective of revolutionary mass political action as the only road out of the endless horrors that imperialist capitalism presented to humanity.

The "lack of stability", wrote the Bolshevik leader Leon Trotsky in the early 1920s, "the uncertainty of what tomorrow will bring in the personal life of every worker, is the most revolutionary factor of the epoch in which we live". The resulting "absence of stability drives the most imperturbable worker out of equilibrium. It is the revolutionary motor power", Trotsky (1972) added. This, above all, is what imperialist capitalism offers to the working people of the world in the twenty-first century—a prolonged period of political and economic shocks, insecurity and uncertainty, a prolonged period of deepening class polarisation and potential revolutionary political crises.

REFERENCES

Gittings, John (1967), "The Origins of China's Foreign Policy", in D. Horowitz (ed), *Containment and Revolution*, New York: Monthly Review Press.

Horowitz, D. (1971), *Imperialism and Revolution*, London: Penguin.

Lenin, V.I. (1977) *Collected Works*, Vol. 22, Moscow: Progress Publishers.

Preobrazhensky, Ye. (1965), *The New Economics*, Oxford: Oxford University Press.

Trotsky, L. (1972), *The First Five Years of the Communist International*, Vol.1, New York: Monad Press.

Williams, W. (1962), *The Tragedy of American Diplomacy*, New York: Delta.

Dynamics of American Foreign Policy:
Economic Aspects

William K. Tabb

There are two faces of US imperialism which I wish to discuss. The first is economic coercion which today is exercised through what I call global state economic governance institutions to foster regime changes in the areas of trade, investment and finance. It is these institutions such as the World Trade Organization, the International Monetary Fund, the World Bank, managed in substantial degree by the executive branch of the American government which function to gain acceptance of the rules transnational capital and international finance would have others follow acceptable and enforceable. The changes imposed by the leading capitalist countries, primarily by the Americans in consultation with Europe and to a lesser extent Japan come at the expense of weaker capitals and the working class. Matters of course are not put this way. There is much talk about how everyone benefits from free trade, transparency, democracy and human rights. These high sounding motivations are the occasion for insistence on rules demanding privatization, deregulation, fiscal and monetary austerity, labour discipline and other aspects of what are called liberalization that structure the world system today. The second face of American foreign policy is the employment of the threat, and the actual use of force.

For an imperial power there are always these two faces of the ruling class. The first is its seemingly more reasonable face, at least as it is presented in the home country. In an earlier era it explained colonialism as a white man's burden, the obligation to civilize the savage races, presumably as an act of Christian charity. Today the leading sectors of capital and their government representatives say the goals are good governance, free markets, and free trade which are declared to be in the general interest. All the while under such self-righteous cover imperial powers impose unequal exchange, exploitation, and domination which these days they call partnership. Its second face is revealed when it takes the mask off and the gunboats and the laser guided bombs impose order on the natives, the uncooperative local rulers who in a cynical perversion of the reality are deemed a threat to the imperial power(s). Those who for whatever reason are unwilling to obey are taught a brutal lesson. The face the United States representing transnational capital's most powerful centre now shows the world is of a war without end declared on "evil". It is in fact a strategy to subjugate all those who would fail to follow its wishes.

The imposition of neoliberalism today has been linked tightly to the US war on terrorism. When US Trade Representative Robert Zoellick, touring the world to drum up support for a new trade round in 2002, made the link that free trade would help stamp out terrorism, his comments were generally taken as opportunist rhetoric. However, President Bush's threat that if countries are not with us they are with the terrorists had a huge impact on trade negotiations and particularly the outcome of the WTO's Fourth Ministerial Conference at Doha. As Ninan Koshy (2002:11) writes, "The links between launching new trade talks and security issues only remotely connected earlier, became one and the same issue." Of course, it is possible they always were the same issue. As Thomas Friedman (1999) has famously proposed: "The hidden hand of the market will never work without the hidden fist—McDonald's cannot flourish without McDonnell-Douglas, the designer of the F-15. And the hidden fist that keeps the world safe for Silicon Valley's technologies is called the United

States Army, Air Force, Navy and Marines." Indeed we have a whole lot of writing mostly by right wing ideologues on the need for imperialism and colonialism in the pages of the business press. (Johnson, 2001; Wolf, 2001) The Bush people hardly need prompting. This after all is an Administration which is drawn not just from corporate American but from the oil and what is called the "defense" industries. It has managed to frighten the American public and so in effect extort much of the support it is able to claim from the American people. It has shown repeatedly whenever there is bad news such as the President's close ties with "Kenny Boy" Lay, the CEO of Enron and Mr. Bush's largest campaign contributor, or news of wrong doings by Halliburton while Vice President Cheney was its head, or even the embarrassing testimony to the Congress by an FBI agent, Coleen Rowley who accused the Bureau of bungling September 11th, an event they were forewarned about, Attorney General Ashcroft can be counted upon to announce the capture of a dangerous terrorist, typically one who has been in custody for awhile or under close surveillance ready to be picked up when the White House wants to command the media and bury a potentially embarrassing alternative story. (Lewis, 2002)

Globalist Economics

The Washington Consensus, so named because the leading institutions guiding the development process, the World Bank and the International Monetary Fund are for some reason headquartered in Washington D.C., suggests that neo-liberalism, the privatization of as many government functions as possible and opening markets without restrictions to foreign banks, investors and producers will bring about more rapid growth. While most countries accepted the Washington Consensus neoliberal advice and opened themselves to foreign investment and trade only a few attracted significant foreign investment and for almost half of all countries the trade ratio fell. (Otsubo, 1996) Growth of foreign investment and the growth of exports as a percentage of GDP was limited to fewer than a dozen countries even though overall global trade (as measured by its ratio to gross domestic product) more than doubled over the 35 years from 1960 to 1994 going from 21% to 46% and for the low and middle income economies from 31% to 47%, world growth rates slowed over these decades. As globalization trends, including liberalization, the removing of state regulation of capital movements, have taken their toll, world growth rates have slowed and there have been more crises, recessions, financial meltdowns, and these have become more widespread.

As importantly, many countries which in the World Bank's view were successful "globalizers" succeeded despite, or perhaps because they did not follow Washington Consensus advice. The most impressive growth came in East Asia where South Korea, Taiwan and China, all countries in which state subsidies, protection and guidance played central roles. There has been failure in the very countries the Bank has held up as models in their respective parts of the world: Ghana in Africa, (where, by the Bank's calculations, 16 % of Ghanaians lived on a mere $1.08 in 1987 and an incredible 78% lived on this amount in 1997) or Argentina in Latin America where, after being the star pupil, the country had to painfully devalue and is now in collapse. It is in truth difficult for the Bank to point to any country where its advice has worked for the economy and its people.

World Bank statisticians conclude that in the aggregate, and for some large regions, all measures suggest that the 1990s "did not see much progress against consumption poverty in the developing world". (Otsubo, 1996:18) The United Nations Development Program's *Human Development Report, 2000* tells us that at the end of the 1990s over 80 countries had lower per capita incomes than at the end of the 1980s. While some, especially the upper end of the income distribution in some of the poorer countries may be better off and even where average incomes may have gone up (a minority of the nations of the developing world), as Amartya Sen (2002:5) has written: "Even if the poor were to get just a little richer, this would not necessarily imply that the poor were getting a fair share of the potentially vast benefits of global economic interrelations. It is not adequate to ask whether international inequality is getting marginally larger or smaller. In order to rebel against the appalling poverty and the staggering inequalities that characterize the contemporary world – or to protest against the unfair sharing of benefits of global cooperation – it is not necessary to show that the massive inequality or distributional unfairness is also getting marginally larger. This is a separate issue altogether." The question is: do the policies pursued by the US government close the development gap?

The insistence on financial deregulation has in fact led to crisis after crisis in developing and transitional economies. Deregulated international capital flows lead to rapid short term inflow of speculative monies, to a bidding up of assets which rise to unsustainable levels, the bubble pops, capital flees, and the country is left with debts it cannot pay denominated in foreign currencies forcing it to go to the IMF which offers help on the harshest terms. Such economic upheavals lead to rising inequalities, increased suffering by the poorest and make programs to help the poor impossible for these governments to finance. Such episodes can also destroy the middle class and produced state failure and collapse and sometimes threaten social revolution. It is important not to see these episodes in isolation. We have had a series of such crises from Mexico, to Russia, Thailand, to Argentina. How many have there been? An UNCTAD study found no case in any country, developed or developing where a large increase in liquidity in the banking sector did not lead to overextended lending, lax risk management and a worsening in the quality of assets. (UNCTAD, 1998) A 1996 IMF study found that 133 of the Fund's 181 member countries had suffered at least one crisis or episode involving significant banking difficulties between 1980 and 1995. (UNCTAD, 1998) The World Bank identifies over 100 major episodes of bank insolvency in 90 developing countries and transitional economies (former communist regimes) from the late 1970s to 1994. These crises were found in advanced and underdeveloped economies, newly industrializing, and transitional economies. While in each case policy errors could be blamed, the pervasiveness of financial sector crises suggested that broader and more systemic problems were at work. The fact that two-thirds of IMF members experienced banking problems between 1980 and 1996 can hardly be a coincidence. The very deregulation the global state economic governance institutions forced on these countries produced crises which in turn allowed global state economic governance institutions to demand more deregulation resulting in still greater foreign control.

One of the most important critics of these policies is Joseph Stiglitz whose evaluation of the Washington Consensus has been stinging. This is because Stiglitz was a Chief Economist at the World Bank until he was fired by Lawrence Summers, Secretary of the Treasury of the Clinton Administration for being too critical of Washington policies. Professor Stiglitz is a Nobel Prize winning economist and formerly chair of the Clinton Council of Economic Advisers. He is recognized as one of the brightest economists in the world today and his opinions are hard to dismiss as the mutterings of a malcontent or an incompetent.[1] His stance is hardly anti-imperialist but his testimony gives lie to the cover story the agencies enforcing imperial domination offer for their work.

He agrees with demonstrators and Third World governments that the IMF mishandles economic crises and should not be allowed to force its extensive and controlling conditionalities on debtors. On the East Asian crisis of a few years ago Stiglitz says the IMF's policies brought more trouble not an improvement: "They invoked bad economic analysis. Anybody who has taken Economics 101 would have anticipated there was going to be a recession or a depression. In that case you need to expand government spending; the IMF called for fiscal contraction. It also raised interest rates to very high levels. They focused on inflation in the midst of a depression." Asked about the IMF's decade-long effort to help Russia transform from communism to capitalism he told *Business Week* a year ago, "They bungled the transition in Russia. More than 50% of the people are impoverished vs. 2% just 10 years ago. Gross domestic product is 50% of where it was. It's startling. We told these countries that, if you go to a market system, you're going to see things you've never seen before. It was like nothing they had seen before but it was the opposite of what we told them to expect." Given the mishandling he recommends the IMF's power be limited since the kind of conditionality it imposes "is counterproductive" and suggests the only condition for lending should be they can pay back the loan, a seemingly radical suggestion since most countries don't pay back they simply borrow more money to pay back the loan and interest owing more than they did before. (Business Week, 2001) The chances that the institutions of imperialist domination will in fact back down in their unreasonable and onerous demands would be to hold the IMF itself responsible for loans made to dictatorships which turn up in Swiss banks, which are made for corrupt purposes, and where it is reasonable to believe the loans in any case unlikely to be paid back within the time frame of the original loan. The control exercised by economies which become permanent indentured debtors is one of the most effective tools of imperialist domination.

Where the Washington Consensus has forced governments to sell off publically owned companies Stiglitz has called such privatization "briberization," calling attention to the way government assets when they are sold off find their way into the hands of local elites and their foreign allies who pay the generous bribes to get the deals at low prices and then follow monopoly pricing policies bilking consumers who find there is still no competition for electricity or phone service. Privatization has often been a disaster in practice. More important is Stiglitz's analysis of capital market liberalization advocated by the Washington Consensus, which he is not alone in seeing as the cause of the financial crises which have been the ruin of millions around the world as governments opened their financial markets at US prompting creating speculative bubbles which builds when capital pours in and these countries then suffer the results of the collapse when capital flees after inevitable speculative collapses after countries get in trouble as the result of throwing open their financial markets.

The perpetual indebtedness of IMF clients is as predictable as the demonstrations and IMF riots which follow as the price of necessities rises beyond the means of the masses. As he says, when a country is down and out the IMF "takes advantage and squeezes the last pound of blood out of them. They turn up the heat until, finally, the whole cauldron blows up." (Palast, 2001) At the time Stiglitz was thinking of events particularly in Indonesia and Ecuador but any number of countries have followed this sad scenario. The aid money often must go to buy US Treasury bonds as foreign reserves in an attempt to protect the country from a run on its currency. The country receives four or five percent interest on the money while it borrows from private Western banks at 12 per cent or more. Stiglitz recalls the case of Ethiopia which begged him to be allowed to use the aid money to feed its population instead but he was not permitted to allow them to do this. The money went to the US Treasury. In exchange for loans the global state economic governance institutions demand that countries follow a long list of conditions, on average 111 per nation which require a change in all sorts of policies which are dictated by the Washington approach. When the country fails to recover these institutions demand still more free market policy measures. Stiglitz says, "It's a little like the Middle Ages. When the patient died they would say, 'well, he stopped the bloodletting too soon, he still had blood in him'." (Palast, 2001)

"The IMF makes assertions and predictions concerning its policies that are consistently proven wrong, yet its leaders are seldom held accountable. With each failure, the IMF has looked to others to explain away its mistakes." (Stiglitz, 2001) While the IMF always blames the countries involved for not following its policy demands fully and so bringing further problems on itself, many critics see the IMF and by extension the United States which more or less runs that organization as using financial crises to force changes in economic policies which favour transnational capital. They do so by creating an international financial regime which allows, encourages and even causes crises and then the programs it insists upon are in its interests and not those of the people of the countries involved. I think such criticism is correct but not the whole story since many of these countries have leaders and ruling elites which are corrupt and have chosen policies which have been costly to most of the people who live there. In almost all cases their corrupt leaders came to power in a process shaped by Western powers going back to colonialism which created a system of selecting local strongmen for indirect rule and perpetuated during the Cold War when the CIA and other foreign influences meddled in the internal affairs of these countries to assure leaders friendly to US and other Western interests. To stay in power they spend more on weapons and little on health and education.

In 1989 Barber Conable estimated that the accumulated foreign debt resulting from weapons imports was a third of the total for some of the poorest countries. While he was president of the World Bank its plan to restore economic growth in Africa pointed out that military spending diverted enormous resources from southern Africa's development and consumed nearly 50 per cent of government expenditures in the countries experiencing the worst destabilization. Conable announced that military costs would be a factor in future loan discussions with African countries. But of course America's Cold War foreign policy trumped such concerns. The close to 200 wars waged since the end of the Second World War virtually all have been fought in the Third World with arms supplied by the Cold War powers. Even though communism is gone the great powers continue to sell arms. This suggests the power of the merchants of death in the halls of Western governments, above all in Washington. After all military sales are one of the few plus items on the US merchandise balance. But there is also a foreign policy dimension to the reality that the United States is by far the world's largest arms seller and to the fact that in addition the US has trained death squads who have killed school teachers, trade unionists and peasant leaders to protect the elites of many of these countries and of course US investors.

We should pay particular attention to our training and arming our once friend and asset Osama bin Laden and the Taliban, called freedom fighters by President Ronald Reagan when he welcomed them to the White House and directed their energies against the Soviet Union's support of a government in that country which opened the schools to girls. This man as we all know later turned on us and attacked the Pentagon and the World Trade Center. We have had similar relations with Noriega in Panama who we knew was a drug dealer but as long as he played ball with us could do as he chose in such criminal activity. When he became less cooperative the US military was sent into his country to capture him, killing thousands of civilians in the process. The deposed dictators and people like the murderous Joseph Savimbi who was killed in 2002 after just about destroying Angola have been CIA assets. That we are willing to spend unlimited funds on war and destabilizing governments we don't like but not to rebuild or pay compensation to civilian victims of our actions even now does not, in my view, reflect well on this country. The US offers less foreign aid per capita among the developed nations. At the same time it is willing to spend freely to destroy governments which do not do its bidding.

The Bush Administration rejected an international proposal to double foreign aid in the wake of the war on Afghanistan, contending that poor countries should make better use of the aid they were already getting. It has offered no compensation to the Afghan civilians whose homes were destroyed and loved ones killed in US bombings and has left it to the Europeans to help the devastated civilian population. While attention focuses on the global state economic governance institutions such as the IMF and the World Trade Organization for their harmful policies we should be very aware of the role the US government plays enforcing its will. The two aspects of American foreign policy are complementary. Economic coercion can often do the job. But sometimes physical violence is thought to be needed. These are tactical choices and depend on circumstance and the proclivities of a particular administration in Washington.

US Foreign Policy and the Global State Economic Governance Institutions

The foreign policy aims of the US have guided these institutions from their beginning. There has been a consistency of such intervention starting in the immediate postwar period when the United States State Department informed France that it would have to remove any communist representatives in the cabinet of the coalition government to get loans from the Bank. In 1947 when Poland applied for a loan the Bank team returned from a site visit and reported favourably, the US State Department made it known that it would oppose even a small loan. Bank President John McCloy made it known that he thought Wall Street investors would not approve, and since the Bank depended on loans from Wall Street, Poland was out of luck. Poland and Czechoslovakia, denied loans, withdrew from membership. In its 1948 Annual Report the Bank wrote that existing political difficulties and uncertainties presented special problems.

Other examples can be cited through the history of the Bank. It said no for example to the Aswan Dam loan, after initial approval, when Egypt nationalized the Suez Canal. It denied loans to Chile after the Allende government nationalized copper (the aid was reinstated quickly after General Pinochet seized power in a US-backed coup in which Chile s democratically elected president and thousands of other Chileans were killed). The US opposed loans to Vietnam and manipulated lending in Central America during conflicts in that region. Independent researchers found the Bank had not evaluated the Somoza dictatorship in Nicaragua, a US ally with an even hand, nor Mobutu's Zaire or Marcos's Phillippines. Despite such a pattern, when Ronald Reagan was elected in 1980, the Republican platform urged a return to bilateralism as a tool of American foreign policy. A planning memo for the new administration announced the organs of international aid and so-called Third World development... were infected with socialist error.

There is widespread appreciation that the IMF, the World Bank and other international financial institutions have not simply been concerned with getting repaid. "One of their central missions has been the restructuring of the domestic institutions and policies of borrowing states. In some instances officials of these institutions have occupied positions within the bureaucracies of states that have signed agreements" Stephen Krasner (1999:143) writes. He points out that some of the missions of IFIs are not so different from the bankers' committees that assumed control of state finances in the Balkans in the nineteenth century or the customs receivership established in Nicaragua. David Law suggests that the strategic design and role of these institutions is a new constitutionalism, seeing the process as an attempt to treat the market as a constitutional order with its own rules and institutions that operate to protect the market order from political interference. The presumption in such a frame is that the state does not wither but exhibits strength in new tasks of disciplining domestic constituencies to accept that market regulatory institutions are beyond the reach of transitory political majorities. Such a constitutionalism attempts to construct an economic governance structure of natural economic law and not of voters or their representatives. Such a new economic constitutionalism is not a freeing of the market from state intervention so much as it is an insulating of regulatory global state economic governance institutions and their local correspondents from political interference protecting the market as reconstructed under their guidance from domestic politics.

The WTO is an arena for bargaining over market access and "free" trade is not the typical outcome, nor as Dani Rodrik and others have pointed out, is consumer welfare what negotiators prioritize. "Instead," Rodrik (2001:7) says, "the negotiating agenda has been shaped in response to a tug-of-war between exporters and multinational corporations in the advanced industrial countries on one side, and import-competing interests (typically, but not solely, labour) on the other. He notes such examples as the differential treatment of manufactures and agriculture, of clothing and other goods within manufacturing, and the intellectual property rights regime as being a result of this political process. "There is little in the structure of the negotiations to ensure that their outcomes are consistent with development goals, let alone that they seek to further development." The rich countries, and not only the United States, have used their greater negotiating strength to impose unequal gains and losses as a result of the way regime rules and their enforcement are constructed.

But it is the US as the hegemonic power which typically gets its way, even against almost universal opposition. It has rejected the Kyoto Accords, imposed steel tariffs and the huge agricultural subsidies, abrogated the ABM treaty so a new generation of nuclear weapons can be produced, failed to accept treaties on land mines, or to protect the rights of children, the establishment of an international criminal court, it has tried to rewrite the UN plan intended to reinforce the convention against torture, it refuses to accept an agreement on controlling the international flow of small arms, the list goes on and on. With the Cold War over, Washington under George W. Bush now sets its sights on a unilateralist domination which brooks no competition or constraint on its activities. In this it produces popular resentments and a broad understanding of its goal of domination. In trying to establish an American Empire the US therefore creates a broad front of opposition encompassing the leading powers of Europe and forces conflict between the comprador bourgeoisies and nationalist, socialist and other popular movements everywhere.

To carry out its unilateral interventions the United States is dramatically increasing its military spending so that by year 2003 it spent over $300 billion, an amount equal to the entire Gross Domestic Product of Russia. Its total military spending will be more than the rest of the world's put together. The US currently spends more on just military research and development that either Britain or Germany spend in total on defence. There have been Pentagon announcements that the US is now planning to use tactical nuclear weapons in future conflicts. In post-Soviet Asia it is establishing huge military bases and completing its encircling of the globe from Japan to China's western border. It is militarizing space with an objective, as the Space Command's Vision 2020 declares, of "dominating the space dimension of military operations to protect U.S. interests and investments... The emerging synergy of space superiority with land, sea and air superiority will lead to Full Spectrum Dominance." Given this capacity it can be argued that the central issue of our time is what to do about the US.

The Bush Doctrine of preemptive strikes at evil ones by declaring that "the war on terrorism will not be won on the defensive" puts the world on notice he is discarding the conventions which have governed relations between nations for more than half a century and is re-interpreting self-defence to mean the US will attack whatever enemy it finds appropriate. Even conservative commentators find the implications of such domineering profoundly troubling. As Philip Stephens (2002:15), the *Financial Times* columnist writes, "Where do we draw the line between pre-emptive action against an obvious and imminent menace and what one senior US official called 'preemptive retaliation' to head off more distant threat?" And it worries him that "Mr. Bush seems to presume that the US alone would make all these judgments." This bothers many of us. If the US has the ability to do whatever it wants in the world ordinary people must become active participants in shaping the kind of world we shall live in, to do what their governments are often unwilling to do, stand up to Empire. The US approach which focuses on violence to extend US economic and political power is the immediate threat to the world. It is embedded in a larger system of structural injustice which must be addressed and resisted.

Military Force and Oil

It has been pointed out by vulgar Marxists and some other observant folks that the US seems in need of fighting evil primarily where it doesn't control oil. It is becoming heavily involved in the Caspian Sea region, for example. This is suggested in such communist publications as *Business Week* where in a recent article Paul Starobin (2002:92) writes: "The game the Americans are playing has some of the highest stakes going. What they are attempting is nothing less than the biggest carve-out of a new US sphere of influence since the US became involved in the Middle East 50 years ago. The result could be a commitment of decades that exposes America to the threat of countless wars and dangers." There are already thousands of US troops in new bases and Defense Secretary Donald Rumsfeld says they will stay "as long as necessary". US investments in the region, one of the world's last undeveloped cluster of fields, which hardly existed five years ago are now $20 billion and growing. The US is manoeuvering to break Russia's monopoly over oil transport routes. Such considerations explain much else. Russia's only operational pipe line for Caspian oil goes through

Chechnia which may explain the virulence for their war on terrorists there. China which imported 20 per cent of its petroleum needs in 1995 will need to import 40 per cent by 2010 and the China National Petroleum Corporation is active in Kazakhstan. The Chinese are helping equip the Kazakh military and our relations with China seem to resonate in relation to their involvement in the region.

Washington worries about plans by some of the oil majors to have a pipeline across Iran and does not like European governments talking of constructive engagement with that country. They want to help their friends and punish their enemies in the region and so prefer a more costly route from Baku through Georgia to Turkey, a NATO ally. As the *Business Week* article reports, Georgia "has been wracked by civil war, organized crime and terrorism" (Starobin, 2002:54)—clearly another possible site for countering evil. The Russians of course are involved. While Putin wants to make deals with the US, a group of ex-military officers recently wrote him a letter describing his foreign policy as "the policy of licking the boots of the West". Perhaps more work there for the CIA.

Oil is found in many places around the world and control over energy resources is always a matter of concern to political leaders of powerful states. It is not surprising then that the US government under a president and a vice president who come from the oil industry and who have filled their administration with oil people in their war of good against evil concentrate on areas of interest to the industry. Terrorist sanctuaries and a map of principle energy resources from Indonesia to Venezuela have a certain overlap. The nations of West Africa—Angola, Nigeria, Congo, Gabon, Cameroon and Equatorial Guinea—will collectively supply 25 per cent of US oil by 2015 and have already been designated "an area of vital US interest". Most important is Central Asia. Estimates of the Caspian Sea area vary from 200 billion barrels which is on level with Saudi Arabia to fewer than 100 barrels, on par with the reserves of the North Sea which would at current prices be worth about $2.7 trillion. Bringing this non-OPEC source on line would also undermine the cartel and give control over oil prices to the major oil companies and their governments, diminish any threat of blackmail from Mideast producers, indeed would allow the pressure to be exerted effectively against OPEC countries. The Caspian area, as Jan Kalicki (2001:2) points out in *Foreign Affairs*, "Located at the crossroads of western Europe, eastern Asia, and the Middle East, the Caspian serves as a trafficking area for weapons of mass destruction, terrorists, and narcotics – a role enhanced by the weakness region's governments. With few exceptions the fledgling Caspian republics are plagued with pervasive corruption, political repression, and virtual absence of the rule of law." Looks like more work for Uncle Sam.

The dissolution of the Soviet Union opened the vast oil and gas resources of the region and unleashed a high stakes contest for regional hegemony over the world's largest untapped reserves. Haliburton, the company not long ago headed by Vice President Cheney has long been a player planning the construction of a pipeline to exploit the energy resources of the region once security was established which the US invasion of Afghanistan has, some believe, achieved. Afghanistan is the most convenient route to the Pakistani coast on the Arabian Sea which would reduce dependence on the Gulf as a shipping lane. Whether any of this has anything to do with Operation Enduring Freedom is an interesting question. Brown and Root, a division of Haliburton was the contractor for the construction of Camp Bondsteel, one of the many new bases the US has established for what appears to be a long stay in the region. This is an area where economic analysis and politics are intertwined with rumour and conspiracy theory so that, for example, it is said that US-led operations in Kosovo were to secure a route from the Caspian through the former Yugoslavia to Central Europe. Commentators point out the potential gains for other US industries – "from infrastructure to telecommunications to transportation and other sectors" which could also benefit. (Kalicki, 2001)

Just behind the oil industry at the heart of the economic coalition supporting current policy are the so-called defence contractors who for a price promise a new generation of weapons which will make all of this possible without loss of American lives. Coming on stream or already in use are ground sensors dropped from drone planes which self-activate and listen and watch for enemy troops and vehicles which they can recognize from memory. Unmanned planes with stealth design can then bomb them. Human soldiers will carry micro air vehicles so small they can be carried in back packs which use tiny cameras to get bird's eye views of enemy territory. The hornet munitions, small canisters which can be dropped, right them-selves and then their sensors detect and attack with armour-piercing projectiles. The list of such new war toys is a long one. They are expensive and so profitable, and are likely to be as accurate as the so-called smart bombs which have killed so many civilians where they have been used. It is a pretence of course that the dirty job of killing accurately can be done by remote control but the Pentagon is pushing these scenarios of video war game.

The Bush people plan to increase their budget by $120 billion or so each year for the next five years with most of the money going to new weapons systems. This will increase the Pentagon budget by a quarter of a trillion dollars above what it would be if increases in spending are kept proportional to what it is now adjusting for inflation. By 2007 the estimate is for a 30 per cent increase in Pentagon spending which, along with the Bush tax cuts, will force down all other spending. These numbers are only projections. If the president gets his way military costs will stay high, crowding out expenditures for social needs at home and instead of considerations of development aid and debt cancellation we will get more focus on militarization of societies around the world. The strategy of empire is one of permanent garrison states led by Washington increasing the police presence everywhere and repressing dissent.

The trilateralist focus on reasonable discussion and gentle coercion coaxing the world into line, of avoiding obvious brutality as much as possible, although always bringing out the club when needed to make a point, the current Bush administration using fear generated by its clear message that anyone who is not with us is with the terrorists, makes clear it will act alone whenever it likes. In the president's words, the

US "will not hesitate to act alone, if necessary, to exercise our right of self-defense by acting pre-emptively". Iraq will not be the end of such regime changes, if Mr. Bush gets his way. While the US has surely overthrown many governments in the past, the Bush Doctrine is a very public statement of a muscular unilateralism. As Steven Mufson (2002:22) has written in the *Washington Post* of the Bush approach, "Because it stresses the hatred and ambition of `evil doers,' it stands in stark contrast to the outlook of his father as well as former president Bill Clinton, both of whom stressed nations' self-interest in achieving freedom and prosperity. Bush senior may have waged war against Iraq, but throughout his career he placed greater faith in diplomacy than confrontation. And Clinton... mostly promoted a positive vison of a world where `democratic enlargement' and free trade would spread stability and liberal values."

Bush's view is darker, more black and white, a war of good and evil, a war without end. It can be said that the difference is September 11th. In some ways it is but it is useful to remember that Ronald Reagan also came to the presidency announcing that a war on terrorism would be the core of US foreign policy. Reagan condemned the "evil scourge of terrorism", a plague spread by "depraved opponents if civilization itself", as Reagan's Secretary of State George Schultz said in 1984. At the time Donald Rumsfeld was Mr. Reagan's special envoy to the Middle East where we were active fighting evil even if the main action was in Central America where the World Court found the US guilty of terrorism and ordered it to terminate its crimes against the Nicaraguan government. The US financed and actively planned a war aimed at soft targets—schools, clinics, teachers, doctors, nurses—to undermine the Sandinista government. It mined the harbor to keep food, medicine and other supplies from arriving. The US is the only country ever found guilty of terrorism by the World Court. The US ignored the decision and continued its activities. Claiming one's enemies and those seen as not sufficiently opposing them as equally terrorists and so worthy targets of American military action has however reached new heights with the well advertised preparation for war against

Iraq because it may, or in the Administration's view must inevitably be a threat and will use weapons of mass destruction against us if we do not destroy them.

From the perspective of the other themes I have developed and as the passage from Mufson suggests, the Bush people have changed the subject and the terms on which globalization will be carried on. This is however a difference of degree and not of kind. The US was and continues to be an imperialist power even if it is perhaps likely that the Clinton people would not have been quite as obvious and single minded about grabbing the oil at whatever cost and would have consulted their allies more. This difference in emphasis is not without importance but we are talking about tactical differences not any real difference over the interests of US-based transnational capital coming first and foremost. The only government which stands clearly with the United States is Tony Blair's. This is in part because US and British capital have merged to a large extent. British Petroleum has now merged with the American Oil Company (Amoco) which had already eaten Atlantic Richfield. The company is one of the largest if not the largest oil company in the world. There have also been Anglo-American mergers in defence contracting and of course in financial services.

Concluding Thoughts

Unfortunately the discussion addressing poverty, oppression, and the need for economic justice is being pushed aside by the rising tide of military escalations as the United States sees its amorphous enemies, one day an axis of evil, less frequently these days Osama bin Laden but always a shadowy al Qaeda network which is everywhere the US wants the occasion for intervention, a new conspiracy to replace the Cold War and justify Empire. We need to address both the economic designs of neoliberalism, the cost to the lives of ordinary people of these policies, at the same time draw attention to the expanding militarism and the price ordinary civilians who are in no manner terrorist threats are paying for this unholy crusade, and finally we need to develop a framework large enough to encompass these two aspects of what are surely a single policy design. I want to conclude with a few thoughts on this comic book clash of civilizations, comic only in the sense of the puerile level of the ideological excuses and rhetoric, not of course in the dire implications for millions of human beings.

What began as a demonizing of anti-American Moslem extremists became a war to save Western civilization. There is a great deal of writing these days about the desirability of a benign imperialism as these "predatory societies" and "premodern barbarous states" in need of the civilizing influence of the West become the topic of a rationalizing rhetoric for an endless Manichean war of good against evil. The world is divided, we are told. The West is presented as a reasonably cohesive, open multi-nation democratic entity with a free press, a competitive electoral process bounded by acknowledged rules of unquestionably peaceful transitions and in which member states work out their differences with mutual respect through discussion and compromise. The non-West is violent, weakly involved in international cooperation, ambivalent, indeed suspicious, of the West and composed of authoritarian, semi-authoritarian, weak quasi democracies, rogue states and failed states where, if there are elections they are manipulated, where the press manipulates and manages the news under government direction. These are lands of unfreedom, repression and violence with little respect for the rule of law or Western norms generally. What we are seeing according to Martin Shaw (2000:254) is a new bipolar world in which "The West marks the boundaries of a large, relatively pacified, prosperous, democratic and law-bound social universe. These are widely acknowledged, both within and beyond its borders, as the major lines of economic and social as well as political division in the contemporary world".

If such clash of civilization views are not to dominate the foreign policy discussion it is necessary that the nature of Western imperialism in the region be better understood, both in terms of the historic behaviour of the West, the origin of the regimes which now rule in the region and the current policies of the United States. Indeed, an imperialism framing of the issues is required to make proper sense of what is going on, the reality of the so-called war on terrorism. Complaints against the United States have little to do with our purported love of democracy and everything to do with our support of injustice in the region.

Let me conclude by saying that the policies which will ease tensions in the Middle East and address the support that terrorists in the region now receive overlaps quite substantially with the demands of the global justice movement. These are the recognition of the rights of oppressed people including of course the Palestinians and an end to the blind support of Israeli occupation and oppression of Palestinians, an end to the condoning of violations of essential human rights, and of course not only in the Middle East. A respect by the rich countries of the core of the needs of peoples and societies of the rest of the world, including the cancellation of odious debt, sharing technology and not monopoly control in the name of protecting intellectual property, in general a focus on fairness and not arrogance, and the development of a social safety net for all people everywhere as citizens of our global society. To achieve these sensible goals will require a strong popular movement with a basic understanding that these evils are a result of a system, a capitalist system in which inequality and violence are essential to class rule. To consider the economic aspects of US foreign policy that have been stressed in this presentation is to discuss as well the nature of imperialism in the age of globalization, the duty to confront the American Empire, and the need for international solidarity.

NOTES

1. For an interesting discussion of why Stiglitz was fired see Robert Wade (2001). For earlier criticisms by another World Bank (and IMF) economist, see Davison Budhoo (1990).

REFERENCES

Budhoo, Davison (1990) *Enough is Enough: Open Letter of Resignation from the International Monetary Fund.* New York: New Horizons Press.

Business Week (2001) "Acid Words for the IMF", April 24.
Friedman, Thomas (1999) "What the World Needs Now", *New York Times*, March 28.
Johnson, Paul (2001) "The Answer to Terrorism? Colonialism?", *Wall Street Journal*, October 9.
Kalicki, Jan H. (2001) "Caspian Energy at the Crossroads", *Foreign Affairs*, September/October.
Koshy, Ninan (2002) *Globalization: The Imperial Thrust of Modernity*. Mumbai: Vikas Adhyayan Kendra.
Krasner, Stephen D. (1999) *Sovereignty: Organized Hypocrisy*. Princeton: Princeton University Press.
Lewis, Neil A. (2002) "Questions of Timing Arise With New Information", *New York Times*, June 12.
Mufson, Steven (2002) "Bush's Stark World View", *Washington Post National Weekly Edition*, February 25-March 3.
Otsubo, Shigeru (1996) "Globalization – A New Role for Developing Countries in an Integrated World". *World Bank Policy Research Working Paper #1628*, July.
Palast, Greg (2001) "The Globalizer Comes in From the Cold", *Observer*, October 10.
Rodrik, Dani (2001) "Trading in Illusions", *Foreign Policy*, March-April.
Sen, Amartya (2002) "How to Judge Globalism", *The American Prospect*, Special Supplement, Winter.
Shaw, Martin (2000) *Theory of the Global State: Globality as an Unfinished Revolution*. Cambridge: Cambridge University Press, 2000.
Starobin, Paul, Belton, Catherine and Crock, Stan (2002) "The Next Oil Frontier: America carves out a sphere of influence on Russia's borders", *Business Week*, May 27.
Stephens, Philip (2002) "The American Way of Defense", *Financial Times*, June 14.
Stiglitz, Joseph (2001) "Failure of the fund: rethinking the IMF response", *Harvard International Review* 23(2).
UNCTAD (1998) *Trade and Development Report*. New York: Oxford University Press.
Wade, Robert (2001) "Showdown at the World Bank", *New Left Review*, January-February.
Wolf, Martin (2001) "The Need for a New Imperialism", *Financial Times*, October 10.

God's Cowboy Warrior: Christianity, Globalisation, and the False Prophets of Imperialism

Peter McLaren and Nathalia E. Jaramillo

At this particular historical moment democracy seems acutely perishable. Its contradictions have become as difficult to ignore as sand rubbed in the eyes. While dressed up as a promise, democracy has functioned more as a threat. Spurred on by feelings of 'righteous victimhood' and by a 'wounded and vengeful nationalism' (Lieven, 2003) that has arisen in the wake of the attacks of September 11, and pushing its war on terrorism to the far reaches of the globe, the United States is shamelessly defining its global empire as an extension of its democratic project. The US National Security Strategy of 2002 states quite clearly that the US will not hesitate to act alone and will "pre-emptively" attack against "terrorists" that threaten its national interests at home or abroad. And one of its national interests is to bring free market democracy to the rest of the world.

Despite the fact that tens of millions of people—many of whom were presumably within a hair's breadth of Saddam's weapons of mass destruction—marched in the streets of cities on every continent to denounce the US decision to launch an unprovoked invasion of Iraq, the US pressed ahead with its plan to seize its oil fields, privatise its industries, demonstrate to would-be 'evildoers' what was in store for them, and secure a strategic geopolitical stranglehold on the Middle East. Those nations that supported its imperial design on behalf of fighting terrorism are now being rewarded with some of the spoils of victory (i.e., sub-contracts to rebuild the infrastructure of Afghanistan or Iraq) or at least that assurance they will not to be invaded. Nearly 5 billion dollars in military aid and training will be distributed to countries that have contributed to the so-called global war on terrorism or to the war in Iraq (a war whose definition remains unknown) in the coming months. Human Rights Watch International warns that these same nations have a recent history of committing human rights violations. The Philippines is primed to receive 19 million dollars worth of sniper rifles, mortars, grenade launchers and helicopters. A broadened US role in Colombia has extended from counter-narcotics to a unified campaign against insurgents. In the case of Colombia, this signals the connivance of US special operations protecting oil pipelines working side-by-side with right-wing paramilitaries. Indonesia, Uzbekistan, Tajikistan, the Republic of Georgia and Kyrgyzstan, will soon profit from the global market for terror – they too will receive millions in military aid from the US.

But perhaps the most alarming case is that of India and Pakistan. Two nations that have taunted each other with nuclear warfare have had their sanctions lifted and are being provided with millions of dollars worth of artillery for their support to the US Rather than trying to quell the possibility of nuclear warfare over Kashmir, the US has equipped India with 78 million dollars of artillery, while Pakistan, a much more visible force post-9.11, stands to gain fighter jets and armoured personnel carriers with a price tag of over 1 billion dollars.

In a fit of familiar paradoxical behaviour that is consistent with symptoms of clinical paranoia, the US is seeking help from countries to contribute troops to Iraq while at the same time threatening countries, including members of the "coalition of the willing"—Bulgaria, Latvia, Lithuania, Estonia, Slovakia, and Slovenia—who have not signed bilateral agreements, exempting US citizens from prosecution by the International Criminal

112 : *The Politics of Imperialism and Counterstrategies*

Court. The US has threatened to cut 150 million of the Pentagon's annual aid to Bogota unless it signs the exemption. Not surprisingly, John Bolton, Undersecretary of State for arms control and international security explains: "We have not been pressuring countries".

With promiscuous persistence, the US distributes itself around the world in gleeful anticipation of being welcomed with open arms as long-awaited liberators. The problem is that those welcoming arms have been, more often than not of late, severed at the joint by US imperialism's signature cluster bombs, shells of depleted uranium, and cruise missiles. When democracy does announce itself, it arrives under the sign of its own negation. Claiming to bring freedom and liberation to the Iraqi people, the US invasion, according to some estimates, has been responsible for the death of approximately ten thousand innocent civilians. The occupying force has prohibited the Iraqi people from forming their own government, preferring to select its leaders for them from a group of perfumed and pampered exiles, already thoroughly Westernised and plumping for the creation of an Iraqi neo-liberal state. They have begun to stage manage the country for democracy's free market drama: privatisation of its oil, agriculture, and just about everything that will put US dollars in investors' pockets. Like hyenas descending on a carcass, the trade lawyers, consultants, bankers, and CEOs of transnational corporations are licking their chops in anticipation of the US fulfilling its mission of opening up Iraq to foreign (mainly US and British) investment, and bringing Washington's neo-liberal imperative to the uncivilised territories of the Middle East.

When the Ministry of Oil claimed the dubious status of the only Ministry the US troops deemed worthy of protection after the fall of Baghdad, the Iraqi people should have known at that very moment that America's self-designation as a bastion of freedom was vacuous. By now they should realise that the US is also an oil-producing nation since so much snake oil drips persistently from the lips of its politicians and policy-makers.

A sandstorm has erupted in the hourglass of history where the liberators from Fort Hood or Fort Benning squint through steel burqas affixed with turrets and cannons and treads while dreaming they are back home rollerblading down Venice Boulevard, eating Krispy Kremes at the Valley drive-thru, renting the latest Arnold video at Blockbusters and watching the terminator dunk a woman's head in a toilet bowl; maybe these young recruits are thinking life might be better in the golden state under the Gropenfuher's red robotic eye in Sacramento. Maybe they are thinking they can caress a woman's breast whenever and wherever they please and do all the things their fraternity brothers bragged about doing. Now they can publicly apologise for all their sins and at the same time claim that they didn't commit them; now maybe they are dreaming about that trip to the Moonlight Bunny Ranch brothel in Nevada where the proprietor is offering a 50 per cent discount for a night with Air Force Amy.

The accelerating bellicosity of the liberating army can be put in its proper perspective when you recognise that its overall goal is to open up Iraq to the free market. But the end results will not be what the many Iraqis believe them to be. Once the transition to the neo-liberal marketplace has been accomplished, the Iraqi business elite will be able to purchase for themselves the best democracy money can buy, and the bogus freedom that goes with it (i.e., the freedom to be rich or poor, to own a palace or to lack shelter, to shop at an upscale supermarket or to starve in the streets).

In the light of present historical circumstances, it was a bad idea to think that what Washington's vision of a post-Saddam Iraq resembled anything like Baywatch reruns. Now that the country lies in tatters, its infrastructure in ruins, its water and electricity supplies failing to meet even the most basic needs of the people, its museums and hospitals looted and destroyed beyond redemption, and Iraqi protesters shot like animals, is it any wonder the US occupation has produced such an incandescent anger among the Iraqi populace? Any occupying power that decides in advance who will rule their conquered territories cannot lay claim to being liberators. US forces are currently engaged in Vietnam-style operations eerily similar to the "search-and-destroy" tactics of 40 years ago with predictable responses from an increasingly tense civilian population whose anger against the US troops is growing steadily to a fever pitch.

The United States is following a "carrot-and-stick" approach to occupational warfare. The military raids civilian homes and "enemy outposts" at night, before the scorching 120-degree heat begins to set in—in targeted missions that appear patterned after the occupation of Palestine—in an attempt to intimidate and frighten an already humiliated and degraded population into acquiescence. However, this is sure to increase resentment and armed reprisals. An Iraqi truck driver captured this resentment following the armed search of his truckload of potatoes. Stoically facing the lens of an American photographer, he asked, "Do they think we are monkeys?" In another scenario, 39 Iraqi men were seized for 'questioning' following a military raid. Shortly upon being released, the men took with them an austere consolation, "If you fight against your government, we will hunt you down and kill you". How ironic that US colonels rely on Saddam Hussein-style governance to control the 'liberated'.

Some may argue that the Iraqi post-war state is better off than before and that nation-building takes time, perhaps decades. But from where will democracy arise? Will it arise from the leadership of Paul Bremer, the appointed Iraqi governor who is better known among the ruling elite as a terror expert entrepreneur? Following 9.11 and the subsequent attacks on Afghanistan and Iraq, Bremer helped to form "Crisis Consulting Practice", a business designed to assist US multinationals in taking advantage of nations newly destroyed on behalf of democracy. Meanwhile, millions of Iraqis remain jobless, without electricity, and wondering – when will the occupation end?

The ongoing war in Iraq has signalled to the world that the US is willing to use any means necessary in its fanatical plight for world dominance. A recent survey by the Pew Research Center unveils the stark reality that a majority of civilians in the predominantly Muslim nations of Indonesia, Nigeria, Pakistan, Turkey, Kuwait, Lebanon, and Jordan fear a military strike from the United States. About the only place where people of colour do not appear threatened by patterns of merciless war and imperialism is on the moon or other uninhabited celestial bodies, which cautions us about the prospect of interplanetary travel.

Citizens of the world have placed their hope in the hands of international organisations such as the United Nations, designated to halt unilateral massacres. However, the UN has proven to be more like a vaudeville stage for the political charades of Powell and Blair than a viable organ for peace. While the Security Council staged a temporary revolt, it has now obediently fallen back into line. No longer content to play Edgar Bergen to the UN's Charlie McCarthy or Mortimer Snerd,[1] the US recognises that in a world with only one superpower, it's no longer in need of ventriloquism. If you are in control of the most powerful military force in world history, you can speak directly without a mediator, even if your words fall from both sides of your mouth.

Having used the Reagan-Shultz doctrine to interpret Article 51 of the UN Charter as giving license to the US to resort to force in "self-defense against future attack" (Chomsky, 2003), the US administration is now transforming itself into the same *junta* it once supported in the person of Saddam (recall the 1980 photo of Rumsfeld and Saddam shaking hands) but later turned against when it was in their best interest to do so. The US administration looks at the Iraqis like Custer's cavalry looked at the Indians: they couldn't possibly be ready for democracy yet. They inhabit a culture so incommensurable with our own that they are not yet able to grasp fully enough the fiscal advantages and moral superiority of global capitalism and free market democracy. It's a democracy that will enable the US to raid their raw materials and exploit their labour-power (with all those bid-free contracts awarded to Republican-friendly US corporations). It's a democracy that is designed not for the Iraqi people but so that the US can ensure its own economy will reap enough oil profits to be able to keep any upstart country from challenging its sole military superpower status for another century and beyond (Bush's inner circle of neocon zealots don't belong to a think tank called the Project for the New American Century without taking the name seriously). Of course, the US will make sure that a new class of Iraqi businessmen will become rich beyond their wildest dreams, maybe even as rich as Saddam used to be.

The key point to be made is recognising that the US is out to weaken and cheapen labour in order to compensate for a major loss of profits and dramatic increase in debts over the last several years. As further evidence one need only witness Bush invoking the Taft-Hartley Act against the West Coast dockworkers' union or his granting of federal aid to failing airlines on condition that management purges the airline unions. How many social services will need to be cut in order to finance Homeland security? How much rebuilding can occur in Iraq in the face of US budget deficits as a result of the current recession? How will tax cuts for corporations and the wealthy help to pay for the war and occupation? Is reducing domestic budget deficits by exclusive US control of Iraqi oil production worth the price of further enraging France, Germany, Russia, and China and making Trotsky's concept of inter-imperialist rivalry seen tame by comparison? Is it worth increasing the number of terrorist recruits who will dedicate themselves to eliminating the US military presence in the Middle East? Here it is easy to recognise how capitalism has been turned into a quasi-natural force by the corporatised lawmaking of the International Monetary Fund and World Bank of which workers are the passive, unnamed victims. The US has successfully alienated much of both the developed and Third World, and has sent an unmistakable message to both Russia and China that Washington's new-found military brinkmanship and aggression are a profound threat to their strategic interests and geopolitical influence. As if the lessons of Afghanistan and Iraq were not enough, Washington is now clearly preparing the ground for a possible attack on Iran.

Here at home the pusillanimity and fecklessness of the Democrats has been as difficult to stomach as Bush *hijo's* bumptious belligerence towards the nation's poor and his failure to recognise how he is in ironic violation of democracy's own fundamentals. Their integrity addled, the Democrats for the most part remain unwilling to name Bush the liar and deceiver that he is. What worries them is the spin that the media are likely to give their criticisms of Bush; they feat that going too far in attacking a wartime president will condemn them irrevocably in the public eye as unpatriotic.

The relatively compliant US citizenry should have known they were orbiting disaster when, as early as July 2001, Attorney General John Ashcroft was warned not to fly commercial airlines due to a CIA threat assessment but did not share with the public what that assessment was, when Bush delayed to release the Reagan presidential papers, violating a post-Watergate law and protecting those in his administration who were involved in the Iran-Contra crimes when they worked for Reagan and Bush *padre*, when the House of Representatives passed the U.S. Patriot Act without reading it or holding a hearing or public debate about it, when Bush and Cheney urged Tom Daschle not to make an inquiry related to 9.11, when thousands of librarians started destroying records so federal agents would have nothing to seize under the Patriot Act, when convicted felon Vice Admiral John Poindexter began to run a clandestine new government agency known as Information Awareness Office, when the government created a no-fly list in order to prevent certain political dissidents (like some members of the Green Party) from flying, when CIA director Tenet told the country there was no 9.11 intelligence failure, when the US military unveiled the Total Information Awareness System, when FBI director Mueller denied that information related to any aspect of the September 11 plot crossed his desk before that fateful day when the Twin Towers collapsed, when the Pentagon started to consider the creation of execution chambers for Camp Delta in Guantanamo Bay, when Bush *hijo* opposed establishing a special independent commission to probe how the government dealt with terror warnings before 9.11 (he finally consented to a 'token' commission after public pressure), when Ashcroft permitted government agents to monitor domestic religious and political groups without advanced approval from superiors, and when Bush unveiled Operation Tips, a program encouraging Americans to spy on each other. But these incidents don't seem to phase the American public, partly because they are played down in the news shows and partly because many citizens have become exceptionally adept at hearing only what they want to hear (McLaren, 2003). And that's really not such a difficult task when the official media are there to assist you twenty-four hours a day, seven days a week.

Rarely has any country been in such total control by the media. A recent opinion poll, conducted by the Program on International Policy Attitudes at the University of Maryland, found that one third of the American public believed that American military forces had found weapons of mass destruction in Iraq. Approximately 22 per cent said that Iraq had actually used chemical or biological weapons in the war. Other polls have reported that some 50 per cent of those questioned believed Iraqi citizens participated in the September 11 attacks, while 40 per cent believed that Saddam Hussein directly assisted the hijack-bombers. This reflects the staggering power of the US corporate media as a whole—and not just Fox News—to distort dramatically the facts in favour of the Bush administration and the business elite. Viewed as heroes by the American public, soldiers arrive home in the guise of valiant warriors who have done their patriotic duty by protecting the homeland. Those troops who are not being picked off weekly by Iraqi snipers and have the good fortune of making it back to US soil have been taking advantage of a visit to a legal Nevada brothel—The Moonlite Bunny Ranch—that offers free sex—featuring the likes of Air Force, Army and others—to troops returning from Iraq. The proprietor of the brothel also plans to extend 50 per cent discounts to the military for the next few weeks. As of this writing, 13 men and 3 women in uniform have claimed their free gift.

The captains of US media have realised (perhaps more fully than anyone else) that the more pervasive the lie, the more it will be harmonised with everyday common sense. One glaringly inconspicuous manifestation of this ideological process is the way in which the term 'democracy' is constantly conflated with the 'free market'. These two terms are yoked together as frequently as the term weapons of mass destruction is spoken in the same breath as terrorists or the foreign leader of any county whose resources we have decided to acquire and whose markets we seek to control. The 'free market' is collapsed into exchangeable referents: 'jobs', 'wealth', 'political stability', and 'security'. Capitalism has always been the 'religion' of individualism, of human rights, of constitutional freedom, and of private property. Given this reading, a successful socialist economy would obviously appear threatening to democracy. Democracy and the free market have a sweetheart deal. The capitalist values that adhere to the concept of 'democracy' like flies to a sticky tongue of flypaper, preclude any real challenge to its sacred resting place in the structural unconscious of the US public.

Personally, we believe that the Bush *junta* is so self-discrediting that it doesn't need a commentary such as ours to make a case against it. Yet we offer our perspective nevertheless, if only because of the shameful lack of venues available these days for an analysis of the Bush administration. For all his self-inflating rhetoric about cleaning up the Middle East of its freedom-hating terrorists, his stagy relish for challenging evildoers, and his dyspeptic remarks about his anti-war critics being nothing more than punk ass revisionists, we believe there is a strong case for impeaching our Commander-in-Chief for using misleading evidence to bring the country into war. The Bush administration's lies about Iraq's so-called imminent danger to the safety of the US and world-at-large constitute either an unwitting or witting effort to risk the lives of American soldiers, knowing full well there would be American casualties. The deployment of America's vast military machine was undertaken for reasons Bush and his entire foreign-policy apparatus knew to be based on false and falsified information. No government in Europe or the Middle East regarded Iraq as a serious threat to their safety. The UN weapons inspectors had for months been unable to locate any weapons of mass destruction, despite meticulous searching.

While the White House hawks presented the attack on Iraq as an extension of the "war on terrorism", it was revealed that the Bush administration had drawn up plans to use military force to overthrow the regime of Saddam Hussein well in advance of the attacks on the World Trade Center and the Pentagon. September 11 was seized on as a pretext to shape pubic opinion in favour of the war and now the White House lies about the extent of Saddam's weapons of mass destruction have come to light. Consider the June 15 edition of NBC's *Meet the Press*. During the show, former General Wesley Clark[2] told anchor Tim Russert that Bush administration officials had engaged in a campaign to implicate Saddam Hussein in the September 11 attacks on the very day of the attacks. Clark said that he'd been called on by Bush administration officials on September 11 and urged to link the regime of Saddam Hussein to the terror attacks. Clark declined to do so because of lack of evidence (not surprisingly, there has been very little media coverage of Clark's remarks). Even Deputy Defense Secretary Paul Wolfowitz later admitted that the charge that Iraq possessed weapons of mass destruction was selected for "bureaucratic reasons"—i.e., it was the one allegation that the State Department, the Pentagon and the CIA all agreed could provide a workable cover for a US invasion. The editors of the World Socialist Web Site (2003) captured the essence of this situation with the following remark: "Not since Hitler and the Nazis dressed up storm troopers as Polish soldiers and staged 'attacks' on German positions in 1939 has there been such a flagrant and cynical effort to manufacture a *casus belli*".

Very few Americans know that Bush *hijo's* grandfather helped finance the Nazi Party, or have heard the allegations that the grandfather of Bush's top advisor, Karl Rove, helped run the Nazi Party, and also helped build the Birkenau Death Camp. Further, it's unlikely that that they have heard the news that Arnold Schwarzenegger's Austrian father, Gustav, volunteered for the infamous Strumabteilung (SA), "brown shirt" stormtroopers just six months after the brown shirts played a key role in the bloody Kristallnacht attacks on Germany's Jewish community. Gustav later became a ranking officer (Fitrakis and Wasserman, 2003). While Arnold Schwarzenegger has since renounced Hitler, it remains the case that on October 3, ABC News broke the story of a 1977 interview in which he remarked: "I admire Hitler, for instance, because he came from being a little man with almost no formal education, up to power. I admire him for being such a good public speaker and for what he did with it". (Fitrakis and Wasserman, 2003)

If most US citizens possess little or none of this background information, then it is highly unlikely that they make a connection among Bush, Rove, and Schwarzenegger in the current destabilisation of California or recognise that these three individuals are on the brink of bringing it what Fitrakis and Wasserman (2003) call "a new Reich".

The Bush family ties to the Nazi party are well known among historians but not the general public. The 1994 book written by Mark Aarons and John Loftus, *Secret War Against the Jews*, uses official US documents to establish that George Herbert Walker, George W. Bush's maternal great-grandfather, was one of Hitler's most important early backers who "funnelled money to the rising young fascist through the Union Banking Corporation" Walker arranged to have his new son-in-law, Prescott Bush—father of President George Bush I, grandfather of George Bush II—hired as Vice President at W.A. Harriman and Company in 1926. Prescott became a senior partner when Harriman merged with a British-American investment company to become Brown Brothers Harriman. In 1934 Prescott Bush joined the Board of Directors of Union Banking and assisted in the efforts to put Hitler and the Nazis into power and also to carry out their murderous war campaign. It has also been documented that Prescott Bush knowingly served as a money launderer for the Nazis (Bob Fitrakis and Wasserman, 2003).

According to Fitrakis and Wasserman (2003), Karl Rove has parallel ties. They write:

> The shadowy Rove serves as "Bush's Brain" in the current White House. He is the political mastermind behind the California coup, and is now in the headlines for outing Valerie Plame, the CIA wife of Ambassador Joseph Wilson. A consummate strategist, Rove may have outed Plame in retaliation for Wilson's failure to back up the Bush claim that Saddam Hussein was buying nuclear weapons materials in Africa. According to some published reports, as many as seventy CIA operatives have been put at risk by Rove's

retaliatory strike. According to Wilson, and to Retired US Navy Lt. Commander Al Martin (www.almartinraw.com), Rove's grandfather was Karl Heinz Roverer, the Gauleiter of Oldenburg. Roverer was Reich-Statthalter—Nazi State Party Chairman—for his region. He was also a partner and senior engineer in the Roverer Sud-Deutche Ingenieurburo A. G. engineering firm, which built the Birkenau death camp, at which tens of thousands of Jews, Gypsies, dissidents and other were slaughtered en masse. Rove, who has been based in Utah and associated with the Mormon Church, is widely viewed as the chief engineer of the current Bush administration. He and Tom DeLay are attempting to force the Texas legislature to redistrict its Congressional delegations, adding seven sure seats to the Republican column. By controlling the state houses in New York, Florida, Texas and California, the GOP would have a lock on the four largest states in the union, and thus the ability to manipulate vote counts and strip voter registration rolls in the run-up to the 2004 election. Rove is a prime behind-the-scenes mover in the Schwarzenegger campaign.

Fitrakis and Wasserman (2003) further note:

> According to Bob Woodward's *Bush at War*, Bush attended a New York Yankees game soon after the September 11 World Trade Center disaster. He wore a fireman's jacket. As he threw out the first pitch, the crowd roared. Thousands of fans stuck out their arms with thumbs up. Karl Rove, sitting in the box of Yankee owner George Steinbrenner, likened the roar of the crowd to "a Nazi rally".

Unfettered Capital: War, Globalisation, and Imperialism

A frequently invoked quotation during discussions of contemporary global politics is the one made famous by Prussian military officer, Karl Marie von Clauswitz (1780-1831): "war is the continuation of politics by other means" (cited in Meszaros, 1993, p. 18). However, Istvan Meszaros notes that this definition no longer is tenable in our time. This is because such a definition "assumed the *rationality* of the actions which connect the two domains of politics and war as the continuation of one another" (2003, p. 18). For this definition to hold, war had to be winnable—winnability in war was its absolute condition, for even a defeat in war would not destroy the very rationality of war between competing nation states. This absolute condition for Von Clausewitz's definition no longer exists, maintains Meszaros. If we consider that today, the objective of a winnable or feasible war is tied to the objective requirements of imperialism, which is *"world domination* by capital's most powerful state, in tune with its own political design of ruthless authoritarian 'globalisation' (dressed up as 'free exchange' in a U.S. ruled global market)" (2003, p. 18). This situation is clearly unwinnable and could not be considered a rational objective by any stretch of the imagination. War as the mechanism of global government is untenable because the "weapons already available for waging the war or wars of the twenty first century are capable of exterminating not only the adversary but the whole of humanity, for the first time ever in history" (2003, p. 19). Meszaros warns that Bush's National Security Strategy "makes Hitler's irrationality look like the model of rationality" (2003, p. 19). For Meszaros, humanity entered a qualitatively new phase of imperialism after the structural crisis of the 1960s and early 1970s which he calls "the new historic phase of global hegemonic imperialism" (2003, p. 20) with the US as the preponderantly dominant force. Clearly the logic of capitalist global integration is inextricably linked to this new phase of US military aggression.

Whereas formerly the world economy was composed of the development of national economies and national circuits of accumulation that were linked to each other through commodity trade and capital flows in an integrated international market, while nation states mediated the boundaries between differently articulated modes of production, today national production systems are reorganised and functionally integrated into global circuits, creating a single and increasingly undifferentiated field for world capitalism. The transnationalisation of the production of goods and services has led to a global class formation that has involved the accelerated division of the world into a global bourgeoisie and a global proletariat – a proletariat that has doubled within the last thirty years while the assets of the one-hundred largest multinational corporations has grown by 697 per cent. While the transnational ruling elite and political neocons (a distinction that at times barely deserves mention à la Dick Cheney) would prefer to cast off such disparities as the first step towards a globalised system of trickle-down economics, we are fairly reminded, according to Bill Robinson (2003) that globalisation has indeed led to *global apartheid*.

The distinctions between the poor and the wealthy have become fatally clear as demonstrated by South Korean farmer Lee Kuong-hae who stabbed himself in the heart with a Swiss army knife bearing a sign that read "WTO kills Farmers" during World Trade Organisation protests in Cancun-Mexico. And whereas nation-states in the past, as a consequence of national mass movements that pushed for an equal distribution of wealth, were at times successful in employing policies and economic practices that 'reformed' or 'redistributed' wealth more evenly (social democratic capitalism), neoliberal programs have resulted in a drastic reduction of the so-called welfare state or Keynesian economics (Robinson, 2003, p. 3). It is instructive here to reconsider Lenin's thesis of reformism as one in which "the liberal bourgeoisie grant reforms with one hand, and with the other always take them back, reduce them to naught, use them to enslave the workers, to divide them into separate groups and perpetuate wage-slavery" (1913, p. 373).

Capital's propensity to accumulate does not and cannot take place with a 'soft' or 'liberalised' heart. Without fail, the preponderance of capital production across the globe drives the restructuring of internal economies to extract greater profit and value from the hands of the working poor into the arms of the wealthy few. In conjunction with what Robinson describes as the "worldwide market liberalisation and the construction of a new legal and regulatory superstructure for the global economy" (2003, p.4) transnational capital is able to move freely, deregulated, and unabashed across national borders. This is not to suggest however, that the role of the nation/state has assumed a position of less significance. Power and politics at the level of the nation/state continue to play critical roles in the visceral travel of capital. In the case of the United States, we are witnessing a manifestation of extreme dogma propelled forward by neocons that accept no other alternative than a congenital acceptance to their foreign policy. Further, the "new age of imperialism" defined by strategic shifts made to "preclude the emergence of any potential future global competitor" (Foster, 2003) highlights the necessity of viewing the imperialism of today as one that is not only informed by the global integration of the capitalist market, but which is driven by the dynamic needs of the transnational capitalist class.

Ellen Meiksins Wood (2003) makes the important point that it is wrong to characterise globalisation as the decline of the territorial nation state. What is most unique about the current mode of imperialism is that it is a form of domination managed by a system of multiple states. When commercial exchange gave way to competitive production, it demonstrably affected the logic of imperial expansion in the drive to expand market imperatives of competition and the need to defeat economic rivals. The need for direct colonial coercion and command of trade by military means was dramatically reduced. The early days of capitalist imperialism witnessed colonial appropriation not as conquest or military domination and political jurisdiction but as economic hegemony. The driving force here was John Locke's theory of property and the obligation to produce exchange value. Wood notes that before this stage of economic imperialism, capitalism had passed through the classic age of imperialism with its intense geopolitical and military rivalries. Of course, the fact that we now have economic imperialism in which market imperatives manipulated by the dominant capitalist powers are made to do the work that used to be done by imperial states and colonial settlers, does not mean that military force has disappeared. Far from it, as a recent review of US military operations will clearly attest. The current imperial strategy of the United States is to dictate its conditions to the world, and to impose its economic imperatives on independent states. Many of those that refuse are targeted for military intervention. Developing economies are to be made dependent upon the Washington Consensus, through the instruments of the IMF and World Bank. So-called Third World countries are pressured to produce for export and to remove import controls. They are made market dependent and at the same time vulnerable to competition from highly subsidised Western producers. This is accompanied by the privatisation of public services as well as high interest rates and financial deregulation which has currently given way to the Third World debt crisis (Wood, 2003). Thus, the 'free trade' that describes the defining characteristic of globalisation is anything but free since the global economy that is currently controlled by the United States is being used "to compel other economies to serve the interests of the imperial hegemon in response to the fluctuating needs of its won domestic economy" (Wood, 2003, p. 134). Wood explains:

> Actually existing globalisation, then, means the opening of subordinate economies and their vulnerability to imperial capital, while the imperial economy remains sheltered as much as possible from the obverse effects. Globalisation has nothing to do with free trade. On the contrary, it is about the careful control of trading conditions in the interests of imperial capital (2003, p. 134).

Capital accumulation could not proceed apace without the state creating and maintaining via administrative and military means the conditions necessary for the reproduction of surplus extraction. According to Wood:

> The state, in both imperial and subordinate economies, still provides the indispensable conditions of accumulation for global capital, no less than for very local enterprises; and it is, in the final analysis the state that has created the conditions enabling global capital to survive and to navigate the world. It would not be too much to say that the state is the only non-economic institution truly indispensable to capital. While we can imagine capital continuing its daily operations if the WTO were destroyed, and perhaps welcoming the removal of obstacles placed in its way by

organisations that give subordinate economies some voice, it is inconceivable that those operations would long survive the destruction of the local state (2003, pp. 139–140).

Peter Hudis (2003) has pointed out what distinguishes today's imperialism from that of previous periods. One factor is that the US no longer seeks direct territorial control of the rest of the world, in contrast to its behaviour during the classic stage of imperialist-colonialism of the late 19th and 20th century. After World War II, the US shifted towards more indirect methods of domination through the creation of local surrogates and by relying on economic compulsion. Whereas imperialism once tried to disguise the tendency in the decline of the rate of profits through the extraction of super-profits from exploited lands overseas, the tendency of the rate of profit is now what openly drives capital's quest for imperialist expansion. Hudis further notes that the export of capital was once the prime motive for imperialist expansion whereas now capitalist production compels dominant capitals to incorporate and submit to the domination of foreign national capital. The US, for instance, was once the world's biggest exporter of capital but ever since the Vietnam War it has shifted from a creditor nation to a debtor nation whose importation of surplus capital (mostly from Europe and Asia) has become a defining feature of the world economy. Foreign companies continue to invest in the US because wages are low and health benefits are shrinking, and workers are being laid off, which has created a phenomenon of rising productivity (production increases while employment decreases—a jobless economic recovery). The militarisation of the US economy in its drive for permanent war has also helped to attract foreign capital to the US since the country that rules the world allegedly provides the most stability for investment.

The Question of Empire

The vicissitudes and contingencies of imperialism have brought into question the expansion – or fall – of what is commonly referred to as the American empire. While Peter Hudis expands Lenin's view of imperialism as one that is rooted in state capital and not only private capital, he argues that the new age of imperialism is at a point of rupture. Hudis remarks,

> Just as the emergence of 'classical' imperialism blinded many of its most astute critiques (like Hilferding and Bukharin) into emphasising its role as 'stabiliser' of capitalism rather than that which portends endless, even permanent crises of DISequilibrium, so today, the U.S.'s unmatched global dominance has many thinking the same, when in fact the whole edifice is shaky and prone to severe crisis, if not 'transformation into opposite.' (Personal communication, 2003a).

Unlike Hudis, James Petras believes that US imperial dominance is in no danger of immediate or near future collapse. For Petras, two simultaneously existing US-based economies suggest that in fact, the gluttonous feast is far from over. Rooted in both a domestic and international economy, the US Empire (while on a domestic economic downturn) has demonstrated resilience internationally. In fact, both economies mutually inform one another since "the high profits earned by the MNC's [multinational corporations] relocated throughout the new colonial and semicolonial economies of Asia and Latin America strengthen imperial institutions while weakening the domestic economy, its budget financing and its external accounts" (Petras, 2003, p. 10). According to Petras, US-based multinational corporations (MNCs) represent the impetus of economic empire building. Saturating a handful of economic sectors that include amongst others, oil and gas, US-owned and operated MNCs currently represent nearly half of the top 500 companies of the world while its subservient counterpart, Europe, and eager rival, Japan, lag far behind (Petras, 2003, pp.3-4). Key to this view is the assertion that "no state can aspire to global dominance if its principal economic institutions do not exercise a paramount role in the world economy" (Petras, 2003, p.4). In pursuit of increased profit making and control over competitors such as Europe and Japan, US MNC's currently exist in an ascending phase in the global world order. Petras concludes that an increasing share of profits and the exercise of military force places the US as the dominant empire provocateur.

With a significant portion of the world's wealth tucked neatly under its bedside pillow, the US shamelessly decides how many lives will be relinquished as 'collateral damage', marking it the "most powerful and aggressive superpower" in history (Petras, 2003). But the relationship between the military and economic empire builders is far from fluid. Under the current Bush regime, Secretary of Defense, Donald Rumsfeld, has exacerbated tensions between those who are in sole pursuit of economic conquest by military means and those who consider themselves military professionals by design. Petras describes this phenomenon thusly:

> There is no doubt that Rumsfeld has been the controlling figure in the formulation and execution of the strategy of world military conquest—an imperial strategy which closely resembles that of Nazi Germany. Rumsfeld's concentration of power within the imperial elite and the hostility toward the professionals was dramatically expressed by his nomination of retired General Schoomaker, former commander of the Special Forces 'Delta', which was described to me by senior military officers at the Delta headquarters at Fort Bragg as a collection of 'psychopaths trained to murder.' Clearly the ex-Delta general was selected precisely because his ideological and behavioral profile fits in with Rumsfeld's own Nazi propensities. (2003, p. 15)

And while the military professional 'intelligentsia' may covertly object to ideological demagoguery lacking sufficient military expertise, it hasn't slowed down the momentum of the empire builders. The fact that economic empire builders are able to secure and expand their economic interests at the expense of an overzealous militant cabal is a small price to pay for the inordinate super-profits that will result from obtaining the obvious: control over untapped markets. Key to the expansion of empire is a sophisticated military apparatus that on the surface is seemingly able to 'disarm' its host and force it to submit to "economic empire-building" (Petras, 2003, p.6). All of this leads Petras to the affirmation that "the notion of an 'over-extended' empire is a piece of ahistorical speculation..the benefits of empire building go to the overseas and domestic corporate elite, the costs are paid by US tax payers and the low income families which provide the combat and occupation soldiers" (2003, p. 7). And while the US domestic economy is in decline, the general populace up to the moment has showed no signs of mounting an uprising against a bludgeoning domestic deficit, against the hundreds of corpses returning from Iraq, or against the eviscerated state capacity to offer social services such as health and education. Rather, as stated by Scheer (2003), "too many Americans betray the proud tradition of an independent citizenry by buying into the 'aw shucks' irresponsibility of a president who daily does a grave injustice to the awesome obligations of the office that he has sworn—in the name of God, no less—to uphold".

Currently the majority of US citizens are enjoying the "empire chic" status of the victor and comforting themselves with the notion that, although no weapons of mass destruction were found, mass graves of Saddam's enemies were. This ignores the whole question of organised deception on the part of the Bush administration and his cabal of hawks and conforms to the fascist vocabulary of the newly minted Bush doctrine of preventative war. Those justifying the war on the basis of Saddam's mass graveyards are all too willing to discount the reason that Bush claims to have gone to war and supports the notion that the ends justify the means. Are those people who support the war for humanitarian reasons aware that many of Saddam's victims are the result of his reprisals after 1991, when Bush *padre* exhorted the Iraqis to rise up against Saddam, only to abandon them later on to the ensuing slaughter? It may seem quixotic for us to remark that we believe another world outside of capitalism's military industrial precincts is possible. We believe that calling for a socialist future is more than a hollow paean to the revolution by cross-grained polemicists but a creditable—and necessary—stance given the crisis of over-accumulation and overcapacity that drives capital's endless wars and environmental destruction. Marxists have unpacked the whole discreditable logic upon which capitalism rests, and we would do well to take stock of those arguments today in our struggle to lay the groundwork for a future of peace and prosperity. George Katsiaficas (2003) is correct when he identifies the true "axis of evil" as composed of the World Trade Organisation, the World Bank, and the International Monetary Fund. Their policies and practices clearly means more poverty for nations on the periphery of the world system, and have led to a dynamic "of increasing political democracy in the North coinciding with intensified exploitation in the South" (Katsiaficas, 2003, p. 348).

Towards an Alternative Future

Borrowing from Callinicos (2003), we reject the bourgeois anti-capitalism that critiques civil society but ultimately endorses the proposition that market capitalism is the best solution for meeting the overall needs of humankind. We reject, as well, localist anti-capitalism that endorses economic self-sufficiency by means of micro relationships among producers and consumers because this simply paves the way for market efficiency. Reformist anti-capitalism shares a similar problematic solution, the least of which is an endorsement of a more regulated capitalism at the level of the nation state. The most egregious effects of the capitalist system cannot be eliminated by taming the global corporation, or by trying to make their CEOs more socially conscious. Decentralised networks characteristic of autonomist anti-capitalism advocate a concept of radical democracy in which decentralisation and the deterritorialised multitude replaces the anti-state approach of the proletariat of classic Marxism. We prefer a socialist anti-capitalist approach that is non-sectarian and promotes a conception of the world in which the working class is still the most important agent of social transformation (Callinicos, 2003). We adopt a multi-racial, gender balanced, anti-imperialist approach that struggles to bring about a world in which everyone has equal access to the resources that they need in order to live a valuable and worthwhile life. Such an assertion is based on need and not productive contribution (Callinicos, 2003). We do not focus here on the immediate needs of the workers' that can be met in a 'social partnership' with capital, but on the needs of the global community of immiserated and disenfranchised workers.

The search for social transformation in the form of redistributive justice—i.e. striving to equalise material resources under existing conditions of global capitalism–often works to console those who are oppressed rather than to provoke them to rise up against the world of capitalism. It is a way of temporarily seeking relief from capitalism by ultimately adapting to its inevitability through a struggle to create more humane forms of its instantiation. It helps to soothe or console their alienation by finding temporary relief from their enslavement to capitalism and its attendant suffering. Especially among the privileged strata, the struggle for social justice ultimately rationalises and thus further integrates their parasitic relationship to the oppressed since they can unknot the tightening noose of capitalism without having to cut the rope that is strangling the disenfranchised. It enables them to cling to power and economic security while having the appearance of being progressive. It affords them the opportunity to advertise their discontent with capitalism without having to root out and transform the system of social relations of exploitation and property relations in which their parasitism is uncomfortably nested and upon which the scaffold is built to render a final judgement against the propertyless. Often social justice agendas do more for the privileged strata than they do for the oppressed classes because they address the myriad contradictions that surround the lives of the oppressed and alleviate some of the pain and confusion associated with it. In other words, social justice agendas ease the psychological suffering of the privileged strata while at the same time camouflaging their complicity in a system that is inextricably bound up with the suffering of the masses, a suffering that can only be alleviated by slicing through the gordian knot of capital and moving toward a socialist alternative.

Rikowski (2003) remarks that the social form of the human in society is one shaped by the pervasiveness of capital primarily through the conduit of labour-power. Labour-power takes the form of human capital in capitalist societies, saturating our subjectivities and permeating our personhood, constituting us as transhuman. Coursing through our veins with the force of molten lava are the violent contradictions internal to capital. Scalded into our formation as social agents is subjectivity riven with competing forces spawned by the dialectic *between* and *within* capital and labour. While the nature of our struggle might just prefigure the socialist being of the future, it might not. There are no guarantees.

For many of us who were part of the burgeoning US anti-war movement, protesting at every turn the Bush administration prior to its invasion of Iraq, hope seemed to be within grasp as momentum against the Bush junta was building worldwide. But shortly after the ground invasion began, the anti-war movement began to stagger, as many of the protestors were not prepared to continue their activism once US troops were in the war theatre itself. What seemed like a light at the end of the tunnel for the US left was really Bush *hijo* igniting a flamethrower, incinerating the dream of a new revolutionary dawn. With the mighty chains of his Christian faith, Bush has hoisted his conscience onto the biblical back of God, to whose wrath he has faithfully committed himself and his armies of invasion. As US weapons of mass destruction effortlessly saw through tendon and bone, blast apart organs and incinerate flesh with a vengeful fury, Bush sleeps as soundly as the 10,000 innocent Iraqi civilians that he has killed and the countless thousands that he has left orphaned and crippled. After his routine three-mile jog and bedtime prayers, the former Governor of Texas who set the record for most executions by any Governor in American history, has learned to unburden his heart by invoking the Lord for foreign policy direction. His mind unmercifully devoid of functioning synapses and unburdened by the power of analysis, Bush unhesitatingly made his decision to invade and occupy Iraq "because be believes, he truly believes, that God squats in his brainpan and tells him what to do" (Floyd, 2003, p. 4). The Israeli newspaper Haaretz was given transcripts of a negotiating session between Palestinian Prime Minister Mahmoud Abbas and faction leaders from Hamas and other militant groups. In these transcripts,

Abbas described his recent summit with Ariel Sharon and Bush *hijo*. During the summit, Bush told Abbas: "God told me to strike at al Qaida and I struck them, and then He instructed me to strike at Saddam, which I did, and now I am determined to solve the problem in the Middle East. If you help me I will act, and if not, the elections will come and I will have to focus on them" (Regular, 2003, p. 1). Bush should consult any standard copy of proverbs, maxims, and phrases where he would likely encounter the following saying: He that preaches a war when it might well be avoided, is the devil's chaplain. But perhaps such a maxim doesn't apply to a sitting US President who speaks directly to God.

Joe Conason (2003) has compared Bush *hijo's* compassionate conservatism—which rages against the sins of a welfare state—to Puritanism and feudalism, contrasting it to modern American values as developed over the last hundred years. Conason notes that public support for the poor and powerless represents for Bush and his evangelical fundamentalist ilk an "affront to God" (although they will tolerate it for temporary partisan expedience) and constitutes "an unwholesome stew of libertarian economics and religious orthodoxy" that "exalts church and corporation over the modern democratic state", "condemns democratic initiatives to constrain corporate power or regulate economic activity", and "defines the wealthy as God's elect, even if, like George W. Bush, they have inherited wealth and power that made their lives easy from the beginning" (2003, p. 183). In fact, a case can easily be made that Muslims as a whole have much more favourable opinions about the ideals of democracy than Bush and his cabal of ultraconservative religious sages. Conason writes that Bush's spiritual guru, Marvin Olasky, is financially connected and ideologically aligned to Christian Reconstructionism which Conasan describes as follows:

> The Reconstructionists despise American democracy, the First Amendment, and the separation of church and state. Their ideal society would be ruled by Christians like themselves, according to a literal interpretation of Old Testament biblical law, which prescribes the death penalty

for such offenses as homosexuality, abortion, atheism, juvenile delinquency, adultery, and blasphemy. They openly advocate the suppression of other religions, including that of Christians who don't share their interpretation of God's will. (2003, p. 181)

And while Bush *hijo* has gone out of his way to praise Islam as "a religion of peace" and has invited Muslim clerics to the White House for Ramadan dinners and has publicly opposed labelling Islam a dangerous faith, as is the wont of some evangelical Christian leaders, it is interesting to note that the Pentagon has assigned the task of tracking down and eliminating Osama bin Laden, Saddam Hussein and other high-profile targets to an Army general who characterises the war on terrorism "as a clash between Judeo-Christian values and Satan" (Cooper, 2003). According to Richard T. Cooper of the *Los Angeles Times*, Lt. Gen. William G. "Jerry" Boykin, the new deputy Undersecretary of Defense for Intelligence (whose new high-level policy position at the Pentagon was confirmed by the Senate in June) is a celebrated veteran of covert military operations, from the storied 1993 clash with Muslim warlords in Somalia chronicled in "Black Hawk Down" and the hunt for Colombian drug czar Pablo Escobar to the 1980 failed rescue attempt of American hostages in Iran. He also was an advisor to Atty. Gen. Janet Reno during Waco.

Cooper describes Boykin's new duties as "speeding up the flow of intelligence on terrorist leaders to combat teams in the field so that they can attack top-ranking terrorist leaders". According to Cooper, this former commander and 13-year veteran of the Army's top-secret Delta Force "is also an outspoken evangelical Christian who appeared in dress uniform and polished jump boots before a religious group in Oregon in June to declare that radical Islamists hated the United States 'because we're a Christian nation, because our foundation and our roots are Judeo-Christian ... and the enemy is a guy named Satan'". Last year Boykin is reported to have said: "We in the army of God, in the house of God, kingdom of God have been raised for such a time as this" (Cooper, 2003). Boykin has admitted that radical Muslims who resort to terrorism are not representative of the Islamic faith. Cooper reports that Boykin "has compared Islamic extremists to 'hooded Christians' who terrorised blacks, Catholics, Jews and others from beneath the robes of the Ku Klux Klan".

According to military affairs analyst William M. Arkin (2003), Boykin described his battle in Mogadishu, Somalia, as one that pitted the US forces against a Satanic presence, whose hovering image Boyton claims to have captured in a photograph of the sky over the city:

> In June of 2002, Jerry Boykin stepped to the pulpit at the First Baptist Church of Broken Arrow, Okla., and described a set of photographs he had taken of Mogadishu, Somalia, from an Army helicopter in 1993.
>
> The photographs were taken shortly after the disastrous "Blackhawk Down" mission had resulted in the death of 18 Americans. When Boykin came home and had them developed, he said, he noticed a strange dark mark over the city. He had an imagery interpreter trained by the military look at the mark. "This is not a blemish on your photograph," the interpreter told him, "This is real."
>
> "Ladies and gentleman, this is your enemy," Boykin said to the congregation as he flashed his pictures on a screen. "It is the principalities of darkness. It is a demonic presence in that city that God revealed to me as the enemy."

At the pulpit of the Good Shepherd Community Church in Sandy, Oregon, Boykin displayed slides of Osama bin Laden, Saddam Hussein and North Korea's Kim Jong Il. After posing the question as to why these individuals hate America, he answered his own question: "The answer to that is because we're a Christian nation. We are hated because we are a nation of believers" (Arkin, 2003). Boykin also claimed from the pulpit that America's "spiritual enemy will only be defeated if we come against them in the name of Jesus" (Arkin, 2003). He also proclaimed to the congregation that the faith that the US special operations forces had in God was what gave them victory: "Ladies and gentlemen I want to impress upon you that the battle that we're in is a spiritual battle. Satan wants to destroy this nation, he wants to destroy us as a nation, and he wants to destroy us as a Christian army" (Arkin, 2003).

·Boykin also sees the actions of Providence in the fact that George Bush is now in charge of the White House. While he admits that "George Bush was not elected by a majority of the voters in the United States", he nevertheless was "appointed by God" (Arkin, 2003). Arkin (2003) recounts a story Boykin told a church congregation in Daytona, Florida, in January. With the fervour of a football player bragging in the locker room that his penis is larger than that of his opponent, Boykin claims that his Christian God is far bigger than that of his Muslim warlord rival:

> "There was a man in Mogadishu named Osman Atto," whom Boykin described as a top lieutenant of Mohammed Farah Aidid.
>
> When Boykin's Delta Force commandos went after Atto, they missed him by seconds, he said. "He went on CNN and he laughed at us, and he said, 'They'll never get me because Allah will protect me. Allah will protect me.'
>
> "Well, you know what?" Boykin continued. "I knew that my God was bigger than his. I knew that my God was a real God and his was an idol." Atto later was captured.
>
> Other countries, Boykin said last year, "have lost their morals, lost their values. But America is still a Christian nation." (Arkin, 2003)

When, on the freshly mopped deck of the carrier, *USS Abraham Lincoln*, the US warrior president emerged in a snug fitting flight suit from an S-3B Viking aircraft, tautened groin accentuating straps strung salaciously between his legs, and glistening helmet clasped snugly against a proud chest (a brazenly hypocritical move considering his military records reveal that he stopped flying during his final 18 months of National Guard duty in 1972 and 1973 and was not observed by his commanders at his Texas unit for a year), his trademark swagger and petulant grin were greeted by patriotic cheers from throngs of wild-eyed officers and sailors. Appearing topside before a bold banner that announced "Mission Accomplished" he declared the "battle of Iraq" a "victory" in the ongoing "war on terror".[3] This event was carefully choreographed by Bush's team of seasoned image-makers that included a former ABC producer, a former Fox News producer and a former NBC cameraman paid for out of an annual budget of 3.7 million that Bush allots for his media co-ordinators. We do not believe that it's coincidental that a comparison clearly can be drawn between this example of rightwing showmanship and Leni Riefenstahl's infamous propaganda film about the 1934 Nazi *Parteitag* in Nuremberg, *Triumph des Willens (Triumph of the Will)* that displayed Adolf Hitler as the world saviour. In the German version, Hitler emerges from a Junker 52 aircraft that had been filmed landing at Nuremberg airport to the lofty strains of a Wagner composition. Thousands of Nazi onlookers chant, *Sieg hiel*! as the musical score builds to a thunderous crescendo. And while the scene was carefully crafted to suggest that Hitler was a modern manifestation of the ancient Aryan deity Odin (see *The Internationalist,* May 2003), the event on the *USS Abraham Lincoln* was pitching George Bush as a major player in the decidedly Christian drama known as the Second Coming. Bush's speech on the carrier paraphrased Chapter 61 of Isaiah, the very book that Jesus used when proclaiming that Isaiah's prophecies of the Messiah had come true, suggesting perhaps that Bush believes the Second Coming has begun (Pitt 2003) and that his war on terror is playing an important role in this Biblical prophecy. Leftist commentators have noted that the Pentagon's "Shock and Awe" bombing strategy was copied from the Nazi strategy of *Blitzkrieg* (lightning war) and the Luftwaffe's doctrine of *Schrecklichkeit* aimed at terrorising a population into surrender, and that the Bush Doctrine of preventative war mirrors the rationale behind Hitler's march into Poland (Hitler had claimed Poland was an immediate threat to the safety of the Reich). And while Bush *padre's* vow to establish a New World Order and Hitler's vow to create a *Neue Ordung* have to be seen in their historical and contextual specificity, the comparison of the Bush dynasty to the Third Reich does extend beyond fascist aesthetics, media spectacle, and the police state tactics of the Office of Homeland Security. It can be seen in the machinations of capital and the role of the military-industrial complex in imperialist acts of aggression disguised as "freedom".

With Hitler, it was the Jews who were subhuman—the *untermensch*—and with Bush the vermin of choice are the unholy Muslims. Hitler fancied himself as God's chosen leader of the Aryan Race and was in the thrall of a Volkism that prophesised a mighty God-chosen Aryan leader who would lead the people to their rightful destiny through a bloody conquest of the lebensraum (Paul, 2003) while Bush thinks God wears a Stetson hat and speaks in a drawl and is content in his role as God's own Texas Ranger.

Opportunism and hypocrisy are the operative words when it comes to assessing Bush's professed religious beliefs. According to a recent report by John Gorenfeld (2003), Bush *hijo's* Faith Based Initiative has given plenty of financial support to disciples of the Rev. Sun Myung Moon. We know that when John Ashcroft was the incoming Attorney General, he attended Moon's Inaugural Prayer Luncheon for Unity and Renewal just before Bush took office. We know, too, that Moon's *Washington Times* foundation gave a million dollars to the George H. W.. Bush presidential library and has paid the former president large sums as speaking honoraria. We question the so-called 'family values' that, according the Bush *padre*, Moon's organisation is supposed to support, especially in light of a number of uncomfortable facts, such as Moon's own criminal conviction for tax fraud and conspiracy to obstruct justice; his stipulation that his photograph must be placed nearby when spouses have sex; his instructions that spouses wipe their genitalia with the Holy Handkerchief (which is never supposed to be laundered) supplied by Moon's organisation; his labelling of gays as "dung eating dogs" and of American women as "a line of prostitutes"; his claim that the Holocaust was payback for the Jews for the crucifixion of Christ; his claim that he will succeed where Christ had failed in attaining worldly power; his illegal funding of the murderous Nicaraguan Contras during the Iran-Contra affair; his claim that spiritual messages from

Confucius and former US president James Buchanan have verified that he is the saviour of the world; his attack on the crucifix as the final obstacle in keeping Moon from being accepted by the American public as the Messiah; and his instructions to cherish and punish one's sexual organs with pliers, if necessary (Gorenfelf, 2003).

Lacking the enamelled self-importance that often accompanies an aristocratic intellect, Bush *hijo* betrays the spittoon arrogance of the tough-talking, God-fearing Texas oil baron, a ghostly veneer of saloon sawdust coating his forked tongue. His cowboy hauteur affords him a hayseed endearedness among paleocons, radiocons and loyal viewers of Fox News, but positively repulses sober thinkers averse to displays of unvarnished contempt for the world community.

But how is it that Bush can command such respect among everyday, working-class Americans? How is it that the policies that he initiates can destroy their jobs, destroy environmental resources, and yet blue-collar workers still vote for him? How is it that the very sector of American society now poised to keep him in the White House—working-class males or what Arlie Hochschild (2003) describes the prototypical "Nascar Dad" who watches car races on television, who listens to Rush Limbaugh on the drive home from work, who turns on Fox News at dinner, and who is too tired after working overtime to catch more than the headlines —is the one which stands to lose the most from his anti-worker, anti-labour policies? How is it that, as some polls reveal, blue-collar males support massive tax cuts for the rich? Hochschild put the issue thusly:

> Let's consider the situation. Since Bush took office in 2000, the U.S. has lost 4.9 million jobs, (2.5 million net), the vast majority of them in manufacturing. (5) While this cannot be blamed entirely on Bush, his bleed-'em-dry approach to the non-Pentagon parts of the government has led him to do nothing to help blue-collar workers learn new trades, find affordable housing, or help their children go to college. The loosening of Occupational Health and Safety Administration regulations has made plants less safe. Bush's

agricultural policies favor agribusiness and have put many small and medium-sized farms into bankruptcy. His tax cuts are creating state budget shortfalls, which will hit the public schools blue-collar children go to, and erode what services they now get. He has put industrialists in his environmental posts, so that the air and water will grow dirtier. His administration's disregard for the severe understaffing of America's nursing homes means worse care for the elderly parents of the Nascar Dad as they live out their last days. His invasion of Iraq has sent blue-collar children and relatives to the front. Indeed, his entire tap-the-hornets'-nest foreign policy has made the U.S. arguably less secure than it was before he took office. Indeed, a recent series of polls revealed that most people around the world believe him to be a greater danger than Osama Bin Laden. Many blue-collar voters know at least some of this already. So why are so many of them pro-Bush anyway?

Part of the answer is that a large percentage of blue-collar workers are evangelical Christians who regard Bush as possessing a direct line of communication to the Man sitting on the pearly throne. And certainly a large majority of working-class Americans are working far too hard for them to have the time to be as politically informed as they could be. They are also in the thrall of right-wing radio and television talk shows that permeate US airwaves. Many are receptive to the messages of the corporate media that refuse to challenge the Bush administration except in mild mannered ways. Part of the answer is, of course, that Bush reflects the core values of the blue-collar family and his authoritarian father-figure image resonates well with male members, especially after 9/11. Another part of the answer is that Bush has been successful for some time in concealing massive unemployment figures while he has been in office. The Bureau of Labor Statistics ended its Mass Layoff Tracking Study on Christmas Eve of 2002, thanks to the Bush administration. Congressional Democrats successfully raised funding so that the study could be restored in February of 2003 but the loss of 614,167 jobs in those two months went unannounced to the public

(Hochschild, 2003). Another explanation is captured by Nelson Peery, who notes:

> The stability of America has always rested upon that huge section of the population that had just enough to give them the hope that they were going to get some more. So long as they had that hope, they wouldn't change the system for love nor money no matter how hard they were hurting. They weren't going to change the system because they believed there was a golden egg up there somewhere. They were the ones who stabilized America (2002, p. 104).

Equally relevant is the argument that Bush is following a highly successful Republican strategy that began with Nixon and was followed by Ford, which included a deliberate attempt to avoid focusing on the material grievances of the working class, but rather on the 'feeling of being forgotten' among white male workers (Hochschild, 2003). Arlie Hochschild notes that "Nixon appealed not to a desire for real economic change but to the distress caused by the absence of it". Citing Norman Mailer who recently claimed that that the war in Iraq rejuvenated white males by returning to them a lost sense of mastery over the world and offered them a feeling of revenge for their perceived loss of power, Hochschild cites the following statistics:

> In the last thirty years, white men have taken a drubbing, he notes, especially the three quarters of them who lack college degrees. Between 1979 and 1999, for example, real wages for male high-school graduates dropped 24%. In addition, Mailer notes, white working class men have lost white champs in football, basketball and boxing.

Bush has clearly filled the void of the great white hero for the angry white working-class American male. Arnold Schwarznegger is doing the same for the white males of California, who are witnessing large numbers of immigrants from Latin America and feeling overwhelmed by the collapsing economy. But Bush is taking Nixon's blueprint for winning over the working-class male one step further. According to Hochschild, "instead of appealing, as Nixon did, to anger at economic decline, Bush is appealing to fear of economic displacement". He is also "offering the Nascar Dad a set of villains to blame, and a hero to thank". In effect, Bush has been "strip-mining the emotional responses of blue-collar men to the problems his own administration is so intent on causing". Hochschild elaborates:

> Unhinging the personal from the political, playing on identity politics, Republican strategists have offered the blue-collar voter a Faustian bargain: We'll lift your self-respect by putting down women, minorities, immigrants, even those spotted owls. We'll honor the manly fortitude you've shown in taking bad news. But (and this is implicit) don't ask us to do anything to change that bad news.... Paired with this is an aggressive right-wing attempt to mobilise blue-collar fear, resentment and a sense of being lost—and attach it to the fear of American vulnerability, American loss. By doing so, Bush aims to win the blue-collar man's identification with big business, empire, and himself. The resentment anyone might feel at the personnel officer who didn't have the courtesy to call him back and tell him he didn't have the job, Bush now redirects toward the target of Osama bin Laden, and when we can't find him, Saddam Hussein and when we can't find him... And these enemies are now so intimate that we see them close up on the small screen in our bedrooms and call them by their first names.

What makes Bush so frightening is that both the Christian Right and the Pentagon hawks have Bush by his Ponderosa belt buckle, and is in no danger of losing their central role in leading the march towards empire. Even as the economy takes major hits, he still is able to rewrite the losses as a plus for his administration by regulating and channelling the emotions of an angry white male population. Hochschild elaborates:

> George W. Bush is deregulating American global capitalism with one hand while regulating the feelings it produces with the other. Or, to put it another way, he is doing nothing to change the causes of fear and everything to channel the

feeling and expression of it. He speaks to a working man's lost pride and his fear of the future by offering an image of fearlessness. He poses here in his union jacket, there in his pilot's jumpsuit, taunting the Iraqis to "bring 'em on" — all of it meant to feed something in the heart of a frightened man.

This propaganda approach is decidedly costly, not only in terms of human life, but also in terms of US dollars. Because the only way Bush can pull off his image as the great American protector of the white male is if military spending becomes his major priority. Katsiaficas reveals that :

> [s]ince 1948, the U.S. has spent more than $15 trillion on the military—more than the cumulative monetary value of all human-made wealth in the U.S.—more than the value of all airports, factories, highways, bridges, buildings, shopping centers, hotels, houses, and automobiles. If we add the current Pentagon budget (over 346 billion in fiscal 2002) to foreign military aid, veterans' pensions, the military portion of NASA, the nuclear weapons budget of the Energy Department, and the interest payments on debt from past military spending, the U.S. spends $670 billion every year on the military—more than a million dollars a minute. The U.S. military budget is larger than those of the world's next 15 biggest spenders combined, accounting for 36 percent of global military expenditures. (2003, p. 344)

The US military currently is building its tenth supercarrier battle group (no other country possesses even one supercarrier), brags the most advanced fighters and bombers than all the other countries of the world combined, possesses the world's only Stealth aircraft, the world's largest aerial tanker fleet, the heaviest bombers, the most advanced tanks, the most deadly air-to-air and air-to-ground missiles, and the most sophisticated military electronics, including space satellites and drone airplanes (Baker, 2003). And while the US has no storied class of generals who routinely become the country's president, the military rules by proxy. The US has now been transformed into a national-security state, where the military has become the most revered institution in a country now overpopulated by right-ideologues, overburdened with military solutions, unengaged by democratic dialogue, and in the primal thrall of the military industrial complex's inexorable logic of empire. James Baker describes in chilling prose a recent visit by Bush *hijo* to Fort Hood in central Texas on January 3, where the Supreme Commander addressed the troops:

> "The Iraqi regime is a grave threat to the United States," he told them—and the rest of us. "Our country is in a great contest of will and purpose. We're being tested…We must, and we will, protect the American people and our friends and allies from catastrophic violence wherever the source, whatever the threat." (2003, p. 35–36)

What was more frightening than Bush's own words, was the response of the troops who were listening. Baker continues:

> The soldiers answered their commander in chief not with cheers or claps, or any sort of ordinary, civilian applause, but with a sudden, violent roar of "Hu-AH! Hu-AH!" Shouted simultaneously from 4,500 throats, it came across on the evening news as a primal, lusting sound; unexpected and voracious and thoroughly martial, like something one might have expected to hear from the Spartans or a Falangist street demonstration in the 1930s. It was not anything like I had ever heard at a rally convened by an American president. The chant continued throughout the speech, turning Bush's address into a churchy call-and-response. Individual cries of "Yeah!" and "Let's go!" rose from the crowd when he explained why we would invade Iraq though not North Korea, but again and again there was that same swift chant, sweeping all before it—"Hu-AH! Hu-AH! Hu-AH!"—reverberating around the gym until Bush, who just before the rally had exchanged his dark suit coat for a green waist-length army jacket, held up his left hand, palm out, in grand, imperious acknowledgement. (2003, p. 36)

While the steely-eyed generals salivate over the next instalment of the military budget, the US continues to build new military bases throughout the world (the US has over 250,000 troops in 141 countries), works behind the scenes to support a coup against (and likely an assassination of) President Hugo Chavez of Venezuela, stampedes its neo-liberal policies throughout Latin America, and provides funds to so-called 'dissidents' in Cuba in an attempt to undermine the Cuban government. In response to a recent criticism by Colin Powell that Cuba sponsors child prostitution as part of its tourism industry, Cuban author and journalist Rosa Miriam Elizalde captured the current spirit of US diplomacy when she called the Secretary of State *"ese comprador de almas que va como Mefistófeles con una mancha de sangre en la solapa del traje, y que quiere hacernos creer a la fuerza que es apenas un clavelito iraquí."* ("a merchant of souls who goes about like Mephistopheles, bearing a blood stain on his attire, but wanting us to believe that it is merely a little Iraqi carnation").

How quickly the organized fight against terrorism launched by the United States the day after September 11, 2001 has turned into its opposite: the regime of terror. This is not so difficult to fathom when we consider the history of the US empire. The US was founded upon the systematic slaughter of its indigenous peoples. As Katsiaficas (2003, p. 348) notes, "The dialectical irony of history means that [the US] is simultaneously a white European settler colony funded on genocide and slavery as well as on freedom and democracy." Tens of millions of Native Americans were massacred and between 15 to 50 million Africans were killed in the slave trade (with tens of millions more enslaved).

Perhaps not many people realise that when they dine out at the fancy restaurant, the "Lord Jeff", near Amherst College, that the restaurant's namesake, Lord Jeffery Amherst (of whom entire towns have been named after in Massachusetts, New York, and New Hampshire), was celebrated because he devised a method of exterminating indigenous people without risking white lives: delivering to Native Americans blankets carrying the smallpox virus (Katsiaficas, 2003). Of course, even if the patrons of Lord Jeff were conscious of this part of their history, it is doubtful that it would ruin the taste of their fillet minon.

Nineteenth-century US imperialism involved the slaughter of six hundred thousand Filipinos on the island of Luzon alone, and this effort was praised not only by the director of Presbyterian ministries (who noted that the murders were "a great step in the civilisation of the world") but also by both William McKinley and Theodore Roosevelt (Katsiaficas, 2003, p. 344). The latter wrote that the slaughter in the Philippines was "for civilisation over the black chaos of savagery and barbarism" (cited in Katsiaficas, 2003, p. 344). Between 1898 and 1934, the US marines invaded Cuba four times, Honduras seven times, Nicaragua five times, the Dominican Republic four times, and Haiti and Panama twice each. But we shouldn't overlook US slaughter in Indochina, where between three and five million people were killed in Korea, and two million were killed—many by chemical weapons—in Vietnam. Katsiaficas writes:

> For every man, woman, and child in South Vietnam, the U.S. dropped more than 1000 pounds of bombs (the equivalent of 700 Hiroshima bombs), sprayed a gallon of Agent Orange, and used 40 pounds of napalm and half a ton of CS gas on people whose only wrong doing was to struggle for national independence. The kill ratio in these two Asian wars was about 1000 times that of wars in Central America and perhaps just as high for the more than 200 other U.S. military interventions during the "Cold War." (2003, p. 346)

While there has been a great deal of discussion linking US imperialism and the bloody path of military intervention, too little has been said about the intentional targeting of civilians by the US military. As Tariq Ali has argued: "The massacre of civilian populations was always an integral part of U.S. war strategy" (cited in Boggs, 2003, p. 207). Boggs describes the matrix of capitalism, imperialism, and racism that led to the systematic extermination of Native Americans and asserts that the American tradition of war was given ideological meaning through Manifest Destiny and the Monroe Doctrine. He also points out that the US has consistently rejected international treaties and protocols for protecting civilians from the carnage of war. Boggs writes:

> Americans have pursued their global ambitions through every conceivable barbaric method: wars of attrition, carpet bombing, free-fire zones, massacres of unarmed civilians, support for death squads, forced relocations, destruction of public infrastructures, the burning down of cities, use of weapons of mass destruction including atomic bombs. Filled with an imperial contempt for others and a sense of moral supremacy, US leaders have predictably established themselves as beyond the reach of international law, immune to any moral or legal rules of engagement. (2002, p. 208).

The Korean war is just one example. In this war, the infamous "search and destroy" missions

> meant attacking not only combatants but civilians, animals, the whole ecology, as part of effective counterinsurgency operations. When troops came upon any village, they usually came in opening fire, often with support of helicopter gunships. U.S. troops were rewarded according to the well-known "body count," never limited simply to identifiable combatants. (Boggs, 2003, p. 210)

Of course, the US has pursued this logic in most of its wars since that time, up to and including the Gulf War and the bombing of Iraq's civilian infrastructure that lasted for years up to the recent invasion. In a capitalist society—especially in the world's most dominant capitalist society and military superpower—this bloody reality cannot be otherwise. This is because those who are invested in protecting capitalist society and who possess the necessary power (including firepower) not only to defend it but expand its global sweep, are those who have benefited most by it and whose stature has been the most elevated because of it. The guardians of capital represent those whose character has been most fully formed by the ruthless imperatives and unquenchable desires of capital. They have embodied those ensembles of social relations that most estrange them from love and distance them from compassion. Joel Kovel remarks that capitalism cannot be relegated to the social relations of economic production but also represents a "regime of the ego". He reminds us that:

> Each society selects for the psychological types that serve its needs. It is quite possible in this way to mold a great range of characters toward a unified, class purpose. To succeed in the capitalist marketplace and rise to the top, one needs a hard, cold, calculating mentality, the ability to sell oneself, and a hefty dose of the will to power. (2002, p. 78)

Exponents of revolutionary critical pedagogy do not seek capital's self-expansion at the expense of ecologies but rather the emancipation of labour and the creation of a social universe "in which humanity is restored to ecosystemic differentiation with nature" (Kovel, 2002, p. 210). This does not imply the transfer of ownership, but to reject the very idea of ownership. Kovel uses the term 'usufructuary' to describe this relationship, a term used by Marx in *Capital, Volume 3*, which referred to the gratification expressed in freely associated labour beginning with the free association of producers. Kovel importantly notes that "the whole making of the human world is to be taken into account rather than just that which contributes or controls exchange-value" (2002, p. 241). This will require a total break with capitalism's law of value. As McLaren and Faramandpur (forthcoming) have written:

> We do not look to the Heavenly Kingdom of Great Peace, the Paris Commune, or the Russian Revolution for blueprints for our efforts, but the examples of the Taipings, the Communards, and the Bolsheviks—and numerous others—can certainly provide us with inspiration. While socialist struggle must necessarily be international in scope it must not disregard the contextual specificity of regional and local dynamics. We need to remember, too, that we become disinherited from democracy precisely at the moment we believe we have attained it. The struggle never ceases. There are always new unanticipated challenges ahead.

The greatest challenge to the US is itself. The US is advertised as a secular democracy, which it is, but in name only. While its leaders claim to be inspired by providence or guided by the Almighty, the US culture industry continues to profit mightily from the sexualisation of violence. Thousands of young Americans, thrilled and aroused by newspaper accounts of Arnold Schwarzenegger's alleged 'gang bang' of an African-American woman, are posited to cast their votes for "The Terminator" for Governor of California. When Schwarzenegger told assembled US troops that they are "the real terminators", thousands of young people couldn't wait to sign up for the next war. Imperialism has been made sexy by the editors of *People Magazine* who voted Defense Secretary Donald Rumsfeld as one of the sexiest men in the United States. Apparently, many Americans are aroused by the ruthless way he wields war and slaughters the innocent. There is little evidence to indicate that the US is prepared to consider a socialist alternative to its imperialist democracy anytime soon. Freely associated labour can't compete in a capitalist society with being citizens of the world's only superpower, free to conquer and destroy on a scale never imagined by the rulers of ancient Rome. As long as exploitation remains gratifying and continues to accumulate value, there is little motivation for US citizens to create a world outside of capital's value form.

That is why any revolutionary struggle must be dedicated to educating the emotions as much as the intellect, and why anti-imperialist struggle must be waged on the triple continents of reason, faith, and passion. It must take place not only on the picketline or protest march, but in the schools, places of worship, libraries, shop floors, and corporate offices – in every venue where people come together to learn, to labour, and to love.

NOTE

This is an expanded version of Peter McLaren and Nathalia E. Jaramillo, "A Moveable Fascism: Fear and Loathing in the Empire of Sand", *Cultural Studies/Critical Methodologies*, in press.

1. The names of famous puppets that were made popular on US television in the 1950s.

2. Clark is now seeking the Democratic Party's nomination or President, even though he sounded very much like a Republican just a few years ago. He has rightly been criticized for political opportunism and for his ambiguous position on the war on Iraq.
3. From the deck of the USS *Abraham Lincoln*, Bush triumphantly declared the war over; the fall of Baghdad had culminated the one-month long military coup. And yet, when confronted by the media with reports of regular assaults on American troops, Bush had the bombastic arrogance to assert on July 2: "bring 'them on." Since he made that remark (at the time of this writing), 105 US soldiers have been killed.

REFERENCES

Arkin, William, M. (2003). The Pentagon Unleashes a Holy Warrior. *Los Angeles Times* (Thursday, October 16). http://www.latimes.com/news/opinion/la-oe-arkin16oct16,1,6651326.story?coll=la-headlines-oped-manual

Baker, Kevin. (2003). We're in the Army Now: The G.O.P.'s Plan to Militarize Our Culture. *Harper's Magazine*. vol. 307, no. 1841 (October), pp. 35–46.

Boggs, Carl. (2003). Outlaw Nation: The Legacy of U.S. War Crimes. In Carl Boggs, ed., *Masters of War: Empire and Blowback in the Age of American Empire*. (pp. 191–226) New York and London: Routledge.

Callinicos, Alex (2003). *An Anti-Capitalist Manifesto*. Cambridge, England: Polity Press.

Chomsky, Noam. (2003). Wars of Terror. In Carl Boggs, ed., *Masters of War: Empire and Blowback in the Age of American Empire*. (pp. 131–147) New York and London: Routledge.

Conason, Joe. (2003) *Big Lies: The right-Wing Propaganda Machine and How it Distorts the Truth*. New York: St. Martin's Press.

Cooper, Richard, T. (2003). General Casts War in Religious Terms. *Los Angeles Times*. October 16, 2003. http://tm0.com/latte/sbct.cgi?s=406406842&i=916181&m=1&d=5263059

The Editorial Board. (2003). Weapons of mass destruction in Iraq: Bush's "big lie" and the crisis of American imperialism (June 21). http://wsws.org/articles/2003/jun2003/wmd-j21.shtml

Fitrakis, Bob, and Wasserman, Harvey, (2003). Fourth Reich? The Bush-Rove-Schwarzenegger Nazi Nexus. http://

www.counterpunch.org/wasserman10062003.html

Floyd, Chris. (2003). The Revelation of St. George. Counterpunch, June 30. http://www.counterpunch.org/floyd06302003.html

Foster, John Bellamy (2003). The New Age of Imperialism. *Monthly Review*. vol. 55, no.. 3 (July-August).

Gorenfeld, John (2003). Bad Moon on the Rise. *Salon*, September 24. http://www.salon.com/news/feaure/2003/09/24/moon/print.html.

Hochschild, Arlie. (2003). Let Them Eat War. October 2. *ZNet*. http://www.zmag.org/content/showarticle.cfm?SectionID=12&ItemID=4294

Hudis, Peter. (2003). Report to National Plenum of News and Letters Committees, August 30, 2003. Organizational Responsibility for Marxist-Humanism in Light of War, Resistance, and the Need for a New Alternative.

Hudis, Peter (2003a). Personal communication.

Katsiaficas, George. (2003). Conclusion: the Real Axis of Evil. In Carl Boggs (Ed.), *Masters of War: Militarism and Blowback in the Era of American Empire*. (pp. 343-355) New York and London: Routledge.

Kovel, Joel (2002). *The Enemy of Nature: The End of Capitalism or the End of the World?* Nova Scotia: Fernwood Publishing Ltd at London and New York: 2ed Books Ltd.

Lenin, V.I. (1913). Marxism and Reformism. From V.I. Lenin, *Collected Works*, 4th English Edition, Foreign Languages Publishing House, Moscow, 1972 Vol. 13, pp. 372-75. http://www.marx2mao.org/Lenin/MR13.html

Lieven, Anatol. (2003). The Empire Strikes Back. *The Nation* (June 19) http://www.thenation.com/doc.mhtml?i=20030707&s=lieven

Los Ninos Tambien? http://www.infocom.etecsa.cu/prensa/cu/cun_f17.htm

Many Americans Unaware WMD Have Not Been Found. http://www.pipa.org/whatsnew/html/new_6_04_03.html

McLaren, Peter, and Farahmandpur, Ramin (forthcoming). In Arif Dirlik (ed.) Conference proceedings.

McLaren, Peter. (2003). The Dialectics of Terrorism. In Carl Boggs, ed., *Masters of War: Empire and Blowback in the Age of American Empire..* (pp. 149-189) New York and London: Routledge.

Meszaros, Istvan, (2003). Militarism and the Coming Wars. *Monthly Review*, vol. 55, no. 2, (June) pp. 17-24.

Nevada brothel offers free sex to returning troops. Tuesday, June 3, 2003 Posted: 5:02 PM EDT (2102 GMT) CNN.com./U.S. http://www.cnn.com/2003/US/West/06/03/offbeat.brothel.reut/

index.html
Paul, Gregory. (2003). The Great Scandal: Christianity's Role in the Rise of the Nazis. *Free Inquiry* (Oct.-Nov.), vol. 23, no. 4, pp. 20-29.

Petras, James (2003). Empire Building and Rule: U.S. and Latin America. Found at *http://www.rebelion.org* (June 25). (Included in the present book)

Pitt, William (2003). "George W. Christ?" *Truthout* (May 5). Found at *http://www.truthout.org/docs_03/050503A.shtml*.

Peery, Nelsen. (2002). *The Future is Up to US. A Revolutionary Talking Politics with the American People*. Chicago: Speakers for a New America Books.

Regular, Amon. (2003). 'Road map is a life saver for us,' PM Abbas tells Hamas, Haaron, Monday, August 11.
http://www.haaretz.com/hasen/pages ShArt.jhtml?itemNo= 310788 &contrassID=2&subContrassID=1&sbSubContrassID=0&listSrc=Y

Rikowski, Glenn (2003). Marx and the Future of the Human. *Historical Materialism*. vol. 11, no. 2, pp. 121-164.

Robinson, William (2003). Social Activism and Democracy in South Africa: A Globalization Perspective. Remarks for Idasa conference, Cape Town, August 11-13, 2003: "Social Activism and Socio-Economic Rights: Deepening Democracy in South Africa."

Scheer, Robert (2003). Bush Was All Too Willing to Use Emigres' Lies; American experts urged the White House to be skeptical, but they hit a stone wall. *Los Angeles Times* (Sept. 2) pg. B11

Views of a Changing World 2003 War With Iraq Further Divides Global Publics. (June 3, 2003). *http://people-press..org/reports/display.php3?ReportID=185*

The US Imperialism and the Middle East

Samir Amin
(Translated from French by Pratyush Chandra)

The analysis that I propose regarding the importance of the Middle East in the global imperialist strategy of the United States is inscribed in a general historical vision of the capitalist expansion that I have developed elsewhere.[1] Within this vision, capitalism has always been, since its inception, a polarizing system by nature, i.e., imperialist. This polarization - i.e. the concomitant construction of dominant centres and dominated peripheries, and their reproduction deepening in each stage – is immanent in the process of accumulation of capital operating on a global scale, founded on what I have called "the law of globalised value".

In this theory of global expansion of capitalism, the qualitative transformations of the systems of accumulation from one phase of its history to another shape, in their turn, the successive forms of asymmetric centres/peripheries polarization, i.e. of concrete imperialism. The contemporary world system will thus remain imperialist (polarising) throughout the visible future, in so far as the fundamental logic of its deployment remains dominated by the capitalist production relations. This theory thus associates imperialism with the process of capital accumulation on a worldwide scale, which I consider as constituting only one reality whose various dimensions are in fact not dissociable. Thus it differs as much from the vulgarised version of the Leninist theory of "imperialism, the highest phase of capitalism" (as if the former phases of global expansion of capitalism were not polarizing), as from the contemporary postmodern theories that describe the new globalisation as "post imperialist".[2]

1. Permanent Conflict of Imperialisms with Collective Imperialism

In its globalised deployment, imperialism was always conjugated in plural, since its inception (in the XVIth century) until 1945. The conflict of imperialisms, permanent and, often violent, too has occupied in fact a decisive place in the transformation of the world as class struggle, through which fundamental contradictions of capitalism are expressed. Moreover, social fights and conflicts of the imperialisms are closely articulated and it is this articulation that determines the course of really existing capitalism. I also point out that the analysis that I have proposed in this respect differs vastly from that of the "succession of hegemonies".

The Second World War ended in a major transformation with regard to the forms of imperialism: the substitution of the multiplicity of imperialisms in permanent conflict by collective imperialism combining the ensemble of the centres of the world capitalist system (simply, the "triad": the United States and its external Canadian province, Western and central Europe, Japan). This new form of imperialist expansion went through various phases of its development, but it remained all the time present. The eventual hegemonic role of the United States, whose bases will have to be specified as the forms of its articulation with the new collective imperialism, must be located within this perspective. These questions pose problems, which are precisely those that I would wish to point out here.

The United States drew a gigantic benefit from the Second World War, which had ruined its principal combatants–Europe, Soviet Union, China and Japan. It was thus in a position to exert its economic hegemony, since it concentrated more than half of the global industrial production and had specialty in the new technologies that would shape the development of the second half of the century. In addition, they possessed a specialty in the nuclear weapon–the new "absolute" weapon. This is why I situate the break announcing the end of war not at Yalta as what is often told (at Yalta the United States did not have the weapon yet) but at Potsdam (a few days before the bombardment of Hiroshima and Nagasaki). At Potsdam the American tone changed: the decision to engage what was going to be the "cold war" was made by them.

This double absolute advantage was nevertheless eroded in a relatively short period of time (within two decades), by double recovery, economic for the capitalist Europe and Japan, military for the Soviet Union. It will be remembered that this relative retreat of the US power provided at the time a flowering of the discourse on "American decline", and even an ascent of alternative hegemonies (Europe, Japan, later China...).

It is the moment when Gaullism is born. De Gaulle considered that the objective of the United States since 1945 had been to control the entire Old World ("Eurasia"). And that Washington managed to position itself, breaking Europe–the "true" Europe, from Atlantic to the Urals, i.e. including "Soviet Russia", as he said–stirring the spectre of an "aggression" from Moscow, which he never believed in. His analysis was, in my opinion, realistic and perfect. But he was almost alone in saying so. The counter-strategy that he envisaged as a counterpoint to "Atlanticism" promoted by Washington, was founded on Franco-German reconciliation, on whose base the construction of "non-American Europe" could be conceived, carefully keeping out Great Britain, judged rightly as the Trojan horse of Atlanticism. Europe in question could then open the way to reconciliation with "(Soviet) Russia". Reconciling and drawing together the three big European populations–French, Germans and Russians–would put a definite end to the American project of dominating the world. The internal conflict specific to the European project can thus be summarized as the choice between two alternatives: the Atlantic Europe, which is the European wing of the American project or non-Atlantic Europe (integrating Russia in this perspective). This conflict is still not resolved. But later developments—the end of Gaullism, Great Britain's admission in Europe, its extension towards the East, the Soviet collapse—have until now supported together what I call "an obliteration of European project" and its "dual dilution in neo-liberal economic globalisation and in the political-military alignment with Washington."[3] Moreover, this development reinforces the strength of the collective character of the triadic imperialism.

Does it thus stir a "definitive" (non-conjunctural) qualitative transformation? Does it inevitably imply a "leadership" of the United States in one way or another? Before trying to answer these questions it is necessary to express with more precision in what the "project" of the United States consists.

2. The Project of the Ruling Class of the United States: To Extend the Monroe Doctrines to the Whole Planet

This project, which I will describe without much hesitation as overweening, even crazy, and criminal by what it implies, did not come out of President Bush Junior's head, to be implemented by an extreme right junta, seizing power through dubious elections.

It is the project which the ruling class of the United States unceasingly nurtured since 1945, even though its implementation evidently passed through ups and downs, encountered a few vicissitudes and was here and there put to check, and could not be pursued with consistency and violence that this implied in certain conjunctural moments like ours, following the disintegration of the Soviet Union.

The project always rendered a decisive role to its military dimension. It was conceived after Potsdam, as I pointed out, founded on nuclear monopoly. Very quickly, the United States conceived a global military strategy, dividing the planet into regions and allocating the responsibility for the control of each of them under a "US Military Command". I refer to what I wrote on this subject even before the collapse of the USSR, and on the priority position occupied by the Middle East in this global strategic vision.[4] The objective was not only "to encircle the USSR" (and China), but as well to draw up means, making

Washington the ruler in the last resort of all the regions of the planet. In other words, it extended the Monroe Doctrine to the whole planet, which effectively gave the exclusive right of managing the ensemble of the New World to the United States in accordance to what it defined as its "national interests".

The project implies that the "sovereignty of the national interests of the United States" is placed above all the other principles controlling the political behaviours that we regard as "legitimate" means; it develops a systematic mistrust towards all supranational rights. Certainly, imperialisms of the past did not behave differently and those who endeavour to lighten the responsibilities—and the criminal comportments—of the US establishment at the present moment, and find "excuses" for them,[5] continue with this same argument, of indisputable historical antecedents.

But this is precisely what one would have liked to see changing in the history and which begun after 1945. It is because the conflict of imperialisms and the contempt for international law by fascist powers producing the horrors of the Second World War, that the UNO was founded on a new principle proclaiming the illegitimate character of the war. The United States, it could be said, has not only made this principle its own, but has also largely been its early initiator. Soon after the First World War, Wilson advocated to re-found international politics precisely on principles different to those which, since the treaty of Westphalia (1648), have rendered sovereignty to the monarchical States and then to the nations more or less democratic, given that this absolute character was questioned by the disaster to which it had led the modern civilization. It does not matter if the vicissitudes of the domestic policy of the United States have deferred the implementation of these principles. F. Roosevelt, and even his successor H. Truman, played a decisive role in defining the new concept of multilateralism and the condemnation of war that accompanies it, which is the basis of the United Nations' Charter.

This good initiative—supported at the time by the people of the entire world—that represented indeed a qualitative jump and opened the way for the progress of civilization, however never won the conviction of the ruling classes of the United States. The authorities of Washington felt always ill at ease in the concept of the UNO and today brutally proclaim what they were forced to conceal up till now: that they do not accept even the concept of an international law higher than what they consider to be the exigencies of the defence of their own "national interests". I do not believe that it is acceptable to find excuses for this return to the vision, which the Nazis had developed in their time by requiring the destruction of the League of Nations. The plea in favour of the law, developed with talent and elegance by Villepin at the Security Council, is not, in this sense, a "nostalgic look towards the past" but on the contrary a reminder of what the future must be. It was the United States which, on that occasion, defended a past that had been proclaimed definitively outmoded.

The implementation of the project necessarily went through successive phases, shaped by the facts of particular power relations that defined them.

Immediately after the war, the American leadership was not only accepted, but even solicited by the bourgeoisie of Europe and Japan. For if the reality of a menace of the "Soviet invasion" could convince only the feeble-minded, its invocation rendered good services to the Right as well as to the social democrats hounded by their adversary communist cousins. One could then believe that the collective character of the new imperialism was only due to this political factor and that, once their backwardness over the United States is made up, Europe and Japan would seek to get rid of Washington's cumbersome and henceforth useless supervision. That was not the case. Why?

My explanation appeals here to the rise of the national liberation movements in Asia and Africa - the era of Bandung 1955–1975[6] —and to the support that the Soviet Union and China provided them (each one in its own way). The imperialism was then forced "to make up", thus not only accepting the peaceful coexistence with a vast surface which largely escaped it ("the socialist world") but also negotiating the terms of the participation of the Asian and African countries in the imperialist world system. The collective alignment of the triad under the

American leadership seemed useful for managing the North-South relationships of the epoch. This is why the Non-Aligned found itself then confronted with a "Western block" practically impeccable.

The collapse of the Soviet Union and the suffocation of the populist nationalist regimes born out of the national liberation obviously permitted the project of the United States to redeploy itself with an extreme vigour, in the Middle East, along with in Africa and Latin America. The fact remains that the project stays in the service of collective imperialism, up to a certain point at least (which I will try to clarify later). The economic government of the world on the basis of the principles of neo-liberalism, implemented by G-7 and the institutions at its service (WTO, the World Bank, and the IMF), the structural re-adjustment plans imposed on the breathless Third World have come to be the expression. Even on the political level, it will be witnessed that initially Europeans and Japanese agreed to be part of the alignment with the US project, at the time of the wars in the Gulf (1991), then in Yugoslavia and Central Asia (2002), accepting the marginalisation of the UNO for the benefit of NATO. These initial times are still not passed, even if some signs indicate its possible cracking up from the time of the war on Iraq (2003).

The ruling class of the United States proclaims openly that it "will not tolerate" the reconstitution of any economic and military power capable of questioning its monopoly of domination over the planet, and for this purpose, it gave itself the right to lead "preventive wars". Three principal potential adversaries are targeted here.

In the first place is Russia, whose dismemberment, after that of the USSR, constitutes henceforth a major strategic objective of the United States. The Russian ruling class does not appear to have understood this till now. It seems convinced that after having "lost the war", it could "win peace", as what had been for Germany and Japan. It forgets that Washington needed the recovery of these two adversaries in the Second World War, precisely to face the Soviet challenge. The new conjuncture is different, the United States not having more serious competitor. Their option is then to permanently and completely destroy the ravaged Russian adversary. Will Putin understand this and initiate Russia in coming out of its illusions?

In the second place China, whose expanse and economic success worry the United States, whose strategic objective remains here too to dismember this large country.[7]

Europe comes third in this global vision of the new masters of the world. But here the North-American establishment does not appear anxious, at least so far. The unconditional Atlanticism of a few (Great Britain, as well as the new servile powers of the East), the "quicksand of the European project" (the point on which I will come back), the converging interests of the dominant capital of the collective imperialism of the triad, contribute in the effacement of the European project, maintained in its status of "European wing of the US project". The diplomacy of Washington has managed to keep Germany on its trail, the reunification and the conquest of Eastern Europe even seemed to reinforce this alliance: Germany would be encouraged to reclaim its tradition of "thrust towards the East" (the part played by Berlin in the dismemberment of Yugoslavia by the hasty recognition of the Slovenian and Croatian independence was its expression[8]) and, as for the rest, induced to navigate on Washington's trail. Is there a reversing of steam in progress? The German political class appears hesitant and could be divided as far as its strategic choices are concerned. The alternative to the Atlanticist alignment—which seems to have wind in its sails - calls, in counterpoint, a reinforcement of Paris-Berlin-Moscow axis, which would then become the most solid pillar of a European system independent of Washington.

Our main question can be reconsidered now, i.e. the nature and potential strength of the triad's collective imperialism, contradictions and weaknesses of its leadership by the United States.

3. Collective Imperialism of the Triad and Hegemonies of the United States: Their Articulation and Contradictions

Today's world is militarily unipolar. At the same time, some fissures seem to become apparent between the United States and some of the European countries with regard to the political management of a global system so far united on the principles of liberalism, in theory at least. Are these fissures only conjunctural and of limited range, or do they proclaim some lasting changes? Thus, it will be necessary to analyse in all their complexity the logics that command the deployment of the new phase of collective imperialism (North-South relationships in the current language) and the specific objectives of the US project. In this spirit I will approach succinctly and successively five series of questions.

(a) Concerning the Nature of Evolutions which have led to the Constitution of the New Collective Imperialism

I suggest here that the formation of the new collective imperialism finds its origin in the transformation of the conditions of competition. Only a few decades ago, the large firms fought their competing battles essentially over the national markets, whether it is the matter of the United States (the largest national market in the world) or even those of the European States (in spite of their modest size, which handicapped them in relation to the United States). The winners of the national "matches" could perform well on the world market. Today, the size of the market necessary for gaining an upper hand in the first cycle of matches approaches some 500-600 million "potential consumers". The battle must thus be launched straightaway on the global market and won on this ground. And those who perform over this market then assert more over their respective national terrains. Thorough internationalisation becomes the primary setting of the activity of the large firms. In other words, in the pair national/global, the terms of causality are reversed: earlier the national power commanded the global presence and today it is the reverse. Therefore the transnational firms, whatever their nationality, have common interests in the management of the world market. These interests are superimposed on the permanent and mercantile conflicts, which define all the forms of competition specific to capitalism, irrespective of what they are.

The solidarity of the dominant segments of the

transnationalized capital of all the partners in the triad is real, and is expressed by their rallying to globalized neo-liberalism. The United States is seen from this perspective as the defender (military if necessary) of these "common interests". Nonetheless, Washington does not intend "to equitably share" the profits of its leadership. The United States seeks, on the contrary, to reduce its allies into vassals and, thus is only ready to make minor concessions to junior allies in the triad. Will this conflict of interests within dominant capital lead to the break-up of the Atlantic alliance? Not impossible, but unlikely.

(b) Concerning the Place of the United States in the World Economy

General opinion has it that US military power only constitutes the tip of the iceberg, extending the country's superiority in all areas, notably economic, but even political and cultural. Therefore, submission to the hegemony that it pretends would be impossible to circumvent.

I maintain, in counterpoint that, in the system of collective imperialism the United States does not have decisive economic advantages; the US production system is far from being "the most efficient in the world". On the contrary, very few of its sectors would be certain of beating competitors in the truly free market dreamt of by liberal economists. The US trade deficit, which increases year by year, went from 100 billion dollars in 1989 to 500 billion in 2002. Moreover, this deficit involved practically all areas of production system. Even the surplus once enjoyed by the US in the area of high-technology goods, which stood at 35 billion in 1990, has now turned into a deficit. Competition between Ariane rockets and those of NASA, between Airbus and Boeing, testifies to the vulnerability of the American advantages. Faced by European and Japanese competition in high-technology products, by Chinese, Korean and other Asian and Latin American industrialised countries in competition for banal manufactured products, by Europe and the southern cone of Latin America in agriculture, the United States probably would not be able to win were it not for the recourse to "extra-economic" means, violating the principles of liberalism imposed on its competitors!

In fact, the US only benefits from comparative advantages in the armaments sector, precisely because this sector largely operates outside the rules of the market and benefits from state support. This advantage probably brings certain benefits for the civil sphere in its wake (the Internet being the best-known example), but it also causes serious distortions that handicap many production sectors.

The North American economy lives parasitically, to the detriment of its partners in the world system. "The United States depends for 10 per cent of its industrial consumption on goods whose import costs are not covered by the exports of its own products", as Emmanuel Todd recalls.[9] The world produces, and the United States (which has practically no national saving) consumes. The "advantage" of the US is that of a predator whose deficit is covered by loans from others, whether by consent or force. The means put in place by Washington to compensate for deficiencies are of various kinds: repeated unilateral violations of liberal principles, arms exports, search for greater profits from oil (which presupposes systematic control over the producers—one of the real reasons for the wars in Central Asia and Iraq). The fact is that the essential part of the American deficit is covered by contributions of capital from Europe, Japan and the South (from oil-rich countries and comprador classes of every country of the Third World, the poorest included), to which are added the additional sums brought in from servicing the debt that has been forced on almost all the countries on the periphery of the world system.

The growth of the Clinton years, flaunted as the result of a "liberalism" that Europe was unfortunately resisting, was in fact largely fake, and in any case, non-generalisable, depending on capital transfers that meant the stagnation of partner economies. For all sectors of the real production system, US growth was not better than that of Europe. The "American miracle" was fed exclusively by a growth in expenditure produced by growing social inequalities (financial and personal services: the legions of lawyers and private police forces, etc). In this sense, Clinton's liberalism indeed prepared the conditions for the reactionary wave, and later the victory of Bush Junior.

The causes of the weakening of the US production system are complex. They are certainly not conjunctural, and they cannot be corrected by the adoption of a correct rate of exchange, for example, or by putting in place a more favourable balance between salaries and productivity. They are structural. The mediocrity of general education and training systems, and a deep-rooted prejudice systematically in favour of the "private" to the detriment of the public service, is one of the main reasons for the profound crisis that the US society is going through.

One should, therefore, be surprised that the Europeans, far from drawing the conclusions that observation of the deficiencies of the US economy forces upon one, are actively going about imitating it. Here, too, the liberal virus does not explain everything, even if it fulfils some useful functions for the system in paralysing the left. Widespread privatisation and the dismantling of public services will only reduce the comparative advantages that "Old Europe" (as Bush qualifies it) still benefits from. However, whatever damage these things will cause in the long term, such measures offer dominant capital, which lives in the short term, the chance of making additional profits.

(c) Concerning the Specific Objectives of the Project of the United States

The hegemonic strategy of the United States is within the framework of the new collective Imperialism.

The "(conventional) economists" do not have the analytical tools enabling them to understand the paramount importance of these objectives. They are heard repeating *ad nauseam* that in the "new economy" the raw materials coming from the third world are destined to lose their importance and thus it is becoming more and more marginal in the world system. In counterpoint to this naïve and hollow discourse, the Mein Kampf of the new administration of Washington,[10] it is acknowledged that the United States works hard for the right to seize all the natural resources of the planet to meet in priority its consumption requirements. The race for raw materials (oil in the first place, but as much for other resources too—water in particular) has already recovered all its virulence. All the more since these resources are likely to become scarce not only by the exponential cancer of the wastage of Western consumption, but also by the development of the new industrialization of the peripheries.

Moreover, a respectable number of countries from the South are destined to become increasingly important industrial producers as much for their internal markets as in the world market. As importers of technologies, of capital, also competitors in exports, they are destined to push down the global economic equilibrium with an increasing weight. And it is not a question only of some East Asian countries (like Korea), but of immense China and, tomorrow, India and the large countries of Latin America. However, far from being a factor of stabilization, the acceleration of capitalist expansion in the South can only be the cause of violent conflicts, internal and international. Because this expansion cannot absorb, under the conditions of the periphery, the enormous reserve of labour force, which is concentrated there. In fact, the peripheries of the system remain the "zone of tempests". The centres of the capitalist system thus require exerting their domination over the peripheries, to subject their people to the pitiless discipline that the satisfaction of its priorities requires.

Within this perspective, the American establishment has perfectly understood that, in the pursuit of its hegemony, it has three decisive advantages over its European and Japanese competitors: the control over the natural resources of the globe, the military monopoly, the weight of the "Anglo-Saxon culture" by which the ideological domination of capitalism is expressed preferentially. A systematic bringing into play of these three advantages clarifies many aspects of the US policy, in particular the systematic efforts that Washington exerts for the military control of the oil-producing Middle East, its offensive strategy with regard to Korea—taking advantage of this country's "financial crisis"—and to China, its subtle game aiming at perpetuating divisions in Europe—while mobilizing to this end its unconditional British ally - and at preventing any serious rapprochement between the European Union and Russia. At the level of the global control over the resources of the planet, the United States has a decisive advantage over Europe and Japan. Not only because the United States is the sole international military power, and thus no strong intervention in the Third World can be led without it, but more because Europe (excluding ex-USSR) and Japan are, themselves, divested of essential resources steadily from their economy. For example, their dependence in the energy sector, in particular their oil dependence with regard to the Gulf, is and will remain for a considerable long time, even if it were to decrease in relative terms. By militarily seizing the control of this region through the Iraq war, the US has demonstrated that they were perfectly conscious of the utility of this pressure medium, which it brings to bear on its allied-competitors. Not long ago the Soviet power had also understood this vulnerability of Europe and Japan; and certain Soviet interventions in the Third World sought to remind them of it, so as to induce them to negotiate on other grounds. Evidently the deficiencies of Europe and Japan could be compensated in the event of a serious Europe-Russia rapprochement ("the common home" of Gorbachev). This is the very reason for which the danger of this construction of Eurasia becomes Washington's nightmare.

(d) *Concerning the Conflicts that Place the United States and its Partners in the Triad Opposite Each Other within this Framework*

If the partners in the Triad share common interests in the global management of collective imperialism implied in their relationship with the South, they are certainly not less in a serious potential conflictual relationship.

The American superpower sustains itself due to the capital flow that feeds the parasitism of its economy and society. The vulnerability of the United States constitutes, therefore, a serious threat for the project of Washington.

Europe in particular, and the rest of the world in general, will have to choose one of the following two strategic options:

to invest the "surplus" of their capital ("of saving") from which they arrange for financing the US deficit (consumption, investments and military expenditures); or conserve and invest this surplus at home.

The conventional economists are ignorant of the problem, having made the hypothesis (which is not anything, but a nonsense) that "globalisation" having abolished the nations, the economic grandeurs (saving and investment) cannot be managed any more "at national levels". It is a matter of a tautological reasoning where the conclusions at which one wishes to arrive are implied in the very premise: to justify and accept the financing of the US deficit by others since, at the world level, one finds indeed the saving-investment identity!

Why then is such ineptitude accepted? No doubt, the teams "of scholarly economists" who encircle the European (and also, Russian and Chinese) political classes of the right as well as of the electoral left are themselves victims of their economic alienation, which I term as the "liberal virus". Besides, through this option the political judgment of the large transnational capital is expressed which considers that the advantages attained by the management of the globalised system by the United States on behalf of collective imperialism prevail over its disadvantages: the tribute which is needed to pay Washington for ensuring permanence. Because, it was, after all, a tribute and not an "investment" with a good guaranteed return. There are some countries qualified as "poor indebted countries" which are always constrained to ensure the servicing of their debt at any price. But there is also a "powerful indebted country" which has the means enabling it to devalue its debt if considered necessary.

The other option for Europe (and the rest of the world) would thus consist in putting an end to the transfusion in favour of the United States. The surplus could then be used on the original spot (in Europe) and the economy be revived. Because the transfusion requires a submission of Europeans to "deflationary" policies (improper term of the language of conventional economics) that I call as "stagnationist"—so as to release a surplus of exportable saving. It makes a recovery in

Europe—always mediocre—dependent on artificial support from the United States. The mobilization of this surplus in opposite direction for local employment in Europe would permit the simultaneous revival of consumption (by rebuilding the social dimension of the economic management devastated by the liberal virus), investment—and particularly in new technologies (and financing their research), even military expenditure (putting an end to the "advantages" of the United States in this field). The option in favour of this challenging response implies a rebalancing of the social relationships in favour of the labouring classes. National conflicts and social struggles are articulated in this way. In other words, the contrast between the United States and Europe does not fundamentally oppose the interests of dominant segments of the capital of various partners. It results above all from the difference of political cultures.

(e) Concerning the Questions of Theory that the Preceding Reflections Suggest

Complicity-competition between the partners in collective imperialism for the control over the South—the plundering of its natural resources and submission of its people—can be analysed from different angles of vision. I will make, in this respect, three observations, which appear major to me.

First observation: the contemporary world system that I describe as collective imperialist is no "less" imperialist than its precedents. It is not an "Empire" of "post-capitalist" nature. I have proposed elsewhere a criticism of ideological formulations of the "disguise" that feeds this fashionable dominant discourse.[11]

Second observation: I have proposed a reading of the history of capitalism, globalised right from its origin, centred on the distinction between the various phases of imperialism (of centres/peripheries relationships). There exist of course other readings of this same history, in particular that which is articulated around the "succession of hegemonies".[12]

I have some reservations with regard to this last reading, primarily and essentially because it is "Western-centric" in the sense that it considers that the transformations operating at the heart of the system, in its centres, command the global evolution of the system in a decisive, and almost exclusive, manner. I believe that the reactions of the people of the peripheries to the imperialist deployment should not be underestimated. For if they are provoked, it would only be the independence of Americas, the great revolutions made in the name of socialism (Russia, China), the re-conquest of independence by the Asian and African countries, and I do not believe that one can account for the history of world capitalism without accounting for the "adjustments" that these transformations imposed even on central capitalism itself.

Then because the history of imperialism appears to me having been made more through the conflict of imperialisms than by the type "of order" that successive hegemonies have imposed. The apparent periods "of hegemony" have been always extremely short and the said hegemony very relative.

Third observation: internationalisation is not synonymous with "unification" of the economic system by "the de-regulated opening up of the markets". The latter—in its successive historical forms ("the freedom of trade" yesterday, the "freedom of firms" today)—always constituted the project of the dominant capital only. In reality this project was almost always forced to adjust with exigencies that are not the concern of its exclusive and specific internal logic. It thus could never be implemented except in some short moments of the history. The "free exchange" promoted by the major industrial power of its time—Great Britain—was effective only during two decades (1860–1880) which was succeeded by a century (1880–1980) characterized at the same time by the conflict between the imperialists and by the strong de-linking of the countries known as socialist (starting from the Russian revolution of 1917, then that of China) and more modestly the populist nationalist countries (the era of Bandung for Asia and Africa from 1955 to 1975). The current moment of reunification of the world market (the "free enterprise") inaugurated by neo-liberalism since 1980, extended to the whole planet with the Soviet collapse, is probably not destined to experience a better fate. The chaos which it generates - term by which I have described this system since 1990—testifies to its character "of permanent utopia of capital".[13]

4. The Middle East in the Imperialist System

1. The Middle East, henceforth with its extension towards the Caucasus and ex-Soviet Central Asia, occupies a position of particular importance in the geo-strategy/geo-politics of imperialism and singularly of the US hegemonic project. It owes this position to three factors: its oil wealth, its geographical position in the heart of the Old World, and the fact that it constitutes the "soft underbelly" of the world system.

The access to oil at a relative cheap rate is vital for the economy of the dominant triad; and the best means of ensuring this guaranteed access consists in, of course, securing political control of the area.

But the region also holds its importance equally due to its geographical position, being at the centre of the old World, at equal distance from Paris, Beijing, Singapore, Johannesburg. In the olden times the control over this inevitable crossing point gave the Caliphate the privilege to draw the best of benefits from the internationalisation of the epoch.[14] After the Second World War the region, located on the southern side of the USSR, occupied in fact a prime place in the military strategy of encircling the Soviet power. And the region did not lose its importance, in spite of the collapse of the Soviet adversary; while settling in there the United States would simultaneously succeed in reducing Europe to vassalage, dependent for its energy supply, and in subduing Russia, China and India with a permanent blackmail coupled with threats of military interventions if necessary. The control over the region would thus allow indeed an extension of the Monroe Doctrine to the old world, which constitutes the objective of the hegemonist project of the United States.

The efforts made with continuity and consistency by Washington since 1945 to secure control over the region—and in excluding the British and the French—had not been so far crowns of success. One remembers the failure of their attempt to associate the region to NATO through the pact of Baghdad, as later, one of their most faithful allies, Shah of Iran's fall.

The reason is quite simply that the project of the Arab (and Iranian) nationalist populism entered headlong into conflict with the objectives of the American hegemonism. This Arab project had a certain ambition, to impose the recognition of the independence of the Arab world by the Powers. It was the direction of "non-alignment", formulated in 1955 at Bandung by the ensemble of liberation movemen s of Asian and African people, which was making progress. The Soviets quickly understood that, by giving their support for this project, they would render a setback to the aggressive plans of Washington.

The page of this epoch is turned, initially because the populist nationalist project of Arab world quickly exhausted its potential of transformation; the nationalist powers were sunk into dictatorships without program. The vacuum created by this drift opened the way for Political Islam and the obscurantist autocracies of the Gulf, the preferential allies of Washington. The region became one of the underbellies of the global system, producing conjunctures allowing external intervention (including military) that the current regimes are incapable of containing—or discouraging—any more for a lack of legitimacy in the opinion of their people.

The region constituted—and continues to constitute – in the American geo-military apportionment covering the entire planet, a zone considered as that of first priority (like the Caribbean), i.e. a zone where the United States is granted the "right" of military intervention. Since 1990, they are not deprived of anything!

The United States operates in the Middle East in close cooperation with their two unconditional faithful allies—Turkey and Israel. Europe is kept away from the region, accepting that there the United States defends only the global vital interests of the triad, that is to say its oil supply. In spite of the signs of obvious irritation after the Iraq war, the Europeans by and large continue to sail in the region on Washington's trail.

2. Israel's colonial expansionism constitutes a real challenge. Israel is the only country in the world that refuses to recognize its definite borders (and for this reason would not have the

right to be a member of the United Nations). As the United States in the 19th century, it considers that it has the "right" to conquer new areas for the expansion of its colonization and to treat the people inhabiting there after thousand years if not anymore like some Red Skins. Israel is the only country that openly declares not to be considered bound by the resolutions of the UNO.

The war of 1967, planned in agreement with Washington in 1965, pursued several goals: to start the collapse of the populist nationalist regimes, to break their alliance with the Soviet Union, to force them to reposition itself on the American trail, to open new grounds for Zionist colonization. In the territories conquered in 1967, Israel thus set up a system of apartheid inspired by that of South Africa.

It is here that the interests of dominant capital meet up with those of Zionism. Because a rich and powerful modernised Arab world would call in question the guaranteed access of the Western countries to the plundering of its oil resources, necessary for the continuation of waste associated with capitalist accumulation. The political powers in the countries of the triad, such as they are—i.e. faithful servants of dominant transnational capital—do not want a modernized and powerful Arab world.

The alliance between Western powers and Israel is thus founded on the solid base of their common interests. This alliance is neither the product of a guilt feeling of Europeans, responsible for anti-Semitism and Nazi crime, nor that of the skill of the "Jewish lobby" to exploit this sentiment. If the Western powers thought that their interests were harmed by the Zionist colonial expansionism, they would quickly find the means of overcoming their "complex" and of neutralizing the "Jewish lobby". I do not doubt it, not being among those who naively believe that the public opinion in the democratic countries, as they are, imposes their views on these Powers. It is known that opinion "is manufactured" too. Israel is incapable of resisting for more than a few days even moderate measures of a blockade if imposed on it as the Western powers inflicted on Yugoslavia, Iraq and Cuba. It would thus not be difficult to bring Israel to senses and to create the conditions of a true peace, if it were wanted, which is not.

Soon after the defeat of the 1967 war, Sadat stated that since the United States held in their hand "90% of the cards" (that was his very expression), it was necessary to break with the USSR, to reintegrate with the Western camp and that, by doing so, one could get Washington to exert sufficient pressure on Israel to bring it to its senses. Beyond similar "strategic idea" peculiar to Sadat—whose inconsistency the spate of events has proved—the Arab public opinion remained largely incapable of understanding the dynamics of the capitalist world expansion, even more of identifying the true contradictions and weaknesses there. Do not we hear it being said and repeated that "the West would understand in the long run that their proper interest was to maintain good relations with the two hundred million Arabs—their immediate neighbours—and not to sacrifice these relations for their unconditional support for Israel"? This is implicitly thinking that the "West" in question (i.e., the dominant capital) wish a modernized and developed Arab world, and, not understanding on the contrary that they want to maintain it in impotence for which support for Israel is useful.

The choice made by the Arab governments—with the exception of Syrian and Lebanese—which led them through the negotiations of Madrid and Oslo (1993) to subscribe to the American plan of the so-called "definitive peace", could not yield results other than those which it has yielded: encouraging Israel to position itself in its expansionist project. By openly rejecting the terms of the "Oslo contract" today, Ariel Sharon demonstrates merely what was already understood—knowing that it was not a matter of a project of "definitive peace", but of opening a new phase in the Zionist colonial expansion.

The state of permanent war that Israel and the Western powers supporting its project imposed in the region constitutes in its turn a powerful reason allowing the autocratic Arabic systems to be perpetuated. This blockage of a possible democratic evolution weakens the chances of an Arabic revival and thus makes a deal with the deployment of the dominant capital and the hegemonist strategy of the United States. The loop is looped: Israel-American alliance serves perfectly the interests of the two partners.

Initially this system of apartheid deployed after 1967 gave the impression of being capable of achieving its ends, the fearful management of everyday life in the occupied territories by the elites and the commercial bourgeoisie seeming accepted by the Palestinian people. The PLO distant from the region after the invasion of Lebanon by the Israeli army (1982) appeared to have no longer the means of calling into question the Zionist annexation from its remote exile of Tunis.

The first Intifada burst in December 1987. Explosion of a "spontaneous" nature, it expresses the sudden emergence of popular classes on the scene, and remarkably of its poorest segments, confined in the refugee camps. The Intifada boycotted the Israeli power by the organization of a systematic civil disobedience. Israel reacted with brutality; but managed neither in restoring its effective police power nor getting the fearful Palestinian middle classes back in the saddle On the contrary, the Intifada called for the return of exiled political forces in mass, the constitution of new local forms of organization and the adherence of middle classes to the committed fight for liberation. The Intifada was provoked by the youth, Chebab al Intifada, initially not organized within the formal networks of the PLO, but not at all any hostile competitor to them. The four components of the PLO (Fatah, devoted to its chief Yasser Arafat, the DFLP, the PFLP, the Communist Party) surged themselves in the Intifada and for this reason gained the sympathy of the major part of the Chebab. The Muslim Brotherhood outmoded by their activity during these preceding years, despite some actions of Islamic Jihad making its appearance in 1980 yielded its place to a new expression of struggle—Hamas, constituted in 1988.

As the first Intifada gave signs of breathlessness after two years of expansion with the Israeli repression becoming violent (use of firearms against children, closing of the "green line" for the Palestinian workers, almost exclusive source of income for their families, etc.), the scene was mounted for a "negotiation" whose initiative was taken by the US, driving to Madrid (1991), then the so-called Oslo Peace Agreements (1993). These agreements allowed the return of the PLO in the occupied territories and its transformation into a "Palestinian Authority".

The Oslo agreements imagined the transformation of the occupied territories into one or more Bantustans, definitively integrated into the Israeli region. Within this framework, the Palestinian Authority was to be only a false State—as that of the Bantustans—and in fact to be the driving belt of the Zionist order.

Returning to Palestine, the PLO-turned Authority managed to establish its order, not without some ambiguities. The Authority absorbed in its new structures the major part of. Chebab, which had coordinated the Intifada. It achieved legitimacy by the electoral consultation of 1996, in which the Palestinians participated en masse (80%), while an overwhelming majority elected Arafat the President of that Authority. The Authority remained nevertheless in an ambiguous position: would it agree to fulfil the functions that Israel, the United States and Europe allotted it—that of "government of a Bantustan", or would it align with the Palestinian people who refused to submit?

As the Palestinian people rejected the project of Bantustan, Israel decided to denounce the Oslo agreements, whose terms nevertheless it had dictated, by substituting them by the use of pure and simple military violence. The provocation from the top of mosques, engineered by the war-criminal Sharon in 1998 (but with the help of the Labour government that furnished the tanks), the triumphal election of this same criminal at the head of the Israeli government (and the collaboration of the "doves" like Simon Peres with this government), were thus the cause of the second Intifada, which is in progress.

Will this succeed in liberating the Palestinian people from the perspective of its planned submission by the Zionist apartheid? It is quite early to say. In any case, the Palestinian people now have a true national liberation movement. It has its own specificities. It is not of the "unique party" style, of "unanimous" and homogeneous appearance (if not in reality). It has components that conserve their own personality, their visions of future, including their ideologies, their militants and clienteles, but which, apparently, know how to get on to lead the struggle together.

3. The erosion of the regimes of populist nationalism and the disappearance of the Soviet support supplied the United States the opportunity to implement its "project" for the area, without obstacles which were capable of curbing it till now.

The control of the Middle East is certainly a cornerstone of the Washington's project of global hegemony. How then does the United States imagine securing control? It is already a decade since Washington took the initiative of advancing the curious project of a "Common Market of the Middle East" in which some countries of the Gulf would have supplied capital, other Arab countries cheap labour, reserving for Israel the technological control and the functions of the obliged intermediary. Accepted by the Gulf countries and Egypt, the project was confronted nevertheless with the refusal of Syria, Iraq and Iran. It was thus necessary to knock down these three regimes in order to advance. Now that is done for Iraq.

The question then is to know which type of political regime must be set up in order to be able to sustain the project. Washington's propagandistic discourse is about "democracies". In fact, Washington is busy in nothing else but substituting the worn-out autocracies of outmoded populism by the so-called Islamic obscurantist autocracies (obliged by the respect for the cultural specificity of the "communities"). The renewed alliance with a so-called moderate political Islam (i.e. capable of controlling the situation with sufficient efficacy to prohibit the "terrorist" drifts—those directed against the United States and, of course, only against it) constitutes the axis of Washington's political choice, becoming the unique choice. It is within this perspective that the reconciliation with the antiquated autocracy of the system will be sought.

Confronted with the deployment of the US project, Europeans invented their own project, baptized as "Euro-Mediterranean partnership". A decidedly cowardly project, encumbered with incoherent prattling, of course, which too proposed "to reconcile the Arab countries with Israel", while by excluding the Gulf countries from the "Euro-Mediterranean dialogue", these same Europeans recognized consequently that the management of these latter countries concerned the exclusive responsibility of Washington.[15]

The seizing contrast between the bold audacity of the American project and the debility of the European is a good indicator that the really existing Atlanticism ignores "sharing" (shared responsibilities and association in decision-making, placing on equal footing the United States and Europe). Tony Blair, who is made the advocate of the construction of a "unipolar" world, thinks he is able to justify this option because Atlanticism, which would allow it, would be founded on "sharing". Washington's arrogance refutes each day more this hope illusory, if it is not quite simply the means of fooling the European opinions. The realism of Stalin's statement rendered at the time that Nazis "did not know where it was necessary to stop", is applicable to its letter for the junta controlling the United States. And the "hopes" that Blair intends to reanimate resemble only to what Mussolini placed in his capacity of "assuaging" Hitler!

Is another European option possible? Does it take shape? Does Chirac's speech opposing the "uni-polar Atlantic" world (which he seemingly understands well as being in fact synonymous with unilateral hegemony of the United States, reducing the European project to nothing more than the European wing of Washington's project) announces the construction of a "multi-polar" world and an end of Atlanticism?

So that this possibility becomes a reality, it still would be necessary that Europe manage to leave the quicksand on which it slips.

5. Quicksand of the European Project

All the governments of the European States until now are won over to the theses of liberalism. This lining up of the European States thus does not mean anything less than the obliteration of the European project, its double dilution, economic (the advantages of the European economic union are dissolved in economic globalisation) and political (European political and military autonomy disappears). There is not, at the present time, any European project. A North-Atlantic project (or eventually of the triad) under the American command has substituted it.

The "made in USA" wars have certainly stirred the public opinions—everywhere in Europe against the latest, that of Iraq —and even certain governments, initially that of France, but then those of Germany, Russia and beyond that, of China, too. The fact remains that these same governments have not called into question their faithful alignment over the needs of liberalism. This major contradiction will have to be overcome in one way or another, either by their submission to the requirements of Washington, or by a true rupture putting an end to Atlanticism.

The major political conclusion that I draw from this analysis is that Europe cannot leave Atlanticism as long as political alliances defining the blocs in power rest centred over the dominant transnational capital. It is only if the social and political struggles manage to modify the content of these blocs and to impose new historical compromises between capital and labour that then Europe will be able to distance itself from Washington, allowing the revival of an eventual European project. Under these conditions Europe also could—even ought to—be engaged at the international level, in its relationships with the East and the South, on a path other than that traced by the exclusive requirements of collective imperialism, thus initiating its participation in the long march "beyond capitalism". In other words, Europe will be of left (the term left being taken here seriously) or will not be at all.

To reconcile the adherence to liberalism and the assertion of a political autonomy of Europe or the States constituting it remains the objective of certain fractions of European political classes anxious to preserve the exclusive positions of the large capital. Will they be able to manage that? I strongly doubt it.

On the other hand, will the popular classes in Europe, somewhere at least, be able to overcome the crisis that they confront? I believe it possible, precisely for the reasons signifying that the political culture of certain European countries at least, different from that of the United States, could produce this rebirth of the left. The obvious precondition is that it releases itself from the virus of liberalism.

The "European project" was born as the European wing of the Atlanticist project of the United States, conceived just after the Second World War, implemented by Washington in the spirit of the "cold war", the project to which the European bourgeoisies—both weakened and apprehensive with regard to their own working classes—practically adhered to unconditionally.

However, the deployment of this project itself—of doubtful origin—gradually modified some important facts about the problem and the challenges. Western Europe managed, or has the means, "to make up for" its economic and technological backwardness vis-à-vis the United States. In addition, "the Soviet threat" is not there any more. Moreover, the project's deployment erased the principal and violent adversities that had marked the European history during a past century and half: the three major countries of the continent—France, Germany and Russia—are reconciled. All these evolutions are, in my opinion, positive and rich with still more potential. Certainly this deployment is inscribed over the economic bases inspired by the principles of liberalism, but of a liberalism which was tempered until the 1980s by the social dimension taken into account by and through the "social-democratic historical compromise" forcing the capital to adjust itself to the demands of social justice expressed by the working classes. Afterwards, the deployment continued in a new social framework inspired by "American-style", anti-social liberalism.

This last turn has plunged the European societies in a multi-dimensional crisis. Essentially, it is the economic crisis nothing more and nothing less, immanent in the liberal choice. A crisis was aggravated by the alignment of the European countries over the economic requirements of the North American leadership, Europe consenting until now to finance the latter's deficit with detriment of its own interests. Then there is a social crisis, which is accentuated by the rise of resistances and the struggles of the popular classes against the fatal consequences of the liberal option. Lastly, there is the beginning of a political crisis - the refusal to align, at least unconditionally, over the US' choice: the endless war against the South.

How will the European people and states face this triple challenge?

The Europeanists are divided into fairly three different groups:

(i) Those who defend the liberal choice and accept the US leadership, almost unconditionally.
(ii) Those who defend the liberal choice but would wish an independent political Europe, outside the American alignment.
(iii) Those who would wish (and fight for) "social Europe", i.e. a capitalism tempered by a new social compromise between capital and labour operating on an European scale, and simultaneously, a political Europe practising "other relations" (implying friendly, democratic and peaceful) with the South, Russia and China. The general public opinion throughout Europe has expressed, during the European Social Forum (Florence 2002), as well as at the time of the Iraq war, its sympathy for this position on principles.

There are certainly others, the "non Europeans", in the sense that they do not think any of the three pro-European options possible or even desirable. They are still at the moment minorities but certainly called to strengthen themselves. They need to strengthen upon one of the two fundamentally different options:

(i) A "populist" option of right, refusing the progress of political powers—and including economic-supranationals, except obviously for those of the transnational capital!
(ii) A popular option of left, national, citizen, democratic and social.

On what forces is based each one of these tendencies and what are their respective chances?

The dominant capital is liberal, by nature. In fact it is logically inclined towards supporting the first of the three options. Tony

Blair represents the most coherent expression of what I have qualified as "the collective imperialism of the triad". The political class reunited behind the star-studded banner is disposed, if necessary, "to sacrifice the European project"—or at least to dissipate any illusion about it—by maintaining it in the original shackles: to be the European section of the Atlanticist project. But Bush, like Hitler, does not conceive allies other than unconditional aligned subordinates. This is why important segments of the political class, including the right—and although in principle being the defenders of the interests of dominant capital—refuse to line up with the United States as yesterday they did with Hitler. If there were a possible Churchill in Europe, it would be Chirac. Will he be so?

The strategy of the dominant capital can be accommodated in an "anti-Europeanism of right", which would be satisfied with demagogic nationalist rhetoric (mobilising, for example, on the theme of the immigrants, of course) while being subjected in fact to the requirements of a not specifically "European", rather globalised, liberalism. Aznar and Berlusconi constitute the prototypes of these allies of Washington. Likewise, the servile political classes of Eastern Europe.

In fact I believe the second option difficult to hold. It is however, the choice of the major European governments—France and Germany. Does it express the ambitions of a capital sufficiently powerful to be capable of emancipating itself from the US supervision? It is a question to which I do not have an answer: perhaps possible, but intuitively I would say highly improbable.

This choice is nevertheless that of allies facing the North-American adversary constituting the principal enemy of the whole humanity. I say clearly allies because I am persuaded that, if they persist in their choice, they will be driven to leave the submission to the logic of the unilateral project of capital (liberalism) and to seek alliances on the left (the only ones which can give force to their project of independence vis-à-vis Washington). The alliance between two and three groups is not impossible. Just as the great anti-Nazi alliance.

If this alliance takes form, then shall it and will it be able to operate exclusively within the European framework, all the Europeans being unable to renounce the priority given to this framework? I do not believe it, because this framework, such as it is and will remain, systematically favours only the pro-American first group's choice. Will it then be necessary to fracture Europe and renounce its project definitively?

I do not believe it either necessary, or even desirable. Another strategy is possible: to leave the European project "fixed" a while at its present stage of development, and to parallelly develop other axes of alliances.

I would give here very first priority to the construction of a political and strategic alliance between Paris, Berlin and Moscow stretched to Beijing and Delhi if possible. I say clearly political with the objective to restore to international pluralism and to the UNO all their functions; and strategic, in the sense of constructing military forces to the stature of the American challenge. These three or four powers have all the means, technological and financial, reinforced by their traditions of military capacities in front of which the United States is pallid. The American challenge and its criminal ambitions compel it. But these ambitions are disproportionate. It should be proven. To constitute an anti-hegemonist front has today the similar priority, as in the past it was to constitute an anti-Nazi alliance.

This strategy would reconcile the "pro-Europeans" of the second and third groups and the "non-Europeans" of left. It would thus create favourable conditions for the later revival of a European project, integrating even probably a Great Britain liberated from its submission before the United States and an Eastern Europe relieved of its servile culture. Let us be patient, this will take much time.

There will be no progress possible of any European project as long as the US strategy is not routed.

6. Europe vis-à-vis its Arab and Mediterranean South

The Arab world and the Middle East occupy a decisive place in the hegemonist project of the United States. The response that the Europeans render to the US challenge in the region will be one of the decisive tests for the European project itself.

The question is thus to know if the residents of the Mediterranean and its extensions—Europeans, Arabs, Turks, Iranians, countries from the Horn of Africa—are oriented or not towards a representation of their safety differing from what is directed by the primacy from the American world hegemony's safeguards. The pure reason should make them move in this direction. But so far Europe has not given any active indication in this sense. One of the reasons that could explain the European inertia, is that the interests of the partners of the European Union, even if not divergent enough, are at least laden with a range of relative priorities extremely different from one country to the other. The Mediterranean front is not central in industrial polarizations of developed capitalism: the fronts of the North Sea, of Atlantic American North-East and of central Japan have an incomparable density. For Northern Europe—Germany and Great Britain—a fortiori for the United States and Japan, the danger of chaos in the countries located on the South of the Mediterranean does not have the same gravity as for the Italians, the Spaniards and the French.

Various European powers until 1945 had Mediterranean policies suitable for each one of them, frequently conflictive. After the Second World War, the West European states did not have practically any Mediterranean and Arab policy, neither particular, nor common, other than what the alignment with the United States implied. The fact remains that, even within this framework, Great Britain and France, who had colonial possessions in the region, carried out rearguard battles to preserve their advantages. Great Britain renounced Egypt and Sudan in 1954 and, after the defeat in the adventure of the tripartite aggression of 1956, proceeded to a heart-rending reversal, and finally in the 1960s abandoned its influence in the coastal countries of the Gulf. France, eliminated from Syria in 1945, finally accepted the independence of Algeria in 1962, but preserved a certain nostalgia for its influence on Maghreb and Lebanon, encouraged by the local ruling classes, at least on Morocco, Tunisia and Lebanon. At the same time, the European construction did not substitute for the withdrawal of the colonial powers any common policy operating in this sense. One remembers that when, after the Israel-Arab war of 1973, the oil prices were readjusted, communitarian Europe, surprised in its sleep, rediscovered that it had "interests" in the region. But this awakening did not cause any important initiative on its part, for example, concerning the Palestinian problem. Europe remained, in this field as well as in others, irresolute and finally inconsistent. Some progress towards an autonomy with respect to the United States nevertheless were recorded during the 1970s, culminating with Summit of Venice (1980); but this progress was not consolidated and rather eroded eventually during 1980s, finally disappearing with the alignment with Washington adopted during the Gulf crisis. Also the European perceptions concerning the future of the relationships between Europe and Arab-Iranian world must be studied basing on analyses appropriate for each European State.

Great Britain does not have a Mediterranean and Arab policy specific to it any more. In this field, like elsewhere the British society in all its political expressions (Conservative and Labour) made the choice of an unconditional alignment with the United States. It is a fundamental historical choice, amply outmoding the conjunctural circumstances and reinforcing considerably the European submission to the requirements of the American strategy.

For different reasons Germany too does not have any specific Arab and Mediterranean policy and will probably not seek to develop one in a visible future. Handicapped by its division and its status, the F.R.G. devoted all its efforts on to economic development, accepting to hold a low political profile on the simultaneous and ambiguous trail of the United States and "the Europeanism" of the EEC. Initially the reunification of Germany and its re-conquest of a full international sovereignty did not modify its behaviour rather, on the contrary, accentuated these expressions. The reason is that the dominant political forces (conservatives, liberals and social democrats) chose to give the priority to the expansion of German capitalism in Central and Eastern Europe, reducing the relative importance of a common European strategy, as much as on the political level as on that of economic integration. It remains to be known if this tendency is reversed today, as the attitude of Berlin on Iraq War seems to suggest.

French stances are much more balanced. Being at the same time an Atlantic and Mediterranean country, inheritor of a colonial Empire, classified among the winners of the Second World War, France did not renounce being expressed as a power. During the first decade after the war successive French governments tried to preserve the colonial positions of their country by the means of an anti-Communist and anti-Soviet Atlanticist build-up. Washington's support therefore was not sincerely acquired, as the US attitude demonstrated at the time of the tripartite aggression against Egypt in 1956. The Mediterranean and Arab policy of France was then, by force of circumstances, simply retrograde. De Gaulle broke with these palæo-colonial and pro-American illusions simultaneously. He conceived then the triple ambitious project of modernizing the French economy, of leading a process of decolonisation making it possible to substitute a flexible neo-colonialism for henceforth outmoded old formulas and of compensating for weaknesses intrinsic to any average country like France by European integration. Within this latter perspective De Gaulle conceived an Europe capable of being autonomous with respect to the United States not only on the economic and financial plain, but also at political and even, in the long term, military level, just like he conceived, also in the long run, the association of the USSR with the European construction ("Europe from the Atlantic to the Urals"). But Gaullism did not outlive its founder and, since 1968, the French political forces, both the traditional right as well as the socialist left gradually returned to their former attitudes. Their vision of European construction narrowed down to the dimension of the "Common Market", between France and Federal Germany (so much so that when the German unification was realised, people were somewhat surprised and anxious in Paris...) and with the pressing invitation to Great Britain to join EEC (forgetting that England would be the Trojan horse of the Americans in Europe). Naturally, this slide implied the abandonment of any French Arab policy worthy of name, i.e. any policy going beyond the simple defence of immediate mercantile interests. On political level, France behaved objectively in the Arab world as in sub-Saharan Africa, as an auxiliary complementary force of the strategy of American hegemony. It is in this framework that we must put the Mediterranean discourse, that calls the countries of Maghreb to associate with the European tank (in the same manner in which Turkey was associated in today's crisis), which amounts to breaking the prospect of a unitary Arab rapprochement, giving up Mashrek to the Israeli-American intervention. No doubt, the Maghrebi ruling classes are themselves responsible for sympathies, which they showed for this project. Nevertheless, the Gulf crisis gave a serious blow to this project, the popular masses of North Africa having affirmed forcefully on this occasion their solidarity with Mashrek, as that was foreseeable.

Italy, due to its geographical position, is strongly sensitive to the Mediterranean problems. That does not mean that it has —in fact—a real Mediterranean and Arab policy and, even less, that it has efficacy or autonomy. Marginalized for a long time in the capitalist development, Italy was forced to inscribe its Mediterranean ambitions in the wake of a forced alliance with other more decisive European powers. Since it achieved its unity in the middle of the previous century, until the fall of Mussolini in 1943, it always hesitated between alliance with the masters of the Mediterranean—i.e. Great Britain and France – or with those who could contest the Anglo-French positions, i.e. Germany.

Atlanticism, which is exercised in Italy in a vision implying a low profile foreign policy under the tutelage of the United States, has dominated the action and choices of the Italian governments since 1947. It is also dominant, although still in a more ideologised vision, in certain sectors of the secular bourgeoisie (the Republicans and Liberals, certainly socialists). Among the Christian Democrats, it is tempered by the pressure of universalism of the Catholic tradition. Characteristically, papacy often took in fact less retrograde positions with regard to the Arab people (in particular on the Palestinian question) and the Third World than those of many Italian and Western governments, in general. The slide of a section of the Catholic Church towards the left, under the influence of the Latin American liberation theology, today reinforces this universalism whose secular versions are found in the pacifist, ecologist and Third-Worldist movements. The current Europeanist "mittel" (half) has its roots in the 19th century Italy and the North-South divide that the Italian unification did not surmount. Hooked to the interests of big Milanese capital, it suggests giving priority to the economic expansion of Italy towards the European East, in close association with Germany. Within this framework, Croatia constitutes an immediate objective today so much so that certain analysts pinpoint here the Italian expansionist aims in direction of Dalmatia. Of course, this choice would imply that Italy pursues the tradition of low international profile and above all edges out its relationship with the residents of the south of the Mediterranean. A parallel choice of Spain would further isolate France in the European concert, reducing the range to its lower common denominator. The Mediterranean current, which is always weak, in spite of the contribution which universalism could bring it, is expressed, for this reason, in a "Levantine" version: it is a matter of "making deals" here or there without being concerned with the framework of political strategy in which they are inscribed. For another, nobler, consistency, associating Italy to economic openings being inscribed within a perspective of reinforcement of its autonomy and that of its Arab partners to take shape, it would be necessary that a convergence is achieved between this project and the universalist ideals, in particular of a part of the Italian left—Communist and Christian.

The Italian right, reunified under the leadership of Berlusconi in power, has opted for enlisting under the tutelage of the Washington-London Atlantic axis. The behaviour of the police forces at the time of G-8 of Genoa (July 2001) expresses this choice clearly.

Spain and Portugal occupy an important place in the geo-strategy of world hegemony of the United States. The Pentagon considers indeed that the Azores-Canaries-Gibraltar-Balearic

Islands axis is essential for monitoring the North and South Atlantic and sealing the entry in Mediterranean. The United States forged its alliance with these two countries immediately after the Second World War, without feeling least embarrassed of their fascist character. On the contrary, even the fanatical anticommunism of the dictatorships of Salazar and Franco served the US hegemonist cause well permitting the admission of Portugal in NATO and establishing on Spanish soil some American bases of prime importance. In return the United States and its European allies helped Portugal without reservation until its final defeat in its colonial war.

The democratic evolution of Spain after Franco's death was not the occasion of bringing into question the country's integration with American military system. On the contrary, even the formal adhesion of Spain with NATO (in May 1982) was an object of a real electoral blackmail implying that the participation in EEC required this adhesion, to which the majority opinion was opposed.

Since then, the lining up of Madrid with the positions of Washington has been without reservation. In return, the United States would have, apparently, intervened "to moderate" the Moroccan claims on Ceuta and Melilla and even try to convince Great Britain on the subject of Gibraltar. Over this account, we can doubt the very reality of these interventions. The fact remains that the Atlanticist alignment reinforced on Madrid resulted into radical changes in the organization of Spanish armed forces, qualified by the analysts as a "swing towards the South". In Spanish tradition indeed, the army was disseminated throughout the country. Conceived furthermore—after Franco in an obvious manner—as an internal police force more than a deterrent force directed against outsiders, the Spanish army remained rustic and, in spite of the marked attention that Madrid's supreme power paid to the body of the generals and officers, it had not been an object of a true modernization, as were the case with the armies of France, Great Britain and Germany.

The socialist governments and then of right proceeded to a reorganisation of Spanish forces for facing an eventual "southern front", as they engaged in a program of modernization of the Army, aviation and navy. This swing, required by Washington and NATO, is one of the many manifestations of the new American hegemonist strategy substituting the South for the East in the "defence" of the West. It is accompanied, in Spain, by a new discourse that poses in evidence a "hypothetical enemy coming from the South", whose identification does not leave any place for doubt. Curiously, this discourse of Spanish democratic (and socialist) milieus draws on the old tradition of the Reconquista, popular in Catholic circles of the army. The change in Spanish armed forces is thus the sign of a determination of Spain to play an active role within NATO, in the framework of the reorientation of the Western strategies in forecasting a forceful intervention in the Third World. Already the Iberian peninsula constitutes the first post of Washington-Tel Aviv axis, the principal European bridgehead of the American Rapid Deployment Force (which played a decisive part in the Gulf War), supplemented by the bases of Sicily (which too were never used until the operations directed against the Arab World: Libya, Israeli bombardment of Tunisia, etc.) and, curiously, by the facilities granted by Morocco. Of course, this Western choice empties the "Euro-Arab" discourse of all serious content. The new democratic Spain, pretending to stimulate a policy of friendship towards Latin America and the Arab world, started its movement rather in a direction opposed to the exigencies of its proclamations in principle.

The rightist government led by Aznar has confirmed this Atlanticist alignment of Madrid. Even more than Italy, Spain refuses to capitalize its Mediterranean position for the benefit of a new European policy towards the Arab world, Africa and the Third World, distancing from the requirements of the American hegemony. The French idea of a Mediterranean group in the heart of the European Union remains, in fact, suspended in the air, without any serious base of operations. Besides, on the economic level, the Spanish capital, heir to the Francoist tradition, put its principal hope of expansion in the development of agreements with Germany and Japan, invited to participate in the modernization of Catalonia.

As long as it existed, the line of East-West confrontation passed through the Balkans. The obliged affiliation of the local states in the region either to Moscow, or to Washington—the only exception being that of Yugoslavia since 1948, then of Albania since 1960—had then toned down the local nationalist quarrels which made Balkans a European powder keg.

Turkey was placed in the Western camp since 1945, after having hastily putting an end to its rather benevolent neutrality with regard to Hitlerite Germany. The Soviet claims on Kars and Ardahan in Caucasus and concerning the right to passage in the Straits, formulated by Stalin just after the victory, were warded off by Ankara thanks to Washington's decisive support. In return Turkey, a member of NATO, in spite of its little democratic political system, accommodated the American bases closest to the USSR. There is no place to doubt that the Turkish society remains that of the Third World, even if, since Ataturk, the ruling classes of this country proclaim the Europeanism of the new Turkey, knocking the door of the European Union, which does not want it. Being a faithful US ally and of its European partners, does Turkey wish to reintegrate its past and to play an active part in the Middle East, making the West pay for the services that it could render them in this region? It seems that the handicap of its Kurdish question, whose very existence it refuses to recognize, has made it hesitate in making this choice until now. It is the same for a possible Pan-Turkish option—suggested just after the First World War in certain Kemalist milieus was relegated thereafter to the museum of the history of the origins. But today the decomposition of the ex-USSR could constitute an invitation for the power of Ankara to take towards the direction of a Turcophone bloc, which dominates Central Asia from Azerbaijan to Sinkiang. Iran always expressed its real fear of such an evolution, which not only would call in question the status of Iranian Southern Azerbaijan but also the safety of its long North Asian border with Turkmenistan and Uzbekistan.

Greece did not enlist even in the anti-Soviet camp. It was constrained and forced by the British intervention superseded in 1948 by the United States. In conformity with Yalta agreements, the USSR, as we all know, abandoned to its fate the Greek resistance, led by the Communist Party, which however, in this country as in Yugoslavia and Albania, had liberated the country and conquered in fact a large majority of popular support. In this manner, the West was obliged to support the successive repressive regimes and finally a dictatorship of fascistic colonels, against this popular movement without seeing a major contradiction within its discourse, according to which NATO protected the "free world" against the "totalitarian" Satan. The return of Greece to democracy, by the electoral victory of Pasok in 1981 was likely—under these conditions - to call in question the fidelity of this country to NATO. The communitarian Europe then came to help Washington, as in the case of Spain, binding Greek candidature to the EEC with maintaining its participation in Atlantic alliance. This integration in the EEC moreover was itself still strongly discussed in the Greek opinion of the epoch. The choice of Papandreou to rejoin despite everything, after some hesitations and in spite of the option of Pasok's Third-Worldist and neutralist principles, seems to have initiated an irreversible evolution even at the level of mentalities, flattering the aspirations of the Greek people with modernity and Europeanism. However, the new European partners of Greece do not have great thing to offer to this country, called to remain for a long time the poor relative of the communitarian construction.

The fidelity of Athens to the Euro-American West was not even worth of a real support in its conflict with Turkey. The fact remains that, even if the Greek dictatorship had a determined responsibility in the Cypriot tragedy of 1974, the open Turkish aggression (the Attila operation) and the subsequent creation of a "Turkish republic of Cyprus", in frank violation of the island's status, were not only accepted, but probably were in agreement with the services of the Pentagon before which Europe yielded once more. It is obvious that, for the United States, the friendship of Turkey, a considerable regional military power, surpasses that of Greece, even if henceforth democratic.

In 1945, the whole of Balkan-Danubian region (Yugoslavia,

Albania, Hungary, Romania and Bulgaria) had entered in the bosom of Moscow, either by the fact of the Soviet military occupation and the consent of the partners of Yalta, or by the fact of their own liberation and the choice of their people in Yugoslavia and Albania.

The Titoist Yugoslavia, isolated in the years 1948-1953 at the same time by the ostracism of Moscow and the Western anticommunism, had pursued successfully a strategy of construction of a "non-aligned" front, which highlighted its friendship with the Third World, particularly starting from the Bandung Conference (1955). The analysts of the Yugoslav geo-strategic thought of the time show nevertheless this curious fact that this thought was not very sensitive to the Mediterranean dimension of their country. Perhaps Italy's abandonment of its traditional ambitions regarding Dalmatia (and Albania) and the solution found in 1954 to the thorny problem of Trieste were the essence of this "historical lapse of memory". Yugoslavia since then lived itself as a State preoccupied above all by the problems of the equilibrium of its Danubo-Balkan regional relationships and above all by those of the global equilibrium between the Super-Powers. Because in the first place, it had managed to capitalize on its benefit of double attraction—Nordist and Danubian of Croatia-Slovenia and Russian-Balkan of Serbia. The rapprochement initiated by Khrushchev and continued by his successors, recognizing the positive role of Titoist neutralism in the global arena, like the easing of the Warsaw Pact regimes as from 1960s and above all in 1970s, once guaranteed the Yugoslav security which had ceased feeling as the object of any regional conflict. The Yugoslav diplomacy could then be spread in the international arenas, giving this country a weight, out of proportion with its size. But if this diplomacy had incontestably won some points in Asia, Africa and even in Latin America, it made no progress in Europe where its calls to widen the neutralists' front never found favourable echoes. However, vis-à-vis Europe of NATO, from north till the south of the continent, between the two adverse military pacts, Sweden, Finland and Austria could have envisaged some common positive initiatives deviating from the spirit of the cold war. Later Pasok's Greece tried to widen this neutral European camp outlining in 1982 a proposal of a cooperation for de-nuclearisation of the Balkans, addressing itself simultaneously to certain member countries of one or other of the two alliances (Turkey, Romania and Bulgaria) or to the neutrals (Yugoslavia and Albania). These proposals did not find any support.

The decomposition of South-East Europe, since 1989, upset the facts of the problem. The erosion, and then the collapse of the legitimacy of these regimes—which was founded on a certain development, whatever being its limits and negative aspects—shattered the unity of the ruling class whose fractions in desperate straits tried to re-forge their legitimacy over nationalism. The conditions were met not only to allow the offensive of savage capitalism supported by the United States and the European Union, but also so that Germany retakes the initiative in the region, throwing oil on fire—by the hasty recognition of the independence of Slovenia and Croatia, that the European Union itself ratified—thus accelerating the fragmentation of Yugoslavia and the civil war. Curiously, the Europeans tried to impose on Bosnia the coexistence of the communities whose separation they preached elsewhere! If it is possible that the Serbs, Croatians and Moslems coexist in this small Yugoslavia, that is Bosnia, why then they could not have coexisted in large Yugoslavia? Obviously, a strategy of this kind hardly had chances of success, which made it possible for the United States to intervene in its turn, at the heart of Europe! In the strategy of Washington, Balkans—the Caucasus—Central Asia axis extends to the Middle East.

From the analyses suggested above concerning the political-strategic choices of the countries of northern bank of the Mediterranean, I draw an important conclusion: the majority of these countries, yesterday's faithful partners of the United States in the East-West conflict, remain today aligned over the strategy of American hegemony with regard to the Third World, and singularly with regard to the Arab countries and other countries of the Red Sea Gulf region; the others (Balkan and Danubean countries), implicated yesterday in one or other manner in the East-West conflict, have ceased being active agents in the permanent North-South conflict, and has became passive objects of the Western expansionism.

Conclusion: the Empire of chaos and the Permanent war

The project of the US domination—the extension of Monroe doctrines to the entire planet—is disproportionate. This project, that I qualified for this reason as the Empire of chaos since the collapse of the Soviet Union in 1991, will be fatally confronted with the rise of growing resistance of the nations of the old world not ready to be subjected to it. The United States then will have to behave like a "Rogue State" par excellence, substituting the international law with a recourse to the permanent war (starting with the Middle-East, but aiming beyond that, to Russia and Asia), slipping on the fascist slope (the "patriotic law" has already given powers to the police force, equal to those of Gestapo, with regard to foreigners—"aliens").

Will the European States, partners in the system of collective imperialism of the triad, accept this drift placing them in a subordinate position? The thesis that I have developed on this question does not stress so much on the conflicts of interests of the dominant capital as on the difference that separates the political cultures of Europe from that which characterizes the historical formation of the United States and sees in this new contradiction one of the principal reasons for the probable failure of the US project.[16]

NOTES

1. Samir Amin(1981), *Class & Nation: Historically & in the Current Crisis*. New York: New York University; Samir Amin (1989), *Eurocentrism*, New York: Monthly Review Press; Samir Amin, *Au delà du capitalisme sénile: pour un XXI ième siècle non américain*. PUF 2001.
2. For the critique of post-modernism and Negri's theses see Samir Amin (1997), *Critique de l' air du temps*, Paris: Harmattan; Samir Amin (2004), *The Liberal Virus*, New York: NYU Press.
3. Samir Amin (2000), *L'hégèmonisme des Etats Unis et l'effacement du projet européen*, Paris: Harmattan.

4. Samir Amin et al (1992), *Les enjeux stratégiques en Méditerrané* Part 1, Paris Harmattan 1992.
5. As for example: Gérard Chaliand and Arnaud Blin (2003), *America is back*, Paris: Bayard.
6. Samir Amin (1989), *La faillite du développement*, Paris: Harmattan.
7. Samir Amin (1996), *Les défis de la mondialisation*. Paris: Harmattan.
8. Samir Amin (1994), *L'ethnie à l'assaut des nations*. Paris: Harmattan.
9. Emmanuel Todd (2003), *After the Empire: The Breakdown of the American Empire*. New York: Columbia University Press.
10. The National Security Strategy of the United States 2002.
11. Chiefly note 2.
12. Samir Amin (1996).
13. Samir Amin (1992), *Empire of Chaos*. New York: MR Press.
14. Samir Amin (1996).
15. Samir Amin and Ali El Kenz (2003), *Le monde arabe: enjeux sociaux. perspectives méditérranéennes*. Paris: Harmattan.
16. Samir Amin (2004), *The Liberal Virus*, New York: New York University Press; Samir Amin (2003), The American Ideology, *Al Ahram Weekly*, 15-21 May 2003.

Empire Building and Rule:
US and Latin America

James Petras

Introduction

Except for some intellectual dinosaurs, many writers, journalists and academics have re-introduced the concept of imperialism into their analysis of the structure of world power. The earlier discussions focusing on "hegemony" have proven inadequate in explaining the US empire builders' new emphasis on military coercion, invasion and occupation and rule by force. Fifty years ago the Economic Commission on Latin America (CEPAL) described the world economy in terms of "center" and "periphery", twenty years later world-system theorists added a semi-periphery. These terms, long devoid of any historical, class or state specificity are no longer found useful by most critical writers in the contemporary world.

All the major questions we face today regarding the nature and direction of international power relations, the nature of the multiplying conflicts, conquests and resistance revolve around the nature and dynamics of imperialism—particularly the most powerful and aggressive imperial power, the United States of America.

Fundamental questions have been asked about the sustainability of the US empire—at least in its present, military and economic structure. In its simplest form, the most common question is whether the US empire is in ascendancy or whether it is in decline. While on the surface this appears to be the 'central issue' in reality it obscures more fundamental questions that must be addressed, involving the relations between domestic politics and economy to the empire, the class and political relationships sustaining and opposing the empire and the political capacity of the empire to sustain outward expansion and domestic decay. To argue as some academics do, that the empire is declining because it is "over-extended"(Kennedy, Hobsbawm, Wallerstein) overlooks the capacity of the imperial ruling class to continue to re-allocate resources from the domestic economy to the empire, the durable state, media, and party institutions which gird the continuation of empire building and most important, the ability to recruit clients to service the empire.

The continuing dynamic imperial expansion, including the military conquest of three regions (Balkans, Afghanistan and Iraq) takes place with the active approval of the vast majority of US citizens who are suffering the worst social and economic cuts in governmental programs and the most regressive tax legislation in recent history. Clearly the impressionistic commentators who purported to see the occasional mass demonstrations in Seattle, Washington and other cities against globalization and the Iraq war as a challenge and weakening of the Empire were wrong. Once the war began, the large demonstrations ended and no mass movement exists to oppose bloody colonial occupation nor to support the anti-colonial resistance. Equally serious, from the methodological perspective, the critics of imperial power are unable to account for the 'world-wide' nature of the imperial doctrine—of fighting imperial wars "everywhere and for the foreseeable future" according to the Bush doctrine. Latching on to the most visible and obvious objective – in the case of Iraq, oil— the activists critics overlook, the multiple sites of continuing imperialist military intervention, in Latin America, Africa and Asia (Colombia, Djibouti, and Philippines, etc.). Oil is an important component of empire building, but so is power, control and domination of clients, rivals and independent states.

To properly understand the world wide political and military aggression of the US empire builders, we must focus on the scope and extent of the US economic empire. To adequately understand whether the US empire is declining or expanding we must distinguish between the domestic economy (what I will call "the republic") and the international economy (what I call "empire").

The US Economic Empire

One of the key measures of the economic dimensions of the US empire is the number and percentage of its multi-national corporations (MNC) and banks among the top 500 firms in the world in comparison to other economic regions. Almost all economic analysts agree that the driving force of the world economy, the institutions central to international investments, financial transactions and world trade are the MNC's. Equally important, no state can aspire to global dominance if its principle economic institutions, the MNC's, do not exercise a paramount role in the world economy. Any serious discussion of the present and future of US imperial supremacy is obligated to analyze the distribution of power among the competing MNC's.

There are several ways of measuring the "leading MNC's". I have followed the *Financial Times* approach and have used the data they have compiled. The FT ranks companies according to their market capitalization, namely the stock valuation of a company. The greater the stock market value of a company the higher its ranking. Market capitalization is the share price multiplied by the number of shares issued. Only companies where the free float of stocks is over 85% are included thus excluding companies with large state or family holdings.

The US MNC's dominate the listings of the top 500 corporations in the world. Almost half of the biggest MNC's (48%) are US-owned and operated, almost double its next regional competitor, Europe with 28%. Japanese owned MNC's are only 9% of the total and the rest of Asia (South Korea, Hong Kong, India, Taiwan, Singapore etc..) combined possess less than 4 per cent of the 500 biggest firms and banks. The concentration of US economic power is even greater if we look at the 50 largest MNC's—where over 66% are US owned; and the power of the US economic giants is even more evident when we examine the top 20 MNC's, where over 70% are US owned. Among the top 10 MNC's, US controls 80%.

Many impressionistic analysts citing the decline in stock market values of US MNC's as an indicator of a general decline in the US global position failed to recognize that the stock value of the MNC's of Europe, Japan and the rest of the world also fell—in equal or greater degree – thus neutralizing the effect of the decline of the US on the continued dominance by the US MNC's.

We can examine several other measures of the continued and consolidated economic power of the US empire. If we compare the net capitalization of the US MNC's among the top 500 firms to the MNC's of other regions we find that the value of US MNC's exceeds the combined valuation of all other regions. US MNC's valuation is $7.445 billion to $5.141 billion. The US MNC's have a market value more than *double* that of its closest competitor, Europe.

The argument for consolidated and growing US world economic empire is further strengthened if we examine the eight leading economic sectors of the world economy, namely banking, pharmaceuticals, telecommunications, information technology hardware, oil and gas, software and computer services, insurance and general retailers. US MNCs are a majority of the top ranked in five sectors, have 50% in one sector (oil and gas) and are a minority in one sector (insurance). The same pattern is true if we examine the so-called "old economy". The US-owned MNCs in the old economy including mining, oil and automobile, chemical and consumer goods number 45 of the top 100 MNCs. Among the top 45 MNC's connected with manufacturing the US MNC's number 21, Europe 17, Japan 5 and the rest of the world 2. The US has the top ranked company in 23 out of 34 industry groups. US MNC's control nearly 59% of the leading manufacturing and mining firms—almost equal to the combined European and Japanese MNCs. The major area of US weakness is in the electronics sector where the US has only 2 of the top 23 firms.

In so far as the MNCs are the foundation and driving force for economic empire-building, it is clear that the US is still dominant, still controlling and shows little or no signs of "weakening", "declining" or losing ranking to either Japan or Europe. The thesis of an "over-extended" or "declining economy" has little basis. The recent speculative bubble has only affected sectors of the IT (information technology) sector, but this is true for US competitors as well. Moreover while the IT sector declined, sectors of the "old economy" have expanded. And even within the IT sectors, there has been a process of concentration and centralization of capital—with Microsoft, IBM and a few other US giants advancing in ranking while many others declined.

While fraud and corruption have affected investor confidence in US MNC's, it has also been the case in Europe and Japan. The result has been a *general* decline in market valuations of all MNC's in all three competing imperial centres (US, EU, Japan). The worldwide decline in stock valuation is evident if we compare the totals between 2002-2003: in 2002 the net value was $16,250 billion compared to $12,580 billion in 2003—a 22.6% decline. However approximately 50% of the decline took place in the IT hardware sector.

The indisputable fact is that the US economic empire is dominant and in an ascending phase—its depth and scope surpasses its European and Japanese rivals by multiples of two in most instances. The advocates of "declining empire" either fail to grasp the economic structural elements of the US empire or resort to long term forecasts based on historical comparison which conclude that sometime in the future the US empire will, like all empires, decline (Hobsbawm). Long time historical forecasting of an inevitable decline has the virtue of *consoling* the billions of people facing exploitation and destructive wars, and the rulers of nations threatened with military invasion and the takeover of their lucrative natural resources. But it is totally irrelevant in diagnosing the power of the empire today, its dynamic and the forces organized against it. The thesis of decline is based on abstract theorizing, wishful thinking at worst, and at best on extrapolations from the *domestic* economy of the empire.

What needs to be emphasized is that the "contradictions" that threaten the empire are not simple *economic* deductions from an assumed "overextended empire" which presumably will energize "the people" to topple the empire building elite, or force the imperial policy makers to rethink their imperialist project. The US empire is built by and supported by both major political parties, by all branches of the government and has followed an upward trajectory via imperial wars, colonial conquests and MNC expansion, particularly since the defeat in the Indochina wars. Imperial defeats and moments of decline are directly the result of political, social and military struggles —most of which have taken place in Latin America and Asia, and to a lesser extent in Europe and North America.

Militarism and the Economic Empire

There is little doubt that the US global economic empire has had a long term, large scale positive relationship with the US military empire. The US has military bases in 120 countries around the world form the core of the military empire. US militarism, involving wars, proxy interventions via mercenaries, contracted combatants, special forces and covert intelligence operations have created, in many regions of the world over a prolonged period of time, favourable conditions for the expansion of the US economic empire. Regimes which impose restrictions or exclude US foreign investment, refuse to pay debts to US banks, nationalize US overseas holdings or support nationalist movements have been threatened into submission, subverted or invaded, resulting in the imposition of client regimes favorable to US empire building. There is no exact sequence between economic expansion and military action though there is a vast overlap of ties. In some cases, economic interests dictate military bases or CIA intervention (as was the case in Chile in 1973); in other cases military action, including wars, force countries or regions to submit to economic empire building (as in the case of Iraq in 2003).

Nor is there a "perfect symmetry" between imperial military engagement and spending and economic empire building. At times the military engagement "lags" behind the expansion of the US multi-nationals, as occurred during the mid 1950s to the early 1960s and later between the end of the Indo-China wars and the early 1980s. In other moments the reverse takes place, where military involvement dominates the political economic agenda as during the Korean War (1950-1953), the Indo-China War (1965-1974), the Reagan era (1981-1989) and today (2001-?). The "movement" and "construction" of empire-building does not follow a linear line of perfect symmetry between the economic and military components. The periodic, disproportionate emphasis of one or the other does not lead to the demise of the empire, as a review of the past half century of US empire demonstrates.

The notion of an "over-extended" empire is a piece of ahistorical speculation which assumes that empire building must follow some "ideal pattern" where military costs and economic benefits go hand-in-hand. This is false for several reasons: the benefits of empire building go to the overseas and domestic corporate elite, the costs are paid by US tax payers and the low-income families which provide the combat and occupation soldiers. In addition what appear to be military-economic "disproportions" in one period lead to "balance" in the following. For examples US Cold War military expenditures and interventions contributed to the downfall of Communist regimes which later led to windfall profits, cheap labour and lucrative exploitation of mineral resources in the ex-Communist countries and their allies as well as reduction in social welfare programs in the West. In order to argue that "excess" military imperialism is harmful to economic-empire building, it is necessary to specify whether the scope and depth of US MNC control over the world economy has declined, that the access to strategic materials has diminished and that the US citizens are refusing to suffer the social cuts, the regressive tax burdens and budgetary allocations which sustain empire building.

The thesis of the "over-extension" of the US military empire overlooks the capacity of US empire builders to recruit subordinate allies and client states to accept police, administrative and financial duties at the service of the US empire. In the Balkans, the Europeans have over 40,000 troops serving under US-dominated NATO command. In Afghanistan, European military forces, UN administrative personnel and a number of Third World client states supply the personnel to safeguard the US appointed Karzai puppet regime. In Iraq, subordinate allies like Britain and vassal states like Poland and other Eastern European clients supply military and civilian auxiliaries to enforce US colonial rule. Washington's long term, large scale client building in Eastern Europe, dating back to at least the 1980's with Solidarity in Poland, provide a large reservoir of political and diplomatic support, mercenary armies in the current drive for empire building. Huge airbases and troop deployment platforms are currently being constructed in Rumania, Bulgaria to match those in Kosova and Macedonia. The US empire builders have shoved the Russians out of Central and Southern Asia, building airbases in Kazakhstan, Uzbekistan, Georgia and Afghanistan. The recruitment of client regimes from the Baltic to the Middle East, Central Asia and Southern Asia demonstrates the rapid growth of the US military empire and further new opportunities for US MNC's to expand the economic empire. This extended empire has led to the formation of regional imperial dominated alliances which provide new military recruits to bolster and consolidate the expanding empire. Instead of viewing US empire building as a process of "over-extension" it should be seen as a process of *widening the pool* for new recruits to strengthen the US military command. US power has learned to discard multi-lateral power sharing with its European imperial allies-competitors in favor of subcontracting military occupation and police functions to the new clients from Eastern Europe, Central and Southern Asia.

Throughout the growth and expansion of the US empire, the European Union has followed in the wake of its conquests, financing and providing military and civil administrators. The brief interlude of German, French and Belgian dissent, prior to the US invasion of Iraq was followed by almost total subservience to US imperial policies—bellicose and intrusive demands and attacks on Iran, North Korea and Cuba; commitments to follow the US lead in promoting a rapid deployment force; backing for the US occupation of Iraq (Security Council Resolution 1483) and more generally a recognition that in the words of compliant EU Foreign Secretary, Javier Solano, "We don't want to compete with the United States —it would be absolutely ridiculous—but see the problem jointly". The EU accepts its role (as defined by Rumsfeld or Wolfowitz) as a subordinated ally of the US drive for world wide domination, seeking to secure a place at the economic trough and delegated power and minority shares in any of the contracts and privatized companies. Those imperial theorists who argued for heightened European independence and competition as weakening the US empire should read Romano Prodi, President of the European Commission, who in a press statement in Washington on June 2003 said, "When Europe and the US are together, no problem or enemy can face us; if we are not together any problem can be a crises". Prodi and Solano represent the new thinking in Europe: better to collaborate with a winning imperialism and secure minority benefits rather than be chastised, bullied and left out of the new colonies. The US empire builders welcome and encourage the new thinking, given the EU promise of helping to foot the initial costs of occupation and colonial state building without challenging US supremacy.

To date, including the current phase of US wars of imperial conquest, there are no signs that global militarism is eroding economic empire-building in the US. US MNC's continue to dominate key banking, manufacturing, IT, pharmaceutical and oil and gas industries. The Iraqi invasion has strengthened US control over and access to the second greatest reserves of oil and gas in the world. Thirdly, there is no imminent popular revolt or citizen rejection of empire building. In the midst of colonial conquest over three-quarters of US citizens—the highest proportion in the world – say they are "very proud of their country"; more that eight out of ten support the invasion of Iraq even when it is public knowledge that President Bush's justification for the war—to destroy weapons of mass destruction—has been demonstrated to be a pure fabrication. Despite the most regressive tax reduction in recent history, large scale slashing of social spending and huge budget deficits, the citizens of the US show no signs of mass protest. The anti-war movement of January-February 2003, almost completely disappeared with the successful military conquest and occupation of Iraq. In summary, the extension of military activity from the Balkans through the Middle East to South Asia has not adversely affected the international economic position of the US MNCs, nor undermined the domestic political support of the architects of *empire*.

While the empire prospers and the US military bases proliferate, the "republic", the economy within the boundaries of the territorial United States declines, its class society becomes more polarized, its politics become more repressive.

The Republic Declines

There are two distinct but interrelated "economies" and state activities in the US, the *empire* which encapsulates the world of the multi-nationals, the global military apparatus and the international financial institutions linked to the imperial state and the *republic* which is the economy, state institutions and social classes located in the US which provides the soldiers, executives, tax dollars and markets which sustain the empire. The growth of the empire has visibly impoverished the domestic economy in a variety of ways while enriching CEOs (and their extended entourages) who benefit and direct the overseas activities of the MNCs. US empire builders have added over $100 billion to military spending to finance the Iraq and Afghanistan wars, cutting health, education and welfare programs. Today there are more than 50 million US citizens without any health coverage, another 50 million with partial, inadequate coverage and many more millions spending up to one-third of their net income for adequate medical coverage. Pension and social security funds are depleted to cover current expenses and to keep the budget deficit from ballooning out of control. Financing imperialism has led to an estimated $400 billion budget deficit in 2003 which may increase as the military occupation of Iraq will run to at least $80 billion. Domestic industrial production, particularly the auto industry has seen profit margins decline sharply, as Ford has taken several billion dollar losses while the majority of US manufacturers have invested abroad or subcontracted to local producers in Latin America and Asia. The result is that subsidiaries of US MNCs have captured an important share of China's exports to the US market but have increased the US external deficit for 2003 which has climbed toward $500 billion and is rising. The high profits earned by the MNCs relocated throughout the new colonial and semi-colonial economies of Asia and Latin America strengthen imperial institutions while weakening the domestic economy, its budget financing and its external accounts.

The "unbearable costs of global domination" (financier Felix Rohatyn) are indeed "bearable"—there is no mass revolt despite widening inequalities, declining living standards, depleted or non-existent social services, extended working days and higher individual payments to health and pension funds, and massive corruption and fraud—scandals which rob millions of US investors and pensioners of their savings and pension funds. Growing unemployment is now over 10% in 2003 including those who no longer register.

The empire builders spend massive sums to conquer the world based on fabricated claims. They terrorize the population with paranoiac visions of imminent attacks in pursuit of endless wars, world conquest and horrific carnage of defenseless people. They sponsor or protect domestic anthrax terrorists who terrorized the US population and served to justify US state terror. By and large the great majority of the US population "sat back and watched" (Harold Pinter) or worse took pride and vicarious pleasure in being identified with the victorious rampaging armies. While the major US cities are bankrupt or heavily indebted, the Federal Government spends billions subsidizing agro-export elites to the tune of $180 billion dollars over 10 years, handing giant MNC building contractors (Halliburton) with close ties to the empire builders lucrative billion dollar contracts while spending billions to subsidize mercenary armies in Afghanistan, Iraq and Colombia. In the midst of domestic stagnation, the empire builders give massive tax cuts to the corporate elite – those most likely to invest in MNCs that operate abroad.

To attract billions of dollars from overseas investors, the imperial state allows US multi-national banks to launder tens of billions of dollars in illicit funds, from multi-millionaire tax evaders, corrupt bankers and elite political officials from Latin America, China, Africa and elsewhere (US Congress). The funds to sustain the empire is based in part on massive corruption by overseas clients who "invest" in the US economy while opening their countries to imperial pillage. Nevertheless the declining economy of the republic is no longer attracting the high levels of "foreign investment" as the dollar weakens and profitable opportunities shrink. Foreign direct investment has declined from $300 billion in 2000 to $50 billion in 2002. The republic needs $2.7 billion a day in capital inflows to finance the external deficit. The answer to the strengthening empire and weakening republic is greater social sacrifices at home, more protectionism, greater transfers of profits and interest payments from Latin America and other neo-colonial regions, more moralizing crusades, more forceful mass media blitzes, even more blatant official lies and new wars to charge up the endless supply of chauvinist juices.

The big corporate swindle of millions of US investors and pensioners enriched the CEOs and financed the expansion of the MNCs abroad. Corruption was not an anomaly of deviant CEOs—it is a structural feature of US empire building both abroad and at home.

Imperialist Wars and "The Republic"

Despite the occasional criticism by European leaders and inconsequential dissent within the legislature of "the republic", the Bush regime has vastly expanded empire building on the political and military foundations and networks of their predecessors particularly the Clinton presidency. The empire builders under Clinton expanded the military empire from the Baltic to the Balkans and beyond to the partial occupation of Iraq. The Bush militarists expanded the US military empire to the conquest of Iraq, Caucasus, Central Asia, to Afghanistan and Southeast Asia, a vast archipelago of airbases, military supply zones and fortresses from which to attack and conquer the entire southern tier of Asia, up to and including North Korea. In the Middle East, Bush announces a 'free trade zone'—from North Africa to Saudi Arabia, including Israel—controlled by the US. Never has the US military empire grown so widely, so quickly and with such ease—making talk about the "decline of the empire" idle chatter or self–indulgent exercises in "faith healing".

There is no doubt that certain economic sectors have suffered from the empire's hysterical "anti-terrorist" propaganda designed to secure public support for imperial wars and conquests. Those sectors adversely affected include sectors of the civil aeronautic industries, tourism, and related service activities. However large-scale state subsidies and interest-free loans have cushioned the effects for the corporate sector.

Empire building in our time is driven by systemic factors, reinforced by ideological extremism. The simplistic attempts to explain the war by references to the influence of the military-industrial complex fails to take account of the relative decline in rankings of the major aerospace and defense sector between 2001-2002 among the top 500 firms. The imperial conquests today are based on the drive to conquer the world and to open *future* opportunities for US MNCs—the military empire is designed to secure future access to wealth, not to generate it in the process of conquest; war and the network of military satellites is designed to create a world-wide network to facilitate monopoly profits through client rulers disposed to offer exploitation rights to US MNCs.

"Empire building is no tea party", a retired colonel from the US Marines once told me, referring to the systematic human rights violations which accompany imperial wars and conquests. Nothing captures the deliberate, planned, violent conquest and brutal occupation embedded in US empire building, than the US *opposition* to the international criminal court and the vicious arm twisting which has forced over 50 countries to sign bilateral pacts giving US military personnel impunity. But it is not the inhumane nature of imperial wars, nor the gross violations of international law, nor the fabrication of provocations to justify the colonial conquest which cause fissures in the ruling power bloc (state officials and corporate elite) but the relations between the governing military empire builders and the economic empire builders on the best approach to build the empire and consolidate rulership *without undermining the republic's capacity to finance the imperial state.*

Inter-Ruling Class Conflict

There are several levels at which the inter-elite struggle over empire building takes place. The first and most general issue in discussion is the question of the relationship of the militarists and the corporate empire builders. While they both share a common vision of a "dominant US empire", they (or at least some) disagree over the degree of "autonomy" with which the militarists act—at times elaborating military strategies that concentrate on conquest rather than economic costs and benefits. The successful military conquests have increased the power and independence of the militarists in shaping strategic global strategy over and against some of the concerns of the economic empire builders in the private sector.

The second issue is the distortions in US empire building generated by key empire strategists because of their ties to Zionism and the influence this has in shaping imperial policy in the Middle East and beyond. Zionists like Wolfowitz, Feith, Perle and a host of other architects of the strategy of global conquest, following Israeli policy, direct US policy toward destroying Israel's Arab adversaries throughout the Middle East, even when "negotiated" approaches to expanding the US empire are feasible. This is clearly the case with Iran and Syria, despite the emergence of liberal pro-US political movements and personalities who are pursuing non-violent methods.

Equally damaging, in the eyes of conventional military and intelligence strategists, the Zionists empire builders have projected the paranoid Israeli point of view of politics—a world full of enemies, Europeans who can't be trusted, Third World people as potential terrorists. Influential Zionists like Richard Perle follow the precepts of one infamous Israeli military-politicians (Moshe Dayan) " the Arabs only understand force". While the Israeli-Zionist "philosophy" is deadly enough in the Middle East, its exponents in Washington have global power and the capacity to implement it on a world scale. The Israeli world view of "preventive" wars, "colonization", occupation, collective punishment, and unilateral use of force in defiance of international law has been adapted by US militarists who have long standing ties to Israel and have made Israeli practices the doctrinal guide for empire building.

The result of the "Zionist bias" in US strategic empire building has generated several points of conflicts within the imperial elite: among the economic empire builders who look toward alliances with Arab oil rulers to expand their domain; among the professional elite in the US military and intelligence agencies who have been castigated and marginalized by the Zionists for not providing the "right" intelligence to justify the wars of destruction of Israel's enemies. This led Under-Secretary of Defense Paul Wolfowitz to form a parallel intelligence structure compatible with the Zionist policy of "destroying Israel's enemies". This bogus intelligence group calling itself a "cabal" is less an intelligence agency collecting reliable information as it is a propaganda agency to fabricate "reports" justifying pre-determined war policies based on the Israeli world view.

The third level of conflict is between Rumsfeld, the Secretary of Defense, and the military-intelligence professionals. Rumsfeld, as the key figure involved in the military empire building process, has been vigorously involved in concentrating power in his hands and that of his personal coterie led by Wolfowitz, Perle, Boulton and other extremist militarists. Rumsfeld has over ruled the Pentagon professionals on the reorganization of the armed forces, weapon procurement, war strategy and intelligence operations. He has promoted loyalist military officers over those with greater seniority and military experience, and humiliated those who express the slightest dissent. His tyrannical behavior toward high military officials is his method of stifling any elite discussions. His most loyal subordinates and influential advisers are those who adhere to his extremist military empire building strategy: sequential wars which overlap and combine with worldwide terrorist covert assassination programs. There is no doubt that Rumsfeld has been the controlling figure in the formulation and execution of the strategy of world military conquest—an imperial strategy which closely resembles that of Nazi Germany. Rumsfeld's concentration of power within the imperial elite and the hostility toward the professionals was dramatically expressed by his nomination of retired General Schoomaker, former commander of the Special Forces "Delta", which was described to me by senior military officers at the Delta headquarters at Fort Bragg as a collection of "psychopaths trained to murder". Clearly the ex-Delta general was selected precisely because his ideological and behavioural profile fits in with Rumsfeld's own Nazi propensities.

The first major differences and internal conflicts between Rumsfeld and the military/intelligence hierarchies surfaced in the aftermath of the Iraqi war over the issue of the non-existence of weapons of mass destruction (WMD) in Iraq. As WMD was the Bush Administration's major justification for the war, it provoked debate in the mass media and among some congresspeople. The inter-elite conflict surfaced when the "professionals" in the military and the intelligence agencies leaked reports and made statements which questioned the Rumsfeld allegations in the run-up to the war. Clearly the "professionals" were hoping to point to Rumsfeld and the personal "intelligence" coterie as responsible for "cooking the data" to justify the Rumsfeld-Wolfowitz war plans. In short the intensity of the inter-elite struggle for bureaucratic power had reached the point at which the pro-empire professionals were willing the call into question a successful imperialist war to rid themselves of a bureaucratic tyrant who they felt was jeopardizing empire building to advance his narrow personal power within the imperial state apparatus. However the militarists with the aid of Congress and the mass media were able to bury the issue—and even succeeded in securing public compliance with the war.

The fourth issue in debate within the governing imperial

elite is the conflict over the relations between military and economic empire builders. The latter clearly see military action as a *means* to the end—a dominant US economic empire. For the military imperialists, a military definition of world conquest has become the strategic goal, which it is assumed will redound eventually to the benefit of the economic empire builders. This leads critics and ideologues among some economic empire builders to question the militarists knowledge of the economic costs—short and long term—of an indiscriminant policy of military intervention and permanent wars. This may become an important debate over the *methods* of building empire, but not about the empire itself which both support. Added to this discussion is the dispute over "economic cronyism" which afflicts the militarists. They hand over lucrative post-war contracts to favoured MNCs linked to the Rumsfeld-Cheney-Bush clique while ignoring the claims of other corporate sectors.

These disputes between capitalists and the military empire builders however are clearly secondary to the powerful interests and policies which unite them. Despite the occasional and passing concerns expressed by some capitalists of the imperialist war policies, the capitalist class, particularly the MNCs are powerful backers of Bush-Rumsfeld empire building.

There are at least eight reasons why the MNCs back the Bush Administration despite certain misgivings among individual capitalists concerning the neo-Nazi doctrine of permanent warfare. While a few editorial writers in the financial press and individual capitalists have criticized the Bush regime's budget deficits, the weak dollar and the growing external accounts deficits, the majority of the capitalist class continue to provide solid support for the Bush empire building regime for very concrete reasons. The Bush regime has rejected all international treaties, including the Kyoto agreement, which imposes environmental controls on industry, thus lowering the costs of production for US firms. Second, the Bush Administration provides billions in export subsidies particularly to big agro-business export firms, thus increasing their market shares, increasing their "competitiveness" and profits. Third, the Bush Administration provides protective measures for over

200 products, involving tens of thousands of non-competitive producers who sell in the republic's ("domestic") market, thus blocking or limiting the entrance of more efficient competitors. Fifth the Bush regime has decreased taxes for the entire capitalist class—benefiting CEOs of the MNCs and the capitalists operating in the "republic", thus increasing gains from dividends, capital gains and salaries. Sixth, the Bush Administration has largely tolerated (or participated in) the cover-up of billion dollar corruption, fraud and auditing felonies in most of the major MNCs and banks. Seventh the regime continues to tolerate loose banking regulations, in effect promoting billions of dollars of money laundering by US multinational banks. And eighth, the Bush Administration has refused to increase the minimum wage and has pursued an anti-labour agenda, lowering labour costs for big and small business groups engaged in sweatshops and the service sector.

These and similar policies provide the economic bases for long term, large scale structural linkages between the Bush Administration and the capitalist class as a whole. This explains why there is close collaboration between the economic and military empire builders, between the military empire builders and the business class operating in the republic. The 'trade off" (if there even needs to be one!) involves state financial economic payoffs to the local business elite in exchange for the capitalist class's political and financial support for the military empire builders.

What allows the US military empire builders to proceed in their quest for world conquest, despite inconsequential and passing criticism from their European allies is the knowledge that they have the solid backing of Wall Street and "Main Street" (capitalists producing for the domestic market of the republic). Moreover the overseas power and corporate links of US MNC's and banks with their European counterparts has weakened European resolve to challenge US supremacy and strengthened the hand of the right-wing Berlusconi and Aznar regimes in Italy and Spain.

Imperialism: Circuses without Bread

US empire building does not provide payoffs for the workers, employees and small farmers and business people in the empire. Their support of the Empire is based on the consumption of state propaganda via the mass media, symbolic gratification in being part of a victorious 'world power' and a servile attitude to established state authority. The lack of a credible left wing political party or movement further undermines popular opposition. Even worse, what passes for left-wing or progressive journals or intellectuals was in large part supportive of the US wars against Yugoslavia, Afghanistan and to a lesser degree Iraq. What is even more telling, the great majority of the US intellectual left joined the Bush chorus in attacking Cuba over the execution of Cuban terrorists and the jailing of US financed propagandists. The US "progressive" movements and journals have with few notable exceptions never demonstrated solidarity with the current or past anti-colonial resistance movements, national liberation struggles or revolutionary regimes—whether it was the National Liberation Front in Vietnam, the Iraqi resistance or the Cuban revolution. Most of the US opposition is legalist (citing constitutional law), and moralistic (citing universal precepts) divorced from any practical examples, least of all from Third World revolutionary practices.

The state, the mass media and the corporate world encourage mindless, passive engagement in mass spectator entertainment which creates apolitical "identification" (sports and soap opera heroes and heroines) and reinforces the empire world view of "good" and "evil", where the "good guys" defeat the "evil doers" through violence and destruction.

As the empire grows, corporate funded pensions disappear, medical and pharmaceutical costs skyrocket and unemployment and poverty grow beyond the flawed official statistical recordings. As of July 2003, the official unemployment rate was 6.5%—the unofficial close to double. Empire building does not create a "labor aristocracy" which shares the crumbs of empire —at least if we exclude the several thousand trade union officials who draw hundreds of thousands of dollars in annual salaries, pensions and payoffs while the percentage of dues paying union members in the private sector is 9% of the labour force. Inequalities widen: the ratio of CEO income to workers has gone up from 80 to 1 twenty five years ago to 450 to 1 today, and it is still growing. US workers have less vacation time (on average three times less than European workers), a longer working life, more regressive taxes and no representation in the political system, as the two dominant parties are controlled by the empire builders.

The *objective* losses of the working classes has not led to any significant opposition to empire building except among blacks —who opposed the Iraqi war by a substantial margin. The decline of the welfare state and the transfer of wealth upward serves to finance empire building (the end of the Cold War was an "empire dividend"). Large scale corporate corruption in a stagnant speculative economy and rising unemployment has accompanied a dramatic right wing shift in imperial politics. There has been an increase in corporate crime, national chauvinism and the spread of the ideology of individual survival. Unemployed and under-educated minorities choose to join the imperial army, while many poor white workers express hostility to Muslims, Arabs and Middle Eastern peoples. The affluent leaders of the major Jewish organizations give unconditional support to the butcher Sharon and their ideological counterparts in the Bush regime as they plan for new imperial wars particularly aimed at Iran. Meanwhile US "progressives" once again begin their perennial futile effort to transform the Democratic Party from an imperial to a democratic party of the republic.

The major challenges to the empire do not exist in the US, at least in the foreseeable future, neither from dissident capitalists (because of the growing gap between the empire and republic), nor from the working class. The main threat to the empire comes form outside, from the ongoing mass struggles in the Third World, namely Latin America, the Middle East and Asia.

Imperialism and Latin America

Nowhere in the contemporary world have economic relations between Empire and Third World regimes been so one sided—so beneficial to the United States and Europe and so detrimental as in Latin America. In discussing the empire-client state relationship it is important to establish a *periodization*, which distinguishes degrees of domination and control, the specific class collaboraters of empire, and more important identifies the distinct forms of empire building of the last quarter of a century.

To speak of imperialism as "500 years of exploitation and domination" is both *generally true* and *specifically misleading*. While European and US empire builders have exploited many of the countries of Latin America most of the time over half a millenium, its is also true that Latin American popular movements, nationalist and socialist regimes have significantly modified or transformed their relations to empire at different moments. Imperialism is based on class and state relations which by their nature imply conflicts, confrontations and conquests, revolutions, counter-revolutions and transformations.

In recent history, national-populist regimes from the 1930s to the 1960s were successful in partially transforming Latin America from a raw-material based export economy to a diversified urban industrial economy producing for the domestic market. From the 1970s to the present the imperial-led counter-revolution (led by the US imperial state and the IFI's) in alliance with Latin American transnational capitalists (sectors of capital linked to international financial, trade and marketing networks) imposed a "neo-liberal" model through client regimes. By the end of the 1990s, the empire, having taken control of the strategic and dynamic sectors of the economy and consolidated its hold on a client political class, launched the transition toward the re-colonization of the region, dubbing the process the "Free Trade Area of the Americas". The process of re-colonization is well *advanced*, based on traditional right-wing leaders and the recruitment of new client rulers from the ranks of Latin America's renegade leftists and populists.

In brief we can identify three distinct periods of empire-client state relations. The *1930-60* period of relatively limited imperial domination was based on the *eclipse* (not displacement) of the liberal agro-mineral collaborator classes, and the emergence and expansion of national state and private industrial enterprises, foreign trade and exchange control regimes and national banks. The *1970-95* period included massive privatization of public enterprises and the denationalization of banks, industries, telecommunications, strategic energy services etc.. The third phase (the current period) involves the transformation of the strategic economic conquests into a new political-legal regime—the ALCA Commission—which vests the US empire builders with formal rulership of the region.

Empire Building: Phase I

The transition from national-populism to neo-liberalism was consummated through violent conflicts, military coups, massacres, forced exiles, and the establishment of a state apparatus (military and police) loyal to the empire and a political class of willing accomplices of imperial rule. The empire builders and their client rulers, both military and civilian, immediately opened the region to a massive invasion by US and European speculators and MNCs.

Economic empire building was made possible by the military empire builders who directly and indirectly intervened to repress, disarticulate and fragment popular opposition. Military coups in Brazil (1964), Bolivia (1971), Chile (1973), Argentina (1976) and civilian military coups in Uruguay (1972), and Peru (1993) created the political framework and international agreements with the IFIs which reversed the national industrializing project and opened Latin America to conquest by US and European MNCs.

During the mid 1980s under mass pressure the US brokered a "negotiated transition" from military to elite electoral authoritarian political rule, safeguarding the "neo-liberal" economic framework to further the expansion of the economic empire. Between the mid 1980s to 2000, the economic empires expanded—both European (mostly Spanish) and US as trade barriers fell and US, European Union and Asian commodities flooded the Latin American markets, displacing millions of small farmers, local producers, manufacturers and retailers.

The new authoritarian client regimes pillaged the economy,

privatizing and selling off thousands of public enterprises, while the MNCs bought out local banks and manufacturers, land and real estate. According to a recent study (Minella), in Brazil in 1989 foreign banks owned 9.6% of bank stocks, by 2000 they controlled 33%. In 2001, foreign finance capital controlled 12 of the 20 biggest banks in Brazil. The growth of foreign capital is almost exclusively the result of the acquisition of national public and private banks, not the creation of new firms. In Latin America, a study of 212 directors of 19 financial associations representing banks in 14 Latin American countries, revealed that 55% were representatives of foreign banks. A majority of the leaders of financial networks in Latin American are North American or European bankers. These financial networks in turn directly or indirectly control industrial, commercial and real estate properties. Equally important, they establish the conditions for external financing in collaboration with the IFIs. US client ideologues in Latin America are mostly trained at elite propaganda universities like Chicago, Harvard, Stanford etc. Through state terror and coercion they imposed the imperial centered "neo-liberal model". The IFI's reinforced the "model" through their structural adjustment policies supporting the client regimes and benefiting the local financial elites linked to US multi-national banks.

The imperial centred model led to the long term, large scale systematic pillage of every country in Latin America. The latest study, for the year 2002, by the United Nations, Economic Commission for Latin America reveals that over $69.2 billions of dollars in interest payments and profits were remitted to the US home offices. The study did not include the several billion in royalty payments, shipping, insurance and other service fees and the billions more illegally transferred by Latin American elites via US and European banks to overseas accounts. The total pillaged from Latin America is closer to $100 billion dollars. If we multiply this sum for the decade 1992-2002 we can conservatively estimate that Latin America was exploited to the tune of over $1 trillion dollars.

A similar process of empire building is evident in the realm of the imperial takeover of trade, productive facilities and local markets. According to a study by the Banco Bilbao Vizcaya Argentina (BBVA) headquartered in Spain, over one third (56) of the 150 biggest enterprises are foreign owned, half are national private and almost 13% (19) are national state firms. However the 75 national private firms only generate 30% of the total sales of the 150 largest enterprises. The Latin American owned private firms account for only 22% of the exports of the 150 biggest firms, the foreign owned firms 15% and the public firms 63% of export earnings. In other works US and European MNCs control a substantial share of the domestic market, while public national firms are the major foreign exchange earners.

US, European and Japanese MNC's dominate the domestic markets and largely displace local producers. The imperial formula for Latin America is to export capital to capture domestic markets and to import raw materials from the publicly owned enterprises. In 2002, MNCs transferred $22 billion in profits on direct investments of $76 billion—almost a 35% rate of return.

With public enterprises accounting for $245 billion in sales of which 35% represented exports it is clear that the strategic goal of US empire building is to seize control of this sector. The focus is on the state petroleum and gas companies of Mexico, Venezuela, Brazil, Ecuador, Colombia and Bolivia as well as the Chilean Copper Corporation (BBVA quoted in *La Jornada* June 15, 2003.)

Empire building then involves four stages: (1) ideological-military-political intervention to impose "the empire centered model" and the parameters of "realistic" political-economic debate—with some "imperfections" (popular resistance, different timing of implementation, incompetent rulers etc.). (2) Implementation of the first wave of deregulation, privatization and de-nationalization leading to the dominance of local elites linked to the IFI and MNCs. (3)The conversion from national privatization to foreign control via debt payments, loans and buyouts leading to the takeover of large market shares in sales and banking. (4)The drive for direct imperial political-military *control* to repress mass resistance resulting from the pillage of stages 1–3, and to extend and deepen privatization to include the lucrative energy, raw material and light and power public enterprises. Stage four is the preparation for the imposition of ALCA—the final stage of empire building—the re-colonization of Latin America.

How the Empire Rules

The key to empire-building—the dynamic of imperialism—is the dynamic role of the *imperial state* and its "quasi-private/public" auxiliaries in the private sector. The MNCs and financial expansion in Latin America are crucial for accumulation, and to counter the tendency for the rate of profit to decline. But it is also important to recognize the role of the imperial state in resolving the fundamental question of the locations (geographic/economic) where these processes play themselves out, the timing of the resolution or attempted resolution of these economic crises and the necessary political social relations and framework which enable these economic contradictions to be resolved. Over-production may drive the capitalist to turn to the conquest of overseas markets, but the "markets" will not open if local regimes are not forced to lower barriers via military invasions, coups, and the placement of imperial centered economist-ideologues in decision-making positions. The leverage of IFIs linked to the imperial state is also a basic component of market openness. The falling rate of profit of key economic sectors (and their leading MNC's) cannot be reversed if labor legislation in the client states is not "reformed" through the IFIs and mass organized resistance repressed by the police and military apparatus of the clients.

Thirty-five per cent rates of return are not secured in democratic, participatory societies with full employment and labor rights. Exorbitant rates of return, pillage of public resources, saturation of markets, and prompt full payment of debt in the midst of mass poverty requires bloody repression by client rulers, which is far beyond the capability of "market forces".

Strategic openings for the MNCs clearly require the massive systematic involvement of the imperial state. Economic empire building is intimately related to *client regime building* (what imperial ideologues call "nation-building"). The imperial state operating in Latin America not only creates the initial foundations of empire-centered development but is deeply involved in controlling, disciplining, recruiting, corrupting, co-opting and threatening electoral politicians to serve as local collaborators.

The empire rules via the IFIs which enforce economic discipline via loans, conditionality and threats—the purpose being to use debt obligations to deepen privatization and enforce compliance to the "open markets" policy.

The rule of the open market applies to Latin American but not for the US or the EU where selective protectionism reigns. The imperial state has established over 120 military bases throughout the world—including more than two dozen bases and operational locations throughout Latin America to recruit officials and to ideologically train them to identify with the empire, oppose anti-imperial adversaries and to intervene in time of regime crises. Most important, the imperial state intervenes to influence the political elites, financing candidates and parties, buying, co-opting, threatening, and seducing ascending political figures. Imperial policy makers encourage greater links with the MNC's and greater distance from popular constituencies. The latter activity involves long term cultivation of opposition figures from what the State Department calls the "responsible" left or the "democratic left" who provide the "right signals"—supporting electoral as opposed to mass struggle, compromises favoring consequential concessions to MNCs and an affinity for individual over collective mobility. The empire favors a personal profile of personalistic rule which provides an authoritarian setting for implementing harsh austerity rule for the many and large scale concessions to the rich, particularly the foreign rich.

The most recent successes of the imperial state's strategy of client regime building is found in Brazil and Ecuador. In both cases political leaders, Ignacio Da Silva and Lucio Gutierrez were backed by radical popular movements before they "turned" or converted to empire-centred policies via the process of ideological persuasion in line with a rightward shift in the leadership of their party apparatus.

The imperial state through its formal and informal links to US-based cultural institutions—both private and public – recruits media "stars", upwardly mobile intellectuals, students and journalists to design and promote empire-centered cultural practices and institutes which train activists and influence public opinion. The head of US-AID recently demanded that US-funded NGOs drop their "non-governmental" façade and openly declare that they are "an arm of the US government." (*Financial Times*, June 13, 2003). There are many "arms of the US government", admitted or not, which combine cultural entertainment and ideological indoctrination, world news and imperial propaganda, scholarship and foundation grants with empire-centered thinking and acting. The imperial state has created and defended this "public-private" cultural universe for economic empire building in Latin America. In summary Washington spends US tax dollars to finance the expansion of the US economic empire—depleting the republic. Nowhere is the direct ties between political-military empire building and rulership more clearly related to economic empire building than in Latin America and the process marches towards imperial colonial rule.

New Directions of Empire

Empire building has taken a new and more aggressive direction in the new millenium—embarking on a series of imperialist wars and conquests driven by the imperial state and directed by militarist ideologues. In the course of two years the US has engaged in two wars of conquests, innumerable assassinations and interventions throughout the world through clandestine "special forces operations" and the recruitment and co-optation of client rulers throughout Asia, Africa, Latin America and the Balkans. The empire builders have consolidated control over their Eastern European and Baltic clients and moved on to cement ties with the far right regimes of Spain and Italy. Under pressure, the initial resistance of the European Union has given way to becoming *subordinated associates* to the US, protecting US puppet regimes in Afghanistan, providing assistance to the US colonial regime in Iraq, backing the US threats and demands against Iran, and joining the attack on Cuba by supporting US funded Cuban agents.

The US empire builders have accelerated the process of colonization of Latin America via ALCA. There are several reasons why the US is pressing the colonization process: (1) clients and collaborators in Latin America are still in place, but their power is tenuous at best, (2) mass resistance is building up throughout the region, (3) the mercantilist, liberal-protectionist model of empire is provoking opposition among sectors of the Latin American export elites, (4) the US seeks to monopolize the takeover of the remaining major public enterprises as they are privatized—avoiding the losses to Europe, especially Spain, during the previous wave in the 1990s, (5) the military clients are still in place but they are not present everywhere and to the same degree particularly in Venezuela, Brazil, Ecuador, Bolivia, (6) the US has the "momentum" of its military-political conquests in Asia to pressure and blackmail conformity on Latin America political elites, (7) the surprise conversion of two regimes—Da Silva in Brazil, Gutierrez in Ecuador—to ALCA, and their vulnerability to mass opposition causes the empire builders to move with haste.

US empire builders have moved toward colonial domination with naked power and imperial-centered demands, ignoring any concessions to their client regimes, thus severely weakening their bases for compliance. The case of Mexico is clearest: The US has refused President Fox's request to legalize the status of 4 million Mexican migrant workers, or abide by reciprocity in trade agreements on transport, textiles and a number of other commodities. Instead Washington demands the complete privatization of Mexico's public petroleum industry (PEMEX)—the biggest revenue and foreign exchange earning firm in the country.

The historical precedent for the current process of US empire building in Latin America is the mercantilist system of the European colonial empires. The basic common features include: (1) overt imperial controls via a political authority (ALCA) which establishes the economic regulations and legal framework for

US monopolization of a privileged economic position in Latin America; (2) Imperial military command structures, bases, direct involvement in field operations to repress popular insurgencies; (3) Non-reciprocal trade involving total liberalization of Latin American trade and selective protective measures to prevent competitive Latin producers from competing successfully in the US market; (4) The effective exclusion of European, Japanese and others from competing in Latin American markets.

The neo-mercantilist imperial system is explicitly being implemented via ALCA on the economic side, and by Plan Colombia, the Andean Initiative and the continental coordination of military economic for the senior military commanders on the military front.

The perspective for empire building, re-colonization and consolidation rests on three political legs: (1)the co-optation of ex "popular" leaders such as Lula in Brazil, Gutierrez in Ecuador and Kirchner in Argentina; (2) the acceleration of ALCA-military accords in the face of decaying clients (Toledo in Peru, Sanchez de Losada in Bolivia and Uribe in Colombia); and (3) the isolation and/or overthrow of the Venezuelan and Cuban regimes and the defeat of the growing popular opposition in Latin America. ALCA will provide the US empire builders control over an institution, the ALCA Commission, which will make policy on every aspect of trade, investment, public-private relations, services (including education, health, pension, etc.). Just as the debt re-financing of Latin American regimes facilitated liberalization, the current neo-liberal regimes facilitate re-colonization via ALCA. Under US colonial rule the Latin administrative structures will stay in place, reduced and reconfigured, to implement US colonial policies taken within the ALCA commission. The Latin American legislature, executive and judicial powers will be reduced to debating the *methods*, pace and application of the ALCA-US dictated policies. Like all colonial systems vertical authoritarian structures will be superimposed over electoral institutions.

The growing military power of the US and its projections in Latin America have emboldened the empire builders to act more aggressively. In Venezuela a military-civilian coup and employers' lockout were orchestrated by US intelligence agencies. In Colombia, US military involvement has intensified the massacre and displacing hundreds of thousands of peasants to deprive the popular insurgents of recruits, food and logistical support. Against Cuba, Washington has openly organized nuclei of counter-revolutionary cadres (dubbed "dissidents") to engage in propaganda and recruitment, while explicitly including the revolutionary regime as its proximate military target. Throughout Latin America, US military bases have been established as beachhead for intervention in cases where client regimes might be overthrown by popular majorities.

Equally important are the *political conquests* of the empire builders. In Brazil, the Lula regime has been completely converted into a satellite of the empire—indiscriminately embracing the financial and agro-export elites which play an integral role in promoting ALCA and re-colonization. In Ecuador, Lucio Gutierrez and his partners, the Pachacutik party have moved swiftly to privatize the state petroleum and electrical companies, embrace dollarization, US military bases, Plan Colombia and ALCA, breaking strikes, and militarizing petrol refineries in the course of preparing the country for colonial status.

The "new perspectives" for colonization in Latin America *pre-existed* the events of 9/11 and the so-called US "war against terrorism". The new militarism after 9/11 *accelerated* the process of colonization and gave *greater* impetus to militarization and direct intervention. The most significant change since 9/11 was the total exclusion of any consultation and concessions to client regimes—making for even more lopsided relations.

It is futile at best and misleading at *worst* to speculate and take consolation from the fact that in some distant future time "all empires decline". Before that unspecified time takes place millions of lives are at stake, national sovereignty is at risk and popular struggles are taking place. To place "final judgments" in the centre of analysis is to distance oneself form the actors for change and from the real power of empire today, its logic and direction. Tendentious truisms, like "empires decline", provide us with no analytical framework for understanding the driving forces of imperialism and rising forces of opposition. Abstract and non-specific historical analysis and superficial discussion of the empire builders (their decisions are "frivolous") is itself frivolous and superficial. The "long view of history" divorced form concrete analysis of the dominant power of the US empire today and its drive for world-wide conquest and class-based anti-imperialist struggles is a mirror of the style of the ideologues of the empire builders. There is no end of imperial pundits who write of the "American Century", Pax Americana, Global Power and other vacuous "long views" of history.

To understand the current contradictions of empire we have to analyze concrete classes, ethnic-classes, the specific nature of regimes with their class configurations as well as the organizational capacities of the popular movements to mount challenges to imperial clients and the empire. To pontificate from abstract historical analogies and to discover the truism that empires eventually decline, has neither intellectual nor practical political relevance.

Empire: Class Relations and State

US empire building and decay is built on class and state relationships. Collaborator classes are formed through a complex process of internal class and political formation and external integration into subordinate but beneficial relations (for the elite). Hegemony and domination by transnational Latin American ruling classes is essential to shaping and supporting imperial client-states which implement the empire-centered "neo-liberal policies". The role of the imperial state was central to the formation of client states – both in terms of financial and political backing as well as providing the threats and personal rewards which induced active implementation of the privatization of lucrative public enterprises and the one-sided elimination of foreign trade and investment barriers.

What appears to overseas academic critics as "irrational" imperial aggression is in fact a highly rational calculus based on the historical ease with which imperial policy makers have secured a dominant position in the colonized economy, the compliance of client states and the eager support of the financial and speculative transnational Latin elites. Easy success in imposing empire-centered "models", in overthrowing and/or invading recalcitrant or nationalist Latin American regimes (in Chile, Brazil, Panama, Dominican Republic, etc.) has encouraged empire builders to act with greater violence, brazenly wielding force as the most reasonable weapon, given its efficiency in securing imperial goals. We should remember that the US interventionary success in Guatemala (1954) caused the US to repeat its policy with Cuba in 1961 – a policy which led to defeat. The successful US orchestrated military coups in Brazil (1964) and Indonesia (1965) and the invasion of the Dominican Republic (1965) encouraged the US to deepen and extend its military invasion of Indo-China which led to a historic but temporary defeat of imperial policymakers and the profound weakening of domestic political support.

The reconstruction of the empire building project under President Carter focused on political-ideological warfare on the favorable terrain of Eastern Europe and the USSR and the reconstruction of covert military surrogates in South Asia (Afghanistan) in alliance with fundamentalist Islamists. In Southern Africa (Angola and Mozambique) imperial policy makers financed and supplied tribalist surrogates backed by racist South Africa. In South and Central America (Argentina, Chile, Bolivia, El Salvador, and Guatemala) the US acted via client military regimes, and in Nicaragua via client drug-running mercenaries. From the late 1970s to 1990, the empire builders reconstructed the US military imperial apparatus and gradually reconquered domestic political support for overseas conquests through military invasions of Panama and Granada.

The "ideological formula" for imperial conquest is very similar to those used by the Third Reich: opposition leaders are demonized, the invasion and imposition of client regimes are described as liberation and the restoration of democracy and the incorporation into the US sphere of influence is described as becoming part of the "free world". The Carter-Reagan military empire created the foundations for Bush Father's launch into creating a new US-centred "New World Order" with the

Gulf War, a project which was premature and lacked a "colonial occupation" to insure uncontested control.

The Clinton decade (1992-2000) witnessed the massive expansion of empire building on a world scale—wars in the Balkans, conquest of third of Iraq via Kurdish clients in the north and 'no-fly' zones in the south (combined with punishing bombardments and economic blockades to destroy the state and economy), military alliances with new clients and military bases from the Baltic states through Central Europe to the Balkans and the Southern Caucuses. Aggressive military conquest and colonization began under the banner of humanitarian imperialism under Clinton. The doctrinal radicalization came with Bush, Rumsfeld and Wolfowitz. It is a serious and egregious error to view the date '9/11/2001' as the point of departure for military empire building. What occurred after 9/11 is the systematic, unilateral pursuit of empire building through a more explicit doctrine of global warfare, as opposed to the piecemeal but equally violent practice of humanitarian imperialism propounded by Clinton.

Empire and Class, State Relations: Inter-Imperialist and Class/National Conflict

In the first instance, imperial power is embedded in class and state relations: prior to the movement of capital and the imposition of imperial state power, a national-class struggle takes place, a struggle which varies in intensity but recurs throughout the period of imperial occupation and domination. As was pointed out earlier, in Latin America the imposition of the empire-centered neo-liberal regimes was established through a violent class-state struggle "from above". The victorious transnational classes re-configured the state, in order to "reconstruct" social relations (labor-capital relations, public-private and foreign-national property forms) to conform to the empire-centered model. The neo-liberal regimes and neo-mercantilist empires were products of class struggles as are the continuing antagonistic relations which confront the empire builders re-colonization project.

Antagonistic class relations are a constant of contemporary

empire building. However the social relations, class, ethnic and gender forces which confront each other today are different from the recent past due to the transformation of the class structure wrought by a quarter of a century of neo-liberal rulership. It is important to summarize the changes in class formation in order to understand the contemporary social classes confronting the empire builders and local client states. The new class forces have in turn developed new tactics, strategies and leadership which are central to the efforts to overthrow imperial domination.

Basic Changes in Class Structure and Social Relations

Since the onset of neo-liberalism in the 1970s several key political and socio-economic changes have emerged in class structure. The opening of the economy to cheap foreign manufactured imports has had two major impacts on the class structure: it has reduced the size of the industrial working class, established a "captive workforce" in the free trade zones 'maquiladores'/assembly plants, reduced the number of skilled metal workers, and created smaller more exploitative decentralized 'contract labour' industries. As a consequence, the size of the employed stable industrial labour force has declined in most countries (like Bolivia, Peru, Colombia, Brazil and Argentina) while those who remain employed fear their replacement because of the willingness of employers to deploy the reserve army of unemployed. The relative social-political weight of the industrial workers within the working class has declined, as have the percentage of unionized workers and the number of strikes and labor militancy in the industrial sector. On the other hand, the number of unemployed and underemployed workers has increased geometrically, running from 40% to 80% in countries like Argentina, Peru, Bolivia, Colombia, Brazil, Venezuela and Mexico. The older maquiladora industrial regions—the Northern Mexican border regions, the Caribbean—have experienced plant closings as US capitalists relocate to China or to the "rural areas' (Southern Mexico) where salaries are lower and working conditions even more exploitative (longer hours, less safety, health and environmental regulations. The growth of a "critical mass" of unemployed workers has led to the growth of autonomous movements of unemployed workers who attack the capitalist class *outside* of the site of production (the factory) in the streets, blocking the circulation of machinery and raw materials (inputs) and finished products (outputs) transported to the market, putting constraints on the realization of profit.

The promotion of an "export-growth strategy" along with the import of subsidized low-priced food, particularly grains, has led to the displacement of peasants and the bankruptcy of family farmers producing for local markets. Over 90% of state agricultural subsidies are channeled to large scale agro-exporters, denying small producers state credits and financing. Empire centered agricultural policies have increased the percentage and number of landless, rural workers, polarized the countryside and radicalized small family farmers facing extinction because of client state's intervention in favour of food imports and agro-export elites. Growing land concentration, encroachment on indigenous people's land, the high cost of farm inputs and low prices of food products have radicalized the peasant and Indian-peasant communities, depriving them of land, markets and profit margins. The growth of literacy and social interaction with progressive Church and trade union nuclei and the recent experiences of struggle has turned the countryside into a center of anti-imperialist movements.

Contemporary rural movements are not composed of "primitive rebels, backward looking "traditionalists" resisting "modernization". The campesino movements are led by educated sons and daughters of downwardly mobile rural families, seeking to secure credits, and market shares, recover land occupied by capital, and state protection from subsidized cheap imports. Seekers of the modern means of production, market shares, inexpensive credits and 'fair prices', working and struggling collectively are the hallmarks of modern but impoverished rural classes. They are knowledgeable about the negative impact of empire centered policies (ALCA, neo-liberalism). In Brazil, the Rural Landless Workers Movement (MST), in Bolivia (the cocaleros), in Colombia (the peasant and rural guerrilla movements), in Ecuador (sectors of the Indian-peasant movement) and to a lesser extent in Paraguay, Peru and Mexico, peasant-based movements have been the best organized and cutting edges of the anti-imperialist resistance.

The contradiction empire-peasantry has been the most acute, not because of greater exploitation and extraction of surplus value, but because of the threat of *total displacement* (land, home, family, community), *violent appropriation of the means of production,* and denial of a location to 'earn a living'. The rural labor force is highly stratified and in many cases ethnically diverse, leading to socio-political divisions; however where these 'differences" have been overcome, the combative organized rural classes have been most successful in challenging the empire's expansion—in the countryside as well as the cities. The MST has occupied big landholdings and settled 350,000 families in less the 20 years and currently has 120,000 families organized to occupy uncultivated estates (July 2003). In Bolivia over 40,000 families earn a living farming coca in vibrant communities with stable families thanks to the organization and struggles of the cocalero farmers' union. The major military challenge in Latin America to client regimes and the US military empire builders is in the Colombian countryside, where the two major guerrilla groups (FARC and ELN) control over 40% of the countryside. Many of the major national organizations organizing urban demonstrations against ALCA are located, more often than not, among the militant rural organizations.

Given the visible and dominant role of modern rural based agrarian movements in opposing the US empire, it is surprising that *no* systematic discussion occurs in the writing of Hobsbawn, Wallerstein, and other prophets of eventual imperial decline. These writers emphasize inter-imperial rivalries, inter-elite conflicts (capitalists against empire), basing their arguments on specific trade disputes and differences concerning the modes of empire building or general, tendentious and emotionally gratifying notions that "all empires decline", all "capitalist systems eventually go into crises"—leaving it to the magic of the marketplace to bring about what they call "systemic changes" from "chaos". A visit to a meeting of peasants in an occupied estate is likely to provide a sufficient stimulus for these armchair empire-centered prophets to re-think their theories of imperial decline.

The New Urban Proletariat—Public Sector Workers

In June-July 2003, in Ecuador, Bolivia, Peru, Brazil, Argentina and Colombia public employees—mostly public school teachers - were engaged in indefinite strikes, involving millions, and in some cases detonating work stoppages by private sector wage workers. In the cities the public employees have been at the cutting edge of the biggest and most militant urban struggles against the client regimes and their empire centered policies. This is necessarily the case because imperial expansion is premised on the *privatization of public enterprises,* resulting in massive firings, loss of pension and other social benefits and job tenure. Second, the imperial creditors demand budget surpluses to pay the debt to foreign creditors, meaning cutbacks in all social services and public development spending which leads to further slashing of the number of public employees, the reduction of salary, pension and social benefits and greater intensification of workloads (teacher-student ratios and doctor-patient ratios). The loss of tenure and the hiring of contract workers (NGOs) have undermined the job security of public employees—making them subject to the same "market insecurities" as manufacturing workers. In sum, the empire-building strategies of privatization of public firms, the priority of debt payments in budget allocation and the proletarianization of living standards and working conditions are the objective factors driving the public employees into the streets and into prolonged nationwide strikes.

The principle coalition partners in all the major confrontations with client states and their imperial patrons are the public employees, especially the teachers and the peasants. The most militant trade union actions in the provincial and capital cities are led by the public employees, involving the occupation of municipal and federal buildings, the blocking of streets and ousters f public officials. Frequently, public employees have been reduced to near indigence because of delays in payments and/

or payments in devalued currency. In Brazil, public employees have lost 20% of their real income as salaries were frozen from 1998-2003. In the Argentine provinces, municipal workers are delayed payments for 3–4 months and then paid in local, provincial currency.

The new protagonists of anti-imperialist politics include : the rural landless, farmer and peasant movements, the urban unemployed and the self-employed (especially in Argentina, Venezuela, Bolivia and Peru) and the public employees throughout the region particularly the workers in the petroleum and gas industries targeted for privatization. Their specific demands are frequently linked to the rejection of ALCA, US military bases and the empire-centered policies of client regimes.

Empire-Building: Omnipotence is in the Eyes of the Observer

In the US mass media and in the public utterances by the Washington elite the advance of the US empire appears to be an inevitable, always successful, totally justified and irreversible process, to be applauded or suffered. To critics the "internal contradictions" or "over-extension" of empire will lead the empire-builders to their own downfall.

The sense of imperial omnipotence permeates both the celebrants and pessimists who take a long term view of empire. What both "long term" historical speculators and short-term apologists lack is any in depth understanding of the *concrete struggles* which shape the correlation of forces today which will determine whether empire is with us for a few years, a decade or a century.

The US empire-builders have suffered several important defeats in a series of important confrontations. In Venezuela, the urban poor, the unemployed, the self-employed in the hundreds of thousands came down from the 'ranchos' in Caracas and provided the impetus to military loyalists to overthrow the dictatorial Carmona regime imposed by a military-civilian coup orchestrated by the US and to restore the populist elected Hugo Chavez to the presidency. A year later, US–backed economic, media and trade union clients attempted to overthrow the regime by paralyzing the petroleum industry.

Empire Building and Rule : 235

They also were defeated by an alliance of loyalist military officials, sectors of the working class and the mass of urban poor, many organized in "Bolivarian circles", barrio-based mass organizations.

In Colombia, the US effort to establish dominance through paramilitary and state terror campaigns ordered by client President Uribe have been decisively contained by the Revolutionary Armed Forces of Colombia—People Army (FARC-EP) and the National Liberation Front (ELN), despite thousands of US financed mercenaries, contract workers and combat advisers working with a budget of over $2 billion dollars and with the most up-to-date technology and helicopter gunships.

In Bolivia, the cocaleros have successfully resisted the US orchestrated campaign to destroy the coca farmers and their organizations. Despite US client President Sanchez de Losada's violent repression and direct intervention by the US Ambassador in Bolivian politics, the cocaleros have created, in association with miners, the urban poor, the factory workers and self-employed in Cochabamba, La Paz, Sucre and Oruco a formidable coalition capable of blocking neo-liberal policies—such as the privatization of water – building a national political movement which is the main opposition party in Congress, and a national leadership with the capacity to defeat Bolivia's entry into ALCA.

In Cuba, the urban and rural mass movements provided solid support to the revolutionary regime's successful effort to dismantle US-financed terrorist networks as well as embryonic propaganda cells promoted by the head of the US interest section.

The most successful challenges and defeats to US empire-building have taken place in the Third World, by autonomous organized class forces. The least consequential opponents of empire building are the former social democratic, center-left and populist electoral regimes who have largely adopted the empire-centered economic and social strategies and have allied with Latin American transnational capitalists and US and EU multi-nationals. The most striking example is the Inacio "Lula" da Silva and the Workers Party (PT) regime. The PT regime has been converted into a servile client of the US, appointing key economic ministers and a central banker who are totally integrated into empire-centered "development" project. Da Silva's monetarist economic program of reducing public employees' pensions, sharp cuts in social spending, regressive taxation and pro-employer "labor reform" is only part of a pro-empire agenda. Similar processes have occurred with other pseudo-populist electoral politicians in Ecuador with Lucio Gutierrez and in Peru with Toledo. The most significant development is the speed with which the mass of the class-based movements—particularly the public employees, peasants and self-employed—mobilize to confront and attack these new clients of empire. In each instance, the masses who voted for the "center-left" are the identical forces in the streets demanding their resignation as collaborators of imperialism.

Throughout the Latin American continent, there is virtually no organized mass movement organized by the capitalist class —or for that matter by the small and medium sized business people or farmers, though a minority occasionally support particular protests on issues of debt payments, interest rates and protectionism. What precludes inclusion of the bourgeoisie into the mass struggles, is their support of neo-liberal anti-labor legislation, the low level of the minimum wage, the reduction in social security taxes and the regime's tolerance of widespread tax evasion and corrupt links with lower level custom and trade officials regarding import duties and export licenses.

The socio-political movements which have close links with "center-left" regimes, converted into imperial clients, have been severely disoriented and in some cases are in the process of internal debates and discussions. The MST and CUT in Brazil, CONAIE in Ecuador, the unemployed workers movement in Argentina, the trade unions in Uruguay, all face the problem of choosing between anti-imperialist class struggle or collaboration with the new "center-left" electoral client regimes of the empire.

In contrast to the class-based, politically oriented struggle for state power, which have dealt blows to imperial expansion, the amorphous "anti-globalization" movements and World

Social Forums have not defeated any of the empire-building projects nor have they been successful in preventing a single military conquest. Moreover the "anti-globalization"leaders have not created any mass support for the popular anti-imperialist resistance to US military occupation and pillage in the Balkans, Afghanistan or Iraq. The mass demonstrations are ritual events limited in time and space. They lack tactics or strategies which have a major impact on imperial expansion, war preparations, privatizations, structural adjustment policies or any other empire-centered measures. Only when US imperial rivals in Europe (particularly France, Germany, Italy and Spain) take measures to make their MNCs more competitive by lowering pensions or increasing retirement age or slashing social expenditures, do workers demonstrate. Only in France is their any effort by the workers' movement to go beyond limited "ritual" strikes—symbolic protests which may delay but certainly do not eliminate the imposition of domestic burdens to finance imperial expansion.

The orderly time-bounded mass anti-war demonstrations symbolically confront state power—they marched through the city of London to Hyde Park to hear anti-imperialist speeches by speakers but lack the capacity to paralyze the system or engage in serious political warfare. It is the nature of 'crowds' to come and leave as they please, lacking any organized political structures. The leftist sects are confined to selling their newspapers or distributing leaflets for radical forums while self-described anarchists (and police provocateurs) break a few shop windows to convince themselves that they are anti-capitalists.

The strength of the anti-imperialist movement is found among the guerrillas in the jungles of Colombia, the Bolivarian circles in the urban slums of Caracus, the street demonstrations of Cuba, the landless workers occupying the fazendas of Brazil, the coca farmers of Bolivia, the underemployed and unemployed urban poor of Peru and Argentina—in a word the organized classes, displaced, exploited and impoverished by the empire-centered client regimes.

Toward a Theory of Anti-Imperialist Movements

Any theory of anti-imperialism must be by its nature tentative and contingent as it attempts to deal with the fluid nature of class and national subjectivity—consciousness.

A theory of anti-imperialist movements (AIM) must take into consideration several contingent factors: (1) All mass popular AIM are *linked to the struggle for immediate or concrete economic demands*. For example, the coca farmers demand the end of the coca eradication program, the expulsion of the US military bases and oppose ALCA. The Brazilian MST links the expropriation of non-productive land and an agrarian reform to its demands for protection of local food producers and opposition to ALCA. (2) AIM are build upon the *structural weaknesses and economic losses of its constituent supporters*. The Mexican farmers and peasants oppose the North American Free Trade Agreement (NAFTA) because it has permitted the entry into the Mexican market of subsidized US food exports which has impoverished and bankrupted millions of Mexicans. Collective socio-political mobilization and power compensates for the relative market or economic weakness of the Latin American producers. (3) Economic and objective structural conditions are universally necessary but not sufficient conditions for the emergence of AIM.

Throughout Latin America there are hundreds of millions of people exploited and displaced by the empire builders, but only a fraction are conscious and/or organized for struggle. Historical, organizational, structural, political, demographic and geographic factors play a significant role in creating anti-imperialist consciousness. What most AIMs in Latin America have in common is their predominantly, but not exclusively, rural 'center' of organization. The peasants are at the centre of AIM because imperialism has hit hardest at the rural economy even as one can see the negative impact of imperial centered policies on urban unemployment in Argentina, Colombia and elsewhere. The rural social movements are more advanced because their level of organization is stronger and political leadership has emerged which is not beholden to the power brokers of the client regimes. The reasons for stronger agrarian organization are not because the rural sector is larger in size—actually in relative and absolute terms it in declining—but because the militant rural leaders are far more *independent* than the state subsidized urban trade unions, and because they have closer links to their peasant base (in fact most are of peasant or small farmer background). Moreover the rural movements are not confronted with reactionary trade union apparatuses linked to the bosses as is the case in the traditional industrial sectors. In other words, the subjective factor in the countryside is less encumbered with ministerial ties and conservative trade union apparatuses which block the articulation of demands, demobilize popular sectors, and accommodate to the empire building strategies.

The cocaleros, the MST, the FARC, the Zapatistas, and until recently, the CONAIE, play a decisive role in confronting imperialism because their leaders and organizations are able to articulate popular demands free of state commitments, allowing them to mobilize and take direct action which advances the popular struggle. The urban-based AIM movements are more diverse but usually linked to the left-wing trade unions of the public sector workers, the unemployed, the mass of worker-consumers and the beneficiaries of social programs promoted by anti-imperialist regimes in the case of Cuba and Venezuela. Downwardly mobile educated professionals (health workers, teachers), formerly skilled metal workers-turned unemployed, and impoverished consumers hit by declining incomes, rising prices and rising transport and utility rates (power, light, water, telephone, public transport, etc.) of privatized foreign-owned enterprises have spearheaded the urban AIM.

The North American and European "anti-globalization movements" organize in reaction to specific elite events (WTO meetings, European Union summits, etc.) but have no organized links to a mass base. As a result their activities have no real continuity in struggle apart from the specific elite events and have little impact on the ongoing economic and military expansion of empire. Even more seriously, only a very small minority of the northern anti-globalization movements are engaged in ongoing struggles against the imperial colonization and repression of the conquered peoples of Iraq and Afghanistan, and the economic colonization of Latin America via ALCA.

While the mass protests of the anti-globalization and anti-war movements are positive in the sense of demonstrating public opposition, they have no political perspective and little if any links to mass popular struggle or constituencies in contrast to the Latin American AIM. In other words, consequential AIM are decidedly a phenomenon of the oppressed nations—and in particular the exploited rural and urban classes who are economically displaced, downwardly mobile and linked to socio-political movements led by a new generation of grass roots leaders, autonomous of the state and the center-left electoral parties.

Future of Empire

It is difficult to speculate with any accuracy the moment when the US empire will begin to decline. It is even more difficult to determine if the decline is structural or conjunctural. The best that can be done is to delineate the principle contradictions. The major contradictions are political and social as much as they are economic. The fundamental contradiction and challenge today is between Latin America's organized rural and urban masses and the US empire builders and their client rulers, transnational capitalists and NGO/trade union auxiliaries. The second major contradiction is between the expanding empire and the declining republic—and the capacity of the imperial ruling class to transfer wealth, revenues and personnel to empire building. The third contradiction is between the conquest and occupation of colonized countries and the mass national anti-colonial resistance movements—as in Iraq and Afghanistan.

The fourth contradiction is between the growing military empire and the inability to extract profits from the newly colonized regions, future oil revenues notwithstanding.

The centrality of third world struggles to weakening the US empire is best illustrated by the effects of the Iraqi resistance on the US occupation army. The US colonial occupation forces are taking daily casualties—deaths and injuries throughout the country at the hands of the popularly backed Iraqi guerrillas. The most immediate effect is to lower the moral of the US occupying forces. The US military's rapid disenchantment and openly expressed hostility toward any long term occupation is one of the weakest links in the US empire—as it was in the aftermath of the Second World War, and the Korean and Indo-Chinese wars. This key weakness of the US imperial armed forces means that the militarists have a serious problem in sustaining colonial conquests—unless there is a major infusion of foreign legionaires from India, Pakistan, Turkey, Eastern Europe and other client regimes.

The vast technological superstructure of the US imperial war machine, ultimately relies on the ground troops to occupy and consolidate imperial rule. The problem however is that the nature of US ground troops are not compatible with long term policing of colonies. First much of the occupying army is made up of reservists—not life time enlisted soldiers—who joined the military to supplement their civilian pay and secure health and pension benefits not otherwise available. The reservists' idea of "military service" is one night a week training and short term summer exercises, with calls to short term active duty in times of national emergency. This outlook is incompatible with long term colonial occupation. This sector of the military has little stomach for prolonged absence from job, family, school and community, especially in Iraq and Afghanistan facing the harsh conditions of intense heat, lack of water and decent living facilities, widespread popular hostility and frequent sniper attacks. Second, many of the enlisted soldiers joined to escape unemployment or low income dead-end jobs with the hope of 'learning a trade' and returning to civilian life. Few volunteers expected face to face combat on hostile terrain. Third, the "professional soldiers" resent being assigned colonial police activities, particularly given the hostile day to day environment and the total incompetence of the higher echelons of the military command in reconstructing a basic infrastructure. Fourth, there is a profound gap in "soldiering" between the affluent, upwardly mobile, media savvy air conditioned generals and colonels, who fly to the occupied countries for reports, reviews and press conferences and fly out to their secure, well-serviced headquarters in Qatar, Florida or Washington, for fillet mignon dinners, while the occupation forces lodged in flea-bag tents, eating plastic wrap rations, lacking water for showers and toilets and facing the universal hostility of the conquered Iraqi people.

Fifth, the occupation forces are increasingly resentful and frustrated by the lies and deceptions from the high command regarding their tenure of service. The gap between the ideals and promises and the reality is sending shock waves throughout the occupation forces. First, they were told they would be welcomed as a "liberating army"; instead they confront general hostility and are justifiably considered an army of oppressors. They were told they would work with "free Iraqis" to rebuild the country, instead they patrol broken streets in armored carriers, engaging in housebreaking and massive military sweeps. Most significantly, they were told they would fight the war, conquer the country and return home as heroes. Instead, they are now told they will have to spend years ducking grenades and bullets to sustain an inept and universally hated colonial governor.

The US military, which was trained for high tech war, faces urban warfare in the streets, universities, and neighborhoods where the Iraqi resistance has all the advantage of knowing the terrain and having the support of the local people. Rumsfeld's propaganda about the urban resistance being simply a "remnant" of the defeated Baathist forces rings false to the soldiers who experience hostility from grammar school children to the millions of Muslims who were previously persecuted by Saddam Hussein.

The dilemma of the civilian militarists is that the 160,000 US troops in Iraq are inadequate to control 24 million Iraqis demanding self-determination. Given the fact that the US military requires at least 5 non-combat soldiers for every active combatant, and given the decline in recruitment of "volunteers" in the face of the harch demands of being an occupying army, the civilian militarists have no choice but to limit the rotation of troops and to seek "multilateral" assistance from clients and allies. What the civilian militarists are not willing to do is to return to general conscription. As past draft dodgers, the militarists in the Bush administration have no desire to call up their children and grandchildren to risk their lives for their empire. Both upper middle class gentiles and Zionists have no desire to pull their progeny from the elite universities and professional schools or lucrative banking and financial careers to fight "international terrorism".

Finally, the civilian-military rulers in charge of the colonial policy is itself totally divorced , not only from the swelling mass opposition in Iraq and from their own increasing rebellions ground troops, but from sectors of their own military officials. The Rumsfeld-Wolfowitz ideologues discredited and bypassed the military and CIA intelligence sources created their own "inner circles" in order to impose their own highly politicized "intelligence" to justify military conquest. Their obsession with imperial conquest, military dominance is fueled with racist anti-Arab animus and driven by the idea of a greater US-Israel "co-prosperity sphere" in the Middle East. The organizational-ideological division at the top of the imperial military-intelligence organization can over time seriously erode the power of the civilian militarists.

As the "republic" is replaced by the empire, it is more than likely that one of the principle sources of conflict and rebellion may occur within the military and this may eventually have an impact on domestic politics. The war and the drive for colonial control has generalized strong anti-colonial popular resistance in the occupied countries and daily casualties to the imperial ground forces. These factors (resistance, casualties, military discontent) are beginning to effect the popularity of the colonial war. The negative image in the US results form the US casualties, the economic and political chaos in Iraq, the costs of conquest and the incompetence of the colonial rulers. Even noted imperialist apologists are bemoaning the lack of "preparation" or "capacity" of strategists for colonial domination. Unilateral US military action benefited the short term militarists intent on unrestricted warfare, but it undermines the bases for securing multi-lateral financial and military support in post-conquest colony building.

The highly charged and emotional diatribes of the civilian militarists with their neo-nazi "voluntarist" "will to world power" is crashing into the reality of reluctant vassal states, the resurgence of mass Iraqi opposition and the growing rebelliousness of US troops in the occupied lands. Those ideologues and politicians who take their cues from the Israeli-Sharon strategy of massive unilateral force to secure colonies, forget that Sharon cannot exist without the support of the US government and the Zionist Diaspora—the US has neither a supporting power nor affluent benefactors.

Some observers, focusing on discrepancies over tactical and commercial disputes argue for growing inter-imperialist rivalries between the EU and the US. What is significant about these conflicts is how quickly they are defused, how small is their impact and more recently how quickly the disputants are reconciled to jointly pursuing empire building.

For example, the opposition of some European countries to the US-British invasion of Iraq was subsequently followed by an agreement within the European Union to build their own rapid deployment forces. France sent paratroopers into three African countries shortly after the Iraq war. Europe's decision to follow the US is illustrated by its decision to reduce relations with Cuba, collaborate with the US in isolating Iraq, approve US promoted resolutions against the spread of 'weapons of mass destruction', etc.. The imperial linkages between Europe and the US are far stronger than their competing interests. Equally important the strength of the US military and economic empire and its aggressive exercise has intimidated the would-be critics in France and Germany who are surrounded by US satellites in Eastern Europe, the Baltic nations and the Balkans.

The economy of the US republic is built on speculation, fraud, credit, debt, cheap immigrant labor, huge direct and indirect state subsidies, foreign borrowings and large and growing trade and budget deficits. When the economy moves from stagnation into a major recession it will weaken the empire *if* the state is unable to foist the burden of recovery on the backs of the wage, salaried and small business groups and *if* the state is forced to reallocate resources and personnel from empire-building to the republic. Unfortunately the record of the last quarter century tells us that the US public has shown little active resistance to military spending in times of war and only minority opposition to imperial conquest.

The trade unions are politically impotent and linked to the empire through their ties to the Democratic Party. There is no national political and social movement in existence capable of challenging the empire builders, today or in the foreseeable future. With more than 90% of the private sector work force non-union, the workers not only show little if any political influence, they do no even possess the social organization which could potentially reallocate the budget toward greater social instead of military spending. One of the great advantages of the US empire builders over Europe and even Japan is precisely their capacity to exploit workers (longer hours of work, no national health, pension or vacation plans), fire workers easily and cheaply, and relocate firms. US empire builders key comparative advantage against its potential European and Japanese rivals is based on its control over the most backward working class in the industrialized world.

The highly exploitative social relations of productions in the US provide the surplus necessary for overseas expansion and limit the possibilities of the downwardly mobile wage and salaried classes from challenging the decline of the Republic.

The argument for the decline of empire cannot count on any automatic economic collapse or internal rebellion or consequential division between economic and military empire builders. The empire will be defeated from without or it will not be defeated at all. Only with external defeats will internal dissent or opposition emerge, activating the exploited and the poor, particularly the black and Hispanic population. The particularities of the US empire in contrast to Europe, Asia and elsewhere is that it totally lacks a tradition of working class or left-wing anti-imperialism. The opposition in the recent past was directed at "global capital" and the policies and practices of the MNCs. Except for a small minority , there was no sense among the anti-globalization movement that the central issue was the US imperial state. Nor even at the height of the recent anti-war movement was there any understanding of the imperial-colonial nature of the war. This was evident in the subsequent virtual disappearance of the anti-war movement, once the war began. During the US occupation, colonial rule and massacre of Iraqis protesting the US occupation and destruction of their economy, there was virtually no anti-colonial movement. The only long-standing internal opposition to US imperial policy occurred during the Vietnam War *because of the prolonged length and effectiveness of the Indo-Chinese resistance movements, the defeat of the US and the large number of US military deaths and casualties.*

The current empire builders have learned from their previous defeats—they do not hesitate to launch massive aerial attacks, use mini-nuclear weapons (uranium-tipped shells) and mobilize mercenaries from their new client regimes in England, Poland, the Ukraine, etc. They resort to recruiting thousands of private mercenaries subcontracted by the Pentagon in implementing Plan Colombia and the pacification of the Balkans. The problem of "over-extension" is then not an irremediable problem, particularly since the EU has implemented a similar program of rapid deployment forces to invade and occupy countries where clients are in danger or independent states or movements emerge.

The dynamics of the US empire-building are still in full force even as contradictions deepen and fissures appear. The imperialist state commands the allegiance of its domestic ruling class and substantial sectors of a fragmented, chauvinistic, downwardly mobile population despite growing unease among the public as the Iraqi resistance grows. The imperial economy continues to dominate key sectors of world investment, trade and finance through its multi-nationals. The military empire builders have established more military bases in more regions than ever before ,openly embracing a doctrine of permanent warfare and military intervention anywhere in the world—with the acquiescence of Europe and Japan.

Has the US empire "peaked"? Perhaps. But the current imperial projections are for further wars. New imperial colonial networks are being consolidated. In Latin America the conversion of the Da Silva regime to ALCA and the formation of a US-Brazil-Mexico nexus assures the US of new bigger markets and the implementation of vast privileged opportunities for US MNCs. The US-Israel nexus promotes a Middle East "Free Market Zone" dominated by the two powers.

The promoters US imperial-colonial conquest draw no limits, experience no internal constraints and possess willing accomplices among the other great and lesser powers, most of whom are eager to make amends for their meek dissent over US tactics in the run-up to the Iraqi conquest. The evidence is clear—EU has taken up the US cudgels in attacking Cuba, Iran, North Korea with unprecedented vehemence and threats, gaining merit points from Washington. On the bases of the US successful conquest of Iraq, the empire builders in the EU and Japan have decided that it is better to join the US war machine and share the spoils of conquest rather than be excluded in the future.

If our evidence and arguments hold, it is clear that imperial rivalries, internal opposition and economic contradiction will not play a decisive role in the "decline of the empire". Mass political-social struggles in the colonized nations and client states are the driving forces calling into question the durability of the empire, its longevity and its successes and losses. The mass popular resistance in Iraq is delaying oil deliveries, undermining military morale, bringing out all the ugly totalitarian feature of a murderous occupation force. The large scale guerrilla force in Colombia blocks US MNCs expansion and undermines US military strategies. The continuing Palestinian resistance blocks the consolidation of Greater Israel and US-Israeli plans for a wider free trade zone. The urban mass uprising in Venezuela defeated the US-backed bosses lockout and undermined US efforts to monopolize petrol from Venezuela to Iraq. The Cuban revolutionary regime remains a model and hope of resistance to hundreds of millions in the Third World.

Only when these and other struggles *detonate* wider regional uprisings and radical struggles, increasing US casualties and costs, will opposition emerge in the US and the EU. Rival imperial powers may take advantage of the decline to assert their own imperial interests and dissociate themselves from a weakening empire.

US empire building is not merely a product of US "accumulation on a world scale", nor has the military empire builders exceeded the boundaries of economic possibility ('overreach'). The build-up of empire has proceeded with ups and downs for over half a century—accelerating in the recent period with the demise of the Sino-Soviet bloc and its nationalist allies in the Third World. Both Democrats and Republicans, Clinton and Bush Administrations eagerly seized opportunities to extend military bases, launch colonial conquests and impose client regimes, even as the ideological justifications varied between the rulers. Rulers from both major US parties have subordinated the economy of the Republic to the Empire. Both parties pursue ALCA—the first promoted it, the second implemented it. The US political party system, congress, the court system and the mass media are totally embedded in the imperial system. The imperial values and interests of Christian fundamentalists, Zionist ideologues, civilian militarists, bankers and the CEO's of the MNC.s are embedded in the imperial state.

Most US citizens defending the empire do not receive the spoils of empire (rather they finance it), but they are still imbued with a racial-nationalist ideology which arrogates all good to themselves and evil to the critics and overseas adversaries of the state. Change will only come when the reality of Third World resistance and revolts undermine the US military will to conquer.

The Left in Latin America: Questions of Theory and Practice

Ronald H. Chilcote[*]

This essay synthesises generally known information and assesses the current state of the left by focusing on some essential questions of theory and practice. The socialist camp that once offset the dominance and imperial ambitions of the United States no longer exists today, yet the advances of neoliberalism are being countered by newly elected representatives who reject a world that promotes wealth for the few and deepens the poverty of the majority. The emerging progressive governments in Latin America, however, have limited programs and resources, and while the conditions for a profound transformation may be established, the transformation itself may not be possible until well into the future. It may also be useful to recast our understanding of the left which in the past may have been synonymous with being revolutionary or Marxist or with the radical or vanguard political party. Marta Harnecker, a close observer, has suggested that being leftist today "means to fight or be committed to a societal project that opposes the capitalist

---

[*] This essay is drawn from a paper presented to the meetings of the Latin American Studies Association, Dallas, Texas, March 27–29, 2003

logic of profit-making and that seeks to build a society with a humanistic logic" (2002:4). The oasis of the Latin American left, she feels, is found in the World Social Forum, based in Porto Alegre, Brazil, with initiatives emanating from the social movements and nongovernmental organisations and scepticism directed against the political parties of the left whose positioning has often approximated the practices and rhetoric of the traditional conservative and liberal parties.

Theoretical Directions

Many questions face the progressive scholar interested in Latin America. At the top of my list, and what I would briefly like to examine here, is whether a globalisation perspective is useful today and how it relates to the historical experience of US domination and the prospects for real development in a complex capitalist world. Yet we could also consider other important research themes such as the role of the state in public and private capital formation and the provision of essential services to all people in need. Or whether formal or representative democracy can be replaced by new forms of participatory democracy in the political economy. Or assessing the prospects for grassroots and social movements in contrast to the weaknesses of traditional political parties and institutions in the process of mobilising people to become involved in overcoming their conditions of poverty and inequality.

My recent attention has focused on an overview of development in relation to imperialism and globalisation, and here I only wish to summarise my argument. Late in the nineteenth century and until World War II imperialism was the general expression for these relationships, and thereafter up to the late twentieth century development, underdevelopment, and dependency were fashionable, whereas since the 1990s to the present globalisation has become the mode while stimulating debate and controversy.

Imperialism dates to Roman expansion and the Latin word *imperium*, implying command and supreme authority. During the early nineteenth century it was associated with the

Napoleonic empire, later with expanding British colonialism, and by the end of the century it was commonly incorporated into descriptions of the dominance of one nation over another and a "new" imperialism characterised by European and US expansionism. Marx and Engels did not focus on imperialism yet their reference to the expanding international market may be seen as a way to understand later conceptions in the thought of J.A. Hobson, Rudolf Hilferding, Nikolai Bukharin, and V.I. Lenin in a classical Marxist understanding of imperialism with emphasis on the merging of industrial and bank capital into finance capital and monopoly. These theoretical underpinnings of imperialism were assimilated into polemical condemnation and denunciation of capitalist domination and exploitation of the advanced nations over backward areas. (For further detail and analysis, see Chilcote, 2000, 2000a and 2000b).

After World War II, intellectuals in the newly emerging nations began to search for a new theory to explain their backwardness. Understanding imperialism as a manifestation of capitalism in an advanced phase helped in their explanations, but they also attempted to move theory based on external considerations to analysis of why and how imperialism impacted upon their internal national situation, and, in particular, upon social class distinctions and struggle. This theory became known in varying forms, from the attention to economic surplus and backwardness described by Paul Baran to the theory of capitalist development of underdevelopment in André Gunder Frank or the new dependency of Theotónio dos Santos, the subimperialism of Ruy Mauro Marini, to the associated dependent capitalism of Fernando Henrique Cardoso. These theories rarely referred to the early ideas of Marx and Lenin, yet they obscured the old theories of imperialism and became very popular among intellectuals in the regions outside Europe and the United States, and especially in Latin America. Two theoretical directions emerged, one advocating revolutionary and socialist outcomes, based on the promise and example of the Cuban Revolution, and the other that envisaged a reformist path and the development of the capitalist means of production (Chilcote, 1984, and the reader is encouraged to find more background in the excellent syntheses on development in Kay, 1989; Larraín, 1989; and Lehman, 1990).

Among the similarities between the theories of dependency and imperialism were a periodisation around dependency and trade monopolies under colonialism, financial industrialism at the end of the nineteenth century, and capital investment by multinational corporations and penetration in the internal markets of underdeveloped countries after World War II. The theories also were based on structural dichotomies: political (metropole and satellite), geographical (core and periphery) and economic (development and underdevelopment). Finally, both theories emphasised the international implications of unequal or uneven development.

An uncritical and widespread usage of the term globalisation appears to be obscuring attention to the negative impact of capitalist development and imperialism. In a general sense, globalisation is an ideologically and politically motivated concept implying that a harmonious and integrated world order has been evolving to mitigate tensions and struggles that historically have disrupted the international political economy. Globalisation appears to be a concept that may have roots in earlier efforts to characterise the world economy as potentially orderly and harmoniously integrated. Although it is rarely conceptualised within historical theoretical debates, globalisation represents a way of describing a world today reminiscent of the thought of such writers as Karl Kautsky who argued that capitalism eventually would transcend the problems wrought long ago by the imperialist nations and evolve into a peaceful alliance of international finance capital or Joseph Schumpeter who felt that imperialism would eventually disappear in a rational and progressive capitalist era (see Chilcote, 2000: 198-203). Globalisation might be equated to how diffusionist literature has characterised the interdependent world order of nations, diffusionism here implying the assumption that spreading capitalism and technology outward from the developed capitalist part of the world would uplift and allow less developed regions to advance on an equal level. Globalisation also implies that accumulation of capital, trade, and investment no longer are confined to the nation-state. Further, it enhances the idea that capital flows have created a new world order with its own institutions and network of power relationships.

Five questions may help in a critical assessment of whether globalisation is a useful concept. First, does the present stage of capitalism represent a new epoch we can justifiably call globalisation or is it a continuation of the past? Obviously, the world and its conditions have altered substantially in the present era, but are we justified in postulating that a major transformation has occurred that we can call globalisation? I am inclined to believe, to the contrary, that the present trends represent but a continuation of the past, and I will explain my position later. Second, at a theoretical level, is globalisation an adequate term for explaining the fact that capitalism has spread to nearly every geographical region of the world and subsumed local and regional economies under its influence? Although we can speak of global capitalism, my preference is to relate imperialism and its historical theoretical understandings to an analysis of the world today. Third, is globalisation the consequence of a linear and inevitable process toward some better society? Proponents may argue for such outcomes, but the differentiation, inequality, and exploitation we see everywhere more adequately helps in understanding international economy today. Fourth, does globalisation imply a new era of harmony and peacefulness in the world today? In Latin America left revolutionary groups, especially in Central America, have negotiated political pacts allowing them to participate in electoral politics, yet violence and revolutionary activity are evident elsewhere, for instance, in Colombia where politics long has been enmeshed in violent struggle, guerrilla warfare, and the drug cartels, while the Zapatistas in Chiapas and landless peasants in the Brazilian countryside employ varying strategies of pressure and resistance. Although we are in an era of relative calm, it is premature to proclaim an end to resistance, mobilisation at the grassroots, and rapid change favouring the underprivileged peasants and workers of Latin America. Fifth, does globalisation suggest a new era of post-capitalism? This idea has carried on in the various post-forms of contemporary society ranging from post-modernism, post-imperialism, and even post-socialism. It would seem that ideologies counter to these trends remain conspicuous, that there is space for new ideas, and tensions and struggle for change will carry on well into the future.

Globalisation appears everywhere as polemic and controversy in the mainstream and on the left. The mainstream tends to see an evolving process of global integration progressively bringing harmony and integration to the world community. Among left intellectuals, however, there has been debate questioning its importance.

In popular and progressive magazines, the debate has carried on between those acknowledging globalisation as relevant to a critical understanding of the world today and those who reject it as useless and misleading. Controversy over globalisation also rages at a deeper theoretical level. Critical of but influenced by globalisation, William Robinson (1996) links globalisation to US intervention and hegemony and argues: "the focus becomes how accumulation processes that are no longer coextensive with specific national territories determine levels of social development among a globally stratified population" (in Mann et al, 2001-2002: 502). Michael Hardt and Antonio Negri (2000) accept the new world order and reject the idea of autonomy of nation-states. In contrast, Robert Gilpin (2002) and Paul Hirst and Grahame Thompson (1999) remain sceptical of globalisation. The latter proclaim globalisation a myth and favour continuity, believing that investment and trade flows are concentrated in the core rather than the periphery and that advanced capitalist countries will remain dominant. Samir Amin has argued that this theory is fundamentally ideological and can only be considered as "imperialist" globalisation, while James Petras condemns globalisation as "globaloney" and describes the arguments of the globalist theorists as vacuous, tendentious, and tautological (see Chilcote 2000b). While Robert Brenner (1999) and Roger Burbach and William Robinson (1999), and David Held et al (1999) provide overviews of the debate from varying perspectives, the reader may wish to delve into the symposium in the theoretical journal, *Science and Society*, where the argument of neo-Marxist scholars for the existence of a transnational capitalist class is joined by Robinson and Jerry Harris (2000) and criticised by Michael Mann, Giovanni Arrighi, and others (Mann, 2001-2002). Finally, Robert Went (2002-2003) looks at economic globalisation in terms of free trade and free movement of capital reminiscent of the period before World War I characterised by imperialism, yet he also acknowledges important changes have occurred in the international economy.

Just as the old notion of imperialism faded with the attention to developmental theory based on dependency and underdevelopment during the sixties and seventies, the idealised conception of globalisation appeared in the eighties and nineties and has prevailed until the present as an idea that obscures the earlier theory. Yet in reality, the diffusionist assumptions of capitalist development, manifested since World War II, have become incorporated into the presumed "new" theory of globalisation seen as integrating all nations into a harmonious and stable world.

In my recent writings I have emphasised imperialism over dependency and globalisation. Since the nineteenth century imperialist theory generally has focused on global capitalism and its pervasive impact. This attention to capitalism mitigates the tendency to obscure analysis of the underlying capitalist system that dominates the world today.

Practical Considerations

Global capitalism and US hegemony challenge us to reassess old ideas and search for new theories. At the same time it may be helpful to turn to participatory democracy in politics and economic planning. Left participation in formal representative politics offers the possibility of new perspectives. Successful peaceful transitions based on national political alliances may lead to theoretical advances. The question is: how to find a way to provide for the human needs of all people, encourage solidarity and collaboration in the mobilising process of allowing exploited peoples to rise above their miserable conditions? How to implement a transformation in the push toward political and economic egalitarianism if it is to be achieved through the socialisation of the means of production?

More than a decade ago I set forth a left research agenda for the 1990s based on theoretical alternatives and practical realities (Chilcote 1990). In Latin America, the death of Che Guevara in 1967 had resulted in a reassessment of strategies in rural guerrilla warfare; the suppression of urban revolutionary movements (especially in Argentina, Brazil, and Uruguay) during the 1970s impacted on revolutionaries and leftist intellectuals; and the overthrow of Allende in 1973 undermined the movement to seek a peaceful road to socialism. While these developments did not altogether deter revolutionary movements, especially in Nicaragua, Guatemala, and El Salvador the left began to move toward a diversity of perspectives, and the communist parties, long dominant within the Marxist left, continued a trend initiated in the early 1960s and splintered in diverse tendencies, leading to coalitions and alliances with other progressive forces, as in the cases of Brazil and Mexico.

During the 1980s "the Age of Gorbachev" was accompanied by rapprochement with the United States and a gradual withdrawal of Soviet influence and involvement in Latin America. With its collapse the Soviet Union abruptly broke with Cuba where Fidel Castro had already made clear that his country would not pursue the policies of 'glasnost' and 'perestroika'. The continuing US hegemony and policies of undermining revolutionary movements in Central America and elsewhere led to electoral defeat of the Sandinistas in Nicaragua and to peace treaties in El Salvador and elsewhere, signifying a shift from warfare to participation of the left in electoral politics.

During the 1990s US policy under the Clinton administration encouraged electoral regimes, neoliberal favouritism to the private sector, and multilateral trade under NAFTA. The burden of debt continued to weigh heavily on Latin America, and Argentina in particular, whose economy was close to collapse. The early years of the ensuing decade under the Bush administration signified more of the same US policies and dominance for Latin America.

Given these experiences, what issues prevail today? I believe the major concern is how emerging and popular progressive regimes shift resources to begin to deal with basic needs of people. In its transition to socialism, the Cuban revolution early on began to shift resources to basic needs and achieved remarkable results in education and health. The Allende regime in Chile and the Sandinistas in Nicaragua planned for similar needs but were thwarted by counterrevolutionary movements. Contemporary governments advocating popular reforms face the familiar problems of pluralism under minority rule or lack of commitment under majority rule, undermining of state authority, and persistent influence of traditional institutions such as church and military. Under pluralism dominant forces tend to rule through a dispersion of interests, leaving the interests powerless and ineffective in their demands. Popular forces, including the social movements, may fragment in the face of bourgeois dominance while traditional parliamentary groups and parties rise to power. Other obstacles are a low level of development of the capitalist forces of production or external pressures and interventions that interfere with possibilities for development and progress.

The election of Hugo Chávez in Venezuela, Lucio Gutiérrez in Ecuador, and Luiz Inácio da Silva (Lula) in Brazil have raised hopes for change from above that may result in allocations of resources from wealthy to poor segments of the population. Yet Chávez has been confronted with desperate reaction and a lengthy strike with the objective of bringing about his downfall. Gutiérrez, who was elected with support of leftist parties, social movements, and indigenous peoples in rural areas, is untested and the early commitment to reform is questionable. Lula initially has chosen a conciliatory course intending to build on a popular consensus that he offers hope for change. The present conjuncture suggests constraints on available resources but an immediate need for deep reform and decisive measures to shift resources to the broad population.

Where progressive regimes have not emerged and

dominant classes prevail, the left has relied on progressive political parties, organised labour unions, new social movements, and popular alliances in seeking needed changes to benefit people. In the search for participatory democracy, there has been continuing interest in reforming political parties and popular movements. For instance, during the 1990s the meetings of the São Paulo Forum brought left intellectuals and leaders together in search of new strategies and tactics. The ideas that emerged may have benefited successes in urban areas where leftists have risen to political power. The Brazilian Partido dos Trabalhadores (PT) has experienced success in Porto Alegre, São Paulo, and other municipalities. Even more conspicuous have been the actions of the Movimento Sem Terra (MST) in the Brazilian countryside or the Zapatistas in Chiapas. We are less aware of the mobilisation of local peoples in the barrios and favelas of large cities in Latin America where people have directly confronted their problems with limited material but widespread human resources. A close look at the *asambleas populares* in hundreds of neighbourhoods in Buenos Aires illustrates how people at the grassroots are addressing problems of food distribution, healthcare, welfare, and transportation. Similar movements mobilised around the belief that the people can govern themselves are evident in Ecuador and Peru as well as Mexico.

Drawing from my previous attempt to identify priorities for a research agenda, I continue to believe that there is important work to be undertaken in three areas: first, the study of the capitalist state and all its forms (fascist, corporative, bureaucratic authoritarian, national security, neoliberal, socialist, and so on) and that indeed a focus on the state becomes a major question for political study, but that priority must be given to class forces (dominant and popular) and class struggle and that analysis of groups and institutions should be related to a class context; second, continuing investigation of development possibilities, but concretely as capitalist accumulation and development of the forces of production within capitalism and the possibility of transition to socialism; and, finally, a serious look at democracy and socialism in all their forms (social democratic,

democratic socialist, revolutionary socialist, and so on) with careful attention to direct, informal, and participatory democracy and its possibilities.

Among important issues and questions might be the impact of capital on class and institutional forces, especially in the reorganisation of capital both within nations and throughout the international capitalist system. In examining the question of class, we need to look at the new middle classes in the public sector or state and their role at both national and international levels. In view of the inclination of many observers, including some on the left, to depreciate the role of the urban labour movement, we also need to reassess the traditional conflict between labour and capital, strategies in which labour sometimes aligns with capital or the state to obtain short-term benefits and how these strategies relate to the worldwide labour movement and international capital. We also need to pay attention to the ever evolving organisation of labour in the countryside. The break up or unity of labour movements could be assessed along with the implications of intra-class conflict within the domestic and international ruling capitalist classes. In light of the need to develop capitalist forces of production in less developed countries moving toward socialism or strategies which avoid revolutionary or violent means of achieving the transition, it would be useful to examine how progressive forces might penetrate state apparatuses and effect changes from within as well as outside the state?

Given the successes and failures of the various attempts to apply one or another Marxism to the contemporary situation, the intellectual discourse has searched for a "new" democracy and a "new" socialism. The problematic for left intellectuals is, first, how to achieve a transition to a better society, through democracy and socialism. In the democratic openings out of dictatorship, the political rhetoric might have suggested an illusion of a socialist possibility, yet in reality a socialist transition may not occur because the private means of production are not all socialised, and popular classes do not emerge to power with or without the vanguard of a workers' movement or proletarian party; in the end capitalism and bourgeois economic interests are decisive in stemming the tide toward socialism, while the new regimes usually evolve from radical possibilities to representative parliamentary and social democratic forms, and the political parties overshadow the popular and revolutionary movements. Attempts at direct participatory democracy are undermined by formal representative forms. Essential is whether solutions can be found for the economic and political crises without more direct and participatory democracy.

We must also ask what kind of democracy and socialism are possible as mainstream political forces insist on the parliamentary process and the dominance of political parties. Further, if pluralism is premised on individual choice, bargaining and compromise, wither the prospects for alliances and coalitions of popular movements outside the political party system and what are the prospects for resisting the declassing of the socialist project altogether? We need to account for global communication and information transfer through the internet and the web and its potential use and impact on mobilising left forces around the world. There is also the question of revolutionary strategy in a transition to democracy and the drive toward socialism and the role of class and class struggle in the search for a theory of the transformation. At issue is the working class as agency carrying out the revolution.

The road to socialism will be difficult whether an evolutionary or revolutionary course is taken. In Latin America, the level of the productive forces and the seemingly insurmountable problems of external and internal debt, inflation, unemployment, and so on appear to stifle progress toward socialism and democracy. The persistence of capitalism and its pervasive impact makes difficult the implanting of socialism. In their effort to avoid deterministic and reductionist analysis, many progressive intellectuals have retreated from Marxism while favouring a broadly conceived pluralism extending beyond the working class to such other social movements as feminists, ecologists, and pacifists. These movements become relevant with class analysis that examines the mobilising possibilities for both urban and rural workers as well as spontaneous and organised mobilisation of people in poor urban areas and in the countryside. Serious work around these themes may mitigate the crisis of Marxism and stimulate new thinking as theory is applied to the conditions being shaped by people who are determining their own destinies at a local level while confronting the influences and pervasive impacts of a maturing international capitalist order.

REFERENCES

Burbach, Roger and William Robinson 1999. "The Fin de Siecle Debate: Globalization as Epocal shift," *Science and Society.* 63 (Spring), 10-39.

Brenner, Robert. 1999. "Beyond State-Centrism? Space, Territoriality, and Geographical Scale in Globalization Studies," *Theory and Society.* 28:39-78.

Chilcote, Ronald H. 1984. *Theories of Development and Underdvevelopment.* Boulder: Westview Press.

——— 1990. "Tensions in the Latin American Experience: Fundamental Themes in the Formulation of a Research Agenda for the l990s," *Latin American Perspectives* 17 (Spring), 122-128.

——— 2000."Theories of Imperialism," Chapter 5, pp. 175-251 in his *Theories of Comparative Political Economy.* Boulder: Westview Press.

——— (ed). 2000 a. *Imperialism: Theoretical Directions.* .New York: Humanity Book.

——— (ed) 2000 b. *The Political Economy of Imperialism.* Lanham: Rowman and Littlefield, 2000.Cloth edition published by Kluwar Academic Publishers, 1999.

——— 2002. "Globalization or Imperialism?" *Latin American Perspectives* 29 (November), 80-87.

——— Forthcoming. "Theoretical Directions in the Developmental Literature: Imperialism, Dependency, or Globalization?" Introduction to edited volume of selections on development to be published by Rowman and Littlefield in the Series "Latin American Perspectives in the Classroom".

Gilpin, Robert. 2002, *The Challenge of Global Capitalism. TheWorld Economy in the 21st Century.* Princeton: Princeton University Press.

Hardt, Michael, and Antonio Negri. 2000. *Empire.* Cambridge: Harvard University Press.

Harnecker, Marta. 2002. "Marta Harnacker on Latin America Today."

Interview with Manuel Alberto Ramy in *Progreso Weekly* (December 1), 1-10.
Sourced through portside@yahoogroups.com.

Harris, Jerry. 1998-1999, "Globalization and the Technological Transformation of Capitalism," *Race and Class* 40 (No 2-3), 21-36.

Held, David et al.(eds) 1999. *Global Transformations: Politics, Economics, Culture*. Stanford: Stanford University Press.

Hirst, Paul and Grahame Thompson. 1996. *Globalization in Question*. Cambridge: Polity Press.

Kay, Cristóbal.1989. *Latin American Theories of Development and Underdevelopment*. London and New York: Routledge.

Larraín, Jorge. 1989. *Theories of Development: Capitalism, Colonialism, and Dependency*. London: Polity Press.

Lehmann, David. 1990. *Democracy and Development in Latin America*. London: Polity Press.

Mann, Michael et al 2001-2002. "The Transnational Ruling Class Formation Thesis: A Symposium." *Science and Society* 65 (Winter), 464-508.

Marx, Karl, and Frederick Engels. 1958. *Selected Works in Two Volumes*. Moscow: Foreign Language Publishing House.

Robinson, William I. 1996. *Promoting Polyarchy: Globalization, U.S.Intervention, and Hegemony*. Cambridge: Cambridge University Press.

Robinson, William I and Jerry Harris 2000. "Towards a Global Ruling class? Globalization and the Transnational Capitalist Class,' *Science and Society*. 64 (Spring), 11-54.

Went, Robert. 2002-2003. "Globalization in the Perspective of Imperialism," *Science and Society*. 66 (Winter), 473-497).

Beyond Crisis:
On the Nature of Political
Change in Argentina[1]

Ana Cecilia Dinerstein
(Translated from Spanish by Rama Paul)

The complexity of the events of December 2001 in Argentina makes difficult to achieve a balanced evaluation between structural, historical and conjunctural issues, between external and domestic, international, regional and local factors that intervened in the crisis. December 2001 can be seen in fact as the final eruption of a series of medium and long term volcanic processes of diverse kinds with some short-term loose elements.

Acute economic and political crises, together with a high level of social mobilisation, form the regional characteristic of the recent years. In general terms, the processes of democratisation during the 1980s particularly in the Southern Cone, did not facilitate the economic growth with social equity nor did they strengthen democracy, instead they intensified social inequalities and disillusionment with politics. Nation-states became the *terrain* where the fight spread between the requirements of the transnational capital, on the one hand and civil societies of every country in that region on the other. Application of technocratic solutions, primarily directed towards stabilising the economy, and satisfying the demands of credit institutions and international banks did not but widen, and at the same time, made evident the gap between state and civil society. In Argentina, while the process of democratisation (1983–1989) opened up a formidable space for popular mobilisation and expression of postponed and suppressed demands of the major section of the population, they were progressively converting into an obstacle for the 'consolidation' of democracy; the latter understood in terms of processes of gradual legitimisation of economic terrorism openly developed during the 1970s, and now disguised under the garb of economic adjustments, termed cynically as 'policies of stability' (Dinerstein 2003a). Financial speculation and the indiscriminate use of natural, productive and human resources of the countries in the region by transnational enterprises along with their local allies whose actions have systematically fomented the privatisation of the nation-state, the corruption of the political elites and the socialisation of the capitalist risk and external debt, have produced real social disasters such as unemployment and immense poverty, marginality, crime, infirmity and mortality at unusual levels.

As a result, newer forms of social protest and mobilisation emerged to call, not only for the end of neo-liberal policies, but also for the recognition of human dignity and respect for economic and social human rights in Latin America. In many cases, the social protest, motivated either by economic or political reasons, caused at repeated opportunities, the sudden exit of the heads of governments in Brazil, Venezuela, Ecuador, Guatemala, Peru and Argentina (Ollier, 2003)

The intensity of both, crisis and social mobilisation in Argentina 2001 within the Latin American context, brought again in the limelight the question around which reside the finest conceptual and analytical tools to understand the meaning of the post-crisis political change, particularly since the radical call enclosed in "¡que se vayan todos!" found, at the end of the road, a re-composition of the elites in power.

Analysts interested in examining the causes of financial, economic and political crises have to contend with respect to Argentina which functioned badly: 'How could the country which became the darling of both the financial markets and the global policy community for almost a decade, a poster child of desirable reform, fall back into deep and prolonged recession..*What went wrong?*' (Mussa 2002: vii).

Supporters of market ideologies believe that Argentina is a typical case of what can work and what can *go wrong* if healthy macroeconomic policies are not applied consistently (Aguirre-Sacassa, 2002). From an opposed political position others suggest that Argentina is a clear example of "the *failure* of IMF policies to establish the bases for long term economic growth in low-income countries"..."Nowhere has the IMF policy package led to stable, sustained economic expansion" but rather, as in the case of Argentina, have generated "growing inequality." (MacEwan 2002: 2-3, my emphasis). Weisbrot also holds that "the IMF must acknowledge that it played a large role in causing the current crisis of Argentina's economy' by financially supporting a convertibility plan which was *unlikely to succeed* in the long term and imposing austerity conditions on the country for 'opportunistic and ideological reasons"(2002: 2-3, my italics).

Other analysts emphasise structural problems that impede the stabilisation of Argentine capitalism, and that have operated, once again, as unleashing factors of the crisis. Among them are the greed of local and transnational capitalist groups inclined to financial valorisation and their role in destroying regulating and distributive capacity of the State (Basualdo 2002a, 2002b); the corruption of the political elites and their role in sustaining the forms of accumulation associated with financial speculation and the flight of foreign exchange, which have led to the indebtedness of the state with a growth and socialisation of the debt (Basualdo & Kulfas 2002; Llorens & Cafiero 2002; Lozano & Hourest 2002), the dependency of Argentine economy on the flow in financial markets (various authors in *Plan Fenix*; 2001). Finally, political scientists highlight the debility of the democratic state institutions as well as "the form of social contract underpinning the perceived legitimacy of the state's basic democratic role" (Tedesco 2002b: 477-478); the crisis of the system of political representation (Botana 2002); the politico-institutional fragmentation (Ollier 2003: 183) as causes of the crisis.

Though from different perspectives and with distinct political intentions, these analyses share a fundamental problem: guided by the question of *'what went wrong'*, they relegate the popular mobilisation to the state of *undesired effect* of institutional crisis, treating it as a variable dependent (reaction) on the unleashing factors of the crisis. The explanation to this crisis of economic and financial policies is located tautologically in the same institutional dynamics. More importantly, the non-institutional forms of social protest and civil disobedience are seen as *failures* of the channels of participation and articulation of interests. This idea is in some way demoralising because it leads to belief in the existence of an intrinsic incapacity of the Argentines to develop and sustain a stable democracy and capitalism. The crisis and mobilisation are judged from an imaginary model of democratic capitalism with which the Argentine case is compared, thus being able to mark its flaws and abnormalities. Unfortunately, this kind of appeal to the reality to be studied makes difficult the study of the relationship existing between the global capital and national demands and mobilisation, whose forms of interaction and results depend, to a large extent, on the processes of struggle that is uncoiled on the national territory, in a determined historical period.

Other analyses that have tried to bestow on the popular mobilisation the status it deserves, also question *'what went wrong'* in December 2001, but from a distinct political position. The question, in this case, is why the great revolutionary opportunity offered by the 'hegemonic' crisis of capitalism in December 2001 was lost. The popular mobilisation of December is conceived, in this sense, as a fundamental moment of a long-term revolutionary process, wherein the role of the Party is seen as crucial (*Política y Teoría* n° 48, 2002). In this text of December, the political left found an occasion to reaffirm the orthodox ideas regarding the social change.[2] Thus, it was suggested in those days that "the struggle for power is found objectively posed...the bridge for the present consciousness of the workers and that of their complete class character, can be developed consequently to the crisis of power and starting from direct political agitation...the necessary juncture of development of this transition is nothing but the maturity of the masses, which also entails a maturing of the international crisis and the revolutionary development in Latin America." (Altamira 2002: 322)

From this perspective, the recomposition of power in the hands of Presidents Duhalde and Kirchner, along with the gradual decline of the popular movement, led to a profound political disillusionment of the Left. But this vision that supposedly places the popular mobilisation in the foreground is equally or perhaps even more demoralising than that described previously, wherein the mobilisation is a variable dependent on the crisis. However, this disillusionment does not seem to be an outcome of the gradual decline of social mobilisation, but rather it is an effect of an erring intention to subordinate the said mobilisation to the structure, logic and agenda of diverse existing revolutionary parties, following the Leninist criteria of the most orthodox Marxism. Closing the question over the nature of political change, this posture ignored that the popular insurrection of December 2001 in Argentina questioned the dynamics and the strategies of the political structures of the state and the parties, *including* those of the political Left and of organised workers' movement so that these do not escape the logic of power against which, as we shall see later, the mobilisation was directed.

This paper explores the nature of political change in Argentina and reflects briefly upon this new movement in Latin America. The work suggests, in the first place, that in order to appraise the impact of political change produced by the popular mobilisation of December and the forms of mobilisation that followed, it is important to look into the existing relation between the said forms of social mobilisation and the specific form that the capitalist crisis adopted. Establishing this mutual relation helps us avoid, in the first place, tautological explanations of the crisis where its analysis appears disassociated from the analyses of social protest and popular mobilisation, when in reality these play a central role in production and solution of the crisis; in second place, it helps us not to isolate and abstract the popular mobilisation from the institutional transformations and dynamics which gave it life and moulded it, thus avoiding forcing it to respond to a reality which is alien to the subjects involved in the said mobilisation. Any moment of rebellion and popular mobilisation *embody* and put to action profound complex transfcrmations in the social relations of the period under consideration. The virtue of popular mobilisation as that of December 2001 in Argentina does not lie in its capacity to 'alter the established social order', but primarily in its capacity to reveal and make evident the violence intrinsic to the imposition of the capitalist (dis)order.

With this framework of analysis, this paper suggests that the profound institutional crisis, wherein the financial aspects predominated, initiated a movement towards recomposition of the subjectivity and the recuperation of the politics that put a limit to the violence of capitalism. Thus, a process of struggle for 'transforming the civil society in subject' was initiated (Tischler 2001), i.e. a process of fundamental critique not only to the excluding democracy and to the neo liberal economic policies but, principally, to the very forms of democracy and the politics subordinated to the new order imposed by the global capital, the international organisations and the North American imperialism during the 1990s. This critique was expressed for recovering the capacity of collective political action and the re-invention of the political subjectivity of certain sections of the society. Although the very characteristics of the mobilisation (anti-institutional, direct and territorial forms) did not contribute to an institutional level dispute, they constitute however, the fundamental basis for a qualitative change of greater dimensions, whose forms cannot be foreseen yet but which without doubt, will form part of a regional political change in the long term.

The following section analyses the events of December 2001 and the political meaning of the popular insurrection. The second section explores the relationship between the crisis and the form of popular mobilisation in December 2001. The third part will bring forth the common characteristics of the new *territories* for collective action that have emerged or have reinforced since December 2001. The fourth section will indicate the recomposition of the post-December political and economic power. The fifth part will evaluate the nature and meaning of the political change operating in Argentina with relation to the form of crisis and the recomposition of the political and the economic state power of the State.

I. Towards December 2001: Crisis and Mobilisation (2000-2001)

The hope that the triumph of the coalition formed by the traditional *Unión Cívica Radical* (UCR) and the new *Frente País Solidario* (FREPASO) under the leadership of Fernando de la Rua in December 1999 would be putting an end to the neo-liberal project of Carlos Menem (1989-1999) disappeared sooner than expected when the new government, following its predecessor's footsteps, adopted a very harsh position towards social protests and a very soft stance towards the capital and the international credit organisations. Within only five days of his appointment, the Home Minister (Minister of Interiors) ordered repression of the road blockades in Corrientes Province, where two unemployed workers were brutally killed by the police force, while many others were injured and jailed. Simultaneously, and despite acknowledging publicly that the social situation was 'extremely critical' (*La Nación* 28-07-03), the Minister of Economy, José Luis Machinea, assured the IMF in New York at the end of March 2000, that Argentina would comply with all the commitments assumed in the Letters of Intent of December 1997 and January 1999, by implementing an agenda of structural reforms agreed with the said organisation. (*Argentine Letter of Intent* 1999)

Between 1999 and 2001, the tension between the popular expectations and the protests, and the adjustment policies monitored by IMF, along with high level of State corruption and the sustained flight of capitals produced, on one hand, the gradual political deterioration and the collapse of the coalition in power; and on the other, the expansion of social 'bad mood' and the consequent intensification of the popular mobilisation. Both these processes are going to converge in December 2001.

Among the most important factors that drove to the political collapse of the *Alianza* (Alliance) was the resignation of the Vice President of the nation as a consequence of corruption in the Senate over voting on the labour reform; the resignation of those members belonging to FREPASO from the National Cabinet within the Alliance and return of Domingo Cavallo, the creator of the stability, to the Ministry of Economy as the only ally to the President de la Rua. However, the impossibility of consolidating political power in the government was not simply a product of the inability of the persons involved, but was a result of the intensification of contradictory dynamics in the conflictive relationship between international capital and organisations and the civil society mediated by the State, started twenty five years ago.

During the 1990s, the Menem administration *legitimised* the new drive of the national and transnational banks and capitals that were behind the creation and the nationalisation of the external debt during the 1970s and the 1980s, the hyper-inflation episodes of 1989 and 1991, the corrupted process of privatisation of the State's enterprises, the de-regularisation of financial and labour markets and the flight of capital abroad. The uncertainty generated by the Menemist stability rose to unusual levels eroding workers' social and human rights, which were considered untouchable previously, before 1976. The National State subsidised the instability produced by the socialisation of capitalist risk through unemployment, labour precariousness and flexibility, the growth of informal economy, the commercialisation of health, retirement and accidents at work, the reduction of employers' contribution to the social security, destruction of State's institutions of social protection. The Supreme Court of justice started the period of 'absolute majority' in order to legitimise this process of neo-liberal transformation. The law also legitimised the political amnesty to those who perpetuated crimes against humanity during the dictatorship.

The subordination of the nation-State to the logics of international money and organisations initiated in the 1970s, did not affect the process of policy-making externally but rather penetrated it, imposing priorities from within the state structures. The ten years that preceded the crisis of 2001 stood witness to the growing crisis of the traditional political parties such as PJ and UCR, particularly after the disillusionment with the democracy in 1983 and Menem's conversion to neo-liberalism. Also it was evident that now it was not possible for a fragmented political Left to recover from the period of repression and the post 1970s crisis. It also confirmed the crisis of Peronist worker identity, sharpened by the fact that the trade union bureaucracy collaborated with the economic and labour reforms which while facilitating their financial survival, led to a rupture in their capacity of representing their bases in the context of de-industrialisation and unemployment. The de-centralisation and dispersion of the protest paved way for the emergence of new social actors, new identities and organisations with new strategies of struggle that transformed the anatomy and geography of popular mobilisation from an organised, centralised forms predominantly guided by trade unions or by political and human rights parties to more spontaneous, non-institutional, diffused, plural and local forms. The new *movimientista* unionism of the *Central de Trabajadores Argentinos* (CTA) created in 1992 tried persistently to extend trade union's representation and organisation beyond the factories, by incorporating those sectors which were now considered socially marginalised or deeply affected by neo-liberal reforms, such as the national and provincial public sector workers, workers in the informal sector, women, the unemployed, the poor and the street children.

On this scenario unfurled, during 1999–2001, the unsuccessful efforts of the new government to resolve the contradictions of a fragmented (but certainly not less intense) struggle between the 'needs' for global money and the 'needs' of the majority of the Argentines.

The principal form of manifestation of these insurmountable contradictions was the *war* unfolded in favour of and against the 'zero deficit plan', launched by the external Minister Cavallo in order to restrain the crash of reserves in dollars in July 2001 that would lead to the crisis of December 2001. With obvious intention of maintaining the dollar–peso convertibility all through a major recession that would limit the popular demand and consumption, the new plan of austerity was based on 13% reduction in the salaries of public sector and the retirements that would be above 500 pesos/dollars monthly. This reduction of salaries that affected 92% of government employees, and which were disputed fervently in the Parliament, was a key factor for initiating a progressive incorporation of the white-collar workers and the decaying middle class in the trade union mobilisation and the movement of the unemployed. The motives which underlie the social mobilisation of that moment are not only found in the economic questions of that juncture but also in a clear perception that the zero deficit was a new tourniquet of the IMF and the International Banks to force Argentina to a greater social discipline. Despite the fact that the government underestimated their importance, the strikes of CTA, the mobilisation in the streets and the nationalisation of the blockades (which were till then provincial) in July and August 2001, were supported by the middle segment, which marked a *qualitative leap* in popular mobilisation, till then led by CTA and the Movement of the Unemployed Workers in the province of Buenos Aires.

The tension within the State structure, produced by the pressure from the IMF, the US government and the banks for approving the zero deficit law and renegotiating the external debt, and the popular mobilisation that still relied on the bad conditions of the middle class, became practically unsustainable by the middle of the year 2001. While the big corporations and the bondholders outside the country *betted on* the collapse and devaluation, Minister Cavallo tried desperately to stabilise the reserves of the Central Bank in order to *avoid* the devaluation. The zero deficit law was finally approved by the Senate to the joy of Bush administration, also celebrated by Britain's Prime Minister Tony Blair, and the ex-president of Brazil Henrique Cardoso, who considered it a 'great step forward'.(*Clarín* 31-07-01: 4)

The law opened a space for negotiating another aid from the IMF for $1.2 billion, promised with the direct intervention of the government of United States, but it increased the social disquietude.[3] The popular mobilisation showed now not only the support of middle class to the working class or to the unemployed but also its direct participation in the road blockades, neighbourhood meetings, popular kitchens, public classes and marches that demanded, in August 2001, the end to adjustments, meanwhile the negotiations between Daniel Marx and Stanley Fisher got delayed.

Added to the pressures of the social mobilisation and its political subordination to the IMF, the Alliance received a heavy electoral shock in the legislative elections of 14 October 2001, when the *Partido Justicialista* (PJ) won 17 of 24 electoral districts, also acquiring majority in the Senate of the nation. However, the real winner of the elections was not PJ, but the blank vote or *bogus* vote that reached to 10 million heads, coming to 20 % at the national level, 30% in Buenos Aires and 40% in Rosario. (Rodríguez in *Gambina et al* 2002: 23) The fact that a huge percentage of voters would not vote in a country where voting is obligatory made clear the disillusionment of the people with democracy and the political class as well as the immense social marginalisation, among which figured 700,000 youngsters and new voters.

The public appreciation that the IMF was abandoning Argentina to its fate became real on November 2, when it threatened the government with its withdrawal of the agreed $1.26 billion in Washington if the government did not adjust to the law of zero deficit. Confronted with the need to adjust and not emit, the Minister of Economy introduced on December 3, through ministerial decree 1570/01 a new financial measure popularly known as the banking *corralito* (the freezing of deposits in the banking system). The *corralito* restricted the withdrawals from the cash dispensers to $250 weekly for a period of 90 days as well as limited the transfer of money outside, and thus making it impossible for the bank account holders to withdraw their savings from the banks. Agreeing with Cavallo, the *corralito* was directed to prevent the fall in the Central Bank reserves, to force extensive use of credit cards and cheques rather than money in cash, thus blocking tax evasion. Nevertheless, the *corralito* was correctly perceived as 'expropriating' the money savers, among whom figured not only the middle class, but many workers as well who had their compensations for dismissal, invalidity or accidents at work in these banks. The *corralito* also implied lack of money circulation in cash on which depended 40% of the economically active population employed in the informal sectors of the economy as well as those who survived on alms and charity.

Although implementing the *corralito* cannot be considered as the principal motive of the popular insurrection of the 19th and 20th of December, it was without doubt the straw that broke the camel's back, resulting in a chain reaction of furious middle class, workers and the marginalised section of the population. With these *corralito*, those who had savings in the bank or a fixed salary were equally affected as those who had neither any savings nor any fixed salary, united in a general strike called by CTA against the IMF on December 13.

Once again, the popular mobilisation did not merely respond to the economic questions but to the political ones as well, as the perception that the government had decided definitively to favour the groups with economic power and the international banks in detriment to the interests of the population was growing after the implementation of the *corralito*. Such a perception was justified. The government's argument for implementing the *corralito* was the need to put the brakes to the crash of reserves in dollars which according to the government and the IMF was due to the irresponsible attitude of the savers who, scared of the collapse of financial system, were producing the self complied prophecy by withdrawing their money from the banks (See Rock 2002) making the reserves in the Central Bank to crash.

However, the actual cause of the draining of financial system was not the fall of individual deposits, as almost 60% of the deposits trapped in the *corralito* were less than $50,000, i.e. belonging to the people who did not have access to the sophisticated information of the financial market and whose low sums of money remained trapped for this very reason in the *corralito*.

A parliamentary investigation published in April 2002 by

Llorens and Cafiero (2001, 2002) analyses the movement and the changes operated in a section of Banking Institutions' Report presented at the Central Bank in 2001 suspiciously denominated "Other Obligations of Balance of Financial Institutions". The research shows that it was the crash of reserves (and not the deposits) of Central Bank that caused the draining, and this was a consequence of money movement of huge corporations and banks which started months before the crisis as a result of draining strategy, i.e. an 'extensive and silent withdrawal' of money from the financial system by big investors (i.e. ten most important premier banks of the country, mostly foreign banks [Sevares 2002]). (Llorens and Cafiero 2001: 2002)

It is interesting to highlight with regard to the previous, that the said 'draining' took place between March and November 2001, when Minister Cavallo was already in the front of the Ministry of Economy. (Llorens and Cafiero: 2001, 2002). Therefore, the so-called *crisis* of the financial system or the economic coup d'etat was more a yield of financial institutions than that of small savers, and more a gradual and planned process than that of spontaneous reactions of 'markets' to institutional crisis.

The popular perception that the government was entrapped in the logic of international financial power was again confirmed when, despite the promises that were made by the Deputy Minister of Economy, Daniel Marx in Washington, and despite implementing unpopular economic and financial measures that undermined the political authority of the government, on December 5, the IMF changed its opinion and refused to give the promised loan of $1.26 billion, suggesting now that the appropriate policy was *devaluation* and a new plan of fiscal and budgetary adjustment for the year 2002.

Why did the IMF refuse the aid in December 2001, when it had rescued Argentina on repeated occasions in 2000 and in the first half of 2001 even without having zero deficits, is a question without any answer. The argument that Argentina failed to fulfil zero deficits and that it had increased, on the contrary, public spending much higher than what was fixed by the IMF lack empirical support. The official statistics demonstrated, following Weisbrot and Baker, that "it was increasing interest payments on the debt that drove the government's budget from surplus to deficit. Interest payments rose from $2.5 billion in 1991 to $9.5 billion in year 2000, or from 1.2% to 3.4% of GDP". (2002: 7)

Was the generosity demonstrated in the financial loans in 2000 a strategy to postpone the crisis? The argument that the IMF tried to favour the American banks should not be discarded. According to Dávalos (2001) the financial aid in 2000 allowed the big corporations and banks to protect themselves and relocate their investments. After this, the IMF did not have any interest in restraining the unfolding of the announced terminal crisis for four years.

This argument is substantiated firstly by that of Cafiero and Llorens (2002) whose research shows that the planned draining of the financial system was encouraged by the IMF with the direct intervention of Stanley Fisher, the number two ex-official of the organisation, who at the same time, was also the vice president of the Citigroup, when the financial aid to Argentina was carried out in December 2000 (*Shielding*), June 2001(*Mega exchange*, defined by the Congressman Cafiero as the 'robbery of the century') and August 2001 (*Salvaging*). Second, with the fact that the big corporations with international connections betted on devaluation as suggested by the IMF. In November 2001, a group of powerful companies under the leadership of Techint Group, and foreign banks under the leadership of Citibank and Santander Rio, among others, suggested the Argentine economic team, a devaluation of peso and elimination of restrictions so that these institutions could withdraw their money from the country. (Nudler in *Página/12 Online* 06.12.01) Soon after this manoeuvre, the IMF seems to have punished Argentina exemplarily arguing that it was not implementing the suggestions of the IMF appropriately.

The 19th of December 2001 was an inflection point in two senses. Firstly after the refusal from the IMF, the government had to meet 415 millions pesos in obligation to the debt. Anxious, the creditors hoped that the payment would not be made and the official declaration of *default* would be demanded, which they needed to initiate legal actions against the government. The 19th of December was also an important day for popular mobilisation. While the economic team bled to reach the zero deficit mark, 800 people in Concordia (Entre Rios) and 300 more in Mendoza mobilised on 16th December demanding for food in supermarkets, leading in some cases to looting of the same. By the 19th of December the looting had already spread to the city and the provinces of Buenos Aires, Cordoba and Santa Fe. Despite the fact that there were rumours that the opposition PJ had stirred the looting with the intention of destabilising the government, it is clear that this explanation is insufficient for understanding the cases like peaceful mobilisation of 2000 picketers of *Coordinadora de Desocupados de Aníbal Verón* (Organisation of the Unemployed *Aníbal Verón*) who asked for food in supermarkets in Quilmes, Buenos Aires, challenging the police, and indirectly the IMF.

Not only did the looting generate the air of popular mobilisation: more than three million people voted voluntarily in the referendum organised between 13th and 16th December by the *Frente Nacional Contra la Pobreza* (FRENAPO) [National Front against Poverty] and the CTA to which 2,769,831 people attended. Among them, 1,742,327, voted affirmatively for the proposal of introducing a general subsidy for unemployment of $380 a month for all the parents of the family, as well as a minimum pension and benefit of $60 monthly for children. The massive attendance to vote for the proposal of FRENAPO highlighted another qualitative change in popular resistance against the international banks and the IMF, spreading their bases, in contrast with the refusal to vote in the October elections.[4]

Fearing a situation of generalised social unrest, the national government used the famous 'fireman policy', so many times implemented unsuccessfully by the provincial governors to suppress the social protest: on one hand they sent 20,000 boxes of food and, on the other, hundreds of policemen to the areas where poverty had reached incredible proportions and, where consequently, the looting and the mobilisation were intense.

After the failure of attempting to form a unity government due to the refusal of Peronist opposition, the government declared a martial law for a lapse of 30 days by presidential decree 1,678. According to the President, they tried to control, this way, "acts of violence" provoked by "certain groups of people" who encouraged lootings "damaging the private property and putting in danger the lives of the people". The popular reaction to this was unanimous. Declaring martial law released the generalised fury, which turned into a collective delight when people came out in the streets to reject this kind of politics that was deaf to their demands but completely attentive to the directives of the IMF.

The first pan banging was heard in the rich neighbourhood of Buenos Aires: Barrio Norte and Belgrano. (Schuster *et al* 2002) But after the Presidential speech, the noise of casseroles spread gradually throughout the city. As if pleading at another level of communication, away from political speeches or revolutionary slang, the pan banging emerged as an 'emotional' response to political (ir)rationality. The people identified themselves as 'neighbours'. The pan banging kindled a sentiment of street festivity and a sense of 'making history', a moment of liberation of forces, of joy: "everything was emotional, full of unthinkable surprises"..."the noise was incredible"..."the collective power was rediscovered"..."the occupying of public space particularly at night was very important"..."what really united the people who came out on the streets for different reasons was one general sentiment of *'Ya basta!'* [Enough!]"[5]

The spontaneous rebellion became a popular insurrection when pan bangers demanded the resignation of Minister Cavallo, and later at the Plaza de Mayo, the resignation of the President of the nation. The brutal repression in the streets left more than 500 injured and thousands of prisoners and a total of 6 dead, which added to the police killings produced during the lootings and the protests in the rest of the country, coming to a total of 32. The country risk rating rose to 4.619 points and President de la Rua trapped between popular mobilisation and the financial markets, left the Pink House on a helicopter. The popular insurrection forced, thus, the resignation of a President democratically elected two years ago. The noisy popular demands of December did not reclaim the replacement of one government by another, but rather showed an almost irrevocable criticism of the political, economic and legal institutions and of the forms of politics and representative democracy: *"que se vayan todos!"*

II. Financial Collapse versus Pure Rebellion: Recovering the Politics

Although the slogan *"que se vayan todos!"* was aimed against the corrupt and incompetent political class that had become deaf to the popular demands; and against the arrogance of North American imperialism, the greediness of the World Bank and the cynicism of the IMF, it also made apparent a series of processes that were taking place since last ten years but which formed part of a continuity of transformations initiated by the military government of 1976. Among others, (i) the financial valorisation of capital subsidised by the increasing indebted State; (ii) the dependence of the national economy on movements of global capital and international finances, essentially since the external debts and the pressures of the IMF, and the crisis of the said paradigm which began with the Washington Consensus; (iii) the permanent use of the law to legitimise and legalise instability, i.e. the precariousness of labour, the violation of human rights, and the illegitimate transactions to sustain the said forms of accumulation; (iv) the crisis of the representative democratic system, the corruption of the political elites and the crisis of the political parties such as subordination of politics to the logic of money and redefining of new spaces and forms of participation; (v) significant changes in the social structure as a result of unemployment, poverty and gradual ruin of the middle class; (vi) the crisis of primarily Peronist labour identity and the bureaucratic trade union organisations linked to the State; (vii) the emergence of new forms of unionism, social and labour movements (of unemployed, neighbourhood movements and human rights); (vii) the progressive revival of popular mobilisation in fragmented forms through road blockades, marches of the State employees, strikes, *escraches* [6] without any common notion that would articulate the struggle of distinct sectors.

These *qualitative* transformations were generating an increasing *gap* between the conditions of growth and social reproduction imposed by the IMF and the possibilities of rejecting those conditions and resultant changes of the combination of intensifying the *abstract* aspects of the capitalist relations of production (i.e. globalisation, debt, country risk, capital flight, unemployment) and a crisis of political mediations (deterioration of fiscal capacities, definitions and application of social policies, legitimacy and corruption). The financial crisis is undoubtedly a reflection of the recomposition of global capital based on terrorist hegemony of international money (the most abstract form of capital) over the political capacity of the States. The *de-politicisation* of politics and the transformation of democracy in the middle in order to administer social misery and contain the popular mobilisation were sustained for a period of time by short term benefits of stability, but at the same time, the de-politicisation intensified the less visible processes of frustration, individualism, the destruction of social networks, the crisis of identity, political crisis and the organisations which came into limelight in December 2001 when the logic of money dislodged the possibilities of its own reproduction.

The crisis of the neo-liberal *Disutopia* does not simply tells us about a certain political, economic or financial crisis, but rather a crisis of subordination of politics to the logic of money, and with it, the 'virtual disappearance' of human beings in diverse forms like the political repression, poverty, unemployment, social exclusion. As in the rest of the world, wherein "struggles against the intensification of abstraction counter-pose physicality, i.e., seek visibility, in attempts to make themselves concrete against the overwhelming contradictory logic of abstraction" (Dinerstein and Neary 2002: 238), the mobilisation of December 2001 in Argentina proposed re-materialising the abstraction of capital, which in Argentina had adopted graphic forms of *flight*, debt and bankruptcy. In other works, I termed this process as 'the experience of abstraction' (Dinerstein 1999; 2003c), i.e. the collective experience through which the subjects re-signify the processes of social, economic and political exclusion, thus categorised by power, generating alternative forms of collective action that restore materiality to separation, in this case, the abyss created between the subjects and the capital. In December 2001, the pressure of international banks, the financial collapse combined theatrically with the pathetic attitude of the political class and its corruption and the crisis of democracy and law, the expansion of this experience of abstraction from the marginalised sectors to the whole society, revealing thus the violence of capitalist order called stability.

This experience is inevitably an experience of re-invention of *the territories of politics*. The first step towards the re-invention has been the complete negation of institutional politics that sustained the capitalist *irrationality. Que se vayan todos!* put a limit to that irrationality. December 2001 was experienced as a moment of taking hold of oneself, a moment in which the fears and the individual difficulties were transformed in a radical collective action against the power of capital and the State. As a tacit agreement, the popular mobilisation was not guided by a plan of action for a re-change of the government, neither a demand for concrete questions but rather fused a multiplicity of frustrations, necessities, desires and dreams subordinated to the logic of capital. The popular mobilisation embodied in a moment of pure rebellion the collective rejection to the violence of Menemist stability imposed and celebrated during the 90s. (See Dinerstein 2001)

III. New Territories of Popular Mobilisation: Towards the Revival of Political Subjectivity

The moment of initial rejection was followed inevitably by a moment of recomposition of the forms of participation and mobilisation that were born out of the space of subjectivation opened up by the institutional crisis. These forms are inherited, more or less, from the form of crisis. The post December recomposition had four general characteristics:

(1) Reconciliation between people and politics occurred in the form of 'anti-politics' (Dinerstein 2003c) that is the re-politicisation of the society through new forms of collective, direct, radical, joint and democratic participation, mobilisation and action that rejected the

representative and institutional politics. The practice and language of anti-politics, the counter power of anti-capitalism, anti-globalisation developed and expanded territorially through the actions of neighbourhood assemblies, workers' and trade union mobilisations, unemployed workers' movement, co-operative movement and of occupied factories, human rights, retired people, savers and artists movement.[7]

(2) The absence of a centralised political movement that would coordinate the actions of diverse organisational forms, but rather the presence of a horizontally articulated 'rhizomatic' network.

(3) New 'common notions' were born in the core of very collective action, such as dignity, justice, autonomy and democracy that, which while re-introducing the language and practice of rebellion, at the same time rejected the old vocabulary of struggle of the political Left and the organised workers' movement. The new notions motorised the dispute for the sense and meaning of the crisis and insurrection.

(4) During 2002-2003, a recomposition of economic and political state power took place, which though put an end to the Menemist era, did not imply the renovation of political elites or change in the institutional structures.

By looking more closely at some of these organisational forms of popular mobilisation and participation that emerged from the crisis, or whose importance increased after the crisis—neighbourhood assemblies, the autonomous organisations within the movement of the unemployed, and the movements of occupied factories, one can find some common characteristics that, although did not affect the majority of the population, indicate a substantial political change.

First, recomposition of the political and social identities was achieved through the very process of collective action. Disillusioned citizens became active *neighbours*, the unemployed became *picketers* with their own social project, and workers on the verge of losing their jobs became autonomous workers in charge of the organisation of production in their factories. This meant a rejection, or at least, a debate on the existing identities and ideologies of the traditional Left and the workers' movement. In case of neighbourhood meetings, the notion of neighbour is a negative identity that suppresses class differences and refers to a territorial identification of the participants (those who live in the same locality), acting in this sense as a homogenising agglutinin for joint collective actions. Unlike 'citizens', the identity of *neighbour* is concrete and situational, i.e. it exists while the processes of mobilisation and participation take place, rather than being defined in abstract by ideologies and political processes alien to involved subjects. Being neighbours, as well as being picketers or workers in factories taken over and converted to cooperative is not defined *a priori*, but rather it is the involvement in collective actions that paves way for the birth of such identities. The identification and mutual recognition of the members of these meetings through sharing the same problems or disquietudes thus became the basis for action.

Second, we find the physical re-appropriation of public spaces. In all cases, the neighbourhoods became the local territory to reaffirm organisational identity and development. This is true that even at the beginning of taking over the factories; the neighbourhood's support played a crucial role in the success of takeovers. The neighbourhood, thus, is a place of conjunction and meeting (territorial) for deciding (i) survival strategies with high political content (productive economic projects, popular education, occupying abandoned houses for establishing children's dining hall, popular hospitals); (ii) confrontation with local organisations, the State, banks and other service enterprises; (iii) organisation of artistic events, political debates; and (iv) coordination of protests and articulation of grievances and expression of resistance against repression and against the state political coercion.

Third, one observes in all the cases the practice of direct or radical democracy defined as "people's power" or "democracy in its essential form" (Esteva, 1999:155). The *assembly* is used by all these organisations as a way of deliberating and deciding. In case of picketing movement, the assembly is used for deciding the date and the forms of blockade, as well as the forms of utilising the employment programs for local productive projects like creating bakeries, brick kilns and schools.

Fourth, the post-December mobilisation and participation operates on *'here* and *now'*. Though there are substantial differences among them, for example between the movement of the unemployed and the neighbourhood meetings, it can be said that, in general, the political commitment of the neighbours, *picketers*, workers in the occupied factories along with their organisations is permanently recreated while they participate in the meetings. One is not a picketer if she does not participate in the movement; neither is she a neighbour if she does not attend the neighbourhood meetings. The organisation itself exists as long as the meetings keep on taking place. These new territories are, therefore, relatively flexible and the identitarian identifications that reside in their interior, as we say, are superimposed, broken and disappeared as long as the collective action develops. The methods of protests are also direct (meetings, *escraches*,[8] blockades, taking over of factories, marches) and are sustained with political and social communitarian work.

Fifth, what unifies the action of these two new or revitalised organisational forms have been new *common notions* or adequate ideas that allow understanding, and therefore, once again being in possession of the power of action (Deleuze 1992; also Hardt 1995). The emergence of these common notions such as dignity, democracy and autonomy produced a qualitative change in popular mobilisation and simultaneously served for the recovery of the historical forces of opposition to the capital and to the State without reproducing orthodox revolutionary lexicon of social change. In this sense, these common notions helped expand the definition of popular camps and the terms of the 'enemy'.

The defence of *dignity* became, for the organised picketers in the *Coordinadora de Trabajadores Desocupados Aníbal Verón*, not only a fundamental value of the movement, but rather the motor of their political struggle, much beyond the demand for a more just distribution of income and employment programs incited by CTA or the participation in the revolutionary process, as impelled by the picketing organisations of the political Left. In the same sense, the notion of workers' *autonomy*, cooperativism and social solidarity has guided the process of takeovers of 120 factories in which more than 10,000 workers were involved.

In the sixth place, these new territories coordinate the actions through horizontal structures like inter-zone, interneighbourhood assemblies, board meetings, and provincial, regional and national conferences. The interaction among different forms is developed through a virtual network of resistance. The best example of this was the World Social Forum (WSF) in Argentina: "*Another Argentina is Possible!*" (August 22–25, 2002, Buenos Aires). There, more than 600 organisations (neighbourhood assemblies, social movements, unions, professional associates, universities, human rights, unemployed and others) met to discuss the crisis of neo-liberalism and the challenges for the world movement. The WSF in Argentina created a space for meetings, debates, analyses, convergence, and promotion of the mobilisation against the implementation of the FTAA, solidarity and dissemination, without any attribute of representation or resolution. Thus, four days of intense activity that depended on the participation of political and trade union activists of Latin America included marches, academic and political workshops and cultural events in the parks of Buenos Aires.

In the seventh place, all these organisational forms expounded constructing a counter power to reaffirm, thus, the power of civil society against the crisis of the State, the representative democracy, the economy, the law, and therefore, even the forms of politics of previous resistance to the crisis, thus, understanding the possibilities of social change as a "change from bottom" (from neighbourhoods, streets or factories). This was a new characteristics of politics of resistance in Argentina, a country where existed high grade of institutionalisation of the social conflict. The dynamics of the construction of *counter power* is based, as we see, on the daily commitment directed towards recovering the local public spaces, developing territorial communitarian projects, and citizens' and workers' capacity of control and organisation, including the design of a sort of "social policy from bottom", and the resistance to cooptation, coercion and repression by the local and national state, and in lesser degree, by the trade union and political organisations of co-opting the autonomy of counter power.

IV. Recomposition of Political and Economic Power of the State's Elite

The aftermath of December 2001 deployed two contradictory and yet complementary processes: the *rejection of institutional power* and *the search for order* on the other hand. We can identify three phases of this process.

I. In January 2002, the Duhalde administration restarted the process of economic and political stabilisation through devaluation so dear to the financial sectors and the IMF. Despite the clear message of the popular insurrection of December, the government succumbed once again to the dictates of the IMF promoting (*i*) the abolition of the law of Economic Subversion that allowed legal prosecution of those responsible for draining the financial system (*ii*) changes in the law of bankruptcy in order to protect the enterprises from their creditors' demand for a certain period of time so that they can reorganise their debts (Cibilis et al 2002) (*iii*) a compromise with the provincial governors for reducing the deficit to around 60%.

Within this framework, the new agreement with the IMF would facilitate, according to the organisation, 'opening up the resources' for social programs and would help in "building a sound fiscal framework, restoring confidence in the banking sector" (IMF Survey 2003: 1)

The devaluation of Peso, along with the *Peso-ification* of previous debts in dollars, accompanied by tax exemptions, favoured the most concentrated economic power groups, such as the powerful *Asociación de Empresarios Argentinos* (Argentine Entrepreneurs Association) consisting of 47 members of financial, industrial and service enterprises who are practically the owners of the country. The new rescue plan implemented by the government in June 2002 allowed these enterprises, who unemployment among those below 24 years was 31.8%, around 39% of the youth had been unemployed for more than six months and more than one million with the age group of 15-24 years neither studied nor worked (Lozano and Hourest 2002).

During the Duhalde administration, the State criminalised poverty even more and intensified the repression. In tune with the spirit of the 'war against terror' provoked by the United States and British government, and the Bush administration's obsessive concern with the 'volatile region' of Latin America (*La Nación* 7.2.2003), a new parliamentary project was sent to the National Congress in order to re-discuss the participation of intelligence services in repression of 'domestic terrorism'. Like old times, the project defined 'terrorism' as 'all those activities that take place within the national territory' involving 'groups or individuals who use force to achieve political, social, religious, economic or cultural objectives' (Verbitzky 2003; see project 5-02-2239, HCDN).

While this project impelled by the security forces and the government was discussed, the repression against most sections of the unemployed workers movement, the movement of the farmers of Santiago de Estero, the workers of occupied factories, the participants of neighbourhood assemblies and human rights activists intensified reaching to situations of massacre like the killings of Maximiliano Kosteki and Dario Santillán of *Coordinadora de Piqueteros Aníbal Verón* in hands of the police force of Buenos Aires province on June 26, 2002 (Dinerstein, 2003b).

II. The most important moment that defined the course of political change and the dichotomy of power and counter power was the announcement of elections by the Duhalde administration. The problem for the political elite was how to maintain themselves in power, and at the same time, reflect in the political structures and government programmes the spirit of *"que se vayan todos!"* The problem for neighbourhood assemblies, the autonomous picketers' movement and other social forces was how to maintain the critique wielded in December 2001 and the autonomy of the organisations developed thereafter.

are most important debtors of the financial system, to save more than 6, 500 million dollars (Basualdo *et al* 2002 mimeo).

While the government *"peso-ified"* the debts of the big capital, it failed to open the bank *corralitos*, as only six per cent of the deposits were in the public banks, and therefore the decision of returning the sieged savings now were in the hands of foreign banks who refused to bring funds from their head offices.

In accordance with the opinion of the *'Economistas de Izquierda'* (Left Economists), the economic measures of Duhalde administration not only perpetuated the transfer of income from popular sectors to dominant classes, but also implied an explicit expropriation of the former in favour of the latter, this time without any camouflage or demagogy (Katz 2002b: 20).[9] According to Katz, the expropriation was evident not only in *"peso-ification"* of the debts of big capital, the continuation of interest payments on those debts and *corralitos* but also in other mechanisms such as the confiscation of salaries through inflation and price hikes of the family basket, and lack of regulation in the now privatised service enterprises.

In effect, the devaluation produced inflation too, perpetuating through the decline in the incomes of the popular classes, augmenting poverty and unemployment. The rate of unemployment in February 2002 was 21.8% affecting 3, 200, 000 workers. As an absolute record, it is calculated that more than seven million people had fallen under poverty line between October 2001 and 2002. There are 21 million people in the population of 37 million who live under the poverty line; 10 million of these are considered destitute. That is 57.5% of Argentines do not get sufficient income to cover their basic needs. The situation is particularly terrible in North-west (Jujuy, Salta, La Rioja, Santiago del Estero and Tucamán) where these figures ascend to 69% and in the region of Cuyo (Mendoza, San Juan and San Luis) reaches to 61.3% (INDEC in *La Nación* 1.2.2003).

It is important to highlight that 55% of the youth are poor, especially due to the impact of unemployment over poverty. That is to say, unemployment is more acute among the poor than among those who are not. In October 2001, the rate of (which finally only A y L realised) and demanded a Constituent Assembly that would be in charge of organising and controlling the elections.

During May, June, July 2002, the electoral campaign demonstrated an intense fight among the potential presidential candidates, the indifference of civil society and a tremendous political fragmentation. Elisa Carrió, of ARI, represented the proposal of the Left centre with a program that advocated the distribution of the revenues and re-activation of a national economy through reforms in the tax system, implementation of social policies and control over private enterprises. Zamora of A y L, represented the radical proposal of breaking away from the IMF, declaring of *default*, re-nationalisation of private enterprises, as and when would be accompanied by large sections of mobilised population with whom would be constructed new forms of democratic participation and counter power. A third force was constituted by Rodriguez Saa, who was president for a brief period, from the popular insurrection till Duhalde took over. He presented a populist program called the *Bases para la Fundación de la República Argentina* (Foundational Basis of Argentine Republic) that included creation of a million employment and default. On the other side of the political spectrum were the ex-minister de la Rua Lopez Murphy, and the ex-president Menem who represented the continuity of orthodox and repressive economic policies.

Despite the fact, that the electoral campaign witnessed a huge political disillusionment with representative democracy and political class, i.e., days before the elections of April 2003, half of the electorate thought that the elections were not going to change anything (*Página/12* online 17.4.02), the tricky way of electoral system gave the people hardly any choice other than Duhalde and Menem. That is, as time passed the radical and anti-institutional spirit of *"que se vayan todos!"* was overshadowed by clear threats of Menem's return to power. Luis Zamora withdrew from the electoral race, Carrió contested for votes with other candidates and option between Menem and the candidate of Duhalde, Kirchner, was becoming more and more inevitable.

The assemblies and movements refused to participate in the elections. Voting would mean legitimising the political order, and therefore, losing the autonomy and capacity of mobilisation and resistance. Moreover, some members of the movement planned boycotting the elections through different forms of civil disobedience, from marches and protests to graffiti, pan banging and ballots printed with slogans *"que se vayan todos!"* that were to be used to replace the real ballot papers (Hauser 2003a). In various discussions, the members argued that "the elections had the objective of achieving that 'they all should stay!' And nothing can be elected, except different variations of the same regime" ..."we need to be united in order to vote together so that 'they all must go!'" (*Página*/12, 24the March 2003)

The election announcements also produced strong tensions within the picketing movement. Although all sections of the movement agreed that the elections would not reflect any change, and condemned the intensifying of repression by the government against social protest that would be ratified in the popular vote, the attitude towards the elections varied (Dinerstein 2003c). The picketers close to CTA (FTV and CCC) as well as those linked to the political Left decided to participate in the elections, while the more autonomous section like the *Coordinadora Aníbal Verón* refused to vote maintaining thus the politics of constructing a counter power as the fundamental process of change: "we are at bottom and we don't want to go anywhere. We will always be the rebels" (quoted in *Colectivo Situaciones* 2001b).

Some political forces tried to sum up the spirit of *"que se vayan todos!"* in political proposals. In August 2002, the leaders of CTA, along with new political parties *Asociación por una República de Iguales* (Association for a Republic of Equals), headed by Elisa Carrió and *Autodeterminación y Libertad* (A y L–Self determination and Freedom) under the leadership of Luis Zamora, demanded from the government broadening of the election announcements to all political posts. This claim questioned the idea of changing only the head of the State. Some of these forces considered the possibility of abstaining

In an election where 80% of electorate went to vote, when more than 60% of them were choosing a political option which according to them was not going to produce any radical change can be explained partially by the fact that blank vote would have given an advantage to ex-president Menem, as only those votes are counted which are affirmative. The voting of 27 April was a completely anti-Menemist mandate. Kirchner got only 22% in the first round and in the second place was the ex-president Menem. The second round did not take place as Menem renounced his candidature sensing a defeat. The victory of the second round in May 2003 was not 'blank vote' but rather Néstor Kirchner. He was appointed the president and with the Menemism reached its end.

III. Kirchner's appointment, celebrated in Buenos Aires by Fidel Castro, Lula da Silva and Hugo Chávez, initiated a new phase of the processes unleashed in December 2001. The appointment of President Kirchner has changed the social mood and the government enjoys a moment of hope and credibility, particularly from the middle classes. This has a positive impact on the trustworthiness of democratic institutions and the system of political representation.[10] Populist sentiments have been re-energised as some of the new policies took on board some of the demands put forward by the popular insurrection and the organisational forms of participation, which followed it. Kirchner has distanced itself from Duhalde by officially locating at least *discursively* the need for an urgent solution to social needs as a priority in the political agenda, which consequently situates the claims from IMF and the international financial community to a secondary place.

The new administration: (*i*) has shown a shift with regards to human rights and particularly towards the unresolved problem of the trials of the perpetrators of crime against humanity during 1976-1982; (*ii*) started the cleansing of the Supreme Court members accused of several acts of corruption during the Menem administration; (*iii*) confronted the owners of the former state-owned companies as well as public sector concessions many from the European Community (iv) put some limits, at least discursively, to the IMF demands, although this political attitude was reflected neither into a *moratorium* on the external debt nor in any other radical change vis-à-vis the Fund but in the approval of a new loan of US $12.55 billion three-year stand-by credit for Argentina. In return, the IMF demands a three-year programme where includes a fiscal surplus of 3% of the GDP for 2004 (iv) The new administration has agreed with the three central labour confederations CGT, the CGT dissident and the CTA with the cancellation of the last Labour Reform Bill, whose implementation was vigorously demanded by the IMF under Menem and passed under de la Rua. This decision was taken after the results of a legal investigation of the political scandal of the bribes in the Senate around this particular piece of legislation in April 2000 came to light in December 2003. This scandal had contributed to the political disintegration of the Alliance and had led to the resignation of the vice president of the nation Carlos Alvarez in October 2000. The contested bill has been replaced by new legislation to regulate collective bargaining with the agreement of the three central confederations.

However, there are a number of issues that remain unsolved and that are key for the Kirchner administration: the most important being relationship with IMF and the implications of the new agreement for the future, the unemployment rates are expected to remain at two digits during the Kirchner period in office, the present occupational structure and social vulnerability wherein only a minority of workers, that is 3.4 million, are registered as waged labour and wherein poverty remains threatened by the chronic lack of institutional capacity to deliver social policies.; the tension produced by US government pressure on Argentina to participate in the implementation of the unpopular FTAA and the need to reassure alliances with neighbouring countries like Brazil in the context of MERCOSUR, the militarisation of the region following the government's concern with the security of the triangle formed by Argentina, Brazil and Paraguay, together with the Bolivia and Venezuela.

As for social and the labour movements, the *asambleas* have consolidated their territorial communitarian work but have decreased in their capacity to mobilise. Many of them are consolidated as organisational forms, actively involved in the delivering of 'social policy from below', taking on board social problems and needs and sorting out communitarian strategies and solutions to them: popular dining rooms, art workshops, popular education for the illiterate, charity, collaboration with workers in recovered factories, implementation of survival strategies and micro *emprendimientos* (*Página/12* 22.12.03: 6).

The struggles of the most radical sectors of the *Piquetero* movement continue to be under Kirchner, the most significant (only) form of political opposition in Argentina. By the end of 2003, the confrontations between right and centre-left of the neo-Peronist alliance in power, i.e. between Duhalde and Kirchner, over how to deal with the picketers and popular mobilisation in general pointed towards a political rupture of this alliance. Whereas Duhalde demanded tougher controls, Kirchner argued that he would not change his policy of dialogue with the picketers. The latter prevailed and holds so far (February 2004) a strategy aiming to maintain dialogue with the labour and the picketers' movement and hence avoid confrontations with its most radical sectors such as the *Bloque Piquetero Nacional* and obtain support from the most institutionalised ones (FTV/CTA).

The unity between middle and working classes, exceptionally achieved behind the motto '*Piquetes y Cacerolas, la lucha es una sola!*' could not be maintained in the long term as there is an accommodation of the middle classes to the Kirchner's order

V. The Nature of Political Change in Post-Crisis Argentina

The post-crisis mobilisation presented a battle against imperialism, the repressive State, the corrupt law and the exclusionary economic policies, but at the same time it fought against the previous forms of politics, including the participation and resistance, which had become an obstacle to the expression of social rebellion facing the world of power.

The popular mobilisation did not demand in December the renovation of authorities but rather a change in the forms of institutional politics. Anti-politics found its limits in the very organisational forms which allowed the process of rejection to come to light. Labour confronted its own limits as the process of reinvention took place. As a result, despite that the general rejection of neo-liberalism and power was momentous, there was a decline and fragmentation as well of popular mobilisation under Kirchner. Four commemorative acts for the second anniversary of December 2001 gathering, four different sectors of the social and labour movement were held on December 2003, showing the high level of fragmentation of social movements.

This was interpreted as a *failure* that conforms to the country's historical pattern of fragmentation of the social and labour movements and their state-dependence. As a result the impact of the popular insurrection on Argentine politics has been progressively underestimated and reduced to the idea of 'cathartic' event. Indeed, the rebellion did not entail concrete political demand. Unlike other cases, where popular mobilisation entailed an intense clash over defending or attacking a political leader or a state policy, and thus, undoubtedly included a friction on the meaning of civil society itself, as in the case of Venezuela, the Argentine case manifested a momentary but qualitatively important rejection of the state politics *as a whole*, in favour of greater development and recovery of the organisations of the popular sphere. This is a qualitative leap from the earlier years and I have described it as a struggle that rejects practically the notion of civil society as (passive) subsidiary to State in order to articulate a struggle that tries "to transform", in Tischler's words (2001), "civil society into subject". Rejecting the idea of civil society as an object, which can be easily manipulated for endorsing State policies or canalising the movements adequately, the post-December popular mobilisation developed a struggle for transforming the civil society into subject, questioning the political, economic and legal separations and mediations.

Looking at the existing relationship between the forms of popular mobilisation and the forms of crisis, it is evident that the political idea of anti-power was not due to a planned strategy that can be judged as flawed or correct, but rather an outcome of the crisis itself and the limits that the crisis imposed on the popular mobilisation. In this case, the profundity of the articulated and almost total institutional crisis bore a rejection of political, economic and legal mediations, and the consequent opening up of new spaces from where one has to restart the recovery of politics itself and reinvent the democracy. There was a shift in the political dynamics of the country and for the first time, autonomous and 'disorganised' movements became paradoxically *central* to political processes thus overshadowing institutional politics.

So the political change in Argentina since December 2001 is found, first, in the momentous recuperation of the *individual capacity for collective action* and mobilisation after a period of intense individualism and disillusion; second, in the recovery of the *political (collective) subjectivity* understood as the recomposition of identities, organisational forms and action strategies capable of articulating collective action no longer in a totally fragmented fashion but in a broader and universal manner, articulated by new common notions such as the defence of dignity, autonomy, democracy and justice.

Whereas this process certainly helped in strengthening the new organisational forms at territorial, local level, of solidarity action and new networks of resistance, the construction of counter power was, as expected, contradictory and complex, not due to organisational or ideological debility but as a result of the conditions that the capitalist social relations impose on popular mobilisation. The *politics of anti-politics* (Dinerstein 2003a) did not contest the State power, whose recomposition was in the hands of the Peronist elites who were in the government.

Yet, in the capitalist societies, the State mediation is difficult to elude while the State is the principal organiser and feeder of social relations of capitalist production. The success of counter power has not rested on the results obtained at institutional level but in the power to cut across the contradiction presented in and against the State. The struggle of neighbourhood assemblies with the city government of Buenos Aires on participative budget, or the struggle of picketers' movement with the Ministry of Labour for redefining the use of employment programs for joint productive projects designed by the unemployed movement, and the struggle of workers of the occupied factory movements for simultaneous autonomy and the need for legal resolutions of the takeovers, are only three instances of struggle in favour and against the economic and legal state power.

Does this imply that the political change in Argentina has been a failure, as it has not reflected directly in the change of State power? It is not in the sphere of state where we will find answers to the question posed in this paper on the nature of post-December political change, though the new winds brought about the Kirchner administration should not be underrated.

The argument developed in this paper has been that the recovery of collective action and the reinvention of political subjectivities constitute the fundamental basis for any process of significant political change, whose forms yet cannot be foreseen. Although these new developments are expressed at national level, it is obvious that they cannot be understood wholly without taking into consideration the recent developments in the Latin American region, however, at the same time, in other parts of the world. The recovery of politics and renegotiation of the subjectivity developed in these new or revived *territories* of participation and counter power are developing in *local* geographies, in the context of *global* processes where the local or the territorial spheres become the actual terrain of struggle for achieving the expansion of the processes called globalisation, which are undoubtedly processes of fragmentation and unequal development.

It deals, hence, with the *glocal* forms of struggle, which are at the same time local and global, political and economic, for political recognition and a more just distribution of income. Different local forms of demanding social insertions, social policies, beneficent State, participatory democracy, employment generation or securing national citizenship against the power of corporations, related to national processes, show a similar *global* characteristic that underlies differences: a will to recover the ability of political mobilisation in a broad and articulated manner which contains a warning about the absence of rationality in the 'capitalist globalisation', understood as the possibility of human realisation and that it is extending beyond its own limits.

This popular mobilisation, whose latest expression was found in Bolivia in October 2003, poses two fundamental questions that today have spread throughout the whole world and that refers to the possibility of reproduction of capitalist society: what are the limits to the subordination of human life to the movement of global capital? What are the political and organisational forms capable of articulating a collective action around a plural project that combines the universal recognition of the centrality of the human and the particular forms through which that recognition is expressed? New spaces for politics were unlocked again in Argentina in December 2001. The present time does not seem to be about legitimising, adapting or 'democratising' the global terrorism of money but rather I believe, about reflecting on the experience of insubordination and the meaning of politics, democracy and change as the basis for wider political transformation.

NOTES

1. This article contains material that appears in an extended form in the forthcoming book *Against the Violence of Stability: On Labour, Crises and the Politics of Resistance in Argentina*; Verso; London – New York. Translated from *'Más allá de la Crisis. La Naturaleza del cambio político en Argentina'* Revista Venezolana de Economía y Ciencias Sociales, University of Caracas, Caracas, Special Issue on 'Popular Resistance and Political Change in Latin America', January 2004.
2. The term 'left' is used here in a general sense but important differences exist among different parties should to be addressed.
3. The interest of the USA in aiding Argentina was, in the first place, economic given that the American companies are the most important investors in Argentina. And, in the second place, political, as the support of de la Rua administration to the implementation of the Free Trade Area for American Continents

(FTAA) in a near future became indispensable against a negative threat by the Venezuelan President, Hugo Chavez.
4. Different from the fragmented, focalised and subsidiary policies of the State, the proposal of CTA consists of a broader strategy of distribution of income that could have an effect at the level of demand and development of internal market as the principal re-activator of the economy, force the capital to a strategy of production closer to the needs of the people and the State to invest in social policies directed towards the most vulnerable sections of the population instead of subsidising the capital (IDEP-CTA 2002, 2000).
5. Comments extracted from group interviews carried out by the author in June 2002, in Buenos Aires, with ten young participants in the mobilisation of 19th and 20th December 2001, working at the *Observatorio Social para América Latina* (OSAL), *Consejo Latinoamericano de Ciencias Sociales* (CALCSO), Buenos Aires.
6. *Escrache* is a slang term which signifies the act of highlighting a person so that the rest of the people understand his actions. Here the term *escrache* refers to a form of protest introduced by H.I.J.O.S. (*Hijos por la Identidad y la Justicia contra el Olvido y el Silencio*) [Sons/daughters for Identity and Justice against the Oblivion and Silence}, during the 1990s and beginning of 2000. The *escrache* is done after a profound local work in front of the houses of ex-torturers, suppressors and collaborators of the last military dictatorship, who find themselves free, an outcome of the laws of *Obediencia Debida y Punto Final* passed by the Congress during the democratic transition. After the crisis of December, using *escraches* was generalised as a mode of protest against the political class, business class and IMF.
7. This recovery includes the emergence of debates that seemed to be dead such as on reform and revolution, radical, direct or representative democracy, the relationship of the Left with the State, Anarchist or institutionalised resistance, the IMF and globalisation at work places, bars, schools and universities, local areas and homes.
8. See note 8.
9. See EDI documents at *www.geocities.com/economistas_de_izquierda*
10. According to a public poll by *Centro de Estudios de Opinion Publica* (CEOP) in November and December 2003, 64% of Argentineans has a positive view on the new government and believe that the

rate of unemployment will fall and security as well as public education will improve (*Clarín*, 28.12.03: 3)

REFERENCES

Aguirre-Sacassa M, (2002) 'Argentina: A Failure in Market Economics?' *Financial Times* online, FT.com, March 2002, http://news.ft.com

Altamira, J (2002) *El Argentinazo. El presente como historia*, Buenos Aires: Rumbos.

Basualdo E y Kulfas M, (2002) 'Fuga de capitales y endeudamiento externo en la Argentina' *Realidad Económica* nro. 173, IADE, Buenos Aires: 76-103 (http://www.iade.org.ar)

Basualdo, E *et al* (2002), 'Las transferencias de recursos a la cúpula económica durante la presidencia Duhalde. El nuevo plan social del gobierno', paper presentado en la *Asamblea Nacional del FRENAPO*, 2.3.02, mimeo.

Botana N (2002) 'La democracia en zona de riesgo' *La Nación* online, 28.2.02.

Cibils A, Weisbrot M Y Kar D (2002) 'Argentina since default. The IMF and the Depression' *Centre for Economic and Policy Research*, Briefing paper, September 3.

Clarke, S (1992) 'The Global Accumulation of Capital and the Periodisation of the Capitalist State Form' *Open Marxism* Vol. I. 1992: 133-179.

Colectivo Situaciones (2001) *MTD Solano*, Buenos Aires: Ediciones de mano en mano.

Dávalos P (2001) 'Argentina y el FMI', *América Latina en Movimiento* http://alainet.org

Dinerstein A (1999) 'Sujeto y Globalización. La experiencia de la abstracción' *Doxa* 20, Buenos Aires: 87-106.

Dinerstein, A (2001), 'El poder de lo irrealizado. El corte de ruta en Argentina y el potencial subversivo de la mundialización' *Observatorio Social de América Latina (OSAL)*, 5: 11-16.

Dinerstein, A (2003a) 'The Battle of Buenos Aires. Crisis, Insurrection and the Reinvention of Politics in Argentina' *Historical Materialism*. 10.4: 5-38.

Dinerstein A (2003b) 'A Silent Revolution: The Unemployed Workers Movement in Argentina' *Labour Capital & Society/Travail, Capital & Societé*. CDAS, McGill University, Montreal, vol. 34 (2): 166-183.

Dinerstein A (2003c) 'Power or counter power? The dilemma of the *Piquetero* movement in Argentina post-crisis', *Capital & Class* 81: 1-8.

Dinerstein A (2004) *Against the Violence of Stability: On Labour, Crises and the Politics of Resistance In Argentina*; Verso; London – New York, forthcoming

Dinerstein A and Neary M (2002) 'Anti-Value in Motion: Labour, Real Subsumption and the Struggles against Capitalism' in Dinerstein A and Neary M (2002) (coi ip) *The Labour Debate. An Investigation into the Theory and Reality of Capitalist Work*, Ashgate, Aldershot: 226-239.

Esteva G (1999) The Zapatistas and the People's power' *Capital & Class* 68: 153-182.

Gambina, Julio *et al* (2002) 'Rebeliones y Puebladas. Diciembre de 2001 y Enero de 2002. Viejos y Nuevos Desposeídos en Argentina' Buenos Aires, *Cuadernos de la FISyP* no 7 (serie 2).

Hauser I (2003) 'Las Asambleas mantienen el QSVT' *Página/12*, online, 24.3.03 http://200.61.159.98/diario/elpais/1-17958-2003-03-24.html

Holloway (2002) *Cambiar el mundo sin tomar el poder. El significado de la revolución hoy*, Herramienta, Buenos Aires.

Holloway, J. y E. Peláez (1998) *Zapatista! Reinventing Revolution in México*, Pluto: Londres.

IDEP-CTA (2002) *Shock Distributivo, autonomía nacional y democratización*, IDEP-y Editorial La Página, Buenos Aires.

IDEP-CTA (2000) 'Transformar la crisis en una oportunidad: shock redistributivo y profundización democrática' *Mesa de Coyuntura*, June, Buenos Aires, mimeo.

IMFSURVEY (2003) Vol. 32, nro. 1, 20 de Enero de 2003, http://www.imf.org/imfsurvey.

Katz C (2002) 'Una expropiación explícita' in IADE 2002 'Debate: Medidas Económicas, Ganadores y Perdedores', *Realidad Económica* no 186: 20-28.

Krueger, A (2002) 'The lessons to be learned form the Argentine crisis and how these can be used to raise the effectiveness of IMF efforts to prevent and resolve financial crisis', Address to the Last National Bureau for Economic research conference, *IMFSURVEY* 2002 Vol. 31, No 15, August 5, http://www.imf.org/imfsurvey.

Llorens J y Cafiero P (2002) '¿Qué se hicieron de las "cuantiosas" reservas del sistema financiero argentino?' Reporte sobre el Vaciamiento del Sistema Financiero Argentino, *Cámara de*

Diputados de la Nación, http://www1.hcdn.gov.ar/dependencias/ari/Principal/principal.htm

Llorens J y Cafiero M (2001) '¿Por qué se quiere derogar la ley de subversión económica?' Reporte sobre el Vaciamiento del Sistema Financiero Argentino, *Cámara de Diputados de la Nación*, http://www1.hcdn.gov.ar/dependencias/ari/Principal/principal.htm

Lozano C y Hourest M (2002) 'La democracia y el FMI: entre la mentira y el crimen' *Realidad Económica* 187, IADE: 36-55.

MacEwan A (2002) 'Economic debacle in Argentina: the IMF Strikes Again' A Global Affairs Commentary, *Foreign Policy Focus, http://www.fpif.org*, January 2, 2002.

Mussa M (2002) *Argentina and the Fund: From Triumph to Tragedy*, Institute for International: Economics, Washington DC.

Ollier M (2003) 'Argentina: Up A Blind Alley Once Again' *Bulletin of Latin American Research* Vol.22 No.2: 170-186

Política y Teoría no 48, Revista del Comunismo revolucionario de la Argentina, Ediciones HOY, Abril-Julio 2002, Buenos Aires.

Rock, D (2002) 'Racking Argentina' *New Left Review* 17, September-October 2002: 55-86.

Schuster F et al (2002) *La Trama de la crisis*, Cuaderno de Coyuntura No 3, Instituto de Investigaciones Gino Germani, Universidad de Buenos Aires, Buenos Aires.

Sevares J (2002) 'La crisis del sistema bancario' *Le Monde Diplomatique* Junio 2002, Buenos Aires: 6-7.

Tedesco, L (2002) 'Argentina's turmoil: the Politics of Informality and the Roots of Economic meltdown' *Cambridge Review of International Affairs*, Vol. 15 No 3: 469-481.

Tischler, S (2001) 'La "sociedad Civil": ¿Fetiche? ¿Sujeto?' *Bajo el Volcán* Año 2 nro. 3, Puebla: 169-181.

Various Authors (2001) 'Hacia el Plan Fenix. Diagnóstico y Propuestas. Una estrategia de reconstrucción de la economía argentina para el desarrollo y la equidad, *Realidad Económica* no 182: 6-23.

Verbitzky, H. (2003) "Al ataque. Preparativos de represión del conflicto social", Pagina/12, 26.1.03, online, http://www.pagina12web.com.ar/diario/elpais/1-15893-2003-1-26.html

Weisbrot M 2002 *Hearing on 'the State of Argentine Economic Crisis and the Role of the International Monetary Fund DC*, http://www.financialservices.house.gov/media/pdf/030502mw.pdf

Weisbrot M and Baker D 2002 'What happened to Argentina' January 31, 2002 in Weisbrot M 2002 *Hearing on* ...op. cit. appendix.

Anti-Globalisation versus Anti-Capitalism: The Dangers of Nationalism, Racism and Anti-Semitism

Werner Bonefeld

Preface

During the last decade we have seen the deep recession of the early 1990s, the European currency crises of 1992 and 1993, the plunge of the Mexican peso in December 1994 which rocked financial markets around the world, the Asian crisis of 1997, the Russian crisis of 1998, the Brazilian crisis of 1999, and the Argentinean crisis of 2001. Japan teeters on the edge of depression and then there is the speculative bubble in the New York Stock Exchange and the dramatic global slowdown. There is hardly a day without warnings about the immanent burst of the bubble and a worldwide depression. The nightmare of a full-scale world economic crisis, world war and unfettered barbarism cannot easily be excluded as a real possibility. 'We know how rapidly an epoch of global prosperity, underpinning prospects of world peace and international harmony, can become an epoch of global confrontation, culminating in war. If such a prospect seems unlikely now, it seemed equally unlikely a century ago' (Clarke, 2001, p. 91) and it seems more likely today than only yesterday. How many wars have been fought since the end of the cold war and how many will follow in the years to come? And then there is terrorism. The events of September 11th demonstrated with brutal force the impotence of sense, significance, and thus reason and ultimately truth. The denial of human quality and difference was absolute—not even their corpses survived. And the response? It confirmed that state terrorism and terrorism are two sides of the same coin. Between them, nothing is allowed to survive.

Many critics of globalisation urge the creation of new forms of political regulation at the national and international level to humanise global capital, containing its 'neo-liberal' self-destructive force in favour of the common good. What, however, is the common good in a capitalistically constituted form of social reproduction? The 'good' appears to be the creation of wealth that capital is able to achieve for all, if it is made accountable to liberal-democratic forms of regulation. Yet, does the humanisation of inhuman conditions not presuppose these same conditions as eternal? Regardless of its historically changing forms (Agnoli, 1997, Clarke, 1992), the function of the capitalist state has always been to secure the common good of a capitalistically organised form of social reproduction: capitalist accumulation (cf. Agnoli, 2002).

The great scandal of global capital is that it is choking itself up on the pyramids of accumulated abstract wealth. Yet, when looking at social conditions, when listening to the ever more urgent demand for greater labour flexibility, it seems as if the global crisis is really just a consequence of a scarcity of capital. This is indeed the conclusion one would have to reach when one looks at Africa's misery, when one sees the thousands and thousands of children living in poverty, not just in Africa, not just in Latin America and Asia, not just in those areas of the world deemed inessential by global capital but also in the centres of globalisation, in Western-Europe and the USA. Yet, the dramatic increase in poverty and misery across the globe is not caused by conditions of economic scarcity. There is too much capital, too many commodities that can not be sold for profit, too many workers are 'overexploited', on the one hand, and, on the other, too many workers are not even exploitable. Over the last two decades, profits have risen and so too has unemployment. Labour productivity has increased dramatically and poverty has increased, wages have stagnated, and conditions deteriorated. Marx focused this 'constellation' well when he argued that '[S]ociety suddenly finds itself put back into a state of momentary barbarism; it appears as if famine, a universal war of devastation had cut off the supply of every means of subsistence; industry and commerce seem to be destroyed; and why? Because there is too much civilisation, too much means of subsistence; too much industry, too much commerce. The productive forces at the disposal of society no longer tend to further the development of the conditions of bourgeois property; on the contrary, they have become too powerful for these conditions, by which they are fettered, and so soon as they overcome these fetters, they bring disorder into the whole of bourgeois society, endanger the existence of bourgeois property. The conditions of bourgeois society are too narrow to comprise the wealth created by them. And how does bourgeois society get over these crises? On the one hand by enforced destruction of a mass of productive forces; on the other, by the conquest of new markets, and by the more thorough exploitation of the old ones' (Marx and Engels, 1996, pp. 18–19).

The contemporary conditions of poverty, misery, hopelessness, and hunger are not just an appearance of the contradictions of capitalist social reproduction on a global scale. They are also sharp reminders of a conception of progress that entailed barbarism from its inception.[1] Critics argue, rightly, that if unchecked, globalisation will lead to barbarism. However, barbarism has already been. In relation to an earlier resolution to global crisis, Adorno's (1990) insight demands serious consideration: Auschwitz, he argued, not only confirmed the violence of the bourgeois relations of abstract equality and abstract identity. It also confirmed the bourgeois exchange relations of pure identity as death. It is, however, the case that the horror of Auschwitz persists as a barbaric solution to crisis for as long as those social relations exist that made Auschwitz possible (Adorno, 1969, p. 85).

Negt (2001) is surely right when he charges many left critics of globalisation for their failure to offer any views on how the accumulated wealth can be used to liberate millions and millions of people, not only in the 'developing' societies but in the centres of wealth too, from conditions of misery, poverty and starvation; and on how socially necessary labour can be organised to meet human needs. Critics urge the creation of new forms of political regulation at the national and international level to contain capital's 'neo-liberal' self-destructive force in favour of the common good. In opposition to global institutions like the WTO which are seen to affirm neo-liberal values and institutionalise an unfair system of trade, critics urge the renewal of democratic controls of capital so as to regulate trade more fairly and limit the power of global finance and global financial institutions that keep so-called developing nations in debt and force them further into debt. Others call for the de-linking of 'developing' countries from the world market to secure national economic development. Globalisation is seen here as a form of American imperialism and global institutions, like the IMF, are seen as agencies of US imperial power. National self-determination is seen as a socialist opposition to imperialist globalisation. What, however, is anti-capitalistic in anti-capitalism when it seeks to regulate capital without touching the relations of exploitation, when it poses the national state as the sovereign power that places controls on capital to secure the common national good? What is the common national good? The function and role of the national state is to achieve homogeneity of national conditions. In its liberal conception, this means the equality of all before the law. In its Leninist conception, it means the equality of labour. In its nationalist version it means equality as a nation, as a Volk. In its essence, the nationalist conception of equality in terms of Volk entails the projection of a classless 'national community' whose existence is seen to be threatened by the 'external enemy within'.

The anti-globalisation movement of the political Left originated, in Europe at least, against the new anti-immigration populist right led by, for example, Le Pen in France, Haider in Austria, and also Hanson in Australia. The populist right poses national identity and communality as a response to the perceived threats of globalisation. The common feeling of these nationalist forces was well focused by Mahathir Mohamad, the Prime Minister of Malaysia. His assessment of Malaysia's financial collapse in 1997 is symptomatic: 'I say openly, these people are racists. They are not happy to see us prosper. They say we grow too fast, they plan to make us poor. We are not making enemies with other people but others are making enemies with us'.[2] Leaving aside the discrimination of particularly Malaysian citizens of Chinese background aside, what is meant by 'we' and who are the racialised 'they'?

In its structure, the conception of 'speculators' as the external enemy bent on destroying relations of national economy harmony, belongs to modern anti-Semitism. It summons the idea of finance and speculators as merchants of greed and, counterposed to this, espouses the idea of a national community. In the nationalist conception of equality, the 'folk is "subject to blood", it arises from the "soil", it furnishes the homeland with indestructible force and permanence, it is united by characteristics of "race", the preservation of whose purity is the condition of the folk's "health" (Marcuse, 1988, p. 23). Nationalism offers a barbaric solution to globalisation. The evocation of the external enemy serves to displace the focus from the inherent antagonism of capitalism and projects the racialist figure of an external intruder as the cause of national disharmony and misfortune. The traditional figure of this ideological projection is the 'Jew'.

The nerve-centre of barbarism is a fetishistic critique of global relations that projects a class-ridden society as a national community, subsuming, through arson and murder, class relations into the abstract identity of national sameness – the national 'we'. National wealth and autonomy is seen to be undermined by external forces that disrupt the integrity of national economies. Thus 'national disharmony' is merely imported from the outside. The nationalist critique of global capital, then, favours the strong and capable state to restore the cohesion, integrity, and wealth creating potentials of its national economy against threats to stability from the outside. Historically, the restoration of 'national harmony' developed through war and the transformation of economies into war economies. This transformation depends on the creation of the national 'we' and thus on the identification and persecution of the 'external' enemy within. This machination is inherently racist and can easily tip over into anti-Semitism. Racism stands for a barbaric conception of 'equality' and, as this essay argues, anti-Semitism is the objective ideology of barbarism that makes anti-capitalism directly useful for capitalism. It amounts to a fetishistic critique of bourgeois notions of equality in favour of an abstract national identity, of *Volk*.

Racism and anti-Semitism are different-in-unity. All forms of racism project the Other as a disintegrating power, allegedly undermining the integration of the much-praised one-national boat that ostensibly is threatened by globalisation. Racism projects the power of the Other as a 'sub-human' (*Untermenschen*) power. This 'power' is in contrast to anti-Semitism, perceived as a rooted power. That is, the projected Other is seen to be rooted either nationally (Turks should live in Turkey, not in Germany; black Americans come from Africa and are Africans) or should accept their position of inferiority as 'sub-humans' within 'nations' without question. Racism regulates the Other through institutional racism, forced return to 'their homeland', segregation, racial profiling, as well as arson and murder. Racism transposes feudal relations of social hierarchy, position and privilege on to bourgeois society, modernizing, as it were, the relations between master and slave as relations of an 'organic' society sustaining the abstract exchange relations of capital through the racist differentiation of the dependent masses, and that is, the institutional regulation of racialised underclass.

Anti-Semitism, in contrast, projects the Other as rootless. For the anti-Semite, the Jew comes from no-where. Lyotard (1993, p. 159) summaries this projection well. 'The Jews are not a nation. They do not speak a language of their own. They have no roots in a nature...They claim to have their roots in a book'. The anti-Semite does not project the Jew as sub-human. Instead, theirs is the power of an immensely powerful, intangible, international conspiracy (cf. Postone, 1986). Their power cannot be defined concretely. 'Anti-Semitism is the rumour about Jews'

(Adorno, 1951, p. 141). The Jew is seen as the one who stands behind phenomena. Racism's projection of the Other as a real or potential slave contrasts with anti-Semitism's projection of the Jew as evil personified. This Other can thus not be regulated, neither politically nor economically. It has to be, as the anti-Semites have it, destroyed, that is, exterminated.

Introduction

In the Preface to his *Philosophy of Right*, Hegel argued that those who render abstractions effective in social life are engaged in the destruction of social reality. Human values such as honesty, sincerity, tolerance, and especially dignity have no price and cannot be quantified, neither sold nor bought. These values connote individual human distinctiveness, difference, sense and significance, that is, Man (*Mensch*) in possession of himself as a subject. Yet, we are used to think in terms of abstractions, such as capital, the market, the state, the Nation, etc. These, following Sohn-Rhetel's (1970) terminology, are really existing abstractions. The purpose of Marx's critique of fetishism was to demystify their ostensibly objective force and to show that their apparent independence is an objective delusion. He argued that their objective force has a real existence as forms of social relations, that is, as forms constituted and reproduced through human social practice. Their objective delusion is fostered by the capitalist exchange relations themselves. They suggest that rationally acting subjects meet on the market to realise their rational interests, whereas in fact they act as executives of abstract social laws which they themselves have generated historically and reproduce through their rational behaviour and over which they have no control (Reichelt, 2002, p. 143).

In the false totality of bourgeois society it takes courage to demystify abstractions. Dignity has no price. It can however be destroyed when critical-practical judgment is suspended through the identification of really existing humans as mere personifications of abstractions. There is only one human standard which, though unchangeable and indivisible, can be lost—through the imposition of abstract identity (cf. Adorno, 1990). Thinking in terms of abstractions is all-pervasive. This is especially relevant in relation to Israel. Israel is rightly condemned for its policy towards the Palestinians. This condemnation, however, all too easily takes anti-Semitic forms as the difference between really existing individuals and their coercive integration in the form of the state is purged. The mounting scale and sheer extent of the anti-Semitic tidal wave especially in the Middle East has blurred any distinction between the rightful critique of Israeli nationalism and concrete persons, including their class divided mode of existence. Just as the management of the Israeli class conflict through the militarisation of its policy towards the Palestinians, Islamist struggle for national self-determination is commandeered by leaders to achieve, not the emancipation of a people, but their own political emancipation in the form of the national state. Many on the left tend to dismiss rampant Islamist anti-Semitism as a mere epiphenomena of justified anger at Israel and US imperialism. Susan George's (quoted in Callinicos, 2003) description of al Qaeda as fascist fundamentalists drew a rebuke from Callinicos who argued that the Muslim concept *ummah* contrasts to the fascist doctrine of blood and soil because it is a transnational one. al Qaeda, he rightly points out, incorporates activists from many different national backgrounds. He forgets that blood and soil included the 'transnational doctrine' and practice of Lebensraum and that the composition of the SS incorporated many different national backgrounds, including British subjects. Nevertheless, Callinicos is right: historical analogies offer little in terms of analysis and explanation. Yet, if the understanding of fascism is restricted to the experience of European fascist regimes, then fascism has no longer to be feared. Conditions change. It is, however, not the past but the present that demonstrates truth and that is, the potential of fascism's return has to be ascertained against the background of contemporary class struggles and conditions. Herein lies the challenge of George's characterisation. Ideologically, fascist ideology belongs to the far right. However, for fascism to become effective, it has to become an extremism of the political centre. The contemporary transformation of the bourgeois state into a market-liberal security state poses this fascist potential.

Islamic fundamentalism can itself be seen as a reaction against the 'heavy artillery' of global capital to create a world after its own image. Against this, Islamic fundamentalism espouses the quest for authenticity, seeking to preserve through the purification of imagined ancestral conditions and traditions existing social structures. The fight against 'westoxication', as Khomeini called the ideas of liberalism, democracy and socialism, indicates that Islamic anti-Semitism is unlikely to be assuaged by an Israeli-Palestinian settlement. It is more likely to be inflamed. At base, it is the depiction of Israel as an imperialist bridgehead of 'Jewish' capitalist counterinsurgency that fuels the hatred of Israel as a 'Jewish' state. What one may ask is a Jewish state? The attribute might refer to a concrete human being, for example Sharon or Marx, Einstein or Emma Goldman, or it might summon those projected abstract qualities that anti-Semitism calls its own; this deadly displacement from the focus on class antagonism to the racialist other.

In Marx's *Jewish Question* and the writings of the Frankfurt School, the category 'Jew' stands for a social metaphor. In contrast, however, to the affirmative categorisation 'Jew', it was a critical category that challenged 'categorisation'. That is, the meaning and significance of the 'Jewish Question' was approached through the lens of the critique of the fetishism of the commodity form. Expanding on Marx's critical question, 'why does this content [human social relations] assume that form [the form of capital]' (cf. Marx, 1962, p. 95), the Jewish question as a critical category asks why does the bourgeois critique of capitalism assume the form of anti-Semitism? In contrast, the affirmative use of the category 'Jew' rationalises anti-Semitism as a manifestation of the hatred of capitalism, and through its rationalisation, is complicit in the perversion of anti-capitalism that is directly useful for capitalism itself.

The essay focuses on that form of anti-Semitism that found its raison d'être in Auschwitz. Such an examination sheds light on the contemporary connection between globalisation and nationalist anti-globalisation. The essay argues that anti-Semitism is directly related with 'modernity's' attempt at reconciling its constituting contradiction, which is the class antagonism between capital and labour. Horkheimer's (1988, p. 9) dictum that whoever wants to talk about Fascism but not about capitalism should shut up, puts this contention into sharp focus and raises, against the background of the contemporary militarisation of foreign and domestic policies, the issue of its contemporary significance. The conclusion returns to the wider discussion on anti-globalisation and offers some suggestions.

In what follows, I have freely borrowed from Horkheimer and Adorno (1989) and Postone (1986). In their *Dialectic of the Enlightenment*, Horkheimer and Adorno emphasise that Enlightenment's 'reason' obtains fundamentally as 'instrumental reason' or 'instrumental rationality'. The determination of 'reason' as reason being denied in the form of 'instrumental reason' entails that instrumental reason is reason's false friend and that, as such a friend, it negates reason's promise to destroy all relations where humanity exists as a resource. Horkheimer and Adorno build on discussion of anti-Semitism as a form of hatred that identifies Jews as the representatives of the sphere of capital circulation, especially in its most elementary form of M...M', and argue that anti-Semitism projects Jews as personifications of global capital, leading to the murderous demand that the liberation from capital amounts to the liberation from Jews. Postone deepens this insight arguing that anti-Semitism amounts to a fetish critique of capital and thus to a critique on the basis of capital. Anti-Semitism is a constituted form of the capital fetish: it amounts to a perverted, bourgeois form of anti-capitalism that is directly useful for capitalism. The critique of anti-Semitism amounts thus to a critique of those forms of anti-capitalism that do not oppose, but rather derive their rational from constituted capitalist forms (see Marx, 1964).

Reason, Anti-Semitism and Equality

Anti-Semitism does not 'need' Jews. The category 'Jew' has powers attributed to it that cannot be defined concretely. It is an abstraction that excludes nobody. Anyone can be considered a Jew. The concept 'Jew' knows no individuality, cannot be a man or a woman, and cannot be seen as a worker or beggar; the word 'Jew' relates to a non-person, an abstraction. 'The Jew is one whom other men consider a Jew' (Sartre, 1976, p. 69). For anti-Semitism to rage, the existence of 'Jews' is neither incidental nor required. 'Anti-Semitism tends to occur only as part of an interchangeable program', the basis of which is the 'universal reduction of all specific energy to the one, same abstract form of labour, from the battlefield to the studio' (Horkheimer and Adorno, 1989, p. 207). Thus, anti-Semitism belongs to a social world in which sense and significance are sacrificed in favour of compliance with the norms and rules of a political and economic reality that poses sameness, ritualised repetition, and object-less subjectivity as Man's only permitted mode of existence. Difference, and therewith the elevation of human dignity to a purpose of social existence, beyond and above the ritualised mentality of empty and idle thought stands rejected. The mere existence of difference, a difference that signals happiness beyond a life of rationalised production and its expansion into every area of social life fosters the blind resentment and anger that anti-Semitism focuses and exploits but does not itself produce (cf. ibid., pp. 207-8).

Anti-Semitism differentiates between 'society' and 'national community'. 'Society' is identified as 'Jewish'; whereas community is modelled as a counter-world to society. Community is seen to be constituted by nature and 'nature' is seen to be at risk because of 'evil' abstract social forces. The attributes given by the anti-Semite to Jews include mobility, intangibility, rootlessness and conspiracy against the values and cohesion of an 'ancestral', that is, original community. The presumed 'well-being' of this community is seen to be at the mercy of evil powers: intellectual thought, abstract rules and laws, and the disintegrating forces of communism and finance capital. Both, communism and finance capital are seen as uprooting powers and as entities of reason, and both are seen as the property of the rootless intelligence of 'Jews', an intelligence based on reason and critical judgment.[3] Reason stands rejected because of its infectious desire to leave behind relations of domination and exploitation. Reason is the weapon of critique. It challenges conditions where Man is degraded to a mere resource that stands to attention clicking his heels to receive the commands of those who demand the transformation of the world into one huge factory of commandeered labour. For the anti-Semite independence of thought and the ability to think freely without fear, is abhorrent. It detests the idea that *'Man is the highest being for Man'* [*Mensch*] (Marx, 1975, p. 182). Instead, it seeks deliverance through murder. It the anti-semites that produce the 'Jew', and the anti-Semites' portrayal of the Jew as evil personified is in fact their own self-portrait.

Anti-Semitism has always been based on an urge, which its instigators held against the Social Democrats: the urge for equality. Social Democracy sees equality as emanating from the project of the Enlightenment. It urges equality to achieve a just and fair society. This demand focuses on citizenship rights for all and on the sphere of distribution where equality of opportunity is seen as a civil good compensating for the absence of humanity at the point of production. Anti-Semitism urges a different sort of equality. It derives equality from membership in a national community. This equality is defined by the mythical 'property' of land and soil based on the bond of blood. Blood and soil are configured as the mythical bond of a national community. The fetish of blood and soil is itself rooted in the capital fetish where the concrete in the form of use value obtains only in and through the abstract in the form of exchange value. Anti-Semitism construes blood, soil, and also machinery as concrete counter-principles of the abstract. The abstract is personified in the category Jew. The anti-Semitic revolt, then, against the abstract amounts to a conformist rebellion in favour of the fascist extension of the capitalist factory discipline to society at large. For the apologists of market liberalism, the reference to the invisible hand operates like an explanatory refuge. It explains everything with reference to the Invisible. 'Starvation is God's way of punishing those who have too little faith in capitalism' (Rockefeller Sr., quoted in Marable, 1991, p. 147). For the anti-Semites, however, the power of the invisible can be explained—the Jew is its personification and biologised existence. It transforms anti-capitalist anger about social injustice into a conformist rebellion against the projected personification of capitalism.

The nationalist conception of equality defines 'society' as the Other—a parasite whose objective is deemed to oppress, undermine and pervert the 'natural community' through the 'disintegrating' force of the abstract and intangible values of bourgeois civilisation. The category 'Jew' is seen to personify abstract thought and abstract equality, including its incarnation, money. The Volksgenosse, then, is seen as somebody who resists 'Jewish' abstract values and instead upholds some sort of natural equality. Their 'equality' as Jews obtains as a construct to which all those belong who deviate from the conception of the *Volksgenosse*, that is, mythical concrete matter. They myth of the Jew is confronted with the myth of the original possession of soil, elevating nationalism's 'regressive equality' (Adorno, 1951, p. 56) to a liberating action. The *Volkgenosse* sees himself as a son of nature and thus as a natural being. He sees his natural destiny in the liberation of the national community from allegedly rootless, abstract values, demanding their naturalisation so that everything is returned to 'nature'. In short, the *Volksgenosse* portrays himself as rooted in blood and ancestral tradition to defend his own faith in the immorality of madness through the collective approval of anger. This anger is directed towards civilisation's supposed victory over nature, a victory that is seen as condemning the *Volksgenosse* to sweat, toil and physical effort, whereas the Other is seen to live a life as banker and speculator. This the *Volksgenosse* aspires for himself with murder becoming the climax of his aspiration. The *Volksgenosse* speculates in death and banks the extracted gold teeth.

For the *Volksgenossen*, the Jews 'are the scapegoats not only for individual manoeuvres and machinations but in a broader sense, inasmuch as the economic injustice of the whole class is attributed to them' (Horkheimer and Adorno, 1989, p. 174). Pogroms are not only conceived as a liberating action but, also, as a moral obligation: anti-Semitism calls for a 'just' revenge on the part of the 'victimised' national community against the powers of 'rootless' society. 'Community' is seen to be both victimised and 'strong'. Strength is derived from the biological conception of the national community: blood constituted possession and tradition. This biologisation of community finds legitimation for murder in the biologisation of the 'action': biology is conceived as a destiny. From this follows the demand to overturn and break society's hold on community in order for the latter to reassert its assumed authenticity and purity.

Reason that escorted the primitive accumulation of capital with the promise of human dignity, appears transformed into the idle occupation of killing for the sake of killing. Kant's notion that reason was to lead mankind to maturity formulated reason's claim to think beyond itself in order to find deliverance in significance and meaning, in humanity. This is reason's revolutionary imperative. However, reason is not one-sided; it has a darker side, as de Sade showed. This darker side subsists as instrumental rationality, a joyless rationality interested only in calculability be it in terms of an all pervasive market rationality or fordist production processes. Instrumental rationality does not know human values. Everything and everybody is just a tool, a utility, in the forward march of accumulation for accumulation's sake. For instrumental rationality, human values are a scandal for they inhibit the full utilisation of technical efficacy and humanity is merely conceived as an irritating factor of production, a living resource that has to be integrated into the well-oiled systems of economic production and political machines. Reason's claim to lead the exodus to a better world and the resourceful rationality of instrumental reason are two halves of the same walnut: Revolution and its containment in the name of revolution itself. 'The thought of happiness without power is unbearable because it would then be true happiness' (ibid., p. 172). Instrumental reason allows merely technological revolutions and is interested merely in the corrosion of character - Men with no qualities, humans of standardised and yet flexible issue, always prepared to be called upon to function as resourceful tools for profitable calculations, whatever the 'product'. All that instrumental rationality wishes for itself is how best to achieve the optimum result, how best to increase efficiency be it in terms of produced cars or gassed corpses. It is interested only in quantifiable results regardless of content.

The efficient organisation and the cold, dispassionate execution of the deed - the cruelty of silence in the house of the hangman —is mirrored by its disregard for individuality: corpses all look the same when counting the results and they are equal to each other; and nothing distinguishes a number from a number except the difference in quantity—the measure of success. The mere existence of happiness is a provocation. Judgment is suspended. Everybody is numbered and assessed for use.

Anti-Semitism's stigmatisation of reason and money as evil not only mythologises reason and money as forces that come, like their projected personifications, the Jew, from no-where. It also produces the legend that those with a 'home', 'tradition', 'roots' and 'soil' are mere objects of evil, abstract forces of darkness. The insight that 'the constitution of the world occurs behind the backs of the individuals, yet it is their work' (Marcuse, 1988, p. 151) is turned against itself: nationalists agree that the world makes itself manifest behind the backs of what they consider as the one-national community. Yet, they deny that it is their work. Instead, it is a world of evil global forces conspiring to undermine relations of national harmony. The evil force is personified in the category 'Jew'. Capitalism becomes Jewish capitalism and globalisation a Jewish conspiracy. In the struggle between 'good' and 'evil' reconciliation appears neither possible nor desirable. Evil needs to be eradicated in order for the 'good' to be set free. The paradox of this claim seems clear, or so it seems. The attack on 'reason' rests on the employment of reason's other self: instrumental rationality, confirming, rather than denying, the circumstance that Nazism was less an aberration in the forward march of instrumental reason than the transformation of the forward march itself into delusion. The attack on reason set 'loose all irrational powers - a movement that ends with the total fictionalization of the mind' (ibid., p. 23). Auschwitz, then, confirms the 'stubbornness' of the principle of 'abstraction' not only through extermination for extermination's sake but also, and because of it, through 'abstractification'. The biologisation of the abstract as 'Jew' denied not only humanity, as the 'Jew' stands expelled from the biologised community of the concrete. The abstract is also made abstract: all that can be used is used like teeth, hair, skin; labour-power; and, finally, the abstract is made abstract and thus invisible itself through gas. The invisible hand of the market, identified as the abstract-biological power of the 'Jew', is transformed into smoked-filled air, into the invisible itself.

Nazism's Anti-capitalist Capitalism

National Socialism projected itself as an anti-capitalist movement. This projection should not be dismissed out of hand. As the late left-wing terrorist Ulrike Meinhoff put it 'finance capital and the banks, the hard core of the system of imperialism and capitalism, had turned the hatred of men against money and exploitation, and against the Jews...Anti-semitism is really a hatred of capitalism' (quoted in Rose, 1990, p. 304).[4] Yet, National Socialism also embraced industrial capital and new technology. Indeed, according to Aly and Heym (1988), the preparation of the Final Solution in occupied Poland was based less on anti-Semitism as an ideology, but, in fact, followed the instrumental reasoning of Neo-Malthusian resource management. Their argument is that, for the Nazis, the economic viability of occupied Poland depended on the reduction of the population per capita in order to secure that capital exported to Poland could be applied efficiently.

What is the relationship between Nazism's anti-capitalist ideological projection and the rational calculation of economic resources that proposes mass murder as a 'solution' to capitalist profitability? Nazi anti-Semitism is different from the anti-Semitism of the old Christian world. This does not mean that it did not exploit Christian anti-Semitism. Christian anti-Semitism constructed the 'Jew' as an abstract social power: The 'Jew' stands accused as the assassin of Jesus and is thus persecuted as the son of a murderer. In modern anti-Semitism, the Jew was chosen because of the 'religious horror the latter has always inspired' (Sartre, 1976, p. 68). In the Christian world, the 'Jew' was also a social-economic construct by virtue of being forced to fill the vital economic function of trafficking in money. Thus, the economic curse that this social role entailed, reinforced the religious curse.

Modern anti-Semitism uses and exploits these historical constructions and transforms them: The Jew stands accused and is persecuted for following unproductive activities. His image is that of an intellectual and banker. 'Bankers and intellectuals, money and mind, the exponents of circulation, form the impossible ideal of those who have been maimed by domination, an image used by domination to perpetuate itself' (Horkheimer and Adorno, 1989, p. 172). The biologically defined possession of land and tradition is counterposed to the possession of universal, abstract phenomena. The terms *'abstract, rationalist, intellectual*...take a pejorative sense; it could not be otherwise, since the anti-Semite lays claim to a concrete and irrational possession of the values of the nation' (Sartre, 1976, p. 109). The abstract values themselves are biologised, the abstract is identified as 'Jew'. Both, thus, the 'concrete' and the 'abstract' are biologised: one through the possession of land (the concrete as rooted in nature, blood and tradition) and the other through the possession of 'poison' (the abstract as the rootless power of intelligence and money). The myth of national unity is counterposed to the myth of the Jew. Jewry is seen to stand behind the urban world of crime, prostitution, and vulgar, materialist culture. Tradition is counterposed to reasoning, intelligence, and self-reflection; and the nationalist conception of community, economy and labour is counterposed to the abstract forces of international finance and communism (Postone, 1986). The *Volksgenossen* are thus equal in blindness. 'Anti-Semitic behaviour is generated in situations where blinded men robbed of their subjectivity are set loose as subjects' (Horkheimer and Adorno, 1989, p. 171). They were set loose as subjects of instrumental reason and are thus robbed of their subjectivity as social individuals to whom reason has and reveals meaning and significance. While reason subsists in and through the critique of social relations, the V*olksgenosse* has only faith in the efficiently unleashed terror of instrumental rationality. The collection of gold-teeth from those murdered, the collection of hair from those to be killed, and the overseeing of the slave-labour of those allowed to walk on their knees for no more than another day, only requires effective organisation.

Nationalism articulates a senseless, barbaric rejection of capitalism that makes anti-capitalism useful for capitalism. 'The rulers are only safe as long as the people they rule turn their longed-for goals into hated forms of evil' (ibid., p. 199). The Jews seem ready made for the projection of horror. 'No matter what the Jews as such may be like, their image, as that of the defeated people, has the features to which totalitarian domination must be completely hostile: happiness without power, wages without work, a home without frontiers, religion without myth. These characteristics are hated by the rulers because the ruled secretly long to possess them' (ibid.). Anti-Semitism invited the ruled to stabilise domination by urging them to de-humanise, maim and kill, suppressing the very possibility and idea of happiness through their participation in the rationally organised slaughter, robbing the projected—capitalist—Others of all possession, including their life. Fascism, then, 'is also totalitarian in that it seeks to make the rebellion of suppressed nature against domination directly useful to domination. This machinery needs the Jews' (ibid., p.185). This insight poses the issue of Nazism's anti-capitalist capitalism, that is, its espousal of capitalist enterprise and its tirades against 'Jewish capitalism'. The fetish critique of capitalism as 'Jewish capitalism' argues that capitalism is in fact nothing more than an unproductive money-making system. The Nation is deemed productive and capitalism is projected on to the image of the rootless 'money Jew'. This critique of global capital is based on a dualist conception between, on the one hand, social relations as relations between creative, industrious individuals and, on the other, their subordination to relations between things, to money.[5]

Marx's critique of fetishism supplied an uncompromising critique of this dualist conception by making clear that the two, use value and exchange value, industrial capital and money capital, do not exist independent from each other but are in fact each other's mode of existence. The critique of capital has to be a critique of economic categories, and that is, a critique of the fetishism of the commodity form which entails the exploitation of labour and the form of money as its presupposition. Without such a critique, it is all too easy to succumb to the objective delusion that the commodity form presents. On the one hand, there is the separation of reality into concrete matter and abstract destructive force, leading to the fetish-like endorsement of the concrete, of creative enterprise and of industry supplying material products that satisfy wants. On the other hand, there is the abstract sphere occupied by money and finance, specifically speculation and global finance capital. The celebration of the concrete goes hand-in-hand with the rejection of the mobility, universality and intangibility of finance capital that is charged with knowing neither national identity nor national 'responsibility'. The Vampire-like figure of capital sucking labour in the quest for surplus value, portrayed by Marx in *Capital*, is thus displaced: the Vampire becomes money. Industrial enterprise, rather than being conceived in terms of an enterprise of exploitation, is projected as the 'national laboratory' of concrete, creative labour. It is projected as a national community where national labour is employed in the much praised one-national boat. The viability of this labour is seen to be threatened by money. Money is conceived as the root of all evil and the cause of all perversion. Enterprise and industry are fetishised as concrete community, as concrete nature. National industrial endeavour is thus portrayed as a 'victim' of the evil forces of abstract values, of money. In sum, modern anti-Semitism is the barbaric ideology of what Marx (1966, p. 438) described in his analysis of the role of credit as the 'abolition of the capitalist mode of production within the capitalist mode of production itself'. National Socialism focuses the resolution of this negative abolition on the national state as the 'harmonies' last refuge' (Marx, 1973, p. 886) that restores in the face of global economic turmoil, the alleged 'national interest' in the exploitation of labour through terror.

For the anti-Semites, the world appears to be divided between finance capital and concrete nature. The concrete is conceived as immediate, direct, matter for use, and rooted in industry and productive activity. Money, on the other hand, is not only conceived as the root of all evil, it is also judged as rootless and of existing not only independently from industrial capital but, also, over and against the industrial endeavour of the nation: all enterprise is seen to be perverted in the name of money's continued destructive quest for self-expansion. In this way, money and financial capital are identified with capitalism while industry is perceived as constituting the concrete and creative enterprise of a national community. Between capitalism as monetary accumulation and national community as industrial enterprise, it is money which calls the shots. In this view, industry and enterprise are 'made' capitalist by money: money penetrates all expressions of industry and thus perverts and disintegrates community in the name of finance capital's abstract values. This destructive force puts claim on and so perverts: the individual as entrepreneur; the creative in terms of a paternalist direction of use-value production; the rooted in terms of *Volk*; the community in terms of a natural community. Instead of community's natural order of hierarchy and position, money's allegedly artificial and rootless force is judged to make the world go round by uprooting the natural order of the *Volksgenossen*. In this way, then, it is possible for the *Volksgenossen* not only to embrace capitalism but, also, to declare that the exploitation of labour creates freedom: *Arbeit macht frei*. 'They declared that work was not degrading, so as to control the others more rationally. They claimed to be creative workers, but in reality they were still the grasping overlords of former times' (Horkheimer and Adorno, 1989, p. 173). By separating what fundamentally belongs together, that is 'industrial' exploitation and money, the differentiation between money on the one hand, and industry and enterprise, on the other, amounts to a fetish critique of capital that attacks the projected personifications of capital rather than the capitalist relations of exploitation themselves.

With the biologisation of creative activity, the unfettered operation of the exploitation of labour in the name mythologised concrete values is rendered attainable by the elimination of the cajoling and perverting forces of the abstract—the 'money Jew'. In this way, the ideology of blood and soil, on the one hand, and machinery and unfettered industrial expansion, on the other, are projected as images of a healthy nation that stands ready to purge itself from the perceived perversion of industry by the abstract, universal, rootless, mobile, intangible, international 'vampire' of 'Jewish capitalism'. The celebration of the *Volksgenosse* as the personification of the concrete, of blood, soil, tradition and industry, allows the killing of Jews without fear. Yet, it manifests 'the stubbornness of the life to which one has to conform, and to resign oneself' (ibid, p. 171): the idle occupation of killing is efficiently discharged.

Everything is thus changed into pure nature. The abstract was not only personalised and biologised, it was also 'abstractified'. Auschwitz was a factory 'to destroy the personification of the abstract. Its organisation was that of a fiendish industrial process, the aim of which was to "liberate" the concrete from the abstract. The first step was to dehumanise, that is, to strip away the "mask" of humanity, of qualitative specificity, and reveal the Jews for what "they really are"— shadows, ciphers, numbered abstraction'. Then followed the process to 'eradicate that abstractness, to transform it into smoke, trying in the process to wrest away the last remnants of the concrete material "use-values": clothes, gold, hair, soap' (Postone, 1986, pp. 313-14).

Conclusion

Adam Smith was certain that capitalism creates the wealth of nations and noted that 'the proprietor of stock is properly a citizen of the world, and is not necessarily attached to any particular country. He would be apt to abandon the country in which he was exposed to a vexatious inquisition, in order to be assessed to a burdensome tax, and would remove his stock to some other country where he could either carry on his business, or enjoy his fortune more at his ease' (1981, pp. 848-49). Ricardo concurred, adding that 'if a capital is not allowed to get the greatest net revenue that the use of machinery will afford here, it will be carried abroad' leading to 'serious discouragement to the demand for labour' (Ricardo, 1995, p. 39). According to Hegel, the accumulation of wealth renders those who depend on the sale of their labour power for their social reproduction, insecure in deteriorating conditions. He concluded that despite the accumulation of wealth, bourgeois society will find it most difficult to keep the dependent masses pacified, and he saw the form of the state as the means of reconciling the social antagonism, containing the dependent masses. Ricardo formulated the necessity of capitalist social relations to produce 'redundant population'. Marx developed this insight and showed that the idea of 'equal rights' in principle a bourgeois right (cf. Marx, 1968). Against the bourgeois form of formal equality, he argued that communism rests on the equality of individual human needs. Adorno and Horkheimer argued that anti-Semitism is a fetishistic, barbaric critique of capitalism that makes the hatred of capitalism functional for capitalism. Luxemburg argued that the fight against barbarism is a fight for socialism.

The history of capitalism shows that the so-called golden age of the capitalism of the 1950s was an exception, if indeed it was golden at all. It did not come about as a result of either cosmopolitan reason or commitments to redistributive justice. As Gambino (1996) has shown, Fascism and Nazism were not in their origins the losing versions of Fordism, but were forced to become such thanks to the class struggles of the 1930s in the United States.[6] This struggle is the practical question of our time.

What is the contemporary meaning of this question? 'The renunciation of internationalism in the name of resurgent nationalism' is the biggest danger (Clarke, 2001, p.91). 'Anti-globalisation' gives in to reactionary forces if its critique of globalisation is a critique for the national state. The history of protectionism, national self-sufficiency and 'national money' has always been a world market history (Bonefeld, 2000)—there are however disturbing exceptions like, for example, Albania during the Cold War and North Korea. The critique of globalisation in favour of 'national socialism' merely offers, whether intentionally or not, the horrors of the past to the present as a solution.

The idea of saving capitalism through institutional reform from its own self-destructive dynamic has to be exposed to reveal its meaning and that is, that money must manage and organise the exploitation of labour. What is the opposite term to the unfettered global accumulation of capital? Is the opposing term the national state that, with transformed regulative powers, forces capital to guarantee the common national good? The ethical appeal of the demand for regulative transformation resides in its critical comparison between the less than perfect reality of capitalist relations and the pleasant norms of equality and justice. Such critical comparison fails to see that the pleasant norms are adequate to their content, the bad reality of a capitalist mode of production. The much desired benevolent regulation of capital presupposes inhuman conditions and these find a political expression in the form of the state which Marx summarised as: 'the concentration of bourgeois society'. Discontent with—neo-liberal—politicians amounts to, paraphrasing Marx, a critique of charactermasks, deflecting from the social constitution of their existence and because of this, it affirms the state as if it were an 'independent being which possesses its own *intellectual, ethical and libertarian bases*' (Marx, 1968, p. 28). It thus amounts to a mere rebellion for a virtuous state - a state, that is, which secures the 'communal interests' of bourgeois society, that is, capitalist accumulation.

Last, the critique of globalisation fails if it is merely a critique of speculative capital and that is, a critique for productive accumulation. It was the crisis of productive accumulation that sustained the divorce of monetary accumulation from productive accumulation (Bonefeld and Holloway, 1996). Globalisation is not responsible for the ever more precarious conditions of work, poverty, and debt, and the ever more destructive force of speculation. Rather, and as Daniel Cohen (1997, p. 15) has argued, it is the restructuring of work that makes globalisation possible and gives globalisation a bad name. This then means that 'anti-globalisation' has to be a critique of the capitalistically constituted relations of production. The critique of, for example, the WTO is not enough. Trade, whether deemed fair or unfair, presupposes capitalist relations of exploitation. Further, without the critique of exploitation, the critique of speculation leads with necessity to xenophobia and anti-Semitic denunciations of money. It conceals the relations of exploitation and is complicit, whether intentionally or not, in the critique of finance as parasitic. Racism and Nazi anti-Semitism shows what that means.

The rejection of the bourgeois relations of abstract equality in favour of nationalist conceptions of equality is reactionary. This is the law of abstract equality: 'The power which each individual exercises over the activity of others or over social wealth exists in him as the owner of *exchange value*, of *money*. The individual carries his social power, as well as his bond with society, in his pocket' (Marx, 1973, pp. 156-57). And the law of the national equality of a people? It is racist. The critique of abstract equality has to be an anti-national critique and that is, a critique of capital and its state—the political master of the national homogenisation of human relations as mere personifications of relations between things.

The theoretical and practical orientation on the utopia of the society of the free and equal is the only realistic departure from the inhumanity that the world market society of capital posits (cf. Agnoli, 2000). In short, those who seriously want freedom and equality as social individuals but do not wish to destabilise capitalism and instead wish to regulate 'abstractions', be it capital or the market, contradict themselves. The attempt to regulate abstractions affirms their constituted existence and thus renders them effective. The struggle for socialism is a struggle against abstractions—and 'abstractifications'—and that is, a struggle for the equality of individual human needs. Paraphrasing Marx (1959, p. 93), 'it is precisely necessary to avoid ever again to counterpose "society" as an abstraction, to the individual'.

Anti-capitalism has, thus, to mean anti-capitalism. It has to mean the complete democratisation of all social forces, making them accountable to individual human needs in and through the democratic organisation of socially necessary labour by the freely associated producers themselves, where the free development of each is the condition for the free development of all. 'Every emancipation is a restoration of the human world and of human relationships to Man [*Menschen*] *himself*' (Marx, 1964, p. 370).

The democratic organisation of economic relations of necessity and the reduction of labour time belong together as each other's presupposition. How much labour time was needed in 2002 to produce the same amount of commodities that was produced in 1992? Twenty per cent? Forty percent or fifty percent? Whatever the percentage might be, what is certain is that labour time has not decreased. It has increased. What is certain too is that the distribution of wealth is as unequal as never before. And how does bourgeois society cope with the expansion of 'redundant populations', on the one hand, and, on the other, the overaccumulation of abstract wealth, of capital? The contradiction between the forces and relations of production does seeks resolution: destruction of productive forces, scrapping of labour through war and generalised poverty and misery, the racist demand for national equality, and all this against the background of an unprecedented accumulation of wealth and the ever more destructive attempts to valorise atoms of time through greater labour flexibility.

Anti-capitalist indifference to the revolutionary project of human emancipation is a contradiction in terms. Such contradictions seek resolution and the grotesque and bloody grimace of the last Century shows what that might mean. The twentieth century has been a lousy century. It was filled with dogmas that one after another have cost us time and suffering. It would, however, be wrong to see it in this one-sided way. It was also a Century of hope in the alternative entelechy of solidarity and human emancipation—from Mexico (1914) to Petrograde (1917) and Kronstadt (1921), from Berlin (1918), Budapest (1919) and Barcelona (1936) to Budapest (1956), from Paris (1968), Chiapas (1994) to the Argentinean *piqueteros* (2001).[7] These, and many more, have been the intense moments of human emancipation, constituting points of departure towards the society of the free and equal.

In conclusion, anti-capitalism has to demand the democratic organisation of socially necessary labour time by the associated producers themselves. This, then, is the splendid category of full employment in and through the emancipation of labour that Marx conceived as the democratic organisation of necessity through the realm of freedom: human self-determination, human sovereignty, and thus human dignity. Anti-capitalist indifference to the project of human emancipation does not pose an alternative to capitalism. It succumbs to abstractions, deprives itself of the weapon of reason, and leaves the door open to socialism's alternative, that is, barbarism. Anti-capitalism has to mean the organised negation of capital and its state, that is, it has to espouse the categorical imperative of human emancipation.

NOTES

1. On this the exchange between de Angelis, Bonefeld and Zarembka in *The Commoner* (www.commoner.org.uk)
2. Quoted in 'Malaysia Acts on Market Fall', *Financial Times*, 4/9/97.
3. For a recent diatribe, see Buchanan's (2002) Aryan dream of a white fortress America that he sees to be in crisis because of the nefarious effects of 'critical theory' for which holds 'those trouble making Communist Jews' responsible.
4. Rose's book offers a conventional conservative critique of revolutionary thought. For a thorough critique of left-wing anti-Semitism, see IFS (2000).
5. This part draws on Postone (1986).
6. As Gambino put it, 'the assembly line is, together with totalitarian state systems and racist nationalism, one of the originating structures which broadly explain the concentration-camp crimes perpetrated on an industrial scale'. The history of so-called Fordism is often seen as a phase where capitalism took on reforming itself in a social-democratic manner. However, as Gambino emphasises, 'Fascism and Nazism were not in their origins the losing versions of Fordism, but were forced to become such thanks to the social and working-class struggles of the 1930s in the United States' (p. 48).
7. For a conceptualisation of the means and ends of human emancipation, see the collection of essays published in Bonefeld and Tischler (2002).

REFERENCES

Adorno, T. (1951), *Minima Moralia*. Frankfurt: Surhkamp.
Adorno, T. (1969), 'Erziehung nach Auschwitz', in ibid., *Stichworte. Kritische Modelle 2*. Frankfurt: Suhrkamp.
Adorno, T. (1990), *Negative Dialectics*. London: Routledge.
Agnoli, J. (1997), *Faschismus ohne Revision*. Freiburg: Ça ira.
Agnoli, J. (2000), 'The Market, the State and the End of History', in Bonefeld, W. and K. Psychopedis (eds.).
Agnoli, J. (2002), 'Emancipation: Paths and Goals', in Bonefeld, W. and S. Tischler (eds.).
Aly, G. and S. Heym (1988), 'The Economics of the Final Solution', *Simon Wiesenthal Centre Annual*, no. 5.
Bonefeld, W. (2000), 'The Spectre of Globalization', in Bonefeld, W. and K. Psychopedis (eds).
Bonefeld, W. and J. Holloway (eds) (1996), *Global Capital, National State and the Politics of Money*. London: Macmillan.
Bonefeld, W. and K. Psychopedis (eds) (2000), *The Politics of Change*. London: Palgrave.
Bonefeld, W. and S. Tischler (eds.) (2002), *What is to be Done?* Aldershot: Ashgate.
Buchanan, P. (2002), *The Death of the West*. New York: Dunne.
Callinicos, A. (2003), 'The Anti-Globalisation Movement after Genoa and New York', in Aronowitz, S. and H. Gautney (eds) *Implicating Empire*. New York: Basic Books.
Clarke, S. (1992), 'The Global Accumulation of Capital and the Periodisation of the Capitalist State Form', in Bonefeld, W. et al (eds.) *Open Marxism*. Vol. I, London: Pluto.
Clarke, S. (2001), 'Class Struggle and the Global Overaccumulation of Capital', in Albritton, R. et al (eds), *Phases of Capitalist Development*. London: Palgrave.
Cohen, D. (1997), *Fehldiagnose Globalisierung*. Frankfurt: Campus.
Gambino, F. (1996), 'A Critique of the Fordism of the Regulation School', *Common Sense*. no. 19.
Horkheimer, M. (1988), 'Die Juden in Europa', in *Schriften 1936-1941*, vol. 4, Frankfurt: Fischer.
Horkheimer, M. and T. Adorno (1989), *Dialectic of Enlightenment*. London: Verso.
IFS (2000), Initiative Sozialistisches Forum, *Furchbare Anti-Semiten, ehrbare Antizionisten*. Freiburg: Ça ira.
Lyotard, J.F. (1993), *Political Writings*. London: University College London Press.

Marable, M. (1991), *Race Reform and Rebellion*. 2nd ed., Jackson: University Press of Mississippi.
Marcuse, H. (1988), *Negations*. London: Free Association Press.
Marx,' K. (1959), *Economic and Philosophical Manuscripts of 1844*. London: Lawrence & Wishart.
Marx, K. (1962), *Das Kapital*. vol. I, Berlin: Dietz.
Marx, K. (1964), *Zur Judenfrage*. MEW 1, Berlin: Dietz.
Marx, K. (1968), *Kritik des Gothaer Programms*. MEW 19, Berlin: Dietz.
Marx, K. (1966), *Capital*. vol. III, London: Lawrence & Wishart.
Marx, K. (1973), *Grundrisse*. London: Penguin.
Marx, K. (1975), 'Contribution to the Critique of Hegel's Philosophy of Law. Introduction', *Collected Works*. vol. 3, London: Lawrence & Wishart.
Marx, K. and F. Engels (1996), *The Communist Manifesto*. London: Pluto.
Negt, O. (2001), *Arbeit und menschliche Würde*. Göttingen: Steidl.
Postone, M. (1986), 'Anti-Semitism and National Socialism', in Rabinbach, A. and J. Zipes (eds.) (1986), *Germans and Jews since the Holocaust*. New York: Holmes & Meier.
Reichelt, H. (2002), 'Die Marxsche Kritik "konomisher Kategorien', in Fetscher, I. and A. Schmidt (eds.) *Emanzipation als Versoehnung*. Frankfurt: Verlag Neue Kritik.
Ricardo, D. (1995), *On the Principles of Political Economy and Taxation*. Cambridge: Cambridge University Press.
Rose, P.L. (1990), *German Question/Jewish Question*. Princeton: Princeton University Press.
Sartre, J-P. (1976), *Anti-Semite and Jew*. New York: Schocken.
Sohn-Rhethel, A. (1970), *Geistige und koerperliche Arbeit*. Frankfurt: Suhrkamp.
Smith, A. (1981), *The Wealth of Nations*. vol. II, Indianapolis: Liberty Fund.

Building a New World, Bottom Up

Massimo De Angelis

Preface

This piece is the edited version of a paper presented at the European Social Forum, workshop on *Commons and Communities*, in Florence 7-10 November 2002 which I helped organize together with a European network of comrades and friends. It first appeared in the web journal I edit, *The Commoner* (http://www.thecommoner.org) together with other important contributions on the subject.

It is an exploratory piece which raises more questions than answers and that was developed in the context of increasing interest and widening debates on "alternatives".[1] This debate is of course fundamental for the constitution of a world of social justice, peace and conviviality. In recent years, its diverse proposals and organizational energies of the underlying diverse movements have contributed to put an end to the claustrophobic discoursive monopoly of the neoliberal *pansée unique*. However, I believe that *broadly* speaking, this debate is still locked in discourses that limit rather than extend the strategic sharpness and political impact of its proposals. To put it simply, the reason why this is so is that most (and fortunately not all) discourses on alternatives see as their referent governments and politicians, rather than people and communities. Instead of starting from our diverse movements as the tip of an iceberg of a constituting process of a new world, they tend to see them simply as a force to pressurize governments to change their policies. Thus instead of making demands on governments and politicians through a clear discourse that makes it explicit that the aims is to constitute new social relations among communities in the world (hence new types of "property rights"), it demands different policies because the current neoliberal policies "do not work". Instead of developing a critique of the type of disciplinary rationale embedded by neoliberal policies which in term of capitalist rationale work very well indeed, as they are increasingly setting people and communities against each other in an endless global competitive rat race they criticize the effect of these policies (income and wealth polarization, poverty, ecological destruction and so on) *as if* it was a miscalculated effect. In a word, current debates on alternatives are not rooted in a strategic understanding of the social force we face (capital). A strategic understanding of capital means to regard the current phase of neoliberalism as a strategic form, historically specific and with its specific features that we should be able to recognize, of capital's attempts to dominate life *vis-à-vis* the needs and aspirations of people and communities expressed in their daily struggles. This is a historical phase of capitalism that despite the different articulations of its institutions and discourses, is based on the same drive shared by *all* phases in which the capitalist mode of production dominates: boundless accumulation, continuous drive to extend commodification to newer social dimension and realms of life, and integration of the social body as boundless work.

I believe that to begin to think of alternatives in terms of commons and communities is the only way we have to avoid the dangers of cooptation, helping instead consolidate a social force that begins to constitute spaces of life beyond capital. Commons and communities are not the slogans, or the ingredients of a recipe for action, nor do they indicate a political line. Nobody has the monopoly of what should constitute a new common and how communities should be formed. The principles of inclusiveness, direct democracy, horizontality and participation so much valued in the practices of current social movements should themselves be seen as constitutive forces of what commons to form and what communities to shape.

Theoretically and politically, commons and communities are two interrelated horizons within which to think of alternatives *while at the same time* keep in mind that the force we face, (capital) is for *enclosures* of commons and for forms of integration of the social body that pit communities against each other. Indeed, enclosure and disciplinary integration are precisely the two coordinates of capital as a social force. So, while the piece here presented deals with commons and communities, let us see very briefly why their opposite, enclosures and disciplinary integration are so important for capital.

At the general theoretical level, the process of capital's accumulation as discussed by Marx in *Capital* can be represented by M-C-M' or more generally, M-$C\{LP;MP\}\ldots P\ldots C'-M'$, in which M is money capital, C is commodity capital, LP is labour power, MP is means of production, P is the human process of production, i.e. capitalist work, and C' and M' are commodity and money accrued in value due to the exploitation of labour. This process has two basic *strategic* components, that is strategic horizons that capital as social force has to pursue in order to proceed with accumulation. These are *enclosures* and spatial-temporal disciplinary integration. The former is the basic premise of accumulation creating and reproducing the commodity-form. The latter is the process of qualitative transformations that constitute the process of accumulation.

Enclosures occurring through the creation of markets and commodities (including the commodity labour power) could be seen in processes that commodify existing "commons" (and thus introducing new laws regulating rights), or by state defence of existing enclosed spaces, vis-à-vis struggles demanding their abolition. In either case, the state deploys institutional force to maintain, protect or extend commodity relations. In different historical contexts the range of these coercions can go from what Marx referred to as "bloody legislation" following the English state defence of enclosure of land in the XVI-XVII century, to modern forms of state protection and safeguard of the existing property right laws and neoliberal policies of dams' construction that expropriates communities from their livelihoods. Social fragmentation (i.e. the destruction of existing communities) is the immediate result of the process of enclosure and correspondent forms of coercion. It is the process of enclosure that creates, reproduces and maintains commodity owners and the structure of entitlements and that give rise to differential degrees of power.

It is important to remember that this process of enclosure is *continuous* in capitalism and not only confined to some "primitive" period[2]. This for at least two reasons. First, because capital's telos, or drive, is to extend and pervade more and more spheres of human life and nature. Commodification is an inherent character of capital. Second, because historically the accumulated result of struggles, or what Karl Polanyi calls "the double movement of society"[3], is effectively constituting new forms of commons that capital, if it cannot administrate in its own terms with new institutional forms compatible with accumulation, must enclose.

On the other hand, both spatial and temporal integration within the M-C-M' circuit requires social cooperation to occur. Cooperation occurs essentially in two ways. Either within productive "nodes" in society i.e. in companies, households, schools or any relatively self-contained and discrete institution or across "nodes". In both cases, the problem of *scale* must be kept in mind in order to analyse the relevant context.[4] In any case, for the sake of this exposition, I will abstract from cooperation within nodes (the realm of *direct* ruling over labour), and will focus mainly on social cooperation across nodes. In capitalist production social cooperation across nodes occurs through market exchange, giving raise to competitive modalities of social interaction. In a word, under capitalist rule we cooperate by competing against each other, thus making cooperation an *emergent* property of social action, rather than the conscious act or project of our actions. To put it differently, instead of having human bodies acting in full self-awareness of their necessary sociality and therefore making the *form* and the *goals* of this sociality the central object of their concerns, we have emergent forms and goals of social interaction that command the alarm clocks, work and life rhythms, as well as desires of individual bodies. In its competitive form, social cooperation which we must remember *is* an unavoidable condition of our *specie being* is turned into an alien force. And the more this force extends and intensifies through the globe, the easier it becomes to react to it with romanticising localism, the myth of "going back" to a idealised past not less alienating and impossible than pure capital's globalism.

The degree of competition depends of course on institutional context. But even in case of near monopoly in some sector, the competitive form of the social interaction is maintained through the opening of markets to trade liberalisation, which fuels if not real at least *threatened* competition, or anti-monopoly laws implemented by the state. Clearly, market interaction is also expression of the configuration of power relations created and/ or maintained by enclosures. These power relations (which concretely depend on the answers to specific questions such as who has what entitlements? who has what commodity and in what amount? who has what financial backing and at what conditions?) play themselves out in strategic competitive interactions in the market giving rise to a particular configuration of systemic integration. Global production chains, speculative capital markets, trade relations are all contemporary specific articulations of today capital systemic integration.

Systemic integration within the social circuit of capital is thus the net results of the interaction of forces each one of which is driven by its own plan and backed by its own power. The emergent result of such interaction is of course unpredictable since the condition of each of the qualitative transformation necessary to allow the reproduction of social capital M-C-M' is ridded with what Marx calls the "possibility" of crisis[5]. Crisis, which Marx roots in the polarity between use value and value of the commodity and in the alienated character of social labour in capitalism, is indeed the all-pervasive condition of commodity production, not only at times of its open manifestation, but also in times of relative business tranquillity. Whatever are the various predispositions of crisis, for the purpose of this analysis they can present two main characters. They either take the form of "disequilibra" in the operations of markets, with consequent ebbs and flows in business activity, changes in market prices, sectors' restructuring and firing and hiring of workers and cyclical and alternate demise and prosperities of communities. Or they take the form of crisis of social stability.

In the first case, crises are inherent part of the disciplinary processes of markets, processes that are founded on competitive modes of interaction among productive nodes in society and, as Hayek reminds us, compel agents to adapt or die. This disciplinary process corresponds ultimately to the degree of subjectification and compliance to a productive *norm* compatible with the full reproduction of the M-C-M' cycle, in both its temporal and spatial dimension. Combining Foucault classical analysis of disciplinary processes in his *Discipline and Punish* (see also Harvey's analysis of the body[6]) with Marx's analysis of capitalist production, we can define subjectification as those social processes that aims at the (re)production of *norms* of behaviour and interaction which are compatible with the compliance to the requirement of capitalist accumulation. For example, the acceptance of the commodity form, its naturalisation in a particular sphere of life, the acceptance as *normal* of a given hierarchy of externally posed goals, the compliance to new methods of doing things, of the parameters of competitive social interaction. The integration over the overall capital's circuit thus passes through a variety of strategies of subjectification, that is the creation of subjects who accepts the norms of the capital's circuits. Following Foucault, we can interpret these strategies of norm creating subjectification as *disciplinary* strategies, that is as repetitive practices of reward and punishment, aiming at co-opting or bypassing resistance and channelling it in "normal" patters of behaviour. Although Foucault's analysis is confined to discrete disciplinary institutions, such as the prison, the hospital or the school, a critical analysis of what Hayek calls the "market order" shows several fundamental similarities with the disciplinary process in these institutions, the most important of which is perhaps that the market disciplinary process contribute to create not only normalised subjects, but also new standards of production, and what Marx referred to as the quantitative aspect of the substance of value, i.e. "socially necessary labour time".[7]

While market discipline, with its systems of rewards and punishment, promotes production of norms and normalised subjects, this always clashes with subjectivities that escape subjectification. Struggles are ubiquitous in capitalism, whether in micro and hidden forms or macro and open conflictuality, and the disciplinary mechanisms of the market are, in normal circumstances, only partially able to co-opt them. Thus, at any given time, the "positive" effect from the perspective of capital that disciplinary processes have on the creation of "normal subjects" is counterpoised to the negative force that struggles have on disciplinary mechanisms: shirking models and principle-agents models in the field of economic theory are just few of the attempts by economists to capture the "market failures" of pervasive micro forms of conflict. The end result between disciplinary processes and struggles is open ended, and depends on historical contingency and balance of forces. But ultimately, to maintain a balance between these "pluses" and "minuses" is the key rationale of disciplinary processes. Modern globalisation processes are disciplinary processes of this kind, forcing and extending a competitive integration over the world social body through the reproduction and spatial displacements of *crises*.

There are however times in which this "balance" cannot be maintained and conflict threatens the particular *forms* of disciplinary mechanisms as well as their very rationale. The "disequilibria" of flows, the cycles, the ebbs and flows of business activity are no longer sufficient to discipline subjects, to channel norms of behaviour, to make them accepting and internalise the normality of competitive market interaction. To the extend this happens, crisis presents itself as a crisis of social stability, a crisis that, whatever its systemic trigger (whether rooted in the financial system, or in a debt default, or in low profitability, or in "animal spirit" and crisis of confidence, or in geo-political factors, or in an eruption of social conflict) puts into question the viability and/or legitimacy of many of the qualitative transformations necessary for accumulation (M-C-M'). It seems that at the present moment we are entering this phase, we are living a crisis as threat of social stability. The ways forward for capital away from this crisis are two, and they do no necessarily exclude each other. First, capital attempts to further extend its domination through further repression and war and corresponding wave of enclosures and the extension of disciplinary integration. This strategy is currently being pursued in the form of the "permanent war on terrorism", both domestically (with the introduction of more stringent laws) and internationally (the war in Iraq is a clear example). Second, capital attempts to co-opt and divide the forces that oppose it. The current discourse on "global governance" goes in this direction, as it was the case for "Keynesianism" in a previous phase.[8] And what is the way forward for the struggling subjects of the world's social body and their communities? The piece here presented is a contribution to a collective exercise in trying to answer this question, but as said, it might even raise more questions that it answers.

1. "Another world is Possible": Yes, but We Need a New Political Discourse

The following reflections emerge out of the overlapping between a two lines of enquiry that I have been pursuing in the last few years. One is drawn from what we may call the critical political economy of globalization, that is the study of trends, processes and the strategies of capital over the last "neoliberal" period. The other is drawn from the participation and, therefore, (self) reflection within the constellation of movements forming the global justice and solidarity movement.[9]

This movement has posed the question of a plurality of "alternatives" to the social processes and arrangements that produce the horrors of modern global capital. In order to take the many calls for and practices of alternatives seriously, we have to make them relevant to the real people at the fringe or outside the movement. In other words, we want to move from movement to society not so much by persuading people to "join" our movement, but through a language and a political practice that by tracing the connections between diverse practices attempts to dissolve the distinctions between inside and outside the movement, i.e., actually moves 'from movement to society'. To make the possibility of a new world that contains many worlds an *actuality*, we have to be able to shape our own discourse in such a way as to echo the needs and aspirations coming from below. We have to give coherence to their plurality, without imposing a model or reiterating dead ideologies.

We need a discourse that helps to articulate the many alternatives that spring out of the points of crises of neoliberal capital, which seriously threaten to dispossess people of their livelihood and impose on them new or more intensified commodified patterns of life. We need a discourse that builds on the plurality of the many concrete struggles and their methods and help us to articulate a vision—not a plan—of the whole. Then we can better evaluate what are the global implications of our local struggles, as well as the local implications of global struggles for the building of a world that contains many worlds.

But most of all, we need a discourse that recognizes the power we have to shape alternatives, at every level in society, that sets out from the simple fact that, contrarily to common belief, alternatives do *exist*, *are* everywhere and plural. To clarify, I think that every social node, that is every individual or network of individuals is a bearer of alternatives. This is evident not only when struggles erupt in any of the waged or unwaged local and trans-local nodes of social production. We just need to look around in the relative normality of daily routines to see that every social node "knows" of different ways to do things within its life-world and sphere of action longs for a different space in which things can be done in different ways. Each social node expresses needs and aspirations that are the basis of alternatives. For example: the alternative to working 10 hours a day is working 6; the alternative to poverty is access to the means of existence; the alternative to indignity is dignity; the alternative to building that dam and uprooting communities is not building that dam and leaving communities where they are; the alternative to tomatoes going rotten while transported on the back of an old woman for 20 miles is not GM tomatoes that do not rot, but access to land near home, or a home, or a road and a truck.

Since every social node is aware of a spectrum of alternatives, the problem is simply *how* to make these alternatives actual? What resources are needed? How to coordinate alternatives *in such a way that they are not pitted against each other* as is the case of the competitive markets' understanding of alternatives? How to solve the many existing problems without relying on the alienating coordinating mechanism of the market and creating instead social relations of mutual enrichment, dignity, and respect? These are I believe the bottom line questions on which a new political discourse must be based.

Once we acknowledge the *existence* of the galaxy of alternatives as they emerge from concrete needs and aspirations, we can ground today's new political discourse in the thinking and practice of the actualization and the coordination of alternatives, so as each social node and each individual within it has the power to decide and take control over their lives. It is this actualization and this coordination that rescues existing alternatives from the cloud of their invisibility, because alternatives, as with any human product, are social products, and they need to be recognized and *validated* socially. Our political projects must push their way through beyond the existing forms of coordination, beyond the visible fist of the state, beyond the invisible hand of competitive markets, and beyond the hard realities of their interconnections that express themselves in today forms of neoliberal governance, promoting cooperation through competition and community through disempowerment. As I will argue, this new political discourse is based on the project of defending and *extending* the space of commons, *at the same time* building and strengthening communities through the social fields.

2. The Need for a New Political Dscourse: An Illustration

To clarify why we need a new discourse, let us take an

example illustrating the limitations of current discourses in the face of a very concrete crisis. As recently as last mid-October, the news that FIAT was in trouble hit the headlines of Italian and international newspapers. This was followed by a typical vociferous debate, in which the different positions were outlined.

Very schematically, at the point of the emergence of the crisis, on one side there was the official FIAT line, seeking to sell the lot to GM, with the prospect of closing several plants and turning the plants in Mirafiori into a *maquiladora* factory. On the other side there was the trade union FIOM and Communist Refoundation who, asking for renationalisation, looked forward to large investments, innovation, safeguard of employment and a strong emphasis on research and development. Clearly, if you are a FIAT worker you know which side you are on.

In my lecturers' union in the UK we play this game all the time. We always choose to safeguard jobs and livelihood and rationalize them to the public with stories of regeneration and innovation, even if the implication of our discourse is to accept playing the game of pitting college against college, university against university, teacher against teacher. The point is that from a *broader* political perspective, one that takes the issue of car production in one particular place within the context of global production of cars and, even more broadly, of competitive market interactions and global warming, *both* of these alternatives are quite problematic for *complementary* reasons. They both represent *different* strategies to survive and indeed, fight for domination in the competitive market, measured by profits, rates of growth and market shares. They both imply a competitive relation to the "other". (Here the other can be understood as Renault workers, BMW workers, Ford workers, etc.). Ultimately, anything that "good management" so much hoped for even by the left in the case of FIAT—can do is will contribute to the bankruptcy of Renault, BMW or Ford workers. Until of course it is their turn to restructure and pose with similar urgency the question of new and innovative strategies.

Not to talk of the fact that, in this endless competitive game, the productive effort wasted on global car production is immense, that transport takes on an increasing individualized form, that CO_2 emissions grow exponentially. Before all this, we will meet again next time in Porto Alegre or anywhere else and again demand a different world. However, we will never make a different world if we are not able to acknowledge the needs, aspirations and demands for dignity of, say, the 200,000 FIAT workers across the world *together with* the needs of different, non-competitive, inclusive relations expressed by our movement, *together with* the many demands for participation and empowerment and control over our lives, *together with* the control over our ecosystems. In other words, we will never make a different world if we are not able to acknowledge all this with a new political discourse that makes sense to a multitude that is searching for ways to build bridges with each others and take control of the aims and forms of social production.

How are we to acknowledge this concretely? I do not know. It depends on the context of concrete situations. However I suspect that by posing the question and replicating it for the many instances of crises of social production and reproduction, we are already on the right track, especially if we frame the questions in terms of commons and communities.

3. The Wisdom Emerging from the Movement...

As "coordinates" of a new political discourse, commons and communities can help us organize our thinking and practices of alternatives as enclosures and competitive relations are organizing the thinking of our masters. They are not elements of a fixed ideology, a dogma that we have to subscribe to. They provide both an intellectual and political horizon that we can enrich through our practices and thinking in the context of concretes struggles. Thus, the political discourse I am talking about is one that is not posed from the outside, it is not something that this or that intellectual can "invent" for us all, and then we go out and apply it to our concrete cases. Our new political discourse is one that must acknowledge that the process of creating a new world, as any process of human production, is a praxis, a circular process, from cognition, reflection and imagination to practical intervention in the world making use of some kind of resources, and back to cognition, reflection and imagination. Intellectuals—that is *anybody* who practices the first moment of this loop, *direct action* in the field of thought, communication and reflection—can look at their objects, for example a movement, and distill elements of a discourse. The return of these back to the movement may help the process of a collective self-reflection, coordinate praxis, define strategies and sharpen visions. Then, of course, this will reflect back on the need for direct action in the field of thought, communication and reflection.

Thus my perception is that the aspirations *and* organizational forms that this movement gives itself reveal a field of action grounded upon two main *practices*: the seizure and/or demands for *commons* and the (learning) practice of *communities*. In a nutshell, *commons* suggest alternative, non-commodified means to fulfill social needs, e.g. to obtain social wealth and to organise social production. Commons are necessarily created and sustained by communities, i.e. by social networks of mutual aid, solidarity, and practices of human exchange that are not reduced to the market form. As we will see, the "place" of these networks does not need to be tied to locality. In fact, the many social practices using modern communication technologies create trans-local places in which communities operate to complement local places. Also, as our movements have shown through the organizational forms it practices, communities cannot be separated from the learning practices of direct democracy, horizontality, participation, and inclusiveness. If only we could organize the vast majority of social production along the same principles!

Commons and communities thus represent the two coordinates of a *grounded* vision, that is a vision that emerges out of the *practices* of this movement for global justice and solidarity once this movement is taken as a whole. What does it mean to take this movement as a whole? It means that no matter whether we think that particular positions within it could be politically dangerous, contradictory, naïve, insufficient, "right", "wrong", romantic or idealizing (and each of us make these judgments all the times), the *articulation* of the various practices of the movement is giving rise to something greater than the sum of particular positions. Through a multitude of encounters among different aspirational standpoints rooted in a plurality of struggles, grand narratives about the world or answers to the question of "what is to be done?" are not necessarily getting more coherent. However, two fundamental things are happening.

First, *mutual understanding of subject-positions* within the networks of social production making up the global factory is developing and intensifying. Cross-pollination not just of struggles but also among "life-worlds" and systems of significations, implies that we are remaking ourselves as social subjects with a sensibility towards the "other" which is not just ideological or ethical, but rooted in some experience of communication across life-worlds and subject-positions. Thanks to the struggles of all the invisible people, their refusal to embrace discourses, goals, and worldviews that was not theirs, their rejection of subordination to promises that everything will be OK if only they conformed, we now have to *deal with difference* and we can deal with difference by *exercising the power* of the recognition of "the other" qua dignified and free social subject.

Second, the continuous practice of 'encountering' leads to the consequent "normalization" of the principles of democracy, inclusiveness and horizontality. Those who lament confusion in the movement underestimate the importance of the novel forms through which this confusion is exercised, a creative chaos allowing planting and disseminating seeds of democracy through the social body. The social DNA of a new epoch is *possibly* now emerging, sanctioning a point of no return to forms of politics in which political parties could grant for themselves the knowledge of what *is* the alternative. Alternatives are themselves processes of self-creation of the multitude, and therefore cannot be monopolized by parties or by anybody else. Current parties and political forces, as well as forms of thought still rooted in the belief that they monopolize the true vision of the alternatives (whether "socialism" or any other "ism"), can only try to delay the only inevitable thing: their demise.

These seeds of democracy and conviviality are unstoppable for very simple reasons. The only thing that cannot be fully enclosed is human communication. We are social beings, so how can we enclose our sociality? At most the means of our sociality such as land, water, food, tools, and so on can be enclosed. And when the space of communication is 6 billion human beings, the possible communicative permutations are . . .out of the range of any pocket calculator. If communication is channeled into certain directions, it will then emerge unpredictably in others. Maybe it can be silenced in certain localities, but it pops up in others.

The first immediate impact of this grounded vision is the identification of the state-market nexus as *the* limit set upon the building of concrete alternatives springing from the grassroots. This nexus that all want to channel, control and discipline in pre-established competitive modes of social interaction expresses the terror of economic, financial and political elites for anything alive and free. In front of this barrier to our freedom to interact and develop local and trans-local communities of social production and mutual aid, this movement is developing instead strategic alternatives which extend new types of commons and strengthen communities.

Also, this grounded vision underlines a tacit (and in the case of Argentina, not so tacit) call for systematic *"removal policies"* to dispose of, bit by bit, all the crap of traditional politics, left or right, socialist or conservative, all forms of hopelessness, of the "there is no alternative" kind or "the alternative begins after we take power". It is a disenchanted wisdom that recognizes the power-seeking and manipulating practices of traditional politics for what they are. It is totally cynical towards testimonial campaigning and brand politics. It is outraged at the politicians' seeming to address needs before a vote and spitting out the emptied shells of bodies after elections. Increasingly, the wisdom emerging is that this is the case not just because individual politicians are corrupted—and, of course, many are – but because the system of global corruption is more powerful than well-intentioned politicians. Thus, the wisdom of this movement is a demand, first of all, for respect!

Does this mean that the movement is demanding withdrawal from engagement with the state? No, it means that it increasingly regards the articulation of our communities as "the state", and the existing state bureaucracy as a nuisance we inherit from another era in which we thought that power was "up there". A nuisance that we have to push back from our lives inch by inch, while at the same time using it to suit our purposes where the articulation of our communities cannot yet reach.

But the opportunities to build communities on the basis of commons are everywhere, whether within the bellies of transnational corporations or outside, in fields or in the streets of our cities. The goals and aspirations of these communities are as diverse as the recognition of union rights with which to fight battles for the reduction of working rhythms and increase in wages, or win individual and communities' access to land, social knowledge, transports health, education, communication and means of existence.

Articulation of communities on the basis of commons means regarding the interactions among individuals and communities as human interactions that give rise to many different kinds of exchanges. These human exchanges on the basis of commons are different from the current market exchanges grounded on enclosures that have come to dominate our lives. This latter form of human exchange, the forms it takes, the concentration of power over resources behind it, and its drive to dominate every other human exchange, make poverty and plenty two sides of the same coin and make us run like rats no matter how much we produce. Scarcity is the ongoing *result* of our competitive participation in this market. The seizure and demands for commons put an end to this by ending the specific "lack" that is its foundation: the artificial lack of access to the plentiful means for producing our existence.

Again, bit by bit, wherever it can reach, this movement seems to identify the lacks that stand in the way of our very concrete empowerments. It points at this or that barrier, at this or that property concentrated in the hand of modern *rentiers*, at this or that accumulation of social wealth detached from its common-sense human purpose, at this or that corporate monopoly over social knowledge. Some sections of the movement at times identify a barrier and decide to overcome it, by seizing property as in the case of the landless brothers and sisters in Brazil, the millions on the internet who defy corporate enclosures of music. Sometimes other extensions of the movement identify needs that are not met, and campaign demanding commons to make it possible to meet them thus releasing resources for social reproduction. This is what we do when we fight for entitlements in health and education, and against privatization. Sometimes there are movements to limit the activities of major transnational corporations, by building barriers to their private cost-minimizing dumping of waste, or exposing for everybody to see their profit-maximizing use of child labour in the sweatshops of the worlds.

However, other times the movement appears unable to reach its object, not even with words, as if paralyzed by the task at hand. Looking at those global production chains, large transnational corporations mobilizing an immense amount of social resources, we try to build our struggles for jobs, working conditions, wages, or for responsible environmental practices, often afraid to think about the broader implications of our struggles when taken as a whole. Thus, we seldom construct political discourses that directly challenge corporate's *property* of the means of existence, almost in fear we could be damned by the wrath of the money-god that rules our lives and makes us relate to each other competitively. We are afraid that the experience of past alternatives bureaucratic state property which was as exploitative and oppressive as corporate property demonstrate that maybe actually there is no alternative.

Ultimately however, the movements will have to face this *impasse*. If we keep setting limits to capital *in every sphere of social life*, saying no to war and enclosures, environmental destruction and indignity, growth for growth sake and exploitation, human relations based on competition or despotism, *and if we are effective in doing so*, there will be nothing else left that the beast can feed upon. Capital, that depends on growth for growth's sake, barrier overcoming and colonization of life, collapses if it is unable to overcome the barrier posed by socialized humanity. We will have to take responsibility and say what must be said: the expropriators must be expropriated so that we can rebuild our lives through new forms of sociality. We will have to take responsibility and find ways to go beyond the invisible hand of the market and the visible fist of the state to coordinate our social practices. Ironically, that would imply looking at the equipment and machines of the most efficiently integrated transnational corporation and say: "What a waste of social wealth!"

4. . . . and the Movement of the Wisdom: The Space of the Commons . . .

Commons are forms of *direct* access to social wealth, access that is not mediated by competitive market relations. The fact that we can today pose the question of their actualisation, that they enter the imagery space of modern political discourse, is due to the fact that in last two decades we have witnessed and practiced numerous struggles against their opposite, neoliberal capitalist enclosures.

Commons acquire many forms, and they often emerge out of struggles *against* their negation. Thus, struggles against intellectual property rights opens up the questions of knowledge as commons. Struggles against privatization of water, education and health, opens the question of water, education and health as commons. Struggles against landlessness open up the question of common land. Struggles against environmental destruction open up the question of environmental commons. In a word, struggle against actual or threatened enclosures opens the question of commons. . . .

Note: they *open* the question of commons, they do not immediately and uniquely pose it. Between the struggle against enclosure and the positing of commons there is a political space in which co-optation that is the acknowledgment of struggles *in order to subsume them* into a new modality of capital accumulation can still take place. Examples of this are endless and our political discourse should be aware of this always-present danger. For example, governments' practical solutions devised to deal with the struggles against the enclosures in health and education as well as their crises, instead of fully recognizing them as commons, deploy new forms of private participation in these sectors without formal privatization. This formally acknowledges public entitlements, but at the same time shapes the nature of their services in tune with the markets, by pitting nurses against nurses, teachers against teachers, and "service consumers" against "service deliverers". At the same time, the exports of service industries are promoted, thus threatening "service consumers" and "service deliverers" in other localities. The way of cooptation is here the way of trans-local community destruction through competition.

Another example is the acknowledgment of "commons" but without their link "to communities", that is when commons are not referred to community practices for their access and reproduction. For example, behind the emerging concept of "global commons" there is, at most, an abstract concept of "global community" but no concrete communities, no problematic of their constitution, protection and empowerment, and articulation with each other. However, we cannot have commons (not even "global") without community.

Another opening to co-optation may occur when, in pursuit of "legitimacy", the movement too heavily relies on emerging critical voices from within the camp of international financial institutions. For example, uncritically relying on economists like Joseph Stiglitz, thinking that he could give us legitimacy because he *acknowledges* many of the movements' denunciation of the IMF and the Washington consensus policies, could be a risky strategy. Behind these denunciations there is no agenda that is *alternative* to competitive market interaction between people on the planet and capital accumulation with all its consequences. There is no promotion of "communities" at the basis of these criticisms, but an agenda that attempts to use our struggles to push accumulation to a possibly new phase. *If it does not succeed in pushing for an autonomous discourse on alternatives, the movement risks to capitulate to an alternative form of co-optation.*

Having said this, this struggle for commons, even as the yet nebulous political space opened with struggles against enclosures, have an immediate crucial effect: they contribute to bring capital to crisis by posing the question of *limit* to capitalist accumulation. It is like this movement, once taken as a whole, is drawing a line in the sand against growth for growth's sake, against accumulation as a panacea for the solution of all the evils of the world. In the last two decades, struggles around the world and through a process of political recomposition have seen Seattle only as the media's tip of the iceberg. To downplay this emergent quality of the movement is, in my opinion, a big mistake. It represents a big cultural shift in politics away from the mythologies of socialist growth or other strategies of growth with a "human face". The thinking of alternatives today cannot abstract from the widespread intolerance towards the various forms of "economicism" that accompany capital's own alternatives.

Clearly, we have to acknowledge, there are many ambiguities and contradictions within the movement. For example, those who ask for a fairer liberalization of trade to the advantage of the South, are doing so to establish fair play in the competitive rules of the game, rather than attacking the game itself. This may risk of being instrumental in the co-optation of poorer communities to the logic of competitive markets, and thus contributes to their doom. Indeed, declining terms of trade, both in primary products and manufacturing, are the recurring emergent results of this competitive war among the poor. To take another example, there are environmentalists who fetishise "place" as "locality" and insist that the latter is *the* only locus of an environmentally sustainable community. They forget that the composition of large sections of the global proletariat *is* de facto today, in aspiration and composition, trans-local, and a political discourse that identifies the "place" of social cooperation only with "locality" risks being instrumental in the co-optation of "locality" against migratory flows.

As we have seen, it is despite or perhaps because of the ambiguities and contradictory positions between its different components that the movement, taken as a whole, is able to pose the question of a limit to capital accumulation. And this has an important consequence: posing the question of the limit to capital means simultaneously posing the question of the limit that capital places upon human free enterprise and vice versa. In other words, saying "no" to further accumulation, means saying "yes" to a plurality of *alternative* activities. This implies *reclaiming the discourse of freedom* and taking it away from the hands of business and its neoliberal political and cultural acolytes. Yes, this movement is the true and the only force for "free enterprise" in the world today! We see it for example in the worldwide production of indymedia, of that of social fora, in the assemblies in Argentinian barrios and in the networks of production cooperatives in that country, in the practice of sharing knowledge and resources while confronting Monsanto and the like by Indian farmers. Professor Hayek's followers, please take note! Look at all these instances of human beings cooperating with each other with no need of capitalist market to do the coordinating job for them! No market and no plan! Almost magic, if seen through the eye of a politician who can only think in terms of false dichotomies such as the market and the state.

And this is of course only the tip of the iceberg, the bit of social production that not only practices non-market social cooperation, but is also self-aware of its stand vis-à-vis capital's enclosures. Indeed, we are all aware of other huge yet invisible local and trans-local areas of social cooperation that go on all the time, uncoordinated by the market: software production, domestic work, transmission of historical memory, emotional work, community building, and so on and on, and on.

The "free enterprise" posed by this movement can be understood in two senses. First, free *from* the restrictions of property and rent positions in the capitalist market, as its struggles are against enclosures and open the space of commons. This implies understanding "free enterprise" as free flow of social cooperation, invention and innovation driven by need and aspiration and not by profit. Free in the sense that the organisational means of this free social cooperation is free from relations of domination, exclusion and oppression. In other words, this "free enterprise" is recognizable in the form of a plurality of *powers to*, "potentia", that are longing to get rid of all the *powers over*, or "potestas", that condition them. This second aspect opens the question of definition and learning practices *of communities*.

5. . . . and the Learning Practices of Communities

Alternatives become actualised through the power of seizing control of our lives, of transcending alienation beginning from our life-worlds and spheres of action. Our life-worlds define communities we belong to immediately, and these are nothing other than networks of *real* individuals, living real conditions, having real needs and aspirations and enjoying real relations among them. *Seizing power over our lives implies therefore not only being able to access resources and means of existence that enable us to organize social production, but also getting on with defending, building and transforming our communities.* Indeed, commons and communities are two sides of the same coin.

In what follow we need to look at what are the communities we belong to, where is their "place" and what is their transformative potential.

The Communities We Belong To

Communities are social networks of mutual aid, solidarity, and practices of human exchange. In this sense, communities are everywhere there are sustaining non-competitive relations among human beings, and their potential existence is in every sphere of social action and, in today's world, they are overlapping.

In common parlance however, we refer to the word "community" to refer to a group of people who share something, and the nature of what they share is what characterizes the specific nature of a determinate community. For example, the business community—a phrase that make us shiver in its paradoxical association of community and business – refers to groups of people who share the same profit-drive and has the power to act upon it. The academic community, refer to all those people working in academia. The neighbourhood community refers to all those people sharing the same neighborhood. The house community refers to all the people who share a same house. The mining community refers to all those people living near a mining establishment and whose livelihood depend, directly or indirectly, on those mines.

This definition of community necessitates the definition of what is *common* among them, yet, it does not tell us anything about the *relations* among them. Certainly, we cannot talk about business community when the daily business of individual people takes the form of cut-throat competition against others. We cannot talk about the academic community when referring to the competition among academic researchers competing for scarce resources or jobs. We cannot talk about the community where we live, when we live in houses or neighborhoods in which nobody knows anybody else; in which people die and nobody notice; in which indifference, to a variety of degrees, seems to be the main mode of interaction between people; in which people *do not* act in fear that action may lead to conflict, when in fact it is the inability to deal constructively with the conflict in and outside our lives that paralyses our actions. We cannot talk about the community of workers, when as workers we go into job centers and compete against each-others for jobs. Or, once found a job, we work in ways that are largely aimed at advancing our company and *therefore*, through competition, undermining the livelihoods of the workers working for other companies.

For the definition of community therefore, we need something more than something shared among a group of people. We need also to be aware that the kind of relations among those people is crucial. Competitive relations, unless expressed as occasional convivial races or football matches on the commons fields, cannot be the center of the production and reproduction of our lives. When we compete in the fields, someone wins and someone loses, but we all end up sharing food, drinks and jokes. When we compete in the global marketplace, we destroy and accumulate, kill and invent, ruin and enrich, pollute and clean up, humiliate and dignify and there are always very concrete people and very concrete places at both ends of each dichotomy. Capitalism, is neither one nor the other side of the dichotomy, it is the endless perpetuation of both, it is the rat-race as an end in itself. In this sense, to defend capitalism as *progress* is as unwise as to condemn it as *doom*. Capital just is, and we need to focus on how to transcend the oppositions at its core.

A political discourse that puts community-building at its core in the context of today's intra-local forms of social cooperation for the production of goods, communication, dreams and life in general, help us to identify opportunities and problems. There are opportunities, because today the range of possible communities of mutual support and enrichment that we can invent are potentially endless. Problems, because due to pervasive market relations, the existence of communities is always intertwined with their negation, i.e. sustained competitive relations. Any node of a social network of mutual aid and solidarity is also *at the same time* whether we like it or not a node within a social network in competition with others. The aim of a new political discourse based on commons and communities is in a sense to help disarticulate and disentangle these two dimensions by first separating them analytically, and then elaborate the next step for political strategies that aim at extending the space of commons and the practices of communities within and among nodes vis-à-vis practices of competition.

The Many Places of Community: Local and Trans-Local Communities

When we think in terms of communities we must make an effort not to idealize or romanticize them. One of the most common ways to romanticize communities is to identify their "place" *exclusively* with their "locality" and therefore build a political discourse that, in the face of the many trans-local trends of "globalisation" aims at "going back to" the local. This romanticism is highly problematic in that "going back to" means not only to go back to things that we may miss, but *also* to things that we certainly *do not* miss. For example, to go back to the economy of the local European village means not only to go back to its conviviality, its culinary traditions, its wealth of embedded knowledge and skills. It also means "to go back to" its patriarchal forms, the particular forms of its relations of oppression and exploitation, its closed cultural environment, its relatively defensive and suspicious attitude to those "others" who do not belong to the community.

In practice, truly "going back to" the local is neither possible nor desirable. It is not possible, because today any locality however localized and isolated, is *at the same time* a node within a trans-local network of social relations. So it has to find ways to *deal with* its connections to the whole. And it deals with its connections to the whole in whatever form it chooses to or is forced to, whether in ways informed by mutual aid or by competitive forms. It is of course true that a locality could certainly choose to reduce its dependence on the outside world, and much of this dependence-reduction does indeed make a lot of sense both in environmental and social terms. But while common sense is one thing; it is quite another to build discourses that think that the needs of XXI century human beings can be squeezed into forms that are compatible with complete independence of locality. No matter whether they are in the North or the South, no matter whether we think of people living in a large metropolis or in a small jungles village. Any discourse of alternative today must conceive a certain degree of intra-local interdependence. If this is the case, our political discourse must be very clear in identifying the general coordinates of *how* this interdependence can be played out without reproducing the same problems of competitive modalities of intra-local interdependence.

In any case, it is only through connecting to the *outside* of locality that a social node in a network can tap into the pool of human resources in general, making it possible to actualize needs and desires emerging from a locality. It is only through connecting to the *outside* that a locality can gain access to the full scale of human wealth necessary to produce and reproduce life. Food, clothing, material goods, technology, know-how, innovation, problem solving, and overall resources in general are today available to such a degree as to meet almost any needs, aspiration, and desires, once we put a stop to a mode of social interaction that pits people against people, networks against networks. It is only through connecting to the outside of locality in non-competitive forms that major problems faced by *any locality* can be in principle solvable.

"Going *back to* the local" is not desirable for two reasons. First, because proximity, locality, *may* help cohesion, but also facilitate destruction and fragmentation. "Going *back to* the local" would mean forcing emerging needs and aspirations into local rules and traditions reflecting needs, aspirations and power relations of *another* era. The clash between the authoritarian act represented by the rigid upholding of rules vis-à-vis the aspirations and needs of the ruled, is the internal opposition helping the disintegration of existing local communities, promoted, of course, by the external force of capital's enclosures. Just think about the exodus from the patriarchal, claustrophobic and authoritarian micro-communities that was the traditional nuclear family, grounded on hierarchical *relations* of oppression within a locality. Or one has to reflect upon the "pull factors" (as opposed to the "push factors" rooted in poverty and enclosures) at the basis of migration from the village to the relative anonymity of the city, whether in the North or the South. In this sense, trans-locality is, and has always been a safety valve allowing exodus away from potentially claustrophobic, enclosing or oppressive communities. The opposite is of course *also* true. Locality also may signify the *refuge* aspired to by social subjects in exodus away from alienating and competitive trans-local relations.

Second, the trans-locality of our current condition allows us much more than "going back to" locality: it allows us to invent ways forward that articulate the best of locality, those aspects that we do not want to miss, together with the best of trans-locality, the world that we want to gain. In fact, modern technology allows the creation of trans-local places in which communities can operate to complement local places, and communities are everywhere and overlapping. In today's world, whether we are aware of it or not, each individual is a node of a series of competitive or communitarian networks, a locus either of cut-throat social relations or relations which are mutually supportive and free. The space of a new politics today is precisely the articulation of this overlapping, which is *both* an individual and collective responsibility. It implies the extension of the realm of community relations into spheres that are ruled by competitive relations. It involves building and defending spaces and commons in which communities can flourish. However, this also shields us from the naïve idea that communities flourish without the continuous learning practice of an *art* of social engagement with the other, of taking individual responsibility, of direct action in any sphere of life.

In terms of the place of community, this new political discourse thus expresses a fundamental aspiration. We want the wealth of localized knowledge and localized traditions to be available to all. We seek patterns of trans-local human exchanges that enrich us all. We want ways that allow anybody and any local or trans-local community to "draw credit" from the "bank" of human ingenuity, paying back to the world the innovation that always accompanies the adaptation of existing resources and knowledge to specific problems and circumstances. Of course, all this with no enslaving interest charged on debt!

Community as Learning Practices of Social Relations

There is of course an opposite risk, an opposite romanticism and idealization. It is the risk that sees COMMUNITY as a singular and written with capital letters. As with the idealized and romanticized illusory community of the past, this one is also an illusory community. However, instead of looking forward by projecting its illusions from the past, it looks below by projecting its illusions from the top. I am talking of the illusory community that is the state, the idea that the state, as a separate realm of social action, is somehow all-powerful, that the state *is* the community of all its citizens, and is the only true agent that can make alternatives actual. And so the corresponding laments follow: If only we could get the right candidate in, if only we could influence the right policies, if only we could democratize it. And so we read the many proposals and manifestos the language and rationale of which is to package a set of alternatives in ways that can be ready for politicians to use. Let's help them make respectable arguments, they say, in ways that can win crumbs of consensus, while at the same time leaving an opening for cooptation.

There is of course some truth in the lament: we do want proper and honest people representing us, even if we know that existing mechanisms of representations are disempowering. We do want policies that help promote social justice, even if we know that competitive relations defended and promoted by states perpetrate injustice. And we do want democratization, in fact, lots of it, even if we know that this is not compatible with existing arrangements of "Western democracies".

However, from the perspective of commons and communities, the "state" can either be a "community of communities" and therefore no longer the "state" as we know it or an illusionary community used to rule our lives. To be a community of communities it has to be the horizontal articulation of communities. The more real are the abilities and powers of communities to decide for themselves, the more real is the community that emerges out of their articulation. But of course, these growing powers imply growing power over resources and the goals of social production, something that actual states today are very careful to protect on behalf of existing business interests and the perpetuation of capital accumulation. It is in this sense, that the state is an "illusionary community". Instead of being the shadow of our social cooperation, it is the divisive knife with which to enforce competition in every sphere of life, thus breaking up communities. Instead of being a simple tool to help, facilitate and promote people to exercise their many powers, the state is the "power over" that channel these "powers to" into forms compatible with capital accumulation.

We said that communities are relations of mutual aid and support, solidarity and concrete practices of human exchange that are not reduced to the market form. In this sense, community is also an art of building what capital destroys. Because, despite the communitarian rhetoric of many of the defenders of capital (of whom UK prime minister Tony Blair is the champion) the endless competitive rat-race destroys communities, whatever they are. In building and strengthening unions, in promoting campaigns, in networking across the globe, in organizing in our neighbourhoods, we are building communities whereas the forces of global capital are destroying them. The recognition of this opposition between construction and destruction of communities should focus our senses both on the risks of cooptation of this community-building and its oppositional potential. Because community is social cooperation, social fabric, and capital depends on this for its stability. Capital co-opts cooperation and mutual support—community—by limiting the scope and power of communities, trying to define the context and the forms of their interaction with each other.

Yet at the same time, capital's competitive drives are set against this social fabric, for its perpetual destruction. So the question becomes: how can we build communities and strengthen them *vis-á-vis* the anti-communitarian forces of global capital and its attempt to co-opt them? I think that the answer rests on two main issues. First, just as commons are created and sustained by communities, so networks of mutual aids and support (communities) can be created and sustained through resources, commons.

Second, the relations within these networks must express needs that are frustrated within capital relations because they cannot be actualized by capital. In this sense, community is the art of building what capital cannot build, of practicing that freedom that cannot be delivered by capitalist social relations, of dreaming those dreams that no Hollywood film can make us dream, and acting upon those dreams in a way that no global commodity chain can do. Our movement of movements, in the articulation of all its dimensions and the innovative organizational forms it gives itself, has shown what these needs and aspirations are. These are social relations that are horizontal instead of being vertical, that are inclusive, instead of being exclusive, that promote empowered participation and dignity, instead of enforcing and promoting exploitation, oppression, estrangement and competition. In a word, a different world springs from a movement that practices what it preaches.

[The author wishes to thank David Harvey, John Holloway and Cyril Smith for their useful comments. The usual caveats apply.]

NOTES

1. This global debate which many saw originating with the World Social Forum movement in Porto Alegre (Brazil) 2000 and others with the Seattle movement in November 1999, was actually given birth by the indigenous people in Chiapas when they organized in 1996 the first international meeting "for humanity against neoliberalism". I have written about the historical importance of this meeting and of the Zapatistas movement in other places. See Massimo De Angelis (1997), "La Realidad in Europe: an account of the first European meeting against neoliberalism and for humanity, Berlin 30 May–2 June 1996." In *Common Sense*, (Journal of the Edinburgh Conference of Socialist Economists), Number 20. Massimo De Angelis (1998), "Introduction to the report on the 2nd Encounter for Humanity and against Neoliberalism". In *Capital and Class*, Number 65, Summer 1998, pp. 135-142. Massimo De Angelis (2000), "Globalisation, New Internationalism and the Zapatistas." In *Capital and Class*, 70, Spring.
2. See Michael Perelman (2000), *The invention of Capitalism*. Durham & London, Duke University Press. A chapter of this book is also available on the web as Michael Perelman (2001), The Secret History of Primitive Accumulation. In *The Commoner*, N. 2, September http://www.commoner.org.uk/02perelman.pdf. For a theoretical discussion see a Massimo De Angelis (2001), "Marx and Primitive Accumulation: the Continuous Character of Capital's Enclosures". In *The Commoner*, N. 2, http://www.thecommoner.org.
3. Polanyi, K. (1944), *The Great Transformation. The Political and Economic Origins of our Time*. Boston, Beacon Press.
4. See for example David Harvey (2000), *Spaces of Hope*. Edinburgh, Edinburgh University Press.
5. See for example Bell, Peter F. and Harry Cleaver (2002/1982).

Marx's Crisis Theory as a Theory of Class Struggle. In *The Commoner*, N5, August 2002, *http://www.commoner.org.uk/cleaver05.pdf*. Originally published in *Research in Political Economy*. Vol 5: 189-261, 1982.
6. Harvey, ibid.
7. See for example Massimo De Angelis (2002), "The Market order as a Disciplinary Order: a Comparattive Analysis of Hayek and Bentham." In *Research in Political Economy* 20; For an earlier analysis available on the web see Massimo De Angelis (2001), Global Capital, Abstract Labour and the Fractal Panopticon. In *The Commoner* N. 1, May, http:/www.commoner.org.uk/fractalpanopt.pdf.
8. On governance, see Massimo De Angelis (2003), Neoliberal Governance, Reproduction and Accumulation. In *The Commoner*, N. 7, Spring/Summer, *http://www.commoner.org.uk/07deangelis.pdf*. For an analysis of Keynesiansim, see Massimo De Angelis (2000), *Keynesianism, Social Conflict, and Political Economy*, London: Macmillan.
9. I must make clear here that whenever I refer to this movement, I mean a galaxy of practices and subjects, a heterogeneous world-wide multitude that comes together as a movement of movements. The aspirational horizons that emerge out of this movement, embedded for example in its organizational network forms (that carry the principles of horizontality, inclusiveness, participation, democracy) and its broad vision for a world that contains many worlds, are an indication that the practices of the multitude include the practices aimed at transcending itself as multitude.

Where is Power?

John Holloway

Behind the discussion of empire and imperialism lie certain assumptions about the location of power. For this reason, this paper focuses on the preliminary question "where is power?" But what do we mean by 'power' and, even more interestingly, what do we mean by 'where'?

In a self-antagonistic society, all concepts (and all people) are self-antagonistic. In a society based on exploitation, all concepts are inevitably battlefields riven by the same binary antagonism between exploiter and exploited, master and slave.

We start from doing. Doing is the basis of any society, including societies based on exploitation. Doing implies power, the power to do, the capacity to do. This power is a social power. The doing of one person implies the (simultaneous or previous) doing of others. Doing is always part of a social flow of doing in which that which has been done by one person is the precondition of the doing of another and the doing of the latter is the development or reproduction of the doing of the former, in which the doing of one flows across time and space into the doing of another and there are no clear boundaries between the doing of one and the doing of another.

There is not necessarily any direct link between the purpose, time or location of one doing and the doing which it develops. When we write a book, we do not know where or when or by whom it will be read (if at all) or from where or when all the influences on our writing come. The social flow of doing meanders through time and space.

In capitalism (and indeed in any society based on exploitation, but it is capitalism that interests us here), the social flow of doing is broken. The done is taken from the doer, broken from the doing and appropriated by the capitalist. This constantly repeated breaking is the basis of capitalist society. Capitalism is based on a movement of breaking, a movement of separating which affects all aspects of human doing (all aspects of life). The separation of done from doing implies the subordination of doing to done. Since the done is the precondition of doing, the capitalist uses his possession of the done to command doing, and he commands doing with the sole purpose of increasing his done and therefore increasing his command over doing. Done commands doing. Power-to-do is transformed into power-over. That which is, the done, that which has been done, is separated from the doing which created it and commands (and denies) that doing. In other words, in a capitalist society, being (that which is) commands doing, doing is subordinated to being. Doing becomes instrumental to the accumulation of the done. What rules is the self-expansion of the done, for doing, like any servant or slave, is invisible, negated.

The subordination of doing to being implies a new spatiality. Capitalist space is in the first place a space of being, not of doing. The fracturing of the social flow of doing is also a fracturing of space, the transformation of the meandering space of the flow of doing into a compartmentalised space of being. Capitalist space is not a space of connections but above all of separations, of frontiers. States defined by frontiers play a central role in capitalist spatiality. The development of citizenship implies the classification of people as beings (not as doers) enclosed within certain frontiers. The organisation of the violence necessary to maintain the system of exploitation follows the same spatial organisation, the same pattern of spatial inclusion/exclusion.

But capitalist space has, inevitably, another dimension. It

cannot simply be a spatiality of being because capitalist being (accumulation of the done) depends on the harnessing (alienation) of doing as work. Behind being is a hidden dependence on work. Behind the fragmented-frontier spatiality, the space of capitalist power-over is bound to follow in perverted fashion the frontier-free flow of doing, and not just to follow it, but to organise and dominate it. Behind the obvious state-organised forms of capitalist domination there has always been a structure of capitalist command going beyond (and largely ignoring) state frontiers. Capitalist command has always had two spatial dimensions: on the one hand, an obvious spatiality of being in which the key figure is the state, and on the other, a more hidden global space of command over work. This global spatiality of global command is not, however, the same as the frontierless flow of social doing: it is based not on unalienated doing but on alienated work, doing organised for the purpose of expanding the done, accumulating capital. Capitalist space is based on a doing organised for a purpose alien to the doing itself, on an instrumentally organised doing. Even its global dimension is a spatiality of straight lines, of railway tracks, highways and airline routes rather than the meandering of free doing.

We have, then, two antagonistic forms of power, characterised by two antagonistic forms of space. On the one hand, the free, frontierless flow of social doing, on the other the fragmented, frontier-dominated and linear space of capitalist command.

In a capitalist world, obviously, our power and our space exist not as timeless truth but as resistance, opposition, as unfulfilled dream and as that upon which capital (as the perversion of our power) ultimately depends. There are many images of this space: the open-road non-instrumental journey praised by Marcuse and idealised by the road movies of Hollywood, the wandering images of romantic poems and novels, the flânerie of Baudelaire and Benjamin, the dérive of the situationists and surrealists, Machado's *'camino que se hace al andar'* ('path made by walking'), the 'caminamos preguntando' (asking we walk') and the intergalacticism of the zapatistas. It is above all a spatiality of self-assertion, of exploration, of non-instrumental creation.

We already have a preliminary answer to the question "where is power?" Our power is everywhere, without frontiers or straight lines. Capitalist power, prior to being in any particular place, lies already in the concept of a spatiality marked out by separations and highways. To accept without criticism the capitalist concept of spatiality (as is done in Leninist theories of imperialism or dreams of national autonomy) is already to enter on to the terrain of capitalist power, to concede the battle before it is begun.

What then do we say of the current controversies stirred up by the publication of Hardt and Negri's Empire? Is capitalist power increasingly centred in the United States or is it an amorphous presence that permeates the whole society and cannot be located in one place?

The answer surely has to be in terms of the two-dimensionality of capitalist power. Capitalist power is a relation of command-over (and therefore dependence upon) the doing of people in all parts of the world. This relation is concentrated in money. The existence of money as the medium of exploitation means that the capitalist relation of exploitation is a-territorial and fluid. This has been true since the origins of capitalism.

However, the intensity of this a-territoriality is not constant. When the insubordination of doers intensifies, so too does capital's hopeless flight from its dependence upon the conversion of doing into labour. Capital then transforms itself into its money form and moves more rapidly through the world. This is essentially what has been happening in the last twenty years or so. The rise of insubordination during the twentieth century, first in the wave of struggles associated with the Russian revolution, and then a second wave in the late 1960s and the 1970s, drove capital to seek refuge in the expansion of credit, an expansion which continues to this day. The expansion of credit is synonymous with the rise of capital in its money form and means therefore the ever more rapid movement of capital throughout the world, the basis of what is generally known as "globalisation". In this sense we can speak of a progressive de-territorialisation of capitalist command.

The rapid movement of capital tends to increase rather than reduce the need for capitalist relations to be protected or enforced by organised violence. The growing deterritorialisation of capitalist command is accompanied by an expansion rather than a diminution of statehood. Nevertheless, the rise of money capital means that states exist in a new environment, in which their limitations, their interdependence but also the antagonism between them is clearer than ever. There is consequently a reorganisation of the political organisation of violence which is inseparable from capitalism. Part of the current reorganisation of political organisation is the frenzied struggle by the US government to maintain or expand the role of the US state.

There is thus no contradiction between the de-territorialisation of capitalist command and the increasingly belligerent politics of the US (and other) governments. Both are aspects of the flight of capital from insubordination, aspects of the protracted crisis of capital.

There is, however, a more interesting question than that of the crisis and reorganisation of capitalist power. To what extent does this crisis and reorganisation stimulate the development of our anti-power, in this case the development of our own spatiality? Probably the answer is contradictory. On the one hand, the reorganisation of capitalist power has led many to want to defend the old organisation of that power, to seek refuge in nationalism or other identitarian responses. On the other hand, the current wave of struggle for a different world indicates a very confident assertion of our own spatiality, in which struggle is not organised on an inter-national basis but simply knows no borders. A space which is conceived not in terms of borders or straight lines, but in terms of spectacles and anti-spectacles, shows and carnivals, events rather than institutions.

This is very important. For too long the left has tried to engage capital on its own spatiality, to organise on national lines and to conceive of change in terms of national states. To some extent it is impossible to avoid engaging with capital on its own terms, but if struggle is to open up any perspective of a different society, it must always be on an against-and-beyond basis, with the emphasis being as strongly as possible on the beyond, with the world of explicitly and consciously social doing always present as a Utopian star.

Analysing Imperialism in the Age of Globalisation: Some Problems

Pratyush Chandra

Although throughout the last century, imperialism has been a theme of recurrent discussion and theorisations; there have been mainly three 'waves of interest' in theories of imperialism. The first wave of interest evolved in the early decades of the 20th century when "the world was finally being divided up among the empires of the European powers". (Owen, 1972) It reflected the saturation of the process of 'internationalisation of capital', which started in 1870s when the financial-industrial monopolies wanting safe territorial havens for their expansion directed the states acting as their agencies to secure colonies (from commercial capital which tends to destroy the productive potentiality of economies through simple reproduction squeeze). The second wave, "beginning in the 1950s, was in large measure a reflection of the new situation produced by the dismantling of these same imperial structures". (Ibid) On the one hand, this was a result of capital accumulation in the colonies and the emergence of strong national capitalist interests, with which the monopoly capital of the advanced countries had to articulate and this could never be done through direct colonialism. The independent regimes intensified the process of capitalisation of local structures and modes of production, which colonialism definitely helped in initiating but could not carry forward; in fact, it acted as a fetter in this process as maintaining the colonies required controlling the process of transition from formal subsumption of labour by capital to actual subsumption.[1] Despite all these changes, however, "monopoly capitalism remains an aggressively expansionist political economic system, but colonialism is seen as merely one form of imperialist domination and frequently an ineffective one at that." (O'Connor, 1970)

The third wave of interest in theories of imperialism came after the East European collapse, which seemingly confirmed the American hegemony. The revival was essentially an attempt to answer the 'hyper-globalists' who have evolved the 'globalisation thesis' in celebration of new strategies of capitalism and its apparent triumphal march—the decay of nation-states, there-is-no-alternative (TINA) to capitalist 'democracy' and new technological changes will not only internationalise capital "but will also radically change our lives". However, this apologetic rhetoric of globalisation is in contrast to the reality. To understand this reality, "one needs a different theoretical frame, one which allows us to see globalisation as a partially new form of modern imperialism. The dominant role of multinationals, the great mobility of huge masses of capital on the international financial markets, the fall of the Soviet Union, the constant introduction of new technologies: all these are real developments. However, the notion which unifies them in one single concept, globalisation, is aggressively ideological." (Carchedi, 1999)

In this introduction, we will start with tracing the trajectory of capitalist development, wherein we will test the 'newness' of the so-called 'globalisation' and fit it in a historical paradigm. Then we will analyse this historical trajectory within the logical framework of Marxist political economy. After this, we will reread Lenin's classic treatise on imperialism as the base on which such framework can be effectively built. We will then interpret the 'post-modern' belligerence that recently some powerful nation-states have shown and the overall rise in jingoistic rightist forces everywhere, followed by a brief survey of political ramifications of the 'ideologies' of globalism and anti-globalism.

GLOBALISATION—A RUPTURE OR CONTINUITY

A Continuity

Capital as a socio-economic force can sustain only through its expansion. This truth was realised even by the classical political economists who saw the plundering wheel of primary accumulation through mercantile and market consolidation. Interdependence was the war cry, which devastated the self-sufficiency of the feuds with the cruel invisible hand of the market. Enclosures created more and more people dependent on the market logic. People were excluded from being propertied but included in the process as non-propertied proletarians in the labour market that slowly became national and international, too. Colonisation was part of this process that created interdependence at the international level. Colonies were made to jettison the self-sufficiency of their village economy and simple commodity production. New areas were included in the reign of capital's logic, but in the process through a 'drain of wealth' they were excluded from the wealthy horizons. They supplied raw materials and indentured labour, and mass production in Manchester competed with the Indian weavers, pauperising the latter. It was not always the coercive power of the colonisers that led to the squeezed economies of the colonised, but essentially the competitive logic of capital accumulation based on the 'equitable' and 'justified' process of competition which killed the weavers of India. Competition creates pauperisation, poverty, and, thus, exclusion. But it simultaneously creates proletarianisation, an interdependence of capital and labour, and thus an inclusion. The debate between Ricardo and Malthus on "free trade" was much more subtle than the usual debate going around globalisation and liberalisation. At that time too, "free trade" signified "freedom of capital" to be trans-national, but it was more trade-oriented, production was still located in the land of the capitalists and the South was mainly a market and raw-material supplier. In fact, Say's law – the supply creates its own demand—could only be sustainable in an ever-growing market expansion.

With the crisis of 1873, globalisation entered a new phase of internationalisation and we see capitalists investing in raw-material extraction, mining and even agricultural production. India, too, after the Victorian takeover from the mercantilist East India Company, saw expansion of railways and 'primary' industries within a few years. Now, the industrial capital of the West had taken over from the mercantile interests, which were increasingly becoming a nuisance in expansion of capital because of their rent-oriented practices and thus thwarting the productive capital that needed secure and cheap sources of oil, metals, rubber, etc. It was a new phase in the global interdependence with a global division of labour taking place in the productive sphere too. World capitalist interests frequently clashed over the partitioning of resources – hence, the two world wars.

With the 30 years of global wars, the process of internationalisation of capital slowed down and the Great Crash of 1929 forced the economies, in order to strengthen their base in the native land, to undergo introversion. Keynesianism was a product of this phase, which sought to regulate and refurbish the native machinery of capital accumulation. We see welfarism seeking to thwart the crisis of over-production and state-regulated basic industries to reproduce the basic infrastructure damaged during the wars and crises. This brief introversion was essentially a consolidation.

State interventionist strategies never reverted the internationalisation of capital rather they enabled the reconstruction the base so that such process could be strongly enforced. It was the New Deal's success and the development of the US as the supreme political force in the capitalist world during the World War II that helped in building the new phase of imperialism in the post-war period. It was Keynes who envisaged the Bretton Woods agreement, laying the foundation of the International Monetary Fund (IMF) and the International Bank for Reconstruction and Development (IBRD) later known as World Bank (WB). They have become the agencies of the latest phase of globalisation. This post-war phase involved further multi-nationalisation of production through setting up of labour-intensive manufacturing units in the cheap labour zones of Asia, Africa and Latin America. These units were initially concentrating on finished goods for direct consumption, like clothing, shoes etc. But in the later years during 1960s and 1970s we find units producing component parts for electronics and other industries concentrated in the advanced countries.

This brief historical survey is perhaps known to all conscious students of economic history; it definitively shows that the process of global interdependence started right from the advent of capitalism. So what is this globalisation we are talking about if it is not a continuation of a process that started a few centuries ago? The newness in it would make it just another phase in the expansion of capitalism, until and unless it shows a fundamental rupture in capital and labour relations overturning the very logic of capital – the logic of expansion of capitalist production and accumulation, its vehicle being competition.

A Change

The new phase of internationalisation of capital, popularly known as 'globalisation', seeks to promote financial integration, financial and trade liberalisation with further internationalisation of production. This is a statement, which perhaps would not be disputed by anyone for or against globalisation. One may, however, argue on the degrees of these processes as they unfold in real life. As mentioned earlier, trans-national corporations concentrated in the 'North' started organising production both in the North and South of the globe after the World War II. We find a consistent and dramatic increase in Foreign Direct Investment (FDI) and doubling of global trade during the post-war phase. But this does not mean only expansion of capital accumulation; it also essentially involved a concentration and centralisation of production and distribution. This becomes clear once we go through the details of the global trade, where we find that one-half to two-thirds of it, since 1945 has been trade between units of the same trans-national corporation.

But what makes this new phase of internationalisation of capital somewhat radically different from the earlier phase is the regulation or rather 'deregulation' to remove the 'obstacles' in the market expansion and integration. National legislations protecting the national capital have to be rationalised to create 'fair' competition for foreign investors and producers. Self-sufficiency of local markets, which was established through provision of subsidies and other benefits to small-scale production, came to be seen as clogs in the integration of demand structure in the economy and as creating price distortions. Historically, such provisions were made to allow the big capital to concentrate on priority industries to help building the newly independent national economies, while small units fulfilled the local and peripheral needs.

In this regard, we have to remember that the rise of financial institutions, which are beyond the control of nations and national laws, make them decisive agencies in facilitating or coercing such changes in the national economic structures. The fear of the 'flight of capital', which is now beyond the control of any country, humbles all the titanic war cry against globalisation. Earlier too, finance capital played a vital role, but in this new phase, its supremacy and independence derives from its speculative pursuit, as 'hot money flow'. Its herd behaviour allows it to set the parameters for financial decisions of the governments without apparently controlling them.

But the more important aspect of this phase, at least from our point of view, is the intensification of capital's control over the workplace and reorganisation of the labour market and work process. It is in this aspect that we can perceive the genesis of 'social exclusion' and deprivation that we recognise today (although it is essentially a realisation of the whole process, as the enumeration and characterisation of different aspects of globalisation have analytical function rather than making any real, political sense).

As profit maximisation and its natural corollary, cost minimisation are the basic motivations that engender competition and thus establish the market, we need to see all these regulatory or de-regulatory policies as part of intensifying competition in the market. The present process of reorganisation of work, too, was essentially a product of this pursuit. This process has been termed by some as 'lean production' and others have called it 'post-Fordism'. The essential nature of the process and its components has been identified more or less in similar fashion. Corporations are seeking to get rid of 'waste' that increases the cost—material, work and workers. Outsourcing or contracting out of work is the basic medium today that integrates the markets locally, nationally and globally, and that too with greater efficiency and less cost. The cutting edge of globalisation and liberalisation, which organises the social life, is lean production, which judges everything and everyone on the basis of speed and productivity. Speeding up, deskilling (breaking the jobs to discrete tasks), multi-tasking (fashionably known as multi-skilling), contracting out of work, utilising casual and contractual labour, flexible working hours – these are what constitute the situation in the labour market and at the workplace, even at the household level, which is now not only a site for the reproduction of labour power but is also for undertaking the production tasks outsourced, facilitating the integration of the cheap feminine workforce.

The so-called 'crisis of Fordism' occurred as "extreme internationalisation of markets and productive networks without a corresponding international harmonisation of wage compromises...brought competitive constraints to centre stage". (Lipietz, 2000:21) It was to rationalise the wage relation with the global needs of capital that flexibilisation and segmentation of the workforce were systematically undertaken.

Globally, as diverse stages of technological development and production techniques coexist, their integration and emerging competition between them evidently structure the global economy in a hierarchy, which may not comply with the geo-historical notions of core and periphery, but definitely such relations exist between all particular capitals through ancillarisation and multilateral capital flows. Concentration and centralisation of capital occurs defeating and accommodating the lower stages of capital formation by giving them places in an invisible hierarchy of capital in general. And this process accommodates the global population and labour force in a hyperbolic curve-like hierarchy where the lowest end always tends towards total exclusion but still not attaining it.

Circuit of Capital and Periodisation of Capitalist Expansion

On the whole, there is a logic operating through these apparent historical realisations of capitalism. The operation of circuit of capital ensuring the capitalist accumulation determines the continuity, break and restructuring in the history of capitalism. It is within this circuit that value (and hence surplus value) is produced and realised. And what is capitalist accumulation, if not "the grabbing of surplus-value and its capitalisation"? (Marx, 1978: 579) If we interpret the historical processes of capital expansion through the logic of capitalist accumulation, we can state that today the whole circuit of capital has been globalised.

The total circuit or movement of capital can be expressed as in (1). It is "a unified process of circulation and production, it includes both." (Marx, 1978: 139)[2]

$$M - C \genfrac{\langle}{}{0pt}{}{L}{MP} ...P...C'(C + c) - (M + m) \quad (1)$$

However, there are moments or levels of phases in this total circuit. The capital value in each phase takes a different form. Marx has demarcated three phases in this circuit, where two takes place in the circulation sphere, and one in production sphere. The forms that capital value takes in the circulation sphere are called *money capital* and *commodity capital* and the circuit according to these forms can be represented as in (2) and (3).

$$M - C...P...C' - M' \quad (2)$$
$$C'-M'-C'...P' - C' \quad (3)$$

In the production sphere, capital value takes the form of *productive capital* and the circuit here can thus be represented (4),

$$P...C'-M'...C'...P \quad (4)$$

In (2) and (3) dots represent a disruption in the circulation sphere, while in (4) they signify that "the entire circulation process of industrial capital, its whole movement within the circulation phase, merely forms an interruption, and hence a mediation, between the productive capital that opens the circuit as the first extreme and closes it in the same form as the last extreme, i.e. in the form of its new beginning".[3] (Marx, 1978: 145)

What we obtain here is the essential mechanism through which capital gets accumulated and expanded. Capital is invested in service of generating more value (its production and realisation). Now as history unfolds, the trade, which is essential to circulate the commodity and money-capital, was the first sphere of human activity that broke the territorial boundaries. Hence, it was its extraordinary ability to mediate between 'spaces and times' that it became the harbinger of world capitalism, of course, when the objective conditions demanded.[4] "Initially, whether accumulation is based on the production of absolute or relative surplus value, accumulation of productive capital guarantees that national capitals expand beyond their boundaries in their search for expanded markets to ensure that realisation and completion of their circuit is possible. Thus commodity capital is the first form of capital to be internationalised, and this can be taken as the index of the first stage of the world economy." (Fine & Harris, 1979) In other words, it was the stage when $C`-M`$ was internationalised, and colonialism signified only "to create a self-sufficient empire, where as much as possible of the raw materials and food needs of England [being the prime coloniser] would come from her own possessions, and in turn the colonies would provide exclusive markets for the mother country's manufactures." (Magdoff, 1974)

After the Industrial Revolution and the complete subjugation of ruling landed interests during the debate on Corn Laws in England, we find the growing need for taming the mercantile interests who in their role as mediators between colonising nations and colonised territories accumulated enormous politico-economic prowess based on pure swindle of buying cheap and selling dear. The birth of railways and other modes of mechanised transportation provided a potentiality to invest in productive mode of raw material extraction in colonies that would serve the industries in metropolitan countries. It was the juncture where we find the internationalisation of financial capital getting an initial stimulus, of which Lenin talks about in his *Imperialism*. The evolution of credit system to facilitate the relative surplus value production brought into the stage monopolies as the product of the coordination of industries and banking capital. Since latter runs as the mediator between productive sphere and circulation sphere, and between various productive zones too, the stage implied a dominance of money-capital. This was the stage when the complete circuit in the circulation sphere M-C-M' was internationalised minus the interrupting agency of *productive capital*. As shown later, the colonial policy was significantly altered to suit the needs of capital accumulation at that juncture. It should be noted that the parasitism of finance capital at this stage derives from its insistence to bypass the dotted zones of the circuit of capital (1), i.e., the operation of the circuit of productive capital, with it obviously even that of commodity-capital. This would mean simply M-M'. In fact, this is symptomatic of an unmanageable clash between the general necessity to realise every phase in the total circuit of capital for the reproduction of the system itself and the particular need to monopolise the surplus value.[5] This accentuates capitalist crises and the 'post-modern' call for local controls indeed evolve from the need to curb (better control) this clash (that is why such call becomes a part of the hegemonic discourse on economic policy at the time of crises, even if they have an apparent 'socialistic' connotation, of course only when they are marginal).

In the post-World War II period, more so after the profitability crises in 1960s and 1970s, it was only through the internationalisation of productive capital that profitability could be revived as the transfer of value through circulation was now ineffective and could have led to further deepening of crisis, as already an enormous political turmoil with a general rise in social unrest was visible internationally. With the increase in the organic composition of capital, there was a general decline in the rate of profit world over leading to the structural crisis of the 1970s. The original cause of the fall in the profit rate was "the disappearance in the late 1960s and early 1970s of certain favourable features of technical change (rapidity and forms) since the Second World War." (Duménil & Lévy, 1999) Since the 1960s, there has been a slowdown in the growth of productivity, the declining profit rate and "the increasing 'burden' of capital in comparison to labour and production". (Ibid) As for the parasitism of money-capital, "the effects of the structural crisis in the 1970s, as it can be accounted for by the evolution of technology and distribution, were prolonged to the present by the policy of high interest rates and the subsequent indebtedness of firms." (Ibid)

It is only through an increase in the intensity of production and through subjugating more and more living labour that variable capital can be decreased restoring the profitability. With the growth in multinationalisation of production and lean production this task is accomplished. "The intensified production of relative surplus value gives rise to a third stage in which productive capital itself is internationalised with multinational corporations controlling production processes which cross national boundaries." (Fine & Harris, 1979) This establishes the full internationalisation of the circuit of capital. The process of "financialisation" or more liberalisation of financial capital evident today, and which has been much talked about, is not negated but included in the overall intensification of capitalist accumulation. Moreover, it is the desperation to consolidate its hegemony over the process of global redistribution of surplus value that has unnerved its ever more liberal spirit to become more and more speculative. But, essentially, as Brunhoff (2003) sees that

> "The visible domination of financial markets does not imply that industrial capital has lost its fundamental importance. Rather, we could say that a new capitalist coalition has emerged, in order to restore profitability after the crisis of the 1970s. When shareholders required very high returns on their financial assets, bosses responded by reorganising production processes: downsizing, subcontracting, relocation of plants and so on. Since the 1980s, company

restructuring has maximised profits *while treating employment and wages as adjustment variables."* (Italics original)

It is important to note that *financialisation* has an important role in securing dependency in the present phase of capitalist development, in opening up the markets in dependent countries and in transfer of surplus value. Further, even if glut may occur (and definitely occurs) during the transition from one phase to another of the total process, we will have to understand with Marx (Capital 1978: 133) that

> "The Capital that assumes these forms (money, commodity and productive capital) in the course of its total circuit, discards them again and fulfils in each of them its appropriate function, is industrial capital – industrial here in the sense that it encompasses every branch of production that is pursued on a capitalist basis…[These forms] thus do not denote independent varieties of capital, whose functions constitute the content of branches of business that are independent and separate from one another. They are simply particular functional forms of industrial capital, which takes on all three forms in turn."

The complete internationalisation of the circuit of capital does not do away with the representation of uneven capitalist development in diverse political and territorial locations, in fact it is accentuated and in turn provides a scope for further expansion of capitalist accumulation necessary for reproducing the system. The international relations still provide the efficacy to the concepts of dependency and domination and hence to Lenin's conceptualisation of imperialism. The role of State in Capitalism too is reasserted as the agency to facilitate the reproduction of the system by mediating the intra-capitalist conflict and coercing the 'living labour' to the reign of capital, which is a necessary precondition for the reproduction of the capitalist mode of production.

Regarding the concept of dependency and its significance in understanding the stage of internationalisation of productive capital, we would simply assert that there is a need to conceive it on the fundamentals of Marxist political economy and derive it from the essential logic of capital. In contrast to the general tendency among *dependentistas* to externalise dependency and present it in terms of the impact of imperial conspiracy, there is a need to visualise it in the internal processes of capital in general of which the total national capitals are parts. Dussel (2001) attempts such a re-conceptualisation of the 'dependency' phenomenon: "Dependency is a moment in the competition of capital." He elaborates on the basis of Marx's understanding of distribution of value via the equalisation of prices:

> "The 'development of the concept of dependency' demands order in the constitution and exposition of categories. The first aspect is the possibility of the existence of products or commodities of different value. The second aspect is to place these products in competition. Thus placed face to face (in reality, so as not to fetishise to unequal exchange of international values, it is not the products but the corresponding national bourgeois classes which are face to face) an equalisation takes place, although not of values (which can never be equalised), but of prices. The law of value regulates or controls this equalisation." (Dussel, 2001: 225)

This equalisation of prices leads to the transfer of value from the economies that produce a particular commodity with a backward technique and hence having greater value to the competing economy that produces that commodity with an advanced technique and thus having less value.

Even the conception of imperialism needs to be reasserted in the dialectical framework of explaining the *concrete* in terms of its *essence*, that "generally exists only *in and through* the phenomena, and the latter are not merely the form of manifestation of the essence but, more strongly, *its mode of existence*." (Saad-Filho, 2002: 10) Most of the discussions on imperialism have been based on an empiricist grounding, constructed through an amalgamation of disparate concepts taken from 'vulgar political economy' informing the national and international statistics and accounts; and then mechanically imposed on Marxism. In fact, we think Lenin's classic treatise on imperialism provides a definite base on which a proper Marxist understanding can be developed. The fact about its Aesopian style and language has been too many times stressed and has been taken as a license to use it to support diverse and contradictory arguments. We feel that one will have to understand Aesop in his own terms and in terms of his stories. To paraphrase Althusser (who said it in the context of *Capital*), we all have read *Imperialism* and "read it every day, transparently, in the dramas and dreams of our history, in its disputes and conflicts, in the defeats and victories of the workers' movement which is our only hope and our destiny. Since we 'came into the world', we have read [it] constantly in the writings and speeches of those who have read it for us..But some day it is essential to read [*Imperialism*] to the letter. To read the text itself.." (Althusser, 1970: 13) We will not submit our reading, at least not here, as to be the only correct one, but as another one, trying to be true to its black letters.

REREADING LENIN'S IMPERIALISM

Lenin's Tasks and Method

Lenin wrote his "popular outline" on imperialism in June 1916, but it was published only in 1917 as *Imperialism, the Latest Stage of Capitalism*, which was later renamed after his death as *Imperialism, the Highest Stage of Capitalism*. (Hobsbawm, 1987: 12; Lenin, 1976: 801) Like other texts written by Lenin, this too was a product of the political need of the time. It was written to expose the imperialist nature of the ongoing World War. Its tone was set by the need, on the one hand, to thwart the chauvinistic and class collaborationist influences of the bureaucratised and petty bourgeois leadership of social democracy throughout the European continent thwarting the revolutionary spirit of the working class. Thus, the pamphlet tried to expose the material reasons for such degeneration. On the other hand, through this polemics and his analysis of the "latest stage of capitalism", Lenin sought to reframe the working class strategy by putting *socialist* revolution once again on its agenda. He explicitly poses the Marxist method of *class analysis* as the most effective methodological standpoint on which capitalism, all its stages and its effects can be understood:

> "Proof of what was the true social, or rather, the true class character of the war is naturally to be found, not in the diplomatic history of the war, but in an analysis of the *objective* position of the ruling *classes* in *all* the belligerent countries." (Lenin 2000: 37, italics original)

Further, this required an analysis of "the *basis* of economic life in *all* the belligerent countries and the *whole* world." (*Ibid*, italics original) Despite his trust, shown at the time of its publication in April 1917, "that this pamphlet will *help* the reader to understand the fundamental economic question, that of the economic essence of imperialism for unless this is studied, it will be impossible to understand and appraise modern war and modern politics" (Lenin, 2000: 35), in 1920 in his preface to French and German editions he explicitly delimits the purpose of the pamphlet and in so doing he cautions the people who have the tendency to read between the lines:

> "As was indicated in the preface to the Russian edition, this pamphlet was written in 1916, with an eye to the tsarist censorship. I am unable to revise the whole text at the present time, nor, perhaps, would this be advisable, since the main purpose of the book was, and remains, to present, *on the basis of the summarised returns of irrefutable bourgeois statistics, and the admissions of bourgeois scholars of all countries, a composite picture* of the world capitalist system in its international relationships at the beginning of the twentieth century — on the eve of the first world imperialist war. (Lenin, 2000: 36; emphasis is added)

This humble and honest admission can come only from a hardcore Marxist revolutionary who is guided by the requirements of praxis. In fact, he presented it as a lesson for the revolutionaries in the bourgeois democratic countries, that if he could achieve so much under the tsarist censorship, they might better him by "making use of even the slight remnants of legality". What did he expect from this collective effort world over? It is presumed from his own admissions that, first, it would be to expose the politics of imperialism and against it, on which only "few necessary observations" were formulated in the pamphlet "with extreme caution, by hints, in an allegorical language – in that accursed Aesopian language". And for a Marxist what else would politics mean, if not thinking and formulating his practical tasks in terms of class struggle? He must have expected, secondly, that comrades would transcend the limitation imposed by hegemonic bourgeois concepts evident in bourgeois statistics and scholarship (even if they are irrefutable, honest and insightful) on his own analysis. Conclusively, he must have expected a return to Marx!

Colonialism, Imperialism and Capital

Lenin explicitly concludes, "We have seen that in its economic essence imperialism is monopoly capitalism." (146) Further, he accounts for different types of monopoly having origins in diverse phases of capitalist production and reproduction:

(1) "monopoly arose out of the concentration of production at a very high stage."
(2) "monopolies have stimulated the seizure of the most important sources of raw materials." (146-47)
(3) "monopoly has sprung from the banks"—achieving "the personal link-up between industrial and bank capital." (147)
(4) "monopoly has grown out of colonial policy." (147)

Lenin differentiates between imperialism (and colonialism) before the 'latest' stage of capitalism and as the latest stage. (107) The colonialism in 'new' imperialism exists as a part of the struggle of the monopoly finance capital "for the sources of raw materials, for the export of capital, for spheres of influence, i.e., for spheres for profitable deals, concessions, monopoly profits and so on, economic territory in general." (147) While talking about the "colonial policy of finance capital", Lenin notes,

"The principal feature of the latest stage of capitalism is the domination of monopolist associations of big employers. These monopolies are most firmly established when *all* the sources of raw materials are captured by one group, and we have seen with what zeal the international capitalist associations exert every effort to deprive their rivals of all opportunity of competing, to buy up, for example, ironfields, oilfields, etc. Colonial possession alone gives the monopolies complete guarantee against all contingencies in the struggle against competitors, including the case of the adversary wanting to be protected by a law establishing a state monopoly." (108)

If we read this analysis with the understanding developed in *State and Revolution* with regard to State, which too was published at the same time, the 'nation-state' too can be comprehended essentially as capitalist 'monopolist' associations, and imperialist aggression as their special mode to enhance accumulation of capital. Fine & Harris (1979: 146) have a cogent explanation on this count:

"The primary function of the state-in-general is to guarantee the reproduction of capitalist social relations—relations which pertain to the existence of capital-in-general. The national state, on the other hand, presupposes the division of social reproduction and also the division of capital into competing blocs (many-capitals)...[T]his division is not a simple one: one cannot assume that capital is divided into national capitals in one-to-one correspondence with national states (a 'British capital' to which corresponds the British state apparatus) and the division of social reproduction is not one which makes the reproduction of nations its main element. Nevertheless the existence of the national state under capitalism is predicated upon the existence of competition between blocs of capitals and the related division of social reproduction. This is to be contrasted with those views which take the national state as the product of 'natural' nations which are defined in terms of unexplained linguistic and cultural characteristics. It is also to be contrasted with those views which see the existence of the national state and its state apparatus only in terms of economic reproduction; for to say that the national state is predicated upon competition between capital means that the political and ideological roles of its national state apparatus as well as its economic are determined in this way."

Lenin was too clear about the role of anti-colonial bourgeois democratic struggles for generating a world revolutionary situation, first, by weakening the colonising bourgeoisie, and, secondly, by unleashing the capitalist transformation and thus sharpening the class struggle within the colonised territories. He drew lessons from Marx's understanding on the Irish question whose solution was according to Marx necessary for the emancipation of both English and Irish working class. "If capitalism had been overthrown in England as quickly as Marx had at first expected, there would have been no room for a bourgeois-democratic and general national movement in Ireland. But since it had arisen, Marx advised the English workers to support it, give it a revolutionary impetus and see it through in the interests of *their own* liberty." (Lenin, 1976: 605) Whenever dealing with the colonial question, Lenin explicitly denied any broad nationalistic framework for evolving the tactics on the question. He was concerned exclusively with developing the *proletarian attitude* towards it. He explicitly concludes in his *The Right of Nations to Self-Determination*:

> "In this situation, the proletariat of Russia is faced with a twofold or, rather, a two-sided task: to combat nationalism of every kind, above all, Great-Russian nationalism; to recognise, not only fully equal rights for all nations in general, but also equality of rights as regards polity, i.e., the right of nations to self-determination, to secession. And at the same time, it is their task, in the interests of a successful struggle against all and every kind of nationalism among all nations, to preserve the unity of the proletarian struggle and the proletarian organisations, amalgamating these organisations into a close-knit international association, despite bourgeois strivings for

national exclusiveness." (Lenin, 1976: 616)

Another important point that he makes clear, throughout the pamphlet and especially against Kautsky and his ilk that imperialism is a 'stage' not a 'policy'. Gerstein (1979) rightly elaborates that

> "What is at the stake is the very definition of the phenomenon to be explained, and thus the shape that the explanation should take.. *The Stage vs. policy dispute is actually a disagreement over the object of study*. For Lenin, operating within the terms of historical materialism, this object is capitalism at a certain stage. For the vast majority of writers (both anti-Marxist and supposedly Marxist) it is the process of expansion of Western Europe into "the less-developed world."[6] (Emphasis is original)

Anti-Imperialism

It is erroneous to identify anti-colonial nationalist struggle with anti-imperialism. The former is just a moment in the latter, and even precedes it if we look at the history of colonialism. Colonialism is just a political form, which due to its primordial historical existence got articulated in every stage of capitalism, even in its new imperialist stage. Hence, anti-colonial struggle cannot be equated with anti-imperialism. Anti-imperialist struggle has to be anti-capitalist. Lenin takes monopolies as necessary outcomes of capitalist competition, hence monopoly capitalism alias imperialism is a new stage in capitalism. "Competition becomes transformed into monopoly." (Lenin, 2000: 52) Further,

> "Translated into ordinary human language this means that the development of capitalism has arrived at a stage when, although commodity production still 'reigns' and continues to be regarded as the basis of economic life, it has in reality been undermined and the bulk of the profits go to the geniuses' of financial manipulation. At the basis of these manipulation and swindles lies socialised production; but the immense progress of mankind, which achieved this

socialisation, goes to benefit...the speculators." (Lenin, 2000: 54)

But this farcical tragedy of capitalist progress cannot be reversed to "'free', 'peaceful', and 'honest' competition, which is nothing but the pipe-dream of "reactionary, petty-bourgeois critics of capitalist imperialism". (Lenin 2000: 54) Lenin scolded "the last of the Mohicans of bourgeois democracy" who simply declared imperialist wars to be 'criminal', illegal, 'treachery' but "shrank from recognising the inseverable bond between imperialism and the trusts, and, therefore, imperialism and the foundations of capitalism". Their anti-imperialism remains "a pious wish". (Lenin, 2000: 135)

Lenin mocks at the Hobsonian-Kautskyite protestors "against the 'inevitability of imperialism' argument, and those "urging the necessity of 'increasing the consuming capacity' of the people (under capitalism!)". He deals in one stroke with "the petty-bourgeois point of view in the critique of imperialism, the omnipotence of the banks, the financial oligarchy", who "contrast imperialism with free competition and democracy, condemn the Baghdad railway scheme, which is leading to conflicts and war, utter 'pious wishes' for peace, etc". (Lenin 2000: 135-6) Lenin questions the Marxism of the 'Marxists' who instead of an analysis of imperialism and an exposure of the depths of its contradictions" utter "a reformist 'pious wish' to wave them aside, to evade them". (Lenin, 2000: 136) He says,

> "Kautsky broke with Marxism by advocating in the epoch of finance capital a 'reactionary ideal', 'peaceful democracy', 'the mere operation of economic factors', for *objectively* this ideal drags us back from monopoly to non-monopoly capitalism, and is a reformist swindle." (Lenin, 2000: 137)

Lenin clearly states quoting Hilferding that the proletarian reply, which was his only concern, to the economic policy of finance capital, to imperialism is nothing but socialism. (Lenin, 2000:137)

A proper and complete rereading of Lenin's text decoding its Aesopian language would demand a complete rewriting of the text, which we believe in turn would require more sophistication and a command over Marxist method and political economy that we do not profess to possess. We have enumerated here the basic controversial arguments that are not frequently raised when talking about this text. In fact, their contemporary tone is quite revealing that can enlighten us even on the politics of a major section if not the majority of vocal sections in the so-called anti-globalisation movement.

POLITICS OF IMPERIALISM

War, American Hegemony and Globalisation

If we delve into the history of discussions on imperialism, it becomes evident that they have been occasioned mainly by the task of understanding the belligerent attitude of nation-states. Lenin's *Imperialism* too was written to execute the task of providing a proletarian perspective on the World War I. The second wave also was immediately effected by Vietnam and Korean wars. And now again, the Gulf War in 1991 became an important point of departure for the discussion on imperialism in the context of globalisation, which has acquired great heights recently with the never-ending 'war on terrorism' and invasion of Afghanistan and Iraq by the US and its vassal states. We do not wish to provide a full-fledged framework for a 'Marxist theory of war', nor will add anything to the understanding of specific wars. We will restrict ourselves to just noting some salient features that characterise belligerence in our times.

War is not intrinsic to capitalism, nor is peace. "Capital tends to require peace but often thrives on conflict." (Cramer, 2002: 156) Hence, to understand wars in capitalism we will definitely require to unearth their essence embedded in capitalist relations (as war is always relational), but the essence must not be confused with the causes, which can be multiple and diverse depending on specific contexts. Cramer has succinctly narrated this point:

> "Nonetheless, there is a final sense in which capitalism might well inherently support the likelihood of violent conflict. For capitalism is by its very nature conflictual: the logic of desperate competition that compels capitalists

– especially perhaps when frames within nation states and the organisation of national interest – could be expected to generate regional and international violence, including violence in the form of war. This tendency might be mitigated, however, by the fact that capitalism is transnational and develops complex interconnectedness between people. The key, however, is to see the independence of the nation state as the principal unit of political organisation and international legitimacy, shaping capitalist competition into a potentially lethal form. There might not be anything inherently warlike about capitalism, but when it is harnessed to national power and competition it easily becomes so." (Cramer, 2002: 155)

Through wars, states reveal their ultimate machinery at an international level necessary for their survival, from where their legitimacy is essentially derived—coercion. The system of multiple states, through which capital accumulation takes place and is supported, howsoever necessary to administer the local flows, exists as potential threat to the same order. This presents a paradoxical situation in which capitalism always finds itself.

In the politico-economic competitive race, the US was ascendant as the supreme runner from the very beginning of the last century. Its victory was partly related to its economy not being essentially dependent on direct colonial expansion. Although it had its own dependent blocs in Latin America, the US economy gained by the post 1870 flight of European capital to its region and the enormous growth in heavy and hi-tech industries enticed both more capital and labour to the New World. This basic reliance on 'internal colonisation' proved positive for its position in international politics too, as colonial reshuffling during the World War I and decolonisation during and after the World War II did not prove damaging to its political economic growth as it did for its other imperialist rivals, especially England, France and Germany. British indebtedness, Russian casualties, and the defeat of Germany and Japan meant the establishment of the US as the supreme command of world capitalism.

The major task for the US was two-fold and this shaped the

character of its foreign policies during the post-colonial Cold War phase. First, it had to make the world safer for capitalism against the looming danger of the spreading of Soviet influence beyond Eastern Europe. The devastated European powers readily accepted the US leadership, more so after witnessing the Chinese Revolution and were anxious to contain this 'evil' from spreading in other newly liberated nations. The second aspect of the US strategic design was to ensure its uncontested primacy within world capitalism.

During the Cold War there was never any grave tension between these two aspects of American foreign policies. The existence of Soviet Union, allowed the tension between these two fundamental objectives of US policy to be minimised. But in 1991, the knot tying them became looser. "Once the Communist danger was taken off the table, American primacy ceased to be an automatic requirement of the security of the established order *tout court*." But "with the erasure of the USSR, there was no longer any countervailing force on earth capable of withstanding US military might." (Anderson, 2002)

In 1990s, an open explosion of potential inter-imperialist rivalries were evaded and the US hegemony was reasserted by buying off two veto-holders in the Security Council (Russia and China); by speeding off NATO's intervention in the Eastern Europe, before the EU could even start off; by balkanising Yugoslavia unilaterally; and, lastly, by the windfall of the Iraqi invasion of Kuwait and ensuing the Gulf Crisis (this too was subtly engineered). The last led to the installation of advanced military bases in Saudi Arabia and the Gulf, establishment of a protectorate in Kurdistan and tied down the Palestinian national movement in an Israeli-dictated waiting zone. In this process, "the UN had become virtually as much an arm of the State Department as the IMF is of the Treasury." (Anderson, 2002)

Recent invasions in Afghanistan and Iraq too do not represent any fundamental change in the strategies of US imperialism. A principal feature of these invasions is that they have significantly altered the international rules of strategy-formation in the sense that all of them were pre-emptive and preventive attacks to anticipate a future danger or based on uncorroborated suspicions. This represented an ideological shift in the US strategy—"Where the rhetoric of the Clinton regime spoke of the cause of inter-national justice and the construction of a democratic peace, the Bush administration has hoisted the banner of the war on terrorism. These are not incompatible motifs, but the order of emphasis assigned to each has altered. The result is a sharp contrast of atmospherics." This was accompanied by two major changes in circumstances—post 9/11 upsurge in jingoism and "the revolution in military affairs" (RMA) that "was a fundamental change in the nature of warfare, by comprehensive application of electronic advances to weapons and communications system" creating "a low-risk power vacuum around American planning, in which the ordinary calculus of the risks or gains of war is diluted or suspended". (Anderson, 2002)

One might ask about the political economic essence of such developments. It is important to note that in the study of imperialism (or even capitalism in general), there is a need to assert the interdependence of capital accumulation and state formation. It is through state and political processes that capital accumulation takes place. "The existence of the national state under capitalism is predicated upon the existence of competition between blocs of capitals and the related division of social reproduction." (Fine & Harris, 1979) Strategies and wars, on the one hand, are results of the competition between blocs of capitals (or monopoly associations) represented by states for hegemony over accumulation. On the other hand, they observe an order in the system of states for accumulation to take place smoothly (smoothness too is relative). The significance of the Gulf for strategic purposes derives from its locus in the global political economy.

Ellen Meiksins Wood (2002) interprets the function of the recent US military efforts (due to its being the most powerful coercive force in the world) as that of "the ultimate enforcer of globalisation." She sees it as high tech bombs "acting as the day-to-day regulator of a complex legal and contractual order, enabling the property transactions and financial dealings that are capitalism's daily bread, to say nothing of the everyday relations between capital and labour. For that, local states are indispensable". She rightly concludes,

> "Controlling a whole global economy, all the time and everywhere, and the many states that are needed to keep it working, is a very different matter from the old imperialist task of capturing territory or dominating particular states, with finite boundaries. So on ways of keeping states in line is regularly to display the military power of the United States and demonstrate that, if it cannot be everywhere all the time, it can go anywhere at any time and do great damage." (Wood 2002: 139)

Open-ended wars, like "war against terrorism", provide legitimacy to intrude anywhere and anytime. The invisible enemy never dies like American comic "forces of evil" which were creations of the Cold War period, but have become a powerful ideology-creating pedagogical tool for inculcating the ethics of globalisation—a constant paranoia.

Pro/anti-globalisation and anti-capitalism

The paranoiac ideologies of globalisation have their beginning in neo-liberalism. Neo-liberalism was the product of the crisis of Keynesianism, which was fast losing its role as the hegemonic economic philosophy feeding the policy designs until the 1960s. Keynesianism in its turn reflected the need to bring the national economies and, through them, the world economy back on track after the devastations of the 1929 crises and world wars. It sought to revamp the economic machinery and infrastructure needed for restoring the process of capitalisation. The increase in effective demand through welfarism and state expenditure was the major policy-level effect of the "Keynesian revolution". Eventually, the economies did revive and a major danger was effectively averted by sidelining any successful working class upsurge in European countries by accommodating its formal leadership into the efforts for national reconstruction – nationalisation, statism and welfarism (to which the concept of socialism was effectively reduced). Revisionism of the Communist Parties in Italy under Berlinguer's leadership, in Spain under Carrillo's leadership, French Communist Party's ambivalence during Gaullist regime and after, and virtual non-existence of British Communist Party after the Soviet invasion of Hungary all were symptomatic of this accommodation (of labour aristocracy!).

But with the crisis of the 1960s-1970s, which was essentially reflected in the productivity and profitability decline, the introversion of Keynesian period became a hurdle. We witness a growing urge to expand the market that was not so much for dismantling the protection of domestic economies, but essentially to increase this protection for monopolies by destroying the barriers imposed by their competitors in their respective economies and in the 'late' capitalist countries. Neo-liberalism was the philosophy of this age inducing monopolistic expansion through Structural Adjustment Policies (SAPs) and forcing every economy to open up. The anti-interventionist policies in effect ironically demanded a heightened intervention of the State for their implementation. Neo-liberalism redefined the role of the State and its relationship with economic processes. The so-called divorcing of politics and economics even at its face value signified that voters or citizens could not affect the economic processes. It tended to belie the illusion of 'relative autonomy' of the state. But this simultaneously reduced the state to an instrument of securing the 'competitive edge' for the financing monopolies through its coercive and consensual function, which includes a regulation (i.e., de-regulation) of labour market in their interest. Effectively, the real function of the state is denuded—now it can be stubborn and unconcerned towards 'citizens', faces may change, yet the policies continue. State politics is reduced to lobby politics as another direct 'political' reflection of monopolistic competition. For general masses, what is left here is herd politics to control them and keep their anti-systemic urge at bay through jingoism and all kinds of physical and spiritual drugging.

Globalisation as neoliberal imperialism in action has induced a plethora of reaction from hyper-globalism to religious bigotry (while the states normally have characteristically combined these two extremes, chiefly the US under Bush and India under

Vajpayee). In between, we find numerous sensible and rational critiques of the politico-economic processes. These critiques of globalism do well in exposing the hypocritical nature of globalisation and neo-liberalism in which imperialist ambitions are rooted. Generally speaking, they view globalisation and global integration as more-or-less illusory because they find them build on the existence of nation-states rather than their transcendence. Trade and investment flows too remain limited between a few developed countries, having a very little macroeconomic effect. Further global neoliberalism has induced "social exclusion" and deprivation. As solutions, some of them propose localisation/decentralisation of the world economy basing on local production and exchange. Some call for democratisation of policy-making with sector-specific trade and industrial policies, and national controls on capital flows. Still others call for a democratic international decision-making through a revitalisation of international institutions like the UN etc. (Saad-Filho, 2003: 10-13)

We feel the main lines of discussion around globalisation today replicate those of Lenin's time, and can be critiqued on same accounts. They propose similar 'petty bourgeois socialist' solutions that were rebuked by Marx in *Communist Manifesto*, *Poverty of Philosophy* and other writings on Proudhon. At one place he says, "They all want competition without the lethal effects of competition. They all want the impossible, namely, the conditions of bourgeois existence without the necessary consequences of those conditions." (Marx, 1846) As noted above, Lenin too confronted similar 'anti-imperialists'. They strategise on the basis of bigness and smallness of firms, proposing localised economy of small firms against 'globalised' economy of monopolies and corporates. They evade the simple truth that the new corporate structure based on flexibility and outsourcing includes small firms too. In fact, Lenin was dealing with a similar structuring although still far from becoming a general reality, when he says:

> "The enormous dimensions of finance capital concentrated in a few hands and creating an extraordinarily dense and widespread network of relationships and connections which

subordinates not only the small and medium, but also the very small capitalists and small masters, on the one hand, and the increasingly intense struggle waged against other national state groups of financiers for the division of the world and domination over other countries, on the other hand, cause the propertied classes to go over entirely to the side of imperialism." (Lenin, 2000: 133)

These critiques uncritically accept the reified notion of capital and capital accumulation inherited from academic 'vulgar political economy'. They do not analyse the essence of capitalist economy in terms of value relations, but in terms of relations of exchange, hence global political economic processes are not understood in terms of the basic capital-labour relations, but in terms of scales of production and exchange, in terms of apparent oppressions at national and communal levels. Berberoglu (2003) has rightly pointed out:

"The distinction...between transnational capitalist industrialisation and national capitalist industrialisation... is grossly exaggerated, as both forms of industrialisation are subject to the laws of the capitalist mode of production, which facilitate capital accumulation for the transnational and/or the national bourgeoisie and prolong capitalist class rule... Under either form of industrialisation, the appropriation of surplus value by the capitalist class continues and expands as an increasing number of peasants and marginal segments of the population are drawn into wage-labor employment. Thus, the de facto emphasis on the "progressive" nature of nation (as opposed to transnational) capital, and the claim that therefore the critique of "blockage" by imperialism of the national industrialisation process should, in effect, be the focus of analysis, as has been the case in most studies adopting such a view, is, I believe, misconceived and misdirected; in practice, they may also lead to wrong (nationalist and class-collaborationist) politics."

For Marx, "capital is a *class relation of exploitation* which allows capitalists to live off the surplus value extracted from the working class". (Saad-Filho, 2002: 41) This definition read with Marx's notion of competition gives the full picture of the essential logic operating through all the apparent realities of national oppressions etc. Marx talks about capital existing only through many capitals in competition. It is in the very "inner nature" of capital that it flourishes through competition, and as long as capital in this sense exist, the *tendency* towards centralisation and concentration, towards monopolies (national, transnational or multinational) will always be there. A refusal to understand this fundamental truth of capitalist society leads the honest critiques of globalisation to committing blunder of preaching "national controls over capital", "democratisation", etc., without changing the fundamental relation between labour and capital that gives shape to every political economic process. Regarding the reliance on the revitalisation of international institutions, it must be noted that to talk about the radical utility of such institutions at the time when they do not figure as the prime means of consent creation even for the hegemonic forces (Gowan, 2003) and with all the major dissenting nations in Cancun and before struggling for better bargains in the global imperialist structure, they are nothing but another "pious wish" of "the last of the Mohicans of bourgeois democracy."

As for the constructive option we quote from an exponent of revolutionary critical pedagogy Paula Allman's marvellous little book, *Critical Education against Global Capitalism* (2001: 130):

"As capitalism has become a fully global, universal system with an abstract form of social domination that increasingly penetrates every aspect of our existence, its contradictions and necessary consequences have become more pervasive and apparent. People in increasing numbers and for various reasons are expressing their desire for change, but thus far their focus has been on the results, or problems, rather than the causes. Thus there is a gap between wanting change and knowing what needs to be changed, or at least knowing what needs to be changed in order to really make a difference —what must be abolished and what can be salvaged if transformed within alternative relation. For example, global campaigns have sprung up to challenge neoliberalism, but neoliberalism is only the most recent and drastic response —that is, the most drastic response thus far devised—to managing capital's contradictions. It may be the immediate enemy, but its elimination would by no means eliminate the contradictions. In other words, we need to understand and name the real enemy. If we do not do so, then the specter of capitalism will simply hover over humanity in an even more menacing form."

> [The author wishes to thank Navin Chandra, Pothik Ghosh and Ganeshan for their constant intellectual support and encouragement during the writing of this article. The usual caveats apply.]

NOTES

1. The concepts of "formal subsumption" and "real subsumption" of labour by capital have been developed by Marx in his *Results of the Immediate Process of Production* published as an Appendix to Marx (1976).
2. Here M=money, C=commodity, L=Labour, MP=Means of Production, P=Production, C'=total commodity produced (which include c=surplus value in commodity form), M' is the total value in money form.
3. See Marx's use of the concept of 'industrial capital' in contrast to the usual narrow usage in terms of sectoral capital.
4. Wood (2002) summarises her significant contribution in successfully showing that capitalism was a product of the internal contradiction of feudal mode of production, rather than caused by external stimulus of mercantilism.
5. "Competition merely *expresses* as real, posits as an external necessity, that which lies within the nature of capital; competition is nothing more than the way in which the many capital force the inherent determinants of capital upon one another and upon themselves." (Marx, 1973: 651)
6. "*For them imperialism is a process that happens between countries;* a process involving expansion and domination both political and economic. Colony and colonisation are at the core of this conception. Not so for Lenin...'Monopoly stage of capitalism' is thus the core notion of Lenin's definition." (Gerstein, 1979)

REFERENCES

Allman, Paula (2001) *Critical Education against Global Capitalism: Karl Marx and Revolutionary Critical Education*. Connecticut: Bergin & Garvey.

Althusser, Louis (1970) "From *Capital* to Marx's Philosophy", in Louis Althusser & Étienne Balibar, *Reading Capital*. NLB.

Anderson, Perry (2002) "Force and Consent", *New Left Review*. 17 Sep-Oct 2002.

Berberoglu, Berch (2003) *Globalization of Capital and the Nation-State: Imperialism, Class Struggle and the State in the Age of Global Capitalism*. Maryland: Rowman & Littlefield.

Brunhoff, Suzanne de (2002) "Financial and Industrial Capital: A New Coalition", in Alfredo Saad-Filho (2003).

Carchedi, Guglielmo (1999) "The Euro and Europe's Labour", in Riccardo Bellofiore (ed.) *Global Money, Capital Restructuring and the Changing Patterns of Labour*. MA: Edward Elgar.

Cramer, Christopher (2003) "War, Peace and Capitalism: Is Capitalism the Harbinger of Peace or the Great Threat to World Peace?", in Saad-Filho (2003).

Duménil, G. and D. Lévy (1999) "Structural Unemployment in the Crisis of the Late Twentieth Century: a comparison between the European and the US experiences", in Riccardo Bellofiore (ed.) *Global Money, Capital Restructuring and the Changing Patterns of Labour*. MA: Edward Elgar.

Dussel, Enrique (2001) *Towards an Unknown Marx: A commentary on the Manuscripts of 1861-63*. London: Routledge.

Fine, Ben & Laurence Harris (1979) *Rereading Capital*. London: Macmillan.

Gerstein, Ira (1979) "What is Imperialism the Highest Stage of? Elements for a Theory of Imperialism", *Research in Political Economy Vol.2*.

Gowan, Peter (2003) "US:UN", *New Left Review*. 24 Nov–Dec 2003

Lenin, V.I. (1976) *Selected Works Vol.1*, Moscow: Progress Publishers

Lenin, V.I. (2000) *Imperialism, the Highest Stage of Capitalism: A Popular Outline*, New Delhi: LeftWord Books.

Lipietz, Alain (2001) "The Fortunes and Misfortunes of Post-Fordism", in Robert Albritton, Makoto Itoh, Richard Westra and Alan Zuege (ed.), *Phases of Capitalist Development: Booms, Crises and Globalizations*. Palgrave: New York.

Magdoff, Harry (1974) "Imperialism: An Historical Survey", in B.

Chattopadhyay, *Imperialism in the Modern Phase.* Vol 1, New Delhi: PPH.

Marx, Karl (1846) Letter to P.V. Annenkov, in Karl Marx & Friedrich Engels (1969), *Selected Works.* Vol.1, Moscow: Progress Publishers.

Marx, Karl (1973) *Grundrisse*, London: Penguin.

Marx, Karl (1976) *Capital: A Critique of Political Economy.* Vol.1, London: Pelican.

Marx, Karl (1978) *Capital: A Critique of Political Economy.* Vol.2, London: Pelican.

O'Connor, James (1970) "The Meaning of Economic Imperialism", in Robert I. Rhodes (ed.) *Imperialism and Underdevelopment – A Reader.* New York: MR.

Owen, Roger (1972) "Introduction", in Roger Owen & Bob Sutcliffe (ed.), *Studies in the Theory of Imperialism.* London: Longman.

Saad-Filho, Alfredo (2002) *The Value of Marx: Political Economy for Contemporary Capitalism*, London: Routledge

Saad-Filho, Alfredo ed. (2003) *Anti-Capitalism: A Marxist Introduction.* London: Pluto.

Wood, Ellen Meiksins (2002) *The Origin of Capitalism: A Longer View.* London: Verso.

Wood, Ellen Meiksins (2003) "Globalisation and the State: Where is the Power of Capital?", in Saad-Filho (2003).

Index

Aarnos, Mark, 121
Abbas, Mahmoud, 133-4
Abstraction, Experience of, 280-1
Afghanistan, 35, 46, 48-9, 103, 204, 207, 209, 215, 240, Attack on, 48, Future of, 34 lesson of, 116 War on, 97
Africa, 28, 67, 91, 96, 121, 280-1
Aideed (Aidid), Mohammad Farah, 34, 137
Albania, 323
Albright, Madeleine, 81
Ali, Tariq, 147
Allman, Paula, 395
Al Qaeda, 106, 134, 309
Alvarez, Carlos, 292
America, 82, 96, 101, 137, 201-2, 207, 209, 216, Stability of, 142, Superiority of, 68, see also United States
American Capitalism, 68
  Empire, 100, 108
  Existence of, 26
  Expansion, 67
  foreign policy, 26, 88, 98, 389, Global Capitalism, 143, Hegemony, 368
  Imperialism, 26, 305

Amherst, Jeffery, 146
Amin, Samir, 254
Angola, 97
Ankara, 191
Anti-American Moslem, Demonizing of, 107
  -Capitalist Revolution, 74
  -Imperialism, 385
  -Semitism, 307, 310-3, 317
Argentina, 30, 39, 77, 91-2, 114, 209, 263, 269, 285
Arkin, William M, 136
Arrighi, Giovanni, 255
Ashcroft, John, 90, 117, 139
Asia, 67, 69-70, 82, 303
Atlanta, 25
Atlanticism, 156, 178-9
Atto, Osman, 137
Auschwitz, 304, 310, 322
Australia, 79-80, 305
Austria, 305
Aznar, J M, 190, 213
Baghdad, 49, Pact of, 176
  Railway Scheme, 386
Baker, D, 276
Baker, James, 146
Balkans, 204, 206
Baran, Paul, 251
Barbarism, 57, 304

Baudelaire, Charles, 363
Beijing, 183
Belgium, 72
Benjamin, Walter, 363
Berberoglu, Berch, 394
Bergen, Edgar, 115
Berlin, 183, 186
Birkenau Death Camp, 120
Black Hawk Down, 135-6
Blair, Tony, 106, 178, 181, 272, 358
Boggs, Carl, 147-8
Bolivia, 235
Bolton, John, 112
Boykin, William G Jerry, 135-7
Brazil, 74, 77
Bremer, Paul, 114
Brenner, Robert, 254
Bretton Woods System, 58, 370
Britain, 26, 28-9, 39-40, 71-2, 82
British Colonialism, 251
    Hegemony, Breakdown of, 32, Sea Power, 29
Brunhoff, Suzanne de, 394
Buchanan, James, 140
Buenos Aires, 258, 272, 277
Bukharin, Nikolai, 251
Burbach, Roger, 254
Bush, Prescott, 121
Bush, George W, 25, 49, 89, 100-1, 116-7, 121, 134, 137-9, 143, 181
Cafiero, P, 276
Callinicos, A, 309
Canada, 79
Canning, George, 29
Capitalism, 37, 43, 119, 125, 316, 322, 353, 362, 392
    Analysis of, 59-60
    Crisis of, 266 Current Phase of, 30, 56
    Global Expansion of, 154

History of, 30, 323, 374
Survival of, 69
Violence of, 268
Capitalist Development, 30, 59, 63, Expansion, 159, Rule 69, Theory of, 251
    World Economy, 34
Cardoso, Fernando Henrique, 251, 272
Carnegie, Andrew, 73
Carrio, Elisa, 289-90
Carter, Jimmy, 228
Castro, Fidel, 256, 291
Cavallo, Domingo, 270-73, 278
Chalabi, Ahmad, 49
Chavez, Hugo, 146, 234, 257, 291
Chebab al Intifada, 175-6
Cheney, Dick, 90, 103, 117
Child Prostitution, 176
Chile, 98
China, 39, 47, 69, 72-4, 76, 84, 91, 100, 102, 116, 155, 161, 171
Chinese Revolution, 389
Christian Nation, 137
    Reconstructionism, 134
CIA, 120 Threat, 117
Civil Disobedience, 289
    Society, 294
Clark, Wesley, 120
Clauswitz, Karl Marie von, 122
Clinton, Bill, 105, 208, 229
Cohen, Daniel, 324
Cold War, 33, 84-5, 96, 100, 106, 147, 156, 216, 303, 389, 391
Collective Imperialism, 178
Colombia, 74, 111, 207, 235
Colonial Expansionism, Policy of, 27 Possessions, 184
Colonialism, 28, 30, 35, 70, 89, 368, 385, History of, 385
Colonisation, 211

Commodification 333
Communist Conspiracy, 69
Communist Manifesto, 60
Conable, Barber, 96
Conason, Joe, 134
Congo, 74
Cooper, Richard T, 135-6
Corn laws, 375
Cramer, Christopher, 387
Credit system, Evolution of, 376
Cuba, 73-4, 76, 146, 173, 215, 235
Cypriot Tragedy, 192
Czechoslovakia, 98
Daschle, Tom 117
da Silva, Lula, 291
Davalos, P, 276
Davan, Moshe, 211
De Gaulle, Charles, 156, 186
De La Rua, Fernando, 269-70, 278, 290
DeLay, Tom, 122
Delhi, 183
Democracy, 110, 114, 118-9
    Crisis of, 281
    Participatory, 258-60
    Radical, 283
    Social, 313
    Transformation of, 280
    Violation of, 116
Democratic Party, 216, 245
de Sade, Marquis, 315
Development Theory, 255
Disraeli, Benjamin, 72
Disutopia, 280
Doha, 89
Duhalde, Eduardo, 267, 290, 293
    Administration, 286-8
Dussel, Enrique, 379
East India Company, 370
Economic Coercion, 88
    Commission, 197
Egypt, 98, 184

Elizalde, Rosa Miriam, 146
Engels, F, 60, 62, 251
England, 375
Escobar, Pablo, 135
Ethiopia, 95
Europe, 27, 68, 77, 100, 103, 119, 156, 159, 172, 217 Political autonomy of, 179
European Colonial Expansion, 72, Powers, Empires of, 367, Social Forum, 330 Union, 244
Extending Control, Principle of, 26, 28
Farahmandpur, Ramin, 149
Fascism, 311, 323
Financial Capital, 66, 71
    Domination of, 71
First World War, 33, 158, 191
Fisher, Stanley, 273, 276
Fitrakis, B, 121-2
Florida, 122
Fordism, Crisis of, 373
Foucault, J, 335
Fox News, 140
France, 44, 69, 72, 82, 97, 116, 180, 186, 305
Frank, A G, 251
Free Market, 118-9
    Movements, 42
    Trade, 105, 126, 369
Friedman, Thomas, 89
Gallagher, John, 26, 28-30
Gambino, F, 323
Gaullism, 156-7, 186
Geopolitics, 116
Germany, 44, 71-2, 116, 180
Gerstein, Ira, 385
Ghana, 91
Gilpin, Robert, 254
Global War, 111
Globalised Value, Law of, 154

Globalisation, 39-40, 47, 50, 53-4, 106, 123, 252-4, 304-6, 324, 371, 392 Critique of, 323, Process of, 56
Gorbachev, Age of, 256
Gorenfeld, John, 139
Great Britain, 26, 29, 156, 161, 183-4
Greece, 191-2
Guevara, Che, 256
Gujarat, Carnage in, 48
Gulf Crisis, 187, 389
    War, 48, 148, 229, 387
Gutierrez, Lucid, 257
Haas, Richard N, 25-6, 28, 34-5
Haider, Joerg, 305
Halliburton, 90, 103
Hamas, 175
Hardt, Michael, 254
Harnecker, Marta, 249
Harriman, W A, 121
Harris, Jerry, 255
Hay, John, 72
Hayek, F, 335, 350
Hegel, G W F, 308
Held, David, 254
Hilferding, Rudolf, 251
Hindutva, 54
Hirst, Paul, 254
Hitler, Adolf, 120-1, 138-9
Hobson, John A, 30, 251
Hochschild, Arlie, 140, 142-3
Horkheimer, M, 311, 323
Horowitz, David, 78-9
Hudis, Peter, 127-8
Human Rights, Violation of, 52, Watch International, 111
Hungary, 392
Hussein, Saddam, 34, 118-21, 135-36, 143, 242
Ignatieff, Michael, 27
Imperialism, 27, 30, 54, 70, 72, 107, 126-7, 150, 155, 217, 248, 250, 293, 367, 376 British, 28, 30, Capital, Expansion of, 30, Debt, 42 Concept of, 197, Critique of, 386, Free trade, 28-30, informal, 29-30, 96, Manifestations of, 96, Politics of, 387, stage of, 78 Theories of, 29, 37, Super-, 44-6, 48-9, 58, Ultra-, 43-4
Imperialist, 25, 28, 30, 154
    Capitalism, 81
    Democracy, 150
    Development, 70
    Power, 46, 106
India, 39, 50, 53-4, 111, 171, 393
Indonesia, 74, 102, 111, 114
Industrial Capitalist, 72
    Revolution, 375
Information Technology, 201
International Monetary Fund, 88, 90, 116, 131, 269, 370
    War Crimes Tribunal, 43
Intifada, 175
Iran, 135, 210 Attack on, 116
Iraq, 34-5, 49, 105, 111, 118-9, 133, 145, 173, 177, 179, 204, 207, 240, 242, Invasion of, 34, 45-6, 48, 110, 114, 119, 141, 204, Lesson of, 116, Occupation of, 207
Islam, 135
Islamic Jihad, 175
    Fundamentalism, 310
Israel, 172-6, 309-10
Israeli Occupation, 108
Japan, 27, 40, 63, 69, 77, 79, 88, 100, 155, 159, 389
    Imperial Expansion, 69
Jewish Lobby, 173
Jews, 307-8, 311-2, 314, 316-7

Jordon, 114
Kabul, 49
Kalicki, Jan, 103
Kant, I, 315
Karbala, 49
Karzai, Hamid, 46, 49
Kashmir, 111
Katsiaficas, George, 131, 144, 146-7
Katz, C, 287
Kautsky, Karl, 43, 252, 385
Kazakhstan, 102
Keynesianism, Crisis of, 391
Khomeini, Ayatollah, 310
Khruschev, N, 193
Kim Jong Il, 136
Kirchner, Nestor, 267, 290-1, 293
Kissinger, Henry, 33
Korea, 76
Korean War, 148
Koshy, Ninan, 89
Kosteki, Maximiliano, 288
Kovel, Joel, 148-9
Krasner, Stephen, 98
Kristallnacht Attacks, 120
Kuong-hae, Lee, 124
Kurds 49
Kuwait, 114 Iraqi Invasion of, 389
Kyoto Accords, 99 Agreement, 213
Labour, Exploitation of, 70
Movements, Unity of, 258
Latin America, 29-30, 91, 142, 216-7
Law, David, 98
Lebanon, 114 Invasion of, 175
Lebensraum, Practice of, 309
Lenin, V I, 30, 37-9, 43-4, 63-4, 67, 71, 81, 251, 380, 382, 384-5
Le Pen, Jean-Pierre, 305

Liberalism, 310
Liberalisation, 91
Liberation Movements, 74
Libya, 34
Lincoln, Abraham, 137-8, 151
Llorens, J, 276
Locke, John, 125
Loftus, John, 121
London, 30
Lunderberg, Ferdinand, 66
Luxemburg, Rosa, 323
Luzon, 147
Machado, Antonio, 363
Machinea, Jose Luis, 269
Madrid, 174
Magdoff, Harry, 32, 35, 36
Mahathir, Mohamad, 306
Mailer, Norman, 142
Malaysia, 306
Manichean War, 107
Mann, Michael, 255
Mao Zedong, 39
Marcuse, Herbert, 363
Marini, Ruy Mauro, 251
Marshall Plan, 76-7
Martin, A I, 122
Marx, Daniel, 273, 275
Marx, Karl, 59-63, 251, 323, 378, 394-5
Marxism, 29-30, 32, 259, 261
Mass Destruction,Weapons of, 110, 118, 120
Mass Insurgency, 75-6, 216
McCarthy, Charlie, 115
McCarthy, Joseph, 69
McCloy, John, 98
McDonnell-Douglas, 89
McKinley, William, 73-147
McLaren, Peter, 149
Meinhoff, Ulrike, 317
Menem, Carlos, 269-70, 290
Meszaros, Istvan, 122-3

Mexico, 77
Middle East, 103, 105, 108, 111, 119, 134, 171, 206, 209-11, 216, 309 Importance of, 154 US Military, Presence of, 116
Military Aid, 111 Dominance, 44 Invasion, 34 Strike, 114
Milosevic, Slobodan, 43
Mogadishu, 136-7
Mommsen, Wolfgang J, 29
Monopoly Capitalism, 77
Monopolistic Corporations, Rise of, 32
Moon, Sun Myung, 139
Moonlite Bunny Ranch, 118
Mormon Church, 122
Moscow, 156, 193
Movimento Sem Terra, 258
Mufson, Steven, 105-6
Murphy, Lopez, 290
Muslim Nations, 114
Mussolini, Fall of, 187
NASA, 144
Nascar Dad, 140-1 143
National Congress, 288
    Liberation Front, 215
    Security Council, 25
    Socialism, 317, 320
Nationalism, 306
Nations, League of, 159
Nazi Crime, 173
    Germany, 212
    Party, 120
Nazism, 316, 323
Negri, Antonio, 254
Negt, O, 304
Neo-liberalism, 47, 90, 106, 249, 391-2, 396 Crisis of, 280, 285, Imposition of, 89 Phase of, 331 Rejection of, 294

New Imperial Wars, 216
    Imperialism, 32
    World Order, 138
New York, 122, 269
New Zealand, 79
Nigeria, 114
North America, 63, 209
North Korea, 145
Olasky, Marvia, 134
Operation Tips, 117
Osama bin Laden, 96, 106, 135-6, 141, 143
Oslo, 174 Peace Agreement, 176
Pakistan, 47, 111, 114
Paris, 183 Committee, 149
Patnaik, Prabhat, 27
Peery, Nelson, 142
Pentagon, 100, 104, 117, 120, 135, 188
Perle, Richard, 210
Peso, Devaluation of, 186
Petras, James, 128-9, 254
Philippines, 111 Annexation of, 73 Slaughter in, 147
Pinter, Harold, 20
Plame, Valerie, 121
Plan Colombia, 246
Poindexter, John, 117
Poland, 47, 97-8, 317
Polanyi, Karl, 333
Political Change, Impact of, 267
    Control, 47
    Democracy, 71
    Islam, 172
    Leadership, Changes in, 34
    Mobilisation, Ability of, 297
Porto Alegre, 341
Post-Soviet Asia, 100
Powell, Colin, 146
Preobrazhensky, Yevgeny 67-8

Prodi, Romano, 205
Putin, 102
Qaddafi, Mohammar, 34
Racism, 307
Reagan, Ronald, 96, 98, 105
Reno, Janet, 135
Ricardo, D, 322-3
Rikowski, Glenn, 132
Robinson, Bill, 124
Robinson, Ronald, 26, 28-30
Robinson, William, 254-5
Rodrik, Dani, 99
Roosevelt, Theodore, 147, 158
Rove, Karl, 120-22
Roverer, Karl Heinz, 122
Rowley, Coleen, 90
Rumsfeld, Donald, 101, 105, 129, 150, 211-2, 242
Russia, 63, 92-3, 100, 116, 160, 171, 180
Russian Revolution, 149, 364
Russert, Tim, 120
Saa, Rodriguez, 290
Sadat, Anwar, 174
Saigon, 74
Sanchez de Losada, 235
Santillen, Dario, 288
Sao Paulo Forum, 258
Saudi Arabia, 34, 209, 389
Savimbi, Joseph, 97
Say's Law, 379
Scheer, Robert, 130
Schoomaker, General, 212
Schultz, George, 105
Schumpeter, Joseph, 252
Schwarzenegger, Arnold, 120, 142, 150
Second World War, 33, 70, 78, 80, 96, 155, 158, 171, 180, 186, 189, 241, 377
Security Council, 115 Resolution, 205

Self-determination, 242
Sen, Amartya, 91
Sharon, Ariel, 134, 174, 244
Shaw, Martin, 107
Silicon Valley, 89-90
Smith, Adam, 322
Snerd, Mortimer, 115
Social Conflicts, 285
    Fragmentation, 333
    Movements, 250
    Resistance against, 54
    Revolution, 92 Stability, Crisis of, 336
Socialism, 149, 391, 258
Solano, Javier, 205
Somalia, 34, 135
South Korea, 77, 91
Soviet Union, 33, 44, 58, 84, 96, 368, 389 Collapse of, 195 Demise of, 27, Invasion, 159 Rise of, 33, 155, 157, 160
Spain 73, 190, 213, 220, 392
Spanish America, 29
Starobin, Paul, 101
Steinbrenner, George, 122
Stephens, Philip, 101
Stiglitz, Joseph, 93-4, 348
Struggle, Plurality of, 343
Suez Canal, 98
Summers, Lawrence, 93
Syria, 184, 210
Taft-Hartley Act, 116
Taiwan, 77, 91
Tajikistan, 111
Taliban, 48-9, 96
Terrorism Act, Prevention of, 53 War against, 27, 34, 49, 85, 100, 105, 107, 110-11, 119, 135, 238, 288, 390
Texas, 122
Thailand, 92

Theotonio dos Santos, 251
Third World, 54-6, 70, 74-7, 93, 98, 116, 190, 193, 204, 210, 216, 236, 248
Tischler, S, 294
Todd, Emmanuel, 164
Torture, Convention against, 100
Trotsky, Leon, 86
Truman, Harry, 69,158
Turkey, 47, 114, 172, 191
Union Bank Corporation, 121
United States, 25-6, 33-4, 72-3, 81, 100, 111, 114, 125, 146, 179-80, 189, 191, 195, 217 Cold War, 203 Defeat, 77 Economic Power, 200 Foreign Policy, 27, Imperialism, 36, 88, 147, 154, 389, National Security Strategy, 100, 110, Patriot Act, 117
Uribe, Alvaro, 235
Uzbekistan, 111
Vajpayee, Atal Behari, 393
Venezuela, 102, 146, 225
Venice, Summit of, 185
Vietnam, 147, 215 War, 34, 74, 76-7, 98, 127, 246
Villepin, Dominique de, 159
Volkism, 139
Volksgenossen, 314, 321
Walker, George Herbert, 121
Warsaw Pact, 193
Washington, 26-7, 33, 67, 74, 90, 95, 100, 102, 116, 126, 156, 161, 170-2,173-4, 189, 211, 275
Wasserman, Harvey, 121-2
Weber, Max, 35
Weisbrot, M, 265, 276
Welfarism, 370, 391
Went, Robert, 255
Western Europe, 63, 69, 77-80
Westoxication, 310
Westphalia, Treaty of, 158
White House 90, 96, 119-20, 135, 137, 140
Wilson, Joseph, 121-2
Wilson, Woodrow, 72, 158
Wolfowitz, Paul, 120, 211
Wood, Ellen Meiksins, 125-6, 390
Woodward, Bob, 122
World Bank, 88, 90-1,93, 96, 116, 131, 160, 279, 370
  Social Forums, 236-7, 250, 285
  Trade Center, Attacks on, 120
Workers' State, 74
WTO, 43, 53-4, 88, 124, 131
Yankees Game, 122
Yugoslavia, 47, 160, 173, 192-3, 215, Dismemberment of, 161, War against, 48, Civil War, 27
Zamora, Luis, 289-90
Zionism, 173, 210, 244
Zoellick, Robert, 89